Beginning Perl

Third Edition

JAMES LEE
with SIMON COZENS

Apress®

Beginning Perl, Third Edtion

ISBN-13 (pbk): 978-1-4302-2793-9

ISBN-13 (electronic): 978-1-4302-2794-6

Printed and bound in the United States of America 9 8 7 6 5 4 3 2 1

President and Publisher: Paul Manning
Lead Editor: Frank Pohlmann
Technical Reviewers: Richard Dice, Ed Schaefer, Todd Shandelman
Editorial Board: Clay Andres, Steve Anglin, Mark Beckner, Ewan Buckingham, Gary Cornell, Jonathan Gennick, Jonathan Hassell, Michelle Lowman, Matthew Moodie, Duncan Parkes, Jeffrey Pepper, Frank Pohlmann, Douglas Pundick, Ben Renow-Clarke, Dominic Shakeshaft, Matt Wade, Tom Welsh
Coordinating Editor: Laurin Becker
Copy Editors: Katie Stence, Sharon Terdeman
Compositor: Kimberly Burton
Indexer: Brenda Miller
Artist: April Milne
Cover Designer: Anna Ishchenko

Distributed to the book trade worldwide by Springer-Verlag New York, Inc., 233 Spring Street, 6th Floor, New York, NY 10013. Phone 1-800-SPRINGER, fax 201-348-4505, e-mail orders-ny@springer-sbm.com, or visit www.springeronline.com.

For information on translations, please e-mail rights@apress.com, or visit www.apress.com.

Apress and friends of ED books may be purchased in bulk for academic, corporate, or promotional use. eBook versions and licenses are also available for most titles. For more information, reference our Special Bulk Sales–eBook Licensing web page at www.apress.com/info/bulksales.

The source code for this book is available to readers at www.apress.com. You will need to answer questions pertaining to this book in order to successfully download the code.

For Polly and Dave Pistole

Contents at a Glance

■About the Author xvi

■About the Technical Reviewers xvii

■Acknowledgements xviii

■Introduction xix

■Chapter 1: First Steps in Perl 1

■Chapter 2: Scalars 13

■Chapter 3: Control Flow Constructs 53

■Chapter 4: Lists and Arrays 81

■Chapter 5: Hashes 115

■Chapter 6: Subroutines/Functions 131

■Chapter 7: Regular Expressions 153

■Chapter 8: Files and Data 179

■Chapter 9: String Processing 207

■Chapter 10: Interfacing to the Operating System 215

■Chapter 11: References 231

■Chapter 12: Modules 257

■Chapter 13: Object-Oriented Perl 287

■Chapter 14: Introduction to CGI 317

■Chapter 15: Perl and DBI 349

■Appendix: Exercise Solutions 387

■Index 409

Contents

■About the Author xvi

■About the Technical Reviewers xvii

■Acknowledgements xviii

■Introduction xix

■Chapter 1: First Steps in Perl 1

Programming Languages 1

Our First Perl Program 2

    Program Structure 6

Character Sets 8

Escape Sequences 8

    Whitespace 9

Number Systems 9

The Perl Debugger 11

Summary 11

Exercises 12

■Chapter 2: Scalars 13

Types of Data 13

    Numbers 14

    Strings 17

    Here-Documents 20

    Converting Between Numbers and Strings 21

Operators 22

    Numeric Operators 22

    String Operators 32

    Operators to Be Covered Later 36

    Operator Precedence 37

Variables 38

    Scoping 43

    Variable Names 46

Variable Interpolation 46

    Currency Converter 48

Two Miscellaneous Functions 50

    The exit() Function 50

    The die() Function 51

Summary 52

Exercises 52

■Chapter 3: Control Flow Constructs 53

The if Statement 54

    Operators Revisited 55

    Multiple Choice: if . . . else 61

    The unless Statement 64

    Expression Modifiers 65

    Using Short-Circuited Evaluation 65

Looping Constructs 66

The while Loop 66

    while (<STDIN>) 67

    Infinite Loops 69

    Looping Until 70

    The for Loop 71

The foreach Loop 71

do .. while and do .. until 72

Loop Control Constructs 74

Breaking Out 74

Going On to the Next 75

Reexecuting the Loop 76

Loop Labels 77

goto 79

Summary 79

Exercises 79

■Chapter 4: Lists and Arrays **81**

Lists 81

Simple Lists 82

More Complex Lists 83

Creating Lists Easily with qw// 84

Accessing List Values 87

Arrays 91

Assigning Arrays 91

Scalar vs. List Context 94

Adding to an Array 95

Accessing an Array 95

Summary 114

Exercises 114

■Chapter 5: Hashes **115**

Creating a Hash 115

Working with Hash Values 117

Hash in List Context 119

Hash in Scalar Context 120

Hash Functions 121

The keys() Function 121

The values() Function 122

The each() Function 123

The delete() Function 123

The exists() Function 124

Hash Examples 125

Creating Readable Variables 125

"Reversing" Information 125

Counting Things 126

Summary 129

Exercises 129

■Chapter 6: Subroutines/Functions 131

Understanding Subroutines 132

Defining a Subroutine 132

Invoking a Subroutine 133

Order of Declaration and Invoking Functions 134

Passing Arguments into Functions 137

Return Values 139

The return Statement 141

Understanding Scope 142

Global Variables 142

Introduction to Packages 144

Lexical Variables (aka Local Variables) 146

Some Important Notes on Passing Arguments 147

Function Arguments Passed by Reference 147

Lists Are One-Dimensional 149

Default Argument Values 150

Named Parameters 151

Summary 152

Exercises 152

■Chapter 7: Regular Expressions 153

What Are They? 153

Patterns 154

Working with Regexes 170

Substitution 170

Changing Delimiters 172

Modifiers 173

The split() Function 174

The join() Function 175

Common Blunders 175

Summary 176

Exercises 177

■Chapter 8: Files and Data 179

Filehandles 179

The open() Function 179

The close() Function 180

Three Ways to Open a File 181

Read Mode 182

Reading in Scalar Context 183

Reading with the Diamond 185

@ARGV: The Command-Line Arguments 187

@ARGV and <> 189

$ARGV 190

Reading in List Context 190

Writing to Files 192

    Buffering 195

Opening Pipes 196

    Receiving Piped Data from a Process 196

    Sending Piped Data to Another Process 198

    Bidirectional Pipes 200

File Tests 200

Summary 205

Exercises 205

■Chapter 9: String Processing 207

Character Position 207

    String Functions 208

    The length() Function 208

    The index() Function 208

    The rindex() Function 210

    The substr() Function 210

    Transliteration 212

Summary 213

Exercises 213

■Chapter 10: Interfacing to the Operating System 215

The %ENV Hash 215

Working with Files and Directories 217

    File Globbing with glob() 217

    Reading Directories 220

    Functions to Work with Files and Directories 221

Executing External Programs 225

    The system() Function 225

Backquotes 227

There's More 228

Summary 228

Exercises 229

■**Chapter 11: References** **231**

What Is a Reference? 231

    Anonymity 232

The Life Cycle of a Reference 232

    Reference Creation 232

    Reference Modification 239

    Reference Counting and Destruction 243

Using References for Complex Data Structures 244

    Matrices 245

    Autovivification 245

    Trees 250

Summary 255

Exercises 255

■**Chapter 12: Modules** **257**

Why Do We Need Them? 257

Creating a Module 258

Including Other Files with use 260

    do 260

    require 261

    use 262

    Changing @INC 262

    Package Hierarchies 263

Exporters 265

The Perl Standard Modules..**267**

    Online Documentation 268

    Data::Dumper... 268

    File::Find 270

    Getopt::Std 271

    Getopt::Long 272

    File::Spec 273

    Benchmark 275

    Win32 276

CPAN...**278**

    Installing Modules with PPM 280

    Installing a Module Manually 281

    The CPAN Module 281

    Bundles... 284

    Submitting Your Own Module to CPAN 285

Summary **286**

Chapter 13: Object-Oriented Perl...**287**

OO Buzzwords...**287**

    Objects.. 287

    Attributes 288

    Methods... 288

    Classes 289

    Polymorphism.. 290

    Encapsulation 290

    Inheritance.. 290

    Constructors 291

    Destructors 292

An Example **292**

Rolling Your Own Classes 295

Bless You, My Reference 296

Storing Attributes 298

The Constructor 298

Creating Methods 301

Do You Need OO? 313

Are Your Subroutines Tasks? 314

Do You Need Persistence? 314

Do You Need Sessions? 314

Do You Need Speed? 314

Do You Want the User to Be Unaware of the Object? 314

Are You Still Unsure? 314

Summary 315

Exercises 315

■Chapter 14: Introduction to CGI 317

We Need a Web Server 318

Creating a CGI Directory 318

Writing CGI Programs 318

"hello, world!" in CGI 319

The CGI Environment 321

Generating HTML 323

Introducing CGI.pm 325

Conventional Style of Calling Methods 331

CGI.pm Methods 332

Methods That Generate Several Tags 332

Methods That Generate One Tag 333

Processing Form Data 333

The param() Method 335

Dynamic CGI 336

Let's Play Chess! 338

Improvements We Can Make 346

What We Did Not Talk About 347

Summary 348

Exercises 348

■Chapter 15: Perl and DBI 349

Introduction to Relational Databases 349

We Need an SQL Server—MySQL 353

Testing the MySQL Server 353

Creating a Database 354

Creating a Non-root User with the GRANT Command 357

The INSERT Command 358

The SELECT Command 361

Table Joins 367

Introduction to DBI 368

Installing DBI and the DBD::mysql 368

Connecting to the MySQL Database 369

Executing an SQL Query with DBI 370

A More Complex Example 372

Use Placeholders 375

DBI and Table Joins 377

Perl, DBI, and CGI 378

What We Didn't Talk About 385

Summary 386

Exercises 386

■Appendix: Exercise Solutions 387

Chapter 1 387

Chapter 2 387

Chapter 3 389

Chapter 4 390

Chapter 5 391

Chapter 6 393

Chapter 7 395

Chapter 8 396

Chapter 9 398

Chapter 10 399

Chapter 11 400

Chapter 13 404

Chapter 14 405

Chapter 15 406

■ **Index**...**409**

About the Author

James Lee is a hacker and open-source advocate based in Illinois. He has a master's degree from Northwestern University, where he can often be seen rooting for the Wildcats during football season. The founder of Onsight, James has worked as a programmer, trainer, manager, writer, and open-source advocate. He is the author of *Open Source Web Development with LAMP* (Addison-Wesley), and a coauthor of *Hacking Linux Exposed, Second Edition* (McGraw-Hill/Osborne). He has also written a number of articles on Perl for *Linux Journal*. James enjoys hacking Perl, developing software for the Web, snowboarding, listening to music on his iPod, reading, traveling, and most of all, playing with his kids, who are now old enough to know why Dad's favorite animals are penguins and camels. You can reach him at `james@onsight.com`.

About the Technical Reviewers

■**Richard Dice** has more than 15 years of experience in the IT industry in many different roles: he has been a software developer, manager of software development groups, and IT director with full responsibility for IT operations and customer deliverables in various operating companies. Richard has also been a IT consultant and corporate technology trainer to internationally recognizable organizations including Intel, Motorola and Unisys. He is an author and frequent speaker at industry conferences. Richard is also the past president of The Perl Foundation, the global organizing body that represented the Perl open-source programming language. Richard has a B.Sc. in Applied Mathematics from the University of Western Ontario and an MBA from the University of Toronto.

■**Ed Schaefer** is an ex-paratrooper, an ex-military intelligence officer, an ex-oil-field-service engineer, and a past contributing editor and columnist for *Sys Admin, the Journal of Unix System Administrators*. He's not a total has-been. He's earned a BSEE from South Dakota School of Mines & Technology, and a MBA from USD. Presently, he fixes microstrategy and teradata problems—with an occasional foray into Linux—for a Fortune 50 company.

■**Todd Shandelman**, who fondly remembers coding assembly language programs on punchcards for IBM System/370 mainframes, has been an ardent Perl devotee since the days of Perl 4. After occupying various other ecological niches in software technology over the years (C, C++, and Java, to name but a few), Todd has now settled comfortably into a mostly-Perl milieu. In his spare time a professional translator of Russian and Hebrew, he also enjoys studying Mandarin Chinese—as a sort of reminder of just how easy learning Perl really is! Todd earned a bachelor of science degree in business administration from the State University of New York and currently lives in Brookline, Massachusetts.

Acknowledgments

I want to start by saying thanks to Simon Cozens for writing an excellent book that I had the privilege of revising, again, for this latest edition. You set the bar extremely high—I hope that my work has not lowered it.

Luckily, I had great tech editors: Richard Dice, Ed Schaefer and Todd Shandelman. Thanks for all your excellent input. This book is better because of your hard work. Any mistakes that remain are all mine.

You folks at Apress are great, especially Frank Pohlmann, Laurin Becker and Fran Parnell. And thanks to Katie Stence and Sharon Terdeman for the copy editing. You all were a pleasure to work with.

Deep appreciation to Larry Wall for creating Perl; the language that has brought me great joy for the last 16 years. I don't think I would like my job as much if I never had Perl to play with. Thanks also to the Perl community for all the selfless work making Perl what it is, especially Lincoln Stein for CGI.pm and Tim Bunce for DBI.

Lastly, thanks to those in my life who help make it worth living: my family and all my friends—I'd list you all by name, but I have no idea who to start with (actually, I do know who to start with). Besides, you know who you are.

Introduction

Perl was originally written by Larry Wall while he was working at NASA's Jet Propulsion Labs. Larry is an Internet legend, known not just for Perl, but as the author of the UNIX utilities **rn**, one of the original Usenet newsreaders, and **patch**, a tremendously useful tool that takes a list of differences between two files and allows you to turn one into the other. The term *patch* used for this activity is now widespread.

Perl started life as a "glue" language for Larry and his officemates, allowing one to "stick" different tools together by converting between their various data formats. It pulled together the best features of several languages: the powerful regular expressions from sed (the Unix stream editor), the pattern-scanning language awk, and a few other languages and utilities. The syntax was further made up out of C, Pascal, Basic, Unix shell languages, English, and maybe a few other elements along the way.

While Perl started its life as glue, it is now more often likened to another handy multiuse tool: duct tape. A common statement heard in cyberspace is that Perl is the duct tape that holds the Internet together.

Version 1 of Perl hit the world on December 18, 1987 and the language has been steadily evolving since then, with contributions from a whole bunch of people (see the file **AUTHORS** in the latest stable release tarball). Perl 2 expanded regular expression support, while Perl 3 enabled the language to deal with binary data. Perl 4 was released so that the "Camel Book" (also known as *Programming Perl* by Larry Wall [O'Reilly & Associates, 2000]) could refer to a new version of Perl.

Perl 5 has seen some rather drastic changes in syntax, and some pretty fantastic extensions to the language. Perl 5 is (more or less) backwardly compatible with previous versions of the language, but at the same time makes a lot of the old code obsolete. Perl 4 code may still run, but Perl 4 style is definitely frowned upon these days.

At the time of writing, the current stable release of Perl is 5.10.1, which is what this book will describe. That said, the maintainers of Perl are very careful to ensure that old code will run, perhaps all the way back to Perl 1—changes and features that break existing programs are evaluated extremely seriously. Everything you see here will continue to function in the future.

We say "maintainers" because Larry no longer looks after Perl by himself—a group of "porters" maintains the language and produces new releases. The perl5-porters mailing list is the main development list for the language, and you can see the discussions archived at **www.xray.mpe.mpg.de/mailing-lists/perl5-porters**. For each release, one of the porters will carry the "patch pumpkin"—the responsibility for putting together and releasing the next version of Perl.

The Future of Perl—Developers Releases and Perl 6

Perl is a living language, and it continues to be developed and improved. The development happens on two fronts. Stable releases of Perl, intended for the general public, have a version number $x.y.z$ where z is less than 50. Currently, we're at 5.10.1; the next major stable release is going to be 5.12.0 (if there is another major release before version 6.0.0). Cases where z is more than 0 are maintenance releases issued to fix any overwhelming bugs. This happens extremely infrequently—for example, the 5.5 series had three maintenance releases in approximately a year of service.

Between stable releases, the porters work on the development track (where y is odd); when 5.8.0 was released, work began on 5.9.0 (the development track) to eventually become 5.10.0. Naturally, releases on the development track happen much more frequently than those on the stable track, but don't think you need to use a development version of Perl to get the latest and greatest features, or just because your stable version from last year seems old in comparison to the bright and shiny Perl released last week—no guarantees whatsoever are made about a development release of Perl. Releases are coordinated by a "patch pumpkin holder," or "pumpking"—a programmer of discernment and taste who, with help from Larry, decides which contributions make the grade and when, and bears the heavy responsibility of releasing a new Perl to the world. They maintain the most current and official source to Perl, which they sometimes make available to the public.

Why a pumpkin? To allow people to work on various areas of Perl at the same time and to avoid two people changing the same area in different ways, one person has to take responsibility for bits of development, and all changes must go through that person. Hence, the person who has the patch pumpkin is the only person who is allowed to make the change. Chip Salzenburg explains: "David Croy once told me that at a previous job, there was one tape drive and multiple systems that used it for backups. But instead of some high-tech exclusion software, they used a low-tech method to prevent multiple simultaneous backups: a stuffed pumpkin. No one was allowed to make backups unless they had the 'backup pumpkin.'"

So what development happens? As well as bug fixes, the main focus of development is to allow Perl to build more easily on a wider range of computers and to make better use of what the operating system and the hardware provides—support for 64-bit processors, for example. The Perl compiler is steadily getting more useful but still has a way to go. There's also a range of optimizations to be done to make Perl faster and more efficient, and work progresses to provide more helpful and more accurate documentation. Finally, there are a few enhancements to Perl syntax that are being debated—the `Todo` file in the Perl source kit explains what's currently on the table.

Perl 6

The future of Perl lies in Perl 6, a complete rewrite of the language. The purpose of Perl 6 is to address the problems with Perl 5 and to create a language that can continue to grow and change in the future. Larry Wall has this to say about Perl 6:

Perl 5 was my rewrite of Perl. I want Perl 6 to be the community's rewrite of Perl and of the community.

There are several changes to the Perl language that are in the works for Perl 6, including enhanced regular expression syntax, more powerful function definitions, some improvements to the constructs (including the addition of a `switch` statement), new object-oriented syntax, and more. Stay tuned for more information—it is definitely a work in progress.

A big change in Perl 6 will be the introduction of Rakudo (`http://www.rakudo.org`) which is based on Parrot (`http://www.parrotcode.org`). Rakudo is the new runtime environment that is being developed from scratch for Perl 6, but it will not be limited to Perl 6—any bytecode-compiled language such as Tcl and Python can use it.

You can read all about the future of Perl at `http://dev.perl.org/perl6/` and `http://www.perl6.org/`. Stay informed, and get involved!

Why Perl?

The name "Perl" isn't really an acronym. People like making up acronyms though, and Larry has two favorite expansions. Perl is, according to its creator, the Practical Extraction and Report Language, or the

Pathologically Eclectic Rubbish Lister. Either way, it doesn't really matter. Perl is a language for doing what you want to do easily and quickly.

The Perl motto is "There's More Than One Way To Do It," emphasizing both the flexibility of Perl and the fact that Perl is about getting the job done. This motto is so important someone has created an acronym for it: TMTOWTDI (pronounced "TimToeDee"). This acronym comes up again and again in this book since we often talk about many ways of doing the same thing. We can say that one Perl program is faster, or more idiomatic, or more efficient than another, but if both do the same thing, Perl isn't going to judge which one is "better." It also means that you don't need to know every last little detail about the language in order to do what you want with it. You'll probably be able to achieve many of the tasks you might want to use Perl for after the first four or five chapters of this book.

Perl has some very obvious strengths:

- It's easy to learn, and learning a little Perl can take you a long way. Perl is a lot like English in this regard—you don't need to know a lot of English to get your point across (as demonstrated by a three-year-old who wants a particular toy for her birthday), but if you know quite a bit about the English language, you can say a lot with a little.

- Perl was designed to be easy for humans to write, rather than easy for computers to understand. The syntax of the language is a lot more like a human language than the strict, rigid grammars and structures of other languages, and so it doesn't impose any particular way of thinking on you.

- Perl is very portable. That means what it sounds like—you can pick up a Perl program and carry it from one computer to another. Perl is available for a huge range of operating systems and computers, and properly written programs should be able to run almost anywhere that Perl does without any change.

- Perl talks text. It can think about words and sentences, where other languages see a character at a time. It can think about files in terms of lines, not individual bytes. Its regular expressions allow you to search for and transform text in innumerable ways with ease and speed.

- Perl is what is termed a "high-level language." Some languages like C concern you with unnecessary, low-level details about the computer's operation: making sure you have enough free memory, making sure all parts of your program are set up properly before you try to use them, and leaving you with strange and unfriendly errors if you don't do so. Perl cuts you free from all this.

However, since Perl is so easy to learn and to use, especially for quick little administrative tasks, "real" Perl users in practice tend to write programs to achieve small, specific jobs. In these cases, the code is meant to have a short lifespan, and be for the programmer's eyes only. The result is often a cryptic one-liner that is incomprehensible to everyone but the original programmer (and sometimes incomprehensible to him a year later). The problem is, these programs may live a little longer than the programmer expects, and be seen by other eyes as well. Because of the proliferation of these rather concise and confusing programs, Perl has developed a reputation for being arcane and unintelligible, one that will hopefully be dispelled during the course of this book.

For starters, this reputation is unfair. It's possible to write code that is tortuous and difficult to follow in any programming language, and Perl was never meant to be difficult. In fact, one could say that Perl is one of the easiest languages to learn, especially given its scope and flexibility.

Throughout this book you'll find examples showing you how to avoid the stereotypical "spaghetti code" and how to write programs that are both easy to write and easy to follow.

It's Open Source

Larry started (and indeed, continued) Perl with the strong belief that software should be free—freely available, freely modifiable, and freely distributable. It is part of a collection of programs known as open source (see `http://www.opensource.org` for details). Perl is developed and maintained by the porters, who are volunteers from the Perl user community, all of who strive to make Perl as useful as possible.

This has a few nice side effects—the porters are working for love, rather than merely because it's their job, so they're motivated solely by their desire to see a better Perl. It also means Perl will continue to be free to use and distribute.

This doesn't mean that Perl is part of the GNU suite of utilities. The GNU project was set up to produce a freely usable, distributable, and modifiable version of the Unix operating system and its tools, and now produces a lot of helpful, free utilities. Perl is included in distributions of GNU software, but Perl itself is not a product of the Free Software Foundation, the body that oversees GNU.

While Perl can be distributed under the terms of the GNU Public License (which you can find at `http://www.gnu.org`), it can also be distributed under the Artistic License (found either with the Perl sources or at `http://www.opensource.org/licenses`), which purports to give more freedom to users and more security to developers than the GPL.

Of course, those wanting to use Perl at work might be a little put off by this—managers like to pay money for things and have pieces of paper saying that they can get irate at someone if it all stops working. There's a question in the Perl Frequently Asked Questions (FAQ) about how to get a commercial version or support for Perl, and we'll see how you can find out the answer for yourself pretty soon.

When we say, "anyone can help" with Perl, we don't mean anyone who can understand the whole of the Perl source code. Of course, people who can knuckle down and attack the source files are useful, but equally useful work is done by the army of volunteers who offer their services as testers, documenters, proofreaders, and so on. Anyone who can take the time to check the spelling or grammar of some of the core documentation can help, as can anyone who can think of a new way of explaining a concept, or anyone who can come up with a more helpful example for a function.

Perl development is done in the open, on the perl5-porters mailing list. The `perlbug` program, shipped with Perl, can be used to report problems to the list, but it's a good idea to check with someone first to make sure that it really is a problem and that it isn't fixed in a later or development release of Perl.

Perl on the Web and the Network

One of the most popular uses of Perl is CGI programming—that is, dynamically generating web pages. This is introduced in Chapter 14. Perl is the power behind some of the most popular sites on the Web: Slashdot (`http://www.slashdot.org`), Amazon (`http://www.amazon.com`), and many others are almost entirely Perl-driven.

Of course, Perl is still widely used for its original purpose: extracting data from one source and translating it to another format. This covers everything from processing and summarizing system logs, through manipulating databases, reformatting text files, and simple search-and-replace operations, to something like `alien`, a program to port Linux software packages between different distributors' packaging formats. Perl even manages the data from the Human Genome Project, a task requiring massive amounts of data manipulation.

For system administrators, Perl is certainly the "Swiss Army chainsaw" that it claims to be. It's great for automating administration tasks, sending automatically generated mail, and generally tidying up the system. It can process logs, report information on disk usage, produce reports on resource use, and watch for security problems. There are also extensions that allow Perl to deal with the Windows registry and run as a Windows service, not to mention built-in functions that enable it to manipulate UNIX passwd and group file entries.

However, as you might expect, that's not all. Perl is becoming the de facto programming language of the Internet—its networking capabilities have allowed it to be used to create clients, servers, and proxies for standards such as IRC, WWW, FTP, and practically every other protocol you can think of. It's used to filter mail, automatically post news articles, mirror websites, automate downloading and uploading, and so on. In fact, it's hard to find an area of the Internet where Perl isn't used. This is kind of like duct tape, really. When was the last time you used duct tape to tape a duct?

Windows, Unix, and Other Operating Systems

Perl is one of the most portable, if not the most portable, programming languages around. It can be compiled on over 70 operating systems, and you can get binary distributions for most common platforms. Most of the programs in this book can run equally well on almost any operating system.

When we're setting up Perl and running our examples, we'll concentrate particularly on Unix and Windows. The term *Unix* here refers to any commercial or free Unix-like implementation—Solaris; Linux; Net-, Free-, and OpenBSD; HP/UX; A/IX; and so on. Perl's home platform is Unix, and 90% of the world uses Windows. That said, Perl is the same for everyone. If you need help with your particular platform, you can probably find a README file for it in the Perl source distribution.

You can also get more information on portable Perl programming from the `perlport` documentation. Again, you'll see how to access this documentation very soon.

Program Names

Perl doesn't care what we programmers name our scripts, but this book uses the conventional file extension `.pl`. For instance, one of our first programs will be named `helloworld.pl`.

The Prompt

If you're primarily using your computer in a graphical environment like Windows or X, you may not be familiar with using the command-line interface, or *shell*. Before those graphical environments came into common use, users had to start a new program not by finding its icon and clicking it but by typing its name. The shell is the program that takes the name from you—the *shell prompt* (or just *prompt*) refers specifically to the text that prompts you to enter a new program name, and also more generally to working with the shell instead of using a graphical interface. Some people still find working with the shell much easier, and sophisticated shells have developed to simplify common tasks. In fact, on Unix, the shell is programmable, and Perl takes some of its inspiration from standard "Bourne Shell" programming practices.

To get to a prompt in Windows, look for Command Prompt or DOS Prompt in the Start menu. Unix users should look for a program called something like `console`, `terminal`, `konsole`, `xterm`, `eterm`, or `kterm`. You'll then typically be faced with a black screen displaying a small amount of text that looks something like one of the following:

```
$
%
C:\>
#
bash$
```

If your shell prompt is #, chances are you're running the shell as the root user. This is usually a bad idea—use with caution!

For this book, we'll use a prompt that looks like this:

```
$
```

We'll show text that you type in using a bold font, and the text the computer generates in normal typeface, like this:

```
$ perl helloworld.pl
Hello, world!
```

More on what this program looks like in just a few pages!

The command line may look scary at first, but you'll quickly get used to it as we go through the examples and exercises.

A note to Unix/Linux/OpenBSD/etc. users: a Perl program can be executed from the shell with

```
$ perl -w helloworld.pl
Hello, world!
```

Or, if the first line of the file resembles

```
#! /usr/bin/perl -w
```

and the file has the proper executable permissions set, it can be executed as

```
$ ./helloworld.pl
Hello, world!
```

Since both methods of invoking the program work in Unix/Linux/OpenBSD/etc., and only the first will work in Windows, the examples in this book will be executed using the first style.

What Do I Need to Use This Book?

First, you need Perl. As mentioned previously, Perl is available for almost any kind of computer that has a keyboard and a screen, but we will be concentrating on Perl for Windows and Unix. Perl 5.10.1 will run on different versions of Windows. It'll run on more or less any Unix, although you may find compilation is difficult if you don't have the latest C libraries. Any 2.x Linux kernel should be fine, likewise Solaris 2.6 or higher. Perl is also available on Apple Macintosh computers—see http://www.macperl.com for Mac OS 9 and below; for Mac OS X, it is found in /usr/bin/perl.

Besides Perl, you'll need a text editor to write and edit Perl source files. We look at a couple of options later in this introduction.

To get the most out of some chapters, you'll also need to have an Internet connection. A helpful place to start on the Internet is http://www.apress.com, where you can download all the source code for the examples in the book.

For Chapter 14, you'll need a web server that supports CGI scripting. Apache is a good bet on Unix machines (and it's included in most Linux distributions). Windows users should also use Apache; check it out at http://www.apache.org.

How Do I Get Perl?

Perl has been ported to many, many platforms. It will almost certainly build and run on anything that looks like (or pretends to be) Unix, such as Linux, Solaris, A/IX, HP/UX, FreeBSD, or even the Cygwin32

UNIX environment for Windows. Most other current operating systems are supported: Windows, OS/2, VMS, DOS, BeOS, the Apple Mac OS, and AmigaOS, to name but a few.

- You can get the source to the latest stable release of Perl from `www.perl.com/CPAN-local/src/stable.tar.gz`.

- Binary distributions for some ports will appear in `www.perl.com/CPAN-local/ports/`. These ports may differ in implementation from the original sources.

- You can get binary packages of Perl for Linux, Solaris, and Windows from ActiveState at `www.activestate.com/ActivePerl/download.htm`.

- Linux users should be able to get binary packages from the contrib section of their distributor's FTP site.

Installing Perl is well-documented at the web sites mentioned, so we won't go through the steps here. Go and install Perl now—reading this book will be much more fun if you can try the examples.

How to Get Help

Perl comes with excellent documentation. The interface to this system is through the `perldoc` command, itself a Perl program. Unix users can also use the `man` command to get at the same information, but `perldoc` allows you to do interesting things, as you're about to see.

Perldoc

Typing `perldoc perl` from a command prompt presents the Perl documentation table of contents and some basic information about Perl.

The pages you're probably going to use the most are the Perl FAQ and `perlfunc`, which describes the built-in functions. Because of this, `perldoc` has a special interface to these two pages. `perldoc -f` allows you to see information about a particular function, like this (the output has been snipped—try it yourself!):

```
$ perldoc -f print
print FILEHANDLE LIST
print LIST
print   Prints a string or a list of strings.  Returns true if success-
        ful.  FILEHANDLE may be a scalar variable name, in which case
        [output snipped]...
```

Similarly, `perldoc -q` allows you to search the Perl FAQ for any regular expression or keyword.

```
$ perldoc -q reverse
Found in /usr/lib/perl5/5.10.1/pod/perlfaq4.pod
   How do I reverse a string?
     Use reverse() in scalar context, as documented in the reverse
     entry in the perlfunc manpage

     $reversed = reverse $string;
```

As well as the documentation pages for the language itself, whose names all start with "perl", there's a whole lot of other documentation out there, too. The reason for this is modules: files containing Perl code that can be used to help with a certain task. We'll examine what modules are available and what they can help us do later, but you should know that each Perl module, whether a core module that comes with the Perl distribution or one you download from the Internet, should contain its own documentation. We'll see how that's constructed later—for now, know that you can use **perldoc** to get at this, too. Here's the beginning of the documentation for the **Text::Wrap** module, which is used to wrap lines into paragraphs:

```
$ perldoc Text::Wrap
5.10.1::Text  User Contributed Perl Documentation  Text::Wrap(3)


NAME
      Text::Wrap - line wrapping to form simple paragraphs

...
```

Perl Resources

There is truly a wealth of Perl information available out there, especially on the Internet. Let's have a look at some of the more prominent sources.

Web Sites

On the web, the first port of call is **www.perl.com**, the main Perl community site. This site contains many good articles of interest to the Perl community and news from Perl's major developers, as well as a wealth of links, tips, reviews, and documentation.

The next stop is CPAN, the Comprehensive Perl Archive Network (**www.cpan.org**), a collection of ready-made programs, documents (notably, the latest edition of the FAQ), some tutorials, and the Far More Than Everything You Wanted To Know About[1] series of more technical notes. Most useful of all, this site contains a huge (and they don't call it comprehensive for nothing!) collection of those Perl modules mentioned previously.

Other important Perl sites are listed here:

- **www.perl.org**: A site with tons of information about Perl

- **www.pm.org**: The Perl Mongers, a worldwide umbrella organization for Perl user groups

- **www.theperlreview.com**: The home of the *Perl Review*, an online Perl magazine

- **www.activestate.com**: The home of Perl on Windows

- **www.perlarchive.com**: Another great source of articles, tutorials, and information

---

[1] Yep, there is an acronym for this phrase – FMTEYWTKA.

Newsgroups

Perl has its own Usenet hierarchy, `comp.lang.perl`.*. The groups in it are listed here:

- `comp.lang.perl.announce` for Perl-related announcements: new modules, new versions of Perl, conferences, and so on

- `comp.lang.perl.misc` for general Perl chat and questions

- `comp.lang.perl.moderated`, which requires prior registration before posting but is excellent for sensible questions and in-depth discussion of Perl's niggly bits

- `comp.lang.perl.modules`, for discussion and queries relating to creating and using Perl modules

- `comp.lang.perl.tk`, for discussion and queries relating to the Tk graphical extensions

IRC

If you've got a more urgent mindbender, or just want to hang around like-minded individuals, come join `#perl` on Efnet (`www.efnet.org`). Make sure you read the channel rules (at `http://pound.perl.org/RTFM/`) and the Perl documentation thoroughly first. Asking questions about CGI or topics covered in the FAQ or the `perldoc` documentation is highly inflammatory behavior.

Books

Of course, reading stuff on the Net is a great way to learn, and it is not difficult to curl up in bed with a good web site (most of us have a WiFi-enabled laptops these days). In the meantime, there are a few good treeware resources available too. Check out the book reviews pages housed at the `www.perl.com` and `www.perl.org` sites.

As for the best book for teaching yourself Perl, just keep reading . . .

Downloading This Book's Example Source Code

As you work through the examples in this book, you might decide you want to type all the code in by hand. Many readers prefer this because it's a good way to become familiar with the coding techniques being used.

Whether you want to type the code in or not, we have made all the source code for this book available at our web site, `www.apress.com`.

If you're one of those readers who likes to type the code, you can use our files to check the results you should be getting—they should be your first stop if you think you might have typed in an error. If you're someone who doesn't like typing, downloading the source code from our web site is a must!

Either way, it'll help you with updates and debugging.

Exercises

At the end of most of this book's chapters, you'll find a number of exercises that we highly recommend you work through. This book will give you the knowledge you need—but it is only through practice that you'll hone your skills and get a true feel for what Perl can help you achieve. You can find our suggested solutions to the exercises in the Appendix at the back of the book and also for download from www.apress.com. But remember TMTOWTDI, so they're not the only ways to solve the exercises.

Who This Book Is For

This book is written for the novice programmer and the experienced programmer alike. Using extensive examples, the features of Perl are introduced and discussed in a way that is easy to learn for the newcomer and useful for the veteran.

If you are looking to learn Perl and get an introduction to its power, this book is for you.

How This Book Is Organized

Chapter 1—First Steps in Perl: The basics of Perl are introduced, including how to execute Perl code. A simple first program is developed.

Chapter 2—Scalars: The most basic Perl data type, the scalar, is described. Perl's arithmetic, logical, and string operators are explained, as are a few of Perl's simplest control flow constructs: `if` and `while`. Several functions are discussed, including `chop()`, `chomp()`, `exit()`, and `die()`.

Chapter 3—Control Flow Constructs: The control flow constructs are discussed, including `if`, `unless`, `while`, `until`, `do .. while`, `do .. until`, `for`, and `foreach`. We also talk about expression modifiers and short-circuited operators as alternative ways of writing constructs.

Chapter 4—Lists and Arrays: We talk about the array data type—a collection of 0 or more scalars. Lists and list operators are also discussed. The array functions `push()`, `pop()`, `shift()`, `unshift()`, `reverse()`, and `sort()` are described, as is the `foreach` loop.

Chapter 5—Hashes: Hashes, the third major data type, are discussed. We describe what hashes are, why we need them, and how to operate on them. We talk about the hash functions `keys()`, `values()`, `each()`, `delete()`, and `exists()`.

Chapter 6—Subroutines/Functions: This chapter talks about user-defined functions. Function definitions are discussed, as well as function invocation, return values, and passing arguments.

Chapter 7—Regular Expressions: This feature that makes Perl a powerful text-processing language is discussed. The basics of regular expressions are introduced, including creating character classes and regex quantifiers. Regex memory, a powerful feature allowing the programmer to extract text, is covered. Several operators, including the match and substitute operators, are introduced.

Chapter 8—Files and Data: Opening files for reading and writing data is discussed, then the topic of reading from files that are provided on the command line using the diamond is covered. Pipes to external processes and pipes from processes are described. File test operators, which test certain qualities of files such as readability and writability, are introduced.

Chapter 9—String Processing: String manipulation functions and operators are introduced, including `length()`, `index()`, `rindex()`, `substr()`, and `tr///`.

Chapter 10—Interfacing to the Operating System: Functions such as `chdir()`, `mkdir()`, `rename()`, and others are discussed. Also, executing external programs with `system()` and backquotes are introduced. Reading the contents of a directory using directory streams is also covered.

Chapter 11—References: A reference is a scalar that refers to another variable in memory. The topics covered include creating references, dereferencing, creating anonymous variables, and complex data types.

Chapter 12—Modules: Using existing modules to easily solve complex problems is described. Several useful modules are discussed and demonstrated. Creating a module from scratch is illustrated.

Chapter 13—Object-Oriented Perl: The basics of creating a class definition in Perl is described, including creating objects with attributes and methods. Inheritance is briefly introduced.

Chapter 14—Introduction to CGI: Perl is a popular language for CGI (that is, web) programming. This chapter introduces `CGI.pm`, a popular Perl module that makes writing CGI programs easy.

Chapter 15—Perl and DBI: The useful DBI module enables a Perl programmer to easily write powerful scripts that connect to and query an SQL database. This chapter introduces the idea of relational databases and SQL. Several Perl scripts for administering a database are described. Then a detailed example is discussed that shows how to use `CGI.pm` and the DBI module to web-enable SQL access.

CHAPTER 1

■ ■ ■

First Steps in Perl

Every programming language has a number of things in common. The fundamental concepts of programming are going to be the same, no matter what language in which you execute them. In this chapter, you'll investigate the things you need to know before you start writing any programs. For instance:

- What is programming? What does it mean to program?

- How do you structure programs and make them easy to understand?

- How do computers see numbers and letters?

- How do you find and eliminate errors in your programs?

Of course, you'll be looking at these from a Perl perspective, and you'll look at a couple of basic Perl programs, see how they're constructed, and what they do. At the end of this chapter, you will be asked to write a couple of trivial Perl programs of your own.

Programming Languages

The first question you should ask yourself when you're learning programming is, "What is programming?" That may sound particularly philosophical, but the answer is easy. Programming is telling a computer what you want it to do; and you do this by writing it a program. The only trick, then, is making sure that the program is written in a way the computer can understand, and to do this, you need to write it in a language that it can comprehend—a programming language, such as Perl.

There's nothing magical about writing a program, but it does call for a particular way of thinking. When you're telling a human what you want them to do, you take certain things for granted.

- Humans can ask questions if they don't understand your instructions.

- They can break up tasks into smaller tasks by themselves.

- They can draw parallels between the current task and a task they have completed in the past.

- Perhaps most importantly, they can learn from demonstrations and from their own mistakes.

Computers can't yet do any of these things very well—it's still much easier to explain to someone how to tie their shoelaces than it is to set the clock on the VCR.

The most important thing you need to bear in mind, though, is that you're never going to be able to express a task to a computer if you can't express it to yourself. Computer programming leaves little room for vague specifications and hand waving. If you want to write a program to, say, remove useless files from your computer, you need to be able to explain how to determine whether a file is useless or not. You need to examine and break down your own mental processes when carrying out the task for yourself—do you mean a file that hasn't been accessed for a long time? How long, precisely? Then do you delete it immediately, or do you examine it? If you examine it, how much of it? And what are you examining it for?

The first step in programming is to stop thinking in terms of "I want a program that removes useless files," but instead think "I want a program that looks at each file on the computer in turn and deletes the file if it is over six months old, and if the first five lines do not contain any of the words 'Larry', 'Perl', or 'Camel'"—in other words, you have to specify your task precisely.

When you're able to do that, you need to translate that into the programming language you're using. Unfortunately, like any human language, the programming language may not have a direct equivalent for what you're trying to say. So, you have to get your meaning across using the parts of the language that are available to you, and this may well mean breaking down your task further. For instance, there's no way of saying "if the first five lines do not contain any of the following words" in Perl. However, there is a way of saying "if a line contains this word," a way of saying "get another line," and "do this five times." Programming is the art of putting those elements together to get them to do what you want.

So much for what you have to do—what does the computer have to do? Once you have specified the task in our programming language, the computer takes your instructions and performs them. This is called *running* or *executing* the program. Usually, you'll specify the instructions in a file, which you edit with an ordinary text editor; sometimes, if you have got a small program, you can get away with typing the whole thing in at the command line. Either way, the instructions that you give to the computer—in this case, written in Perl—are collectively called the *source code* (or sometimes just *source*) to your program.

Our First Perl Program

Assuming that you now have a copy of Perl installed on your machine (perhaps having followed the instructions in the Introduction), you are ready to start using Perl. If not, go back and follow the instructions. The next step is to set up a directory for all the examples used in the rest of the book, and to write your first Perl program.

Here's what it will look like:

```
#!/usr/bin/perl

use warnings;

print "Hello, world!\n";
```

I highly suggest that you type this example in and try to make it work, so before you go any further, a quick note on editors. Perl source code is just plain text, and should be written with a plain text editor, rather than a word processor. Your operating system, whether Unix, OS X, or Windows, comes with a selection of text editors. You may have a favorite already, so feel free to use it. If not, may I suggest vi (www.vim.org), emacs (www.xemacs.org), and nedit (www.nedit.org). Windows provides WordPad and

Notepad, but they lack many features of modern text editors, so they should be avoided. `nedit` is the most WordPad- and Notepad-like, so give it a try.

After an editor is chosen, you need to create a new directory for your work. If you are in Windows, a simple way to do this is to start up a command shell (Start Run cmd) and enter

```
c:> mkdir begperl
c:> cd begperl
```

If you are working in any Unix variant, start a shell and enter

```
$ mkdir begperl
$ cd begperl
```

This directory will hold all the examples that you will do as you go through this book.

The next step is to fire up your editor of choice, type in the code shown previously, and save it into a file named `hellowworld.pl` in the directory you just made. Then, to execute it, type

```
$ perl helloworld.pl
Hello, world!
$
```

Congratulations. You have successfully written and executed your first Perl program!

■ **Note** From this point on, I'll not run through these steps again. Instead, the name you've given the file will be shown as a comment on the second line of the program. You may also have noticed that the output for `hellowworld.pl` on Windows and Unix differs in that Windows adds a blank line at the end of the output for all its Perl programs. From now on, you'll only print the Unix output that is without the additional blank line. Windows users please be aware of this.

Let's look at this program in detail by going through it a line at a time. The first line is

```
#!/usr/bin/perl
```

Normally, Perl treats a line starting with # as a comment, and ignores it. However, the # and ! characters together at the start of the first line tell Unix how the file should be run—in this case the file should be executed by the Perl interpreter, which lives in `/usr/bin/perl` in this example. In the Unix world, this line is known as the *shebang* (short for "hash bang"), and it must be located on the first line starting in the first column.

■ **Note** To Unix users: your version of Perl may reside in a different location than `/usr/bin/perl`. Common alternative locations are `/usr/local/bin/perl` and `/opt/bin/perl`. If your version of Perl resides somewhere other than `/usr/bin/perl`, you will have to adjust your shebang line to point to it.

Unix users can use the invocation shown previously to execute Perl programs:

```
$ perl helloworld.pl
```

But they can also execute Perl programs by making the file executable with the `chmod` command and executing it by name like the in the following:

```
$ chmod +x helloworld.pl
$ ./helloworld.pl
```

Perl also reads the shebang line regardless of whether you are on Unix, Windows, or any other system. The reason for this is to see if there are any special options, or switches, it should turn on. Possible options include `-w` to turn on warnings, `-c` to check the syntax of a Perl program, and many others. Enter `perldoc perlrun` into a shell for more information.

The next line of this program is a blank line. Perl, like C, C++, and many other programming languages, treats blank lines, extra spaces, and tabs as *whitespace*. In Perl, whitespace can be added to the program to make it more readable.

Then you see this line of code

```
use warnings;
```

This line turns on warnings, which will be discussed in detail in the following. Another way to turn on warnings is to use the `-w` option on the shebang,

```
#! /usr/bin/perl -w
```

■ **Note** The use of the `-w` on the shebang is required with older versions of Perl (5.5 and below), so the only reason to use `-w` is if you have a version pre-5.6 Perl release. But since Perl version 5.6 was released in 2000, if you are using a pre-5.6 version it is time to upgrade.

The last line of the program is

```
print "Hello, world!\n";
```

The `print()` function tells Perl to display the given text, without the quotation marks. The text inside the quotes is not interpreted as code, and is called a *string*. As you'll see later, strings start and end with some sort of quotation mark. The `\n` at the end of the quote is a type of escape sequence which stands for "new line." This instructs Perl to finish the current line and take the prompt to the start of a new one. I will talk more about escape sequences later in this chapter.

You may be wondering why `use warnings;` is so helpful. Suppose I altered the program to demonstrate this, and made two mistakes by leaving out `use warnings;` by modifying the code so it looks like this:

```
#!/usr/bin/perl

print "Hello, $world!\n";
```

The string that you are printing now contains the text `$world`. As you will see in the next chapter, `$world` is a variable, and this variable has not been assigned a value. If you attempt to print a variable that has no value, you simply print nothing.

Save these changes in `helloworld2.pl` before exiting your editor. Now let's get back to the command prompt, and type the following:

```
$ perl helloworld2.pl
```

Instead of getting the expected

```
Hello, world!
$
```

the output would be

```
Hello, !
$
```

If you now correct one of the mistakes by including `use warnings;` in your program, then `helloworld2.pl` looks like this:

```
#!/usr/bin/perl

use warnings;

print "Hello, $world!\n";
```

Once you have saved this new change into the program, you can run it again. The output that you get now contains a warning as well as the text printed, so the screen looks like this:

```
$ perl helloworld2.pl
Use of uninitialized value in concatenation (.) or string at helloworld2.pl line 5.
Hello, !
```

On the surface of things, it may seem that you have just given yourself another line of output, but bear in mind that the first line is now a *warning message*, and is informing us that Perl has picked something up that may (or may not) cause problems later on in the program. Don't worry if you don't understand everything in the error message at the moment, just so long as you are beginning to see the usefulness of having an early warning system in place.

Program Structure

One of the things you want to develop throughout this book is a sense of good programming practice. Obviously this will not only benefit you while using Perl, but in almost every other programming language too. The most fundamental notion is how to structure and lay out the code in your source files. By keeping this tidy and easy to understand, you'll make your own life as a programmer easier.

Documenting Your Programs

As mentioned earlier, a line starting with a hash, or pound sign (#), is treated as a comment and ignored. This allows you to provide comments about what your program is doing, something that will become extremely useful to you when working on long programs, or when someone else is looking over your code. For instance, you could make it quite clear what the preceding program was doing by saying something like this:

```
#!/usr/bin/perl

# turn on warning messages
use warnings;

# display a short message to the terminal
print "Hello, world!\n";
```

A line may contain some Perl code, and be followed by a comment. This means that you can document your program "inline" like this:

```
#!/usr/bin/perl

use warnings; # turn on warning messages

print "Hello, world!\n"; # print a short message
```

When you come to write more advanced programs, you'll take a look at some good and bad commenting practices.

Keywords

A *keyword* is a term in Perl that has a predefined meaning. One example would be the term use as you saw in the statement

```
use warnings;
```

Other types of keywords include built-in functions such as print() and control flow constructs such as if and while. I will talk about many built-in functions and control flow constructs in detail as we progress in our discussion of Perl.

It's a good idea to respect keywords and not give anything else the same name. For example, a little later on you'll learn that you can create and name a variable, and that calling your variable $print is perfectly allowable. The problem with this is that it leads to confusing and uninformative statements like print $print. It is always a good idea to give a variable a meaningful name, one that relates to its content in a logical manner. For example, $my_name, @telephone_numbers, %account_info, and so on, rather than $a, @b, and %c.

Statements and Statement Blocks

If functions are the verbs of Perl, then *statements* are the sentences. Instead of a period, a statement in Perl usually ends with a semicolon, as you saw earlier:

```
print "Hello, world!\n";
```

To print some more text, you can add another statement:

```
print "Hello, world!\n";
print "Goodbye, world!\n";
```

You can also group together a bunch of statements into a *block*—which is a bit like a paragraph—by surrounding them with curly braces {...}. You'll see later how blocks are used to specify a set of statements that must happen at a given time, and also how they are used to limit the effects of a statement. Here's an example of a block:

```
{
    print "This is ";
    print "a block ";
    print "of statements.\n";
}
```

Notice how indentation is used to separate the block from its surroundings. This is because, unlike paragraphs, you can put blocks inside of blocks, which makes it easier to see on what level things are happening. Using indentation is a great use of whitespace, making the code easier to read and therefore to maintain later on. The following code serves to illustrate:

```
print "Top level\n";
{
    print "2nd level\n";
    {
        print "3rd level\n";
    }
    print "Where are we?";
}
```

is easier to follow than this:

```
print "Top level\n";
{
print "2nd level\n";
{
print "3rd level\n";
}
print "Where are we?";
}
```

As well as curly braces to mark out the territory of a block of statements, you can use parentheses to mark out what you're giving a function. The set of things given to a function are the *arguments*; and you

7

pass the arguments to the function. For instance, you can pass a number of arguments to the `print()` function by separating them with commas:

```
print "here ", "we ", "print ", "several ", "strings.\n";
```

The `print()` function happily takes as many arguments as it is given, and it produces the expected answer:

```
here we print several strings.
```

Surrounding the arguments with parentheses clears things up a bit:

```
print("here ", "we ", "print ", "several ", "strings.\n");
```

In the cases where parentheses are optional, the important thing to do is to use your judgment. Sometimes something will look perfectly understandable without the parentheses, but when you've got a complicated statement and you need to be sure of which arguments belong to which function, putting in the parentheses is useful. Always aim to help the readers of your code because, remember, these readers will more than likely include you.

Character Sets

Characters such as "A" and "7" have to be respresented in the computer in some way. A system was created called *character encoding* or *character sets*. The first set many of us learn is the ASCII (American Standard Code for Information Interchange), a way of prepresenting a group of 256 characters in 1 byte (8 bits) of information. For instance, in ASCII, the character "A" is represented as the numeric value 65 (0x41 in hexidecimal) and "7" is represented as 55 (0x37).

There are many character sets in use, too many to talk about here. For a good discussion see `http://en.wikipedia.org/wiki/Character_encoding`.

An important character set is called Unicode, which represents over 107,000 characters in over 90 scripts, such as Japanese characters and Chinese characters. Perl supports Unicode.You will see an example of this in the following section.

Escape Sequences

UTF8 gives us 65536 characters, and ASCII gives us 256 characters, but on the average keyboard, there are only a hundred or so keys. Even using the shift keys, there will still be some characters that you aren't going to be able to type. There'll also be some things that you don't want to stick in the middle of your program, because they would make it messy or confusing. However, you'll want to refer to some of these characters in strings that you output. Perl provides us with mechanisms called *escape sequences* as an alternative way of getting to them. You've already seen the use of \n to start a new line. Table 1-1 lists the more common escape sequences.

Table 1-1. Escape Sequences

Escape Sequence	Meaning
\t	Tab
\n	Start a new line (usually called *newline*)
\r	Carriage return
\b	Back up one character (*backspace*)
\a	Alarm (rings the system bell)

In the last example, 1F18 is a hexadecimal number (see the upcoming section "Number Systems") referring to a character in the Unicode character set, which runs from 0000-FFFF. As another example, \x{2620} is the Unicode character for a skull-and-crossbones[1]!

Whitespace

As mentioned previously, *whitespace* is the name you give to tabs, spaces, and newlines. Perl is very flexible about where you put whitespace in your program. You have already seen how you're free to use indentation to help show the structure of blocks. You don't need to use any whitespace at all, if you don't want to. If you'd prefer, your programs can all look like this:

```
print"Top level\n";{print"2nd level\n";{print"3rd level\n";}print"Where are we?";}
```

This is considered a bad idea. Whitespace is another tool you have to make your programs more understandable; let's use it as such.

Number Systems

If you thought the way computers see characters was weird, I have a surprise for you.

The way most humans count is using the decimal system, or what is called base 10; we write 0, 1, 2, 3, 4, 5, 6, 7, 8, 9, and then when we get to 10, we carry 1 in the 10s column and start from 0 again. Then when the 10s column gets to 9 and the 1s column gets to 9, we carry 1 in the 100s column and start again. Why 10? We used to think it's because we have 10 fingers, but then we found out that the Babylonians counted up to 60, which stopped that.

On the other hand, computers count by registering whether or not electricity flows in a certain part of the circuit. For simplicity's sake, you'll call a flow of electricity a 1, and no flow a 0. So, you start off

---

[1] ☠

with 0, no flow. Then you get a flow, which represents 1. That's as much as you can do with that part of the circuit. 0 or 1, off or on. Instead of base 10, the decimal system, this is *base 2, the binary system*. In the binary system, one digit represents one unit of information: one **bi**nary digi**t**, or *bit*.

When you join two parts of the circuit together, things get more interesting. Look at them both in a row, when they are both off, the counter reads 00. Then one comes on, so you get 01. Then what? Well, humans get to 9 and have to carry 1 to the next column, but computers only get to 1. The next number, number 2, is represented as 10. Then 11. And you need some more of your circuit. Number 4 is 100, 5 is 101, and so ad infinitum. If you got used to it, and you used the binary system naturally, you could count up to 1023 on your fingers.

This may sound like an abnormal way to count, but even stranger counting mechanisms are all around us. As this is being written, it's 7:59 p.m. In one minute, it'll be 8:00 p.m., which seems unremarkable. But that's a base 60 system. In fact, it's worse than that—it doesn't stay in base 60, because hours carry at 24 instead of 60. Anyone who's used the Imperial measurement system, a Chinese abacus, or pounds, shillings, and pence knows the full horror of mixed base systems, which are far more complicated than what you're dealing with here.

As well as binary, there are two more important sequences you need to know about when talking to computers. You don't often get to deal with binary directly, but the following two sequences have a logical relationship to base 2 counting. The first is *octal, base 8*.

Eight is an important number in computing; bits are organized in groups of eight to form *byte*s, giving you the range of 0–255 you saw earlier with ASCII. Each ASCII character can be represented by one byte. Octal is therefore a good way of counting bits, although it has fallen out of fashion these days. Octal numbers all start with 0 (that's a zero, not an oh), so know they're octal, and proceed as you'd expect: 00, 01, 02, 03, 04, 05, 06, 07, carry one, 010, 011, 012 . . . 017, carry one, 020, and so on. Perl recognizes octal numbers if you're certain to put that zero in front, like this:

```
print 06301;
```

which prints out the decimal number

```
3265
```

The second is called the hexadecimal system, as mentioned previously. Of course, programmers are lazy, so they just call it *hex*. (They like the wizard image.)

Decimal is base 10, and hexagons have six sides, so this system is base 16. As you might have guessed from the number 1F18 shown previously, digits above 9 are represented by letters, so A is 10, B is 11, and so on, all the way through to F, which is 15. You then carry one and start with 10 (which, in decimal, is 16) all the way up through 19, 1A, 1B, 1C, 1D, 1E, 1F, and carry one again to get 20 (which in decimal is 32). The magic number 255, the maximum number can store in one byte, is FF. Two bytes next to each other can get you up to FF FF, better known as 65535. You met 65535 as the highest number in the Unicode character set, and you guessed it, a Unicode character can be stored as a pair of bytes.

To get Perl to recognize hex, place 0x in front of the digits so that

```
print 0xBEEF;
```

gives the answer

```
48879
```

The Perl Debugger

One thing you'll soon notice about programming is that you'll make mistakes; mistakes in programs are called *bugs*. Bugs are almost entirely unavoidable, and creating bugs does not mean you're a bad programmer. Windows 2000 allegedly shipped with 65,000 bugs, but then that's a special case, and even the greatest programmers in the world have problems with bugs. Donald Knuth's typesetting software TeX has been in use for more than 20 years, and Professor Knuth was still finding bugs until a couple of years ago. Who can tell when all the bugs are out anyway?

While I will be showing you ways to avoid getting bugs in your program, Perl provides you with a tool to help find and trace the causes of bugs. Naturally, any tool for getting rid of bugs in your program is called a *debugger*. Mundanely enough, the corresponding tool for putting bugs into your program is called a "programmer."

To use the debugger, start your program with the -d option as in

```
$ perl -d myprogram.pl
```

See perldoc perldebug for information about the debugger.

Summary

You've started on the road to programming in Perl, and programming in general. You've seen your first piece of Perl code, and hopefully, you were able to get it to run.

Programming is basically telling a computer what to do in a language it comprehends. It's about breaking down problems or ideas into byte-sized chunks (as it were), and examining what needs to be done in order to communicate them clearly to the machine.

Thankfully, Perl is a language that allows us a certain degree of freedom in our expression, and, so long as we work within the bounds of the language, it won't enforce any particular method of expression on us. Of course, it may judge what we're saying to be wrong, because we're not speaking the language correctly, and that's how the majority of bugs are born. Generally though, if a program does what we want, that's enough—TMTOWTDI.

You've also seen a few ways of making it easy for ourselves to spot potential problems, and you know there are tools that can help if you need it. You have examined a little bit of what goes on inside a computer, how it sees numbers, and how it sees characters, as well as what it does to our programs when and as it executes them.

Exercises

1. Create a program `newline.pl` containing `print "Hi Mom.\nThis is my second program.\n"`. Run this and then replace \n with a space or a return and compare the results.

2. Download the code for this book from the publisher's website at `www.apress.com`.

3. Have a look around the Perl homepage at `www.perl.com`.

4. Visit `en.wikipedia.org/wiki/List_of_Unicode_characters` and choose your favorite Unicode character and print it with code that resembles `print "\x{2708}";`.

■ ■ ■

## CHAPTER 2

Scalars

The essence of programming is computation—we want the computer to do some work with the input (the data we give it). Very rarely do we write programs to tell us something we already know. Even more rarely do we write programs to do nothing at all interesting with our data. So, if we're going to write programs that do more than say hello to us, we're going to need to know how to perform computations—operations on our data.

In this chapter, we will discuss several important items basic to programming in Perl:

- Scalars: Single values, either numbers or strings.

- Variables: Places to store a value.

- Operators: Symbols such as + and – that act on data.

- Reading data from the user: Taking data from standard input, also known as the keyboard.

Types of Data

A lot of programming jargon is about familiar words in an unfamiliar context. We've already looked at a string, which is a series of characters. We could also describe that string as a *scalar literal constant*. What does that mean?

By calling a value a *scalar*, we're describing the type of data it contains. If you remember your math (and even if you don't), a *scalar* is a plain, simple, one-dimensional value. In math, the word is used to distinguish such values from a vector, which is expressed as several numbers. Velocity, for example, has a pair of coordinates (speed and direction), and so must be a vector. In Perl, a scalar is the fundamental, basic unit of data, of which there are two main kinds—numbers and strings.

A *literal* is value that never changes. The value 5 is a scalar literal—and is literally 5; it can never be 4. Perl has three types of scalar literals: integers (such as 5), floating point numbers (like 3.14159), and strings (for example "hello, world"). To put it another way, a literal is a *constant*—it never changes.

A *variable*, on the other hand, is a piece of memory that can hold a scalar value, and is so named because the value stored within can vary. For instance, $number can be assigned 5, and then later can be changed to the value 6. We will talk more about variables later in this chapter.

Numbers

As Perl programmers, we are interested in two types of numbers: integers and floating point numbers. We'll come to the latter in a minute; let's work a bit with integers right now. Integers are whole numbers with no numbers after the decimal point, such as 42, –1, or 10. The following program prints a couple of integer literals in Perl.

```
#!/usr/bin/perl
# number1.pl

use warnings;

print 25, -4;
```

```
$ perl number1.pl
25-4$
```

Well, that's not exactly what we want. Fortunately, it's pretty easy to fix. First, we didn't tell Perl to separate the numbers with a space, and second, we didn't tell it to put a new line at the end. Let's change the program so it does that:

```
#!/usr/bin/perl
# number2.pl

use warnings;

print 25, " ", -4, "\n";
```

This will accomplish what we want:

```
$ perl number2.pl
25 -4
$
```

For readability, we often write large integers such as 10000000 by splitting up the number with commas: 10,000,000. This is sometimes known as *chunking*. While we would probably write 10 million with a comma if we wrote a check for that amount[1], don't use the comma to chunk in a Perl program. Instead, use the underscore: 10_000_000. Change your program to look like the following:

```
#!/usr/bin/perl
# number3.pl

use warnings;

print 25_000_000, " ", -4, "\n";
```

----

[1] Ah, if only we could write a check for $10M that would actually cash…

Notice that those underscores don't appear in the output:

```
$ perl number3.pl
25000000 -4
$
```

We will also be working with floating-point numbers, which include everything that's not an integer, like 0.5, –0.01333, and 1.1.

Note that floating-point numbers are accurate to a certain number of digits. For instance, the number 15.39 may in fact be stored in memory as 15.3899999999999. This is accurate enough for most scientists, so it will have to be for us programmers as well.

Here is an example of printing the approximate value of pi:

```
#!/usr/bin/perl
# number4.pl

use warnings;

print "pi is approximately: ", 3.14159, "\n";
```

Executing this program produces the following result:

```
$ perl number4.pl
pi is approximately: 3.14159
$
```

Binary, Hexadecimal, and Octal Numbers

As you saw in the previous chapter, we can express numbers as binary, hexadecimal, or octal numbers in our programs. Let's look at a program to demonstrate how to use the various number systems. Type in the following code, and save it as goodnums.pl:

```
#!/usr/bin/perl
# goodnums.pl

use warnings;

print 255,        "\n";
print 0377,       "\n";
print 0b11111111, "\n";
print 0xFF,       "\n";
```

All of these are representations of the number 255, and accordingly, we get the following output:

```
$ perl goodnums.pl
255
255
255
255
$
```

When Perl reads your program, it reads and understands numbers in any of the allowed number systems, 0 for octal, 0b for binary, and 0x for hex.

What happens, you might ask, if you specify a number in the wrong system? Well, let's try it out. Edit goodnums.pl to give you a new program, badnums.pl, which looks like this:

```
#!/usr/bin/perl
# badnums.pl

use warnings;

print 255,        "\n";
print 0378,       "\n";
print 0b11111112, "\n";
print 0xFG,       "\n";
```

Since octal digits only run from 0 to 7, binary digits from 0 to 1, and hex digits from 0 to F, none of the last three lines make any sense. Let's see what Perl makes of it:

```
$ perl badnums.pl
Bareword found where operator expected at badnums.pl line 9, near "0xFG"
        (Missing operator before G?)
Illegal octal digit '8' at badnums.pl line 7, at end of line
Illegal binary digit '2' at badnums.pl line 8, at end of line
syntax error at badnums.pl line 9, near "0xFG"
Execution of badnums.pl aborted due to compilation errors.
$
```

Now, let's match those errors up with the relevant lines:

```
Illegal octal digit '8' at badnums.pl line 7, at end of line
```

And line 7 is

```
print 0378,       "\n";
```

As you can see, Perl thought it was dealing with an octal number, but then along came an 8, which is not a legal octal digit, so Perl quite rightly complained. The same thing happened on the next line:

```
Illegal binary digit '2' at badnums.pl line 8, at end of line
```

And line 8 is

```
print 0b11111112, "\n";
```

The problem with the next line is even bigger:

```
Bareword found where operator expected at badnums.pl line 9, near "0xFG"
        (Missing operator before G?)
syntax error at badnums.pl line 9, near "0xFG"
```

The line starting "Bareword" is a warning (because we included use warnings;). A *bareword* is a series of characters outside of a string that Perl doesn't recognize. Those characters could mean a number of things, and Perl is usually quite good at understanding what you mean. In this case, the bareword was G; Perl understood 0xF but couldn't see how the G fit in. We might have wanted an operator do something with it, but there was no operator. In the end, Perl gave us a *syntax error*, which is the equivalent of it giving up and saying, "How do you expect me to understand this?"

Strings

The other type of scalar available to us is the string, and we've already seen a few examples. In the last chapter, we met the string `"Hello, world!\n"`. A string is a series of characters surrounded by some sort of quotation marks. Strings can contain ASCII (or Unicode) data, as well as escape sequences such as the `\n` of our example. Perl imposes no maximum-length restriction on strings. Practically speaking, there is a limit imposed by the amount of memory in your computer, but since most computers these days have such a large amount of memory, it's unlikely you'd create a string that would consume all that memory.

Single- vs. Double-Quoted Strings

The quotation marks you choose for your string are significant. So far we've only seen *double-quoted* strings, like `"Hello, world!\n"`. But you can also have *single-quoted* strings. Predictably, these are surrounded by single quotes: `' '`. The important difference is that no processing is done within single-quoted strings, except on `\\` and `\'`. Moreover, as we'll see later, variable names inside double-quoted strings are replaced by their contents, whereas single-quoted strings treat them as ordinary text. We call both these types of processing *interpolation*, and say that single-quoted strings are not interpolated.

Consider the following program, bearing in mind that `\t` is the escape sequence that represents a tab:

```
#!/usr/bin/perl
# quotes.pl

use warnings;

print '\tThis is a single-quoted string.\n';
print "\tThis is a double-quoted string.\n";
```

The double-quoted string will have its escape sequences processed, and the single-quoted string will not. The output is

```
$ perl quotes.pl
\tThis is a single-quoted string.\n     This is a double-quoted string.
$
```

What do we do if we want to have a backslash in a string? This is a common concern for Windows users, as a Windows path looks something like this: C:\WINDOWS\Media\. In a double-quoted string, a backslash will start an escape sequence, which is not what we want it to do.

There is, of course, more than one way to get an actual backslash. You can either use a single-quoted string, as shown previously, or you can *escape* the backslash. One principle you'll see often in Perl, and especially when we get to regular expressions, is that you can use a backslash to turn off any special effect a character may have. This operation is called *escaping*, or more commonly, *backwhacking*.

In this case, we want to turn off the special effect a backslash has, and so we escape it:

```
#!/usr/bin/perl
# quotes2.pl

use warnings;
```

```
print "C:\\WINDOWS\\Media\\\n";
print 'C:\WINDOWS\Media\ ', "\n";
```

This prints the following:

```
$ perl quotes2.pl
C:\WINDOWS\Media\
C:\WINDOWS\Media\
$
```

Aha! Some of you may have got this message instead:

```
Can't find string terminator " ' " anywhere before EOF at quotes2.pl line 7.
```

If you did, you probably left out the space character in line 7 before the second single quote. Remember that \' tells Perl to escape the single quote, turning off its normal meaning of a closing single quote. Perl continues to look for the closing quote, which, of course, is not there. Try this program to see how Perl treats these special cases:

```
#!/usr/bin/perl
# aside1.pl

use warnings;

print 'ex\\ er\\' , ' ci\' se\'' , "\n";
```

The output you get this time is

```
$ perl aside1.pl
ex\ er\ ci' se'
$
```

You'll find it easier to sort out what is happening if you look at each argument individually to determine how the characters are escaped. Remember, there are three arguments to print() in this example. Don't let all the quotes confuse you.

Actually, there's an altogether sneakier way of setting a Windows path. Internally, Windows allows you to separate paths in the Unix style with a forward slash, instead of a backslash. If you need to refer to directories in Perl on Windows, you may find it easier to say C:/WINDOWS/Media/ instead. This gives you the variable interpolation of double-quoted strings without the "Leaning Toothpick Syndrome"[2] of multiple backslashes.

So much for backslashes, what about quotation marks? The trick is making sure Perl knows where the end of the string is. Naturally, there's no problem with putting single quotes inside a double-quoted string, or vice versa:

```
#!/usr/bin/perl
# quotes3.pl
```

_____

[2] Yes, believe it or not the Leaning Toothpick Syndrome (LDS) is real:
http://en.wikipedia.org/wiki/Leaning_toothpick_syndrome

```
use warnings;

print "It's as easy as that.\n";
print '"Stop," he cried.', "\n";
```

This will produce the quotation marks in the right places:

```
$ perl quotes3.pl
It's as easy as that.
"Stop," he cried.
$
```

The problem comes when you want double quotes inside a double-quoted string or single quotes inside a single-quoted string. As you might have guessed, though, the solution is to escape the quotes on the inside. Suppose you want to print out the following quote, including both sets of quotation marks:

```
'"Hi," said Jack. "Have you read Slashdot today?"'
```

Here's a way of doing it with a double-quoted string:

```
#!/usr/bin/perl
# quotes4.pl

use warnings;

print "'\"Hi,\" said Jack. \"Have you read Slashdot today?\"'\n";
```

Now see if you can modify this to make it a single-quoted string—don't forget that \n needs to go in separate double quotes to make it interpolate.

q// and qq//

Wouldn't it would be nice if you could select a completely different set of quotes so there would be no ambiguity and no need to escape any quotes inside the text? The first operators we're going to meet are the *quote-like operators* that do this for us. They're written as q// and qq//, the first acting like single quotes and the second like double quotes. Now, instead of the code we wrote in quotes4.pl, we can write

```
#!/usr/bin/perl
# quotes5.pl

use warnings;

print qq/'"Hi," said Jack. "Have you read Slashdot today?"'\n/;
```

Alternative Delimiters

That's all very well, of course, until we want a / in the string. Suppose we want to replace "Slashdot" with "/."—now we're back where we started, having to escape things again. Thankfully, Perl lets us choose our own delimiters so we don't have to stick with //. Any nonalphanumeric (that is, no letter and no number) character can be used as a delimiter, provided it's the same on both sides of the text. Furthermore, you can use {}, [ ], (), and <> as left and right delimiters. Here are a few ways of doing the print qq/.../;, all of which have the same effect:

```perl
#!/usr/bin/perl
# quotes6.pl

use warnings;

print qq|'"Hi," said Jack. "Have you read /. today?"'\n|;
print qq#'"Hi," said Jack. "Have you read /. today?"'\n#;
print qq('"Hi," said Jack. "Have you read /. today?"'\n);
print qq<'"Hi," said Jack. "Have you read /. today?"'\n>;
```

We'll see more of these alternative delimiters when we start working with regular expressions.

Here-Documents

There's one final way of specifying a string—by means of a *here-document*. This idea was taken from the Unix shell and works in Perl on any platform. Effectively, it means you can write a large amount of text within your program, and it will be treated as a string provided it is identified correctly. Here's an example:

```perl
#!/usr/bin/perl
# heredoc.pl

use warnings;

print <<EOF;

This is a here-document. It starts on the line after the two arrows,
and it ends when the text following the arrows is found at the beginning
of a line, like this:

EOF
```

A here-document must start with << followed by a label. The label can be anything, but is traditionally EOF (end of file) or EOT (end of text). The label must immediately follow the arrows with no spaces between, unless the same number of spaces precedes the end marker. The here-doc ends when the label is found at the beginning of a line. In our case, the semicolon does not form part of the label because it marks the end of the print() function call.

By default, a here-document works like a double-quoted string. In order for it to work like a single-quoted string, surround the label in single quotes. This will become important when variable interpolation comes into play, as we'll see later.

Here-documents are typically used to replace multi-line strings (strings that span multiple lines). A perfect example is a menu that is displayed to the user. Consider this relatively hard-to-read code as a bunch of print() statements:

```perl
print "Enter your selection:\n";
print "    1 - money\n";
```

```
print "    2 - show\n";
print "    3 - get ready\n";
print "    4 - go cat go\n";
```

Or as a here–document:

```
print <<EOMENU;
Enter your selection:
    1 - money
    2 - show
    3 - get ready
    4 - go cat go
EOMENU
```

Converting Between Numbers and Strings

Perl treats numbers and strings as equals and, where necessary, converts between strings, integers, and floating-point numbers behind the scenes. There is a special term for this: *automatic conversion of scalars*. This means you don't have to worry about doing the conversions yourself, as you do in other languages. If you have a string literal, "0.25", and you multiply it by four, Perl treats it as a number and gives you the expected answer, 1. For example:

```
#!/usr/bin/perl
# autoconvert.pl

use warnings;

print "0.25" * 4, "\n";
```

The asterisk (*) is the multiplication operator. All of Perl's operators, including this one, will be discussed in the next section.

There is, however, one area where this automatic conversion does not take place. Octal, hex, and binary numbers in string literals or strings stored in variables don't get converted automatically.

```
#!/usr/bin/perl
# octhex1.pl

use warnings;

print "0x30\n";
print "030\n";
```

gives you

```
$ perl octhex1.pl
0x30
030
$
```

If you ever find yourself with a string containing a hex or octal value that you need to convert into a number, you can use the hex() or oct() functions accordingly:

21

```
#!/usr/bin/perl
# octhex2.pl

use warnings;

print hex("0x30"), "\n";
print oct("030"), "\n";
```

This produces the expected answers, 48 and 24. Note that for `hex()` or `oct()`, the prefix `0x` or `0` respectively is not required. If you know that what you have is definitely supposed to be a hex or octal number, then `hex(30)` and `oct(30)` will produce the preceding results. As you can see from that, the string `"30"` and the number `30` are treated as the same.

Furthermore, these functions will stop reading when they get to a digit that doesn't make sense in that number system:

```
#!/usr/bin/perl
# octhex3.pl

use warnings;

print hex("FFG"), "\n";
print oct("178"), "\n";
```

These will stop at `FF` and `17` respectively, and convert to 255 and 15. Perl will warn you, though, since those are illegal characters in hex and octal numbers.

What about binary numbers? Well, there's no corresponding `bin()` function, but there's actually a little trick here. If you have the correct prefix in place for any of the number systems (`0`, `0b`, or `0x`), you can use `oct()` to convert the number to decimal. For example, `oct("0b11010")` prints 26.

Operators

Now that we know how to specify strings and numbers, let's see what we can do with them. Mostly we'll be looking here at numeric operators—operators that act on and produce numbers—like plus and minus, which take two numbers as *arguments*, called *operands*, and add or subtract them. There aren't as many string operators, but there are a lot of string functions that we'll talk about later. Perl doesn't distinguish very strongly between functions and operators, but the main difference between the two is that operators tend to go in the middle of their arguments—for example: 2 + 2, while functions go before their arguments, which are separated by commas. Both operators and functions take arguments, do something with them, and produce a new value; we generally say they *return* a value, or *evaluate* to a value. Let's take a look.

Numeric Operators

The numeric operators take at least one number as an argument, and evaluate to another number. Of course, because Perl automatically converts between strings and numbers, the arguments may appear as string literals or come from strings in variables. We'll group these operators into three types: arithmetic operators, bitwise operators, and logic operators.

Arithmetic Operators

The arithmetic operators are those that deal with basic mathematics—adding, subtracting, multiplying, and dividing, and so on. To add two numbers together, you'd write something like this:

```
#!/usr/bin/perl
# arithop1.pl

use warnings;

print 69 + 118, "\n";
```

And, of course, you'd see the answer, 187. Subtracting numbers is easy, too, and you can add and subtract at the same time:

```
#!/usr/bin/perl
# arithop2.pl

use warnings;

print "21 from 25 is: ", 25 - 21, "\n";
print "4 + 13 - 7 is: ", 4 + 13 - 7, "\n";
```

Executing this code produces:

```
$ perl arithop2.pl
21 from 25 is: 4
4 + 13 - 7 is: 10
$
```

The next set of operators, for multiplying and dividing, is where it gets interesting. We use the * and / operators respectively to multiply and divide.

```
#!/usr/bin/perl
# arithop3.pl

use warnings;

print "7 times 15 is ", 7 * 15, "\n";
print "249 divided by 3 is ", 249 / 3, "\n";
```

Executing this code produces:

```
$ perl arithop3.pl
7 times 15 is 105
249 divided by 3 is 83
$
```

The fun comes when you want to multiply first and then add, or add then divide. Here's an example of the problem:

```
#!/usr/bin/perl
# arithop4.pl

use warnings;

print 3 + 7 * 15, "\n";
```

This could mean two different things: either Perl must add the 3 and the 7, and then multiply by 15, or multiply 7 and 15 first, and then add. Which does Perl do? Try it and see . . .

Perl should give you 108, meaning it did the multiplication first. The order in which Perl performs operations is called *operator precedence*. Multiply and divide have a higher precedence than add and subtract, and so they get performed first. We can start to draw up a list of precedence as follows:

```
* /
+ -
```

To force Perl to perform an operation of lower precedence first, you need to use parentheses, like so:

```
#!/usr/bin/perl
# arithop5.pl

use warnings;

print (3 + 7) * 15, "\n";
```

Unfortunately, if you run that, you'll get a warning and 10 will be printed. What happened? The problem is that `print()` is a function and the parentheses around `3 + 7` are treated as the only argument to `print()`.

`print()` as an operator takes a list of arguments, performs an operation (printing them to the screen), and returns a 1 if it succeeds, or no value if it does not. Perl calculated 3 plus 7, printed the result, and then multiplied the result of the returned value (1) by 15, throwing away the final result of 15.

To get what you actually want, you need another set of parentheses:

```
#!/usr/bin/perl
# arithop6.pl

use warnings;

print((3 + 7) * 15, "\n");
```

Note that the outer set of parenthesis tells `print()` that what is within are the arguments. The inner set of parenthesis forces the desired precedence. This now gives us the correct answer, 150, and we can put another entry in our list of precedence:

```
List operators
* /
+ -
```

Now let's look at the exponentiation operator,• which simply raises one number to the power of another—squaring, cubing, and so on. Here's an example:

```
#!/usr/bin/perl
# arithop7.pl

use warnings;

print 2**4, " ", 3**5, " ", -2**4, "\n";
```

That's 2*2*2*2, 3*3*3*3*3, and –2*–2*–2*–2. Or is it?
The output we get is

```
$ perl arithop7.pl
16 243 -16
$
```

Hmm, the first two look OK, but the last one's not quite correct. –2 to the 4th power should be positive. Again, it's a precedence issue. Turning a number into a negative number requires an operator, the *unary minus operator*. It's called unary because unlike the ordinary minus operator, it only takes one argument. Although unary minus has a higher precedence than multiply and divide, it has a lower precedence than exponentiation. What's actually happening, then, is -(2**4) instead of (-2)**4. Let's put these two operators in our list of precedence as well:

```
List operators
**
Unary minus
* /
+ -
```

The last arithmetic operator is %, the *remainder*, or *modulo operator*. This calculates the remainder when one number divides another. For example, 6 divides into 15 twice, with a remainder of 3, as our next program will confirm:

```
#!/usr/bin/perl
# arithop8.pl

use warnings;

print "15 divided by 6 is exactly ", 15 / 6, "\n";
print "That's a remainder of ", 15 % 6, "\n";
```

```
$ perl arithop8.pl
15 divided by 6 is exactly 2.5
That's a remainder of 3
$
```

The modulo operator has the same precedence as multiply and divide.

Bitwise Operators

Up to this point, the operators worked on numbers in just the way we'd expect. However, as we already know, computers don't see numbers the same as we do; they see them as a string of bits. These next few operators perform operations on numbers one bit at a time—that's why they're called them *bitwise operators*. They aren't used quite so much in Perl as in other languages, but we will use them when dealing with things like low-level file access.

First, let's have a look at the kind of numbers we're going to use in this section, just so we get used to them:

- 0 in binary is 0, but let's write it as 8 bits: 00000000.

- 51 in binary is 00110011.

- 85 in binary is 01010101.

- 170 in binary is 10101010.

- 204 in binary is 11001100.

- 255 in binary is 11111111.

Does it surprise you that 10101010 (170) is twice as much as 01010101 (85)? It shouldn't; when we multiply a number by 10 in base 10, all we do is slap a 0 on the end, so 21 becomes 210. Similarly, to multiply a number by 2 in base 2, we do exactly the same.

People think of bitwise operators as working from right to left; the rightmost bit is called the *least significant bit* and the leftmost is called the *most significant bit*.

The AND Operator

The easiest bitwise operator to fathom is called the *and* operator, and is written &. This compares pairs of bits as follows:

- 1 and 1 gives 1.

- 1 and 0 gives 0.

- 0 and 1 gives 0.

- 0 and 0 gives 0.

For example, **51 & 85** looks like this:

```
51    00110011
85    01010101
---------------
17    00010001
```

Sure enough, if we give Perl the following:

```
#!/usr/bin/perl
# bitop1.pl

use warnings;

print "51 ANDed with 85 gives us ", 51 & 85, "\n";
```

it tells us the answer is 17. Notice that since we're comparing one pair of bits at a time, it doesn't really matter which way around the arguments go, **51 & 85** is exactly the same as **85 & 51**. Operators with this property are called *commutative operators*. Addition (+) and multiplication (*) are also commutative: 5 *

12 produces the same result as 12 * 5. Subtraction (–) and division (/) are not commutative: 5 – 12 does not produce the same result as 12 – 5.

Here's another example—look at the bits and see what you get:

```
51     00110011
170    10101010
---------------
34     00100010
```

The OR Operator

As well as checking whether the first *and* the second bits are 1, we can check whether one *or* another is 1, the *or* operator in Perl is |. This is how we would calculate 204 | 85:

```
204    11001100
85     01010101
---------------
221    11011101
```

Now we produce 0s only if both bits are 0; if either or both are 1, we produce a 1. As a quick rule of thumb, X & Y will always be smaller or equal to the smallest value of X and Y, and X | Y will be bigger than or equal to the largest value of X or Y.

The XOR Operator

What if you really want to know if one or the other, but not both, are one? For this, you need the *exclusive or* operator, written as ^:

```
204    11001100
170    10101010
---------------
102    01100110
```

The NOT Operator

Finally, you can flip the number completely, and replace all the 1s with 0s and vice versa. This is done with the *not*, or ~, operator:

```
85     01010101
170    10101010
```

Let's see, however, what happens when we try this in Perl:

```
#!/usr/bin/perl
# bitop2.pl

use warnings;

print "NOT 85 is ", ~85, "\n";
```

Depending on the computer, the answer might be

```
$ perl bitop2.pl
NOT 85 is 4294967210
$
```

Your answer might be different, and we'll explain why in a second.

Why is it so big? Well, let's look at that number in binary to see if we can find a clue as to what's going on:

4294697210   11111111111111111111111110101010

Aha! The last part is right, but it's a lot wider than we're used to. That's because the previous examples only used 8 bits across, whereas many computers store integers as 32 bits across, so what's actually happened is this:

85   00000000000000000000000001010101
4294697210   11111111111111111111111110101010

If you get a much bigger number, it's because your computer represents numbers internally with 64 bits instead of 32, and Perl has been configured to take advantage of this.

Truth and Falsehood

True and false are important in Perl. In Perl, false is defined as

- the number 0

- "0" (the string containing the single character 0)

- "" (the empty string)

- Undefined

- Empty list (we'll discuss this in Chapter 4)

Later, we will want to perform actions based on whether something is true or false, like if one number is bigger than another, or unless a problem has occurred, or while there is data left to examine. We will use *comparison operators* to evaluate whether these things are true or false so that we can make decisions based on them.

Some programming languages represent false as 0 and true as 1, and this allows us to use operators very similar to bitwise operators to combine our comparisons, and to say "if this *or* this is true," "if this is *not* true," and so on. The process of combining values that represent truth and falsehood is called *Boolean logic*, after George Boole, who invented the concept in 1847, and we call the operators that do the combining *Boolean operators*.

Comparing Numbers for Equality

The first simple comparison operator is ==. Two equal signs tell Perl to "return true if the two numeric arguments are equal." If they're not equal, return false. Boolean values of truth and falsehood aren't very exciting to look at, but let's see them anyway:

```
#!/usr/bin/perl
# bool1.pl

use warnings;

print "Is two equal to four? ",           2 == 4, "\n";
print "OK, then, is six equal to six? ", 6 == 6, "\n";
```

This will produce

```
$ perl bool1.pl
Is two equal to four?
OK, then, is six equal to six? 1
$
```

This output shows that in Perl, operators that evaluate to false evaluate to the empty string ("") and those that evaluate to true evaluate to 1.

The obvious counterpart to testing whether things are equal is testing whether they're not equal, and for this we use the != operator. Note that there's only one equal sign this time; we'll find out later why there had to be two before.

```
#!/usr/bin/perl
# bool2.pl

use warnings;

print "So, two isn't equal to four? ", 2 != 4, "\n";
```

```
$ perl bool2.pl
So, two isn't equal to four? 1
$
```

There you have it, irrefutable proof that two is not four. Good.

Comparing Numbers for Inequality

So much for equality; let's check if one thing is bigger than another. Just as in mathematics, we use the greater-than and less-than signs to do this: < and >.

```
#!/usr/bin/perl
# bool3.pl

use warnings;

print "Five is more than six? ",         5 >  6, "\n";
print "Seven is less than sixteen? ", 7 < 16, "\n";
print "Two is equal to two? ",           2 == 2, "\n";
print "One is more than one? ",          1 >  1, "\n";
print "Six is not equal to seven? ",  6 != 7, "\n";
```

The results, hopefully, should not be very new to you:

29

```
$ perl bool3.pl
Five is more than six?
Seven is less than sixteen? 1
Two is equal to two? 1
One is more than one?
Six is not equal to seven? 1
$
```

Let's have a look at one last pair of comparisons: we can check greater-than-or-equal-to and less-than-or-equal-to with the >= and <= operators, respectively.

```
#!/usr/bin/perl
# bool4.pl
use warnings;

print "Seven is less than or equal to sixteen? ", 7 <= 16, "\n";
print "Two is more than or equal to two? ",       2 >= 2,  "\n";
```

As expected, Perl faithfully prints out

```
$ perl bool4.pl
Seven is less than or equal to sixteen? 1
Two is more than or equal to two? 1
$
```

There's also a special operator that isn't really a Boolean comparison because it doesn't give us a true-or-false value; instead it returns 0 if the two are equal, –1 if the right-hand side is bigger, and 1 if the left-hand side is bigger—it is denoted by <=>.

```
#!/usr/bin/perl
# bool5.pl

use warnings;

print "Compare six and nine? ",    6 <=> 9, "\n";
print "Compare seven and seven? ", 7 <=> 7, "\n";
print "Compare eight and four? ",  8 <=> 4, "\n";
gives us
```

```
$ perl bool5.pl
Compare six and nine? -1
Compare seven and seven? 0
Compare eight and four? 1
$
```

The <=> operator is also known as the *spaceship operator* or the *shuttle operator* due to its shape.

You'll see this operator used when we look at sorting things, where you have to know whether something goes before, after, or in the same place as something else.

Boolean Operators

As well as being able to evaluate the truth and falsehood of some statements, we can also combine such statements. For example, we may want to do something if one number is bigger than another and two other numbers are the same. The combining is done in much the same way as with the bitwise operators we saw earlier. We can ask if one value *and* another value are both true, or if one value *or* another value are true, and so on.

The operators even resemble the bitwise operators. To ask if both truth values are true, you use **&&** instead of **&**. So, to test whether 6 is more than 3 *and* 12 is more than 4, you can write

```
6 > 3 && 12 > 4
```

To test if 9 is more than 7 *or* 8 is less than 6, you use the doubled form of the | operator, ||:

```
9 > 7 || 6 > 8
```

To negate the sense of a test, however, use the slightly different ! operator; this operator has a higher precedence than the comparison operators, so use parentheses if necessary. For example, the following line tests whether 2 is not more than 3:

```
!(2>3)
```

while this one tests whether !2 is more than 3:
```
!2>3
```

2 is a true value. **!2** is therefore a false value, which gets converted to 0 when we do a numeric comparison. We're actually testing if 0 is more than 3, which has the opposite effect to what we wanted.

Instead of those forms, **&&**, **||**, and **!**, we can also use the slightly easier-to-read versions, **and**, **or**, and **not**. There's also **xor**, for *exclusive or* (one or the other but not both are true), which doesn't have a symbolic form. However, you need to be careful about precedence again:

```
#!/usr/bin/perl
# bool6.pl

use warnings;

print "Test one: ", 6 > 3 && 3 > 4, "\n";
print "Test two: ", 6 > 3 and 3 > 4, "\n";
```

This prints, somewhat surprisingly, the following:

```
$ perl bool6.pl
Useless use of a constant in void context at bool6.pl line 5.
Test one:
Test two: 1$
```

We can tell from the presence of the warning about line 5 and from the position of the prompt that something is amiss (or least Unix users can—Windows users need to be a bit more alert since Windows automatically adds a newline character at the end of the program so the system prompt will be on the next line, but the blank line that is expected will not be there). Notice the second newline did not get printed. The trouble is, **and** has a lower precedence than **&&**. What has actually happened is this:

```
print("Test two: ", 6 > 3) and (3 > 4, "\n");
```

Now, 6 is more than 3, so that returned 1, `print()` then returned 1, and the rest was irrelevant.

String Operators

Let's look at a two string operators.

The first one is the *concatenation operator*, which glues two strings together into one. Instead of saying

```
print "Print ", "several ", "strings ", "here", "\n";
```
you could say

```
print "Print " . "one ". "string " . "here" . "\n";
```

As it happens, printing several strings is slightly more efficient, but there will be times you really do need to combine strings, especially if you're putting them into variables.

What happens if we try and join a number to a string? The number is evaluated and then converted:

```
#!/usr/bin/perl
# string1.pl

use warnings;

print "Four sevens are ". 4*7 ."\n";
```

which tells us, reassuringly, that

```
$ perl string1.pl
Four sevens are 28
$
```

The other string operator is the *repetition operator*, marked with an x. This repeats a string a given number of times:

```
#!/usr/bin/perl
# string2.pl

use warnings;

print "GO! " x 3, "\n";
```

will print

```
$ perl string2.pl
GO! GO! GO!
$
```

You can, of course, use repetition in conjunction with concatenation. The repetition operator's precedence is higher than the concatenation operator's, as you can easily see for yourself:

```
#!/usr/bin/perl
# string3.pl
```

```
use warnings;

print "Ba" . "na" x 4 ,"\n";
```

On running this, you get

```
$ perl string3.pl
Banananana
$
```

In this case, the repetition is done first ("nananana") and then it is concatenated with the "Ba". The precedence of the repetition operator is the same as the arithmetic operators, so if you're working out how many times to repeat something, you're going to need parentheses:

```
#!/usr/bin/perl
# string4.pl

use warnings;

print "Ba" . "na" x 4*3 ,"\n";
print "Ba" . "na" x (4*3) ,"\n";
```

Compare:

```
$ perl string4.pl
Argument "nananana" isn't numeric in multiplication (*) at string4.pl line 6
Ba0
Banananananananananananananana
$
```

Why was the first one Ba0? The repetition happened first, giving us "nananana". Then the multiplication—what's "nananana" times three? When Perl converts a string to a number, it takes any spaces, an optional minus sign, and then as many digits as it can from the beginning of the string, and ignores everything else. Since there were no digits here, the numeric value of "nananana" was 0. Note that if the string that is converted to a number contains any non-numeric characters, Perl will warn you about it, as shown previously.

That 0 was then multiplied by 3, to give 0. Finally, the 0 was turned back into a string to be concatenated onto the "Ba".

Here is an example showing how strings automatically convert to numbers by adding 0 to them:

```
#!/usr/bin/perl
# str2num.pl

use warnings;

print "12 monkeys"    + 0,   "\n";
print "Eleven to fly" + 0,   "\n";
print "UB40"          + 0,   "\n";
print "-20 10"        + 0,   "\n";
print "0x30"          + 0,   "\n";
```

You get a warning for each line saying that the strings aren't "numeric in addition (+)," but what can be converted is:

```
$ perl str2num.pl
Argument "12 monkeys" isn't numeric in addition (+) at str2num.pl line 6.
Argument "Eleven to fly" isn't numeric in addition (+) at str2num.pl line 7.
Argument "UB40" isn't numeric in addition (+) at str2num.pl line 8.
Argument "-20 10" isn't numeric in addition (+) at str2num.pl line 9.
Argument "0x30" isn't numeric in addition (+) at str2num.pl line 10.
12
0
0
-20
0
$
```

Notice how, when each of these strings is converted to a numeric value, Perl complains that the string is not numeric. This happens because the string is not a simple numeric value. But note that Perl does in fact convert the strings to numbers (in the case of three of the strings, the value is 0).

Our first string, `"12 monkeys"`, did pretty well. Perl understood the 12, and stopped after that. The next line of code starts with the word "Eleven"—English words don't get converted to numbers. Our third string was also a nonstarter as Perl looks for a number only at the beginning of the string. If there's something there that isn't a number, it's evaluated as a 0. Similarly, Perl only looks for the first number in the string. Any numbers after that are discarded. Finally, Perl doesn't convert binary, hex, or octal to decimal when it's stringifying a number, so you have to use the `hex()` or `oct()` functions to do that. On our last effort, Perl stopped at the `x`, returning 0. If we had an octal number, such as `030`, it would be treated as the decimal number 30.

Therefore, conversion from strings to numbers can be summed up with these rules:

- A string that is purely a number is automatically converted to the number ("21.42" is converted to 21.42).

- Leading whitespace is ignored (" 12" is converted to 12).

- Trailing nonnumerics are discarded ("12perl" is converted to 12).

- Strings that do not start with numeric values are treated as 0 ("perl12" is converted to 0).

The last three conversions listed will produce a warning message if `use warnings;` is used.

String Comparison

In addition to comparing the value of numbers, we can compare the value of strings. This does not mean we convert a string to a number, although if you say something like `"12" > "30"`, Perl will convert to numbers for you. This means we can compare the strings alphabetically: "Bravo" comes after "Alpha" but before "Charlie", for instance.

In fact, it's more than alphabetical order; the computer is using either ASCII or Unicode internally to represent the string, and so has converted it to a series of numbers in the relevant sequence. This means, for example, "Fowl" comes before "fish", because a capital "F" has a smaller ASCII value (70) than a lowercase "f" (102).[3]

You can find a character's ASCII value by using the ord() function, which tells you where in the (ASCII) order it comes. Let's see which comes first, a # or a *?

```perl
#!/usr/bin/perl
# ascii.pl

use warnings;

print "A # has ASCII value ", ord("#"), "\n";
print "A * has ASCII value ", ord("*"), "\n";
```

This should say

```
$ perl ascii.pl
A # has ASCII value 35
A * has ASCII value 42
$
```

If you're only concerned with one character at a time, you can compare the return values of ord() using the < and > operators. However, when you're comparing entire strings, that can get tedious. If the first character of each string is the same, you move on to the next character in each string, and then the next, and so on.

Instead, you can use string comparison operators to do it. Whereas the comparison operators for numbers are mathematical symbols, the operators for strings are abbreviations. To test whether one string is less than another, use lt. "Greater than" becomes gt, "equal to" becomes eq, and "not equal to" becomes ne. There's also ge and le for "greater than or equal to" and "less than and equal to." The three-way-comparison becomes cmp.

Here are a few examples:

```perl
#!/usr/bin/perl
# strcomp1.pl

use warnings;

print "Which came first, the chicken or the egg? ";
print "chicken" cmp "egg", "\n";
print "Are dogs greater than cats? ";
print "dog" gt "cat", "\n";
print "Is ^ less than + ? ";
print "^" lt "+", "\n";
```

---

[3]This is not strictly true, though. Locales can define nonnumeric sorting orders for ASCII or Unicode characters that Perl will respect.

And the results:

```
$ perl strcomp1.pl
Which came first, the chicken or the egg? -1
Are dogs greater than cats? 1
Is ^ less than + ?
$
```

The last line prints nothing as a result of "^" lt "+" since this operation returns the empty string, indicating false.

Be careful when comparing strings using numeric comparison operators (or numeric values using string comparison operators):

```
#!/usr/bin/perl
# strcomp2.pl

use warnings;

print "Test one: ", "four" eq "six", "\n";
print "Test two: ", "four" == "six", "\n";
```

This code produces

```
$ perl strcomp2.pl
Argument "six" isn't numeric in numeric eq (==) at strcmp2.pl line 5.
Argument "four" isn't numeric in numeric eq (==) at strcmp2.pl line 5.
Test one:
Test two: 1
$
```

Is the second line really claiming that "four" is equal to "six"? Yes, when they are treated as numbers. If you compare them as numbers, they get converted to numbers: "four" converts to 0, "six" converts to 0, and the 0s are equal, so the test returns true and we get a couple of warnings telling us that they were not numbers to begin with. The moral of this story is, compare strings with string comparison operators and compare numbers with numeric comparison operators. Otherwise, your results may not be what you anticipate.

Operators to Be Covered Later

There are a few operators left that we are not going to delve into right now. Don't worry; we will eventually take a look at the more important ones.

- The conditional operator looks like this: a?b:c. It returns b if a is true, and c if it is false.

- The range operators, .. and ..., define a range of values. For instance, (0..5) is shorthand notation for (0,1,2,3,4,5).

- As you've seen, the comma is used for separating arguments to functions like print(). In fact, the comma is an operator that builds a list, and print() works on a list of arguments. The operator => works like a comma but has some additional properties.

- The =~ and !~ operators are used to "apply" a regular expression to a string. We'll look at these operators in Chapter 7.

- As well as providing an escape sequence and backwhacking special characters, \ is used to take a reference to a variable, to examine the variable itself rather than its contents. We will discuss this operator in Chapter 11.

- The >> and << operators "shift" a binary number right and left a given number of bits.

- -> is an operator used when working with references; it will be covered in Chapter 11.

Operator Precedence

Table 2-1 displays the precedence for all the operators we've discussed so far, listed in descending order of precedence.

Table 2-1. Operator Precedence

Operator	Description
List operators	Functions that take list arguments
->	Infix dereference operator
**	Exponentiation
! ~ \	Logical not, bitwise not, reference of
=~ !~	Regex match, negated regex match
* / % x	Multiplication, division, modulus, replication
+ - .	Addition, subtraction, concatenation
<< >>	Left shift, right shift
< > <= >= lt gt le ge	Comparison operators
== != <=> eq ne cmp	More comparison operators
&	Bitwise and
| ^	Bitwise or, bitwise xor

continued

Table 2-1. continued

Operator	Description
&&	Logical and
||	Logical or
.. ...	Range
?:	Conditional
, =>	List separator
Not	Logical not
And	Logical and
or xor	Logical or, xor

Remember that if you need to get things done in a particular order, you will need to use parenthesis. And note that you can use parenthesis even when they're not strictly necessary, and you should certainly do so to help keep things readable. While Perl knows full well what order to evaluate 7+3*2/6-3+5/2&3 in, you'll probably find it easier on yourself if you make it explicit, because by next week you may not remember what you wrote or why.

Variables

Now let's talk about variables. As explained earlier, a variable is storage for your scalars (variables can also store data of different types, which we'll talk about in later chapters). Once you've calculated 42*7, it's gone. If you want to know what it was, you must do the calculation again. Instead of being able to use the result as a halfway point in more complicated calculations, you've got to spell it all out again in full. Talk about tedious. What you need to be able to do, and what variables allow you to do, is store a scalar away and refer to it again later.

A scalar variable name starts with a dollar sign, for example: $name. Scalar variables can hold either numbers or strings, and are limited only by the size of your computer's memory. To put data into a scalar, you assign the data to it with the assignment operator =. (Incidentally, this is why numeric comparison uses two equal signs, ==; the single equal sign = was taken to mean the assignment operator.)

What we're going to do here is tell Perl that the scalar contains the string "fred". Then we can get at that data by simply using the variable's name:

```
#!/usr/bin/perl
# vars1.pl
```

```
use warnings;

$name = "fred";
print "My name is ", $name, "\n";
```

Lo and behold, our computer informs us that

```
$ perl vars1.pl
My name is fred
$
```

Now we have somewhere to store our data, and a way to get it back again. The next logical step is to be able to change it.

Modifying a Variable

Modifying the contents of a variable is easy—just assign something different to it. We can say

```
#!/usr/bin/perl
# vars2.pl

use warnings;

$name = "fred";
print "My name is ",              $name, "\n";
print "It's still ",              $name, "\n";
$name = "bill";
print "Well, actually, now it's ", $name, "\n";
$name = "fred";
print "No, really, now it's ",    $name, "\n";
```

And watch our computer have an identity crisis:

```
$ perl vars2.pl
My name is fred
It's still fred
Well, actually, now it's bill
No, really, now it's fred
$
```

We can also do a calculation in several stages:

```
#!/usr/bin/perl
# vars3.pl

use warnings;

$a = 6 * 9;
print "Six nines are ", $a, "\n";
$b = $a + 3;
print "Plus three is ", $b, "\n";
```

```
$c = $b / 3;
print "All over three is ", $c, "\n";
$d = $c + 1;
print "Add one is ", $d, "\n";
print "\nThose stages again: ", $a, " ", $b, " ", $c, " ", $d, "\n";
```

This code prints

```
$ perl vars3.pl
Six nines are 54
Plus three is 57
All over three is 19
Add one is 20
Those stages again: 54 57 19 20
$
```

While this works perfectly well, it's often easier to stick with one variable and modify its value, if you don't need to know the stages you went through at the end:

```
#!/usr/bin/perl
# vars4.pl

use warnings;

$a = 6 * 9;
print "Six nines are ", $a, "\n";
$a = $a + 3;
print "Plus three is ", $a, "\n";
$a = $a / 3;
print "All over three is ", $a, "\n";
$a = $a + 1;
print "Add one is ", $a, "\n";
```

The = assignment operator has very low precedence. This means that Perl will do the calculations on the right-hand side of it, including fetching the current value, before assigning the new value. To illustrate, take a look at the eighth line of our example. Perl takes the current value of $a, adds three to it, and then stores it back in $a.

Operating and Assigning at Once

Operations, like fetching a value, modifying it, and storing it, are very common, so there's a special syntax for them. Generally

```
$a = $a <some operator> $b;
```

can be written as

```
$a <some operator>= $b;
```

For instance, we could rewrite the preceding example as follows:

```perl
#!/usr/bin/perl
# vars5.pl

use warnings;

$a = 6 * 9;
print "Six nines are ", $a, "\n";
$a += 3;
print "Plus three is ", $a, "\n";
$a /= 3;
print "All over three is ", $a, "\n";
$a += 1;
print "Add one is ", $a, "\n";
```

This works for **=, *=, +=, -=, /=, .=, %=, &=, |=, ^=, <<=, >>=, &&=, and ||=. These all have the same precedence as the assignment operator =.

Autoincrement and Autodecrement

Here are two more operators, ++ and --, that add and subtract one from the variable, but their precedence is a little strange. When they precede a variable, they act before everything else. When they follow a variable, however, they act after everything else. Let's examine this behavior in the following example:

```perl
#!/usr/bin/perl
# auto1.pl

use warnings;

$a = 4;
$b = 10;
print "Our variables are ", $a, " and ", $b, "\n";
$b = $a++;
print "After incrementing, we have ", $a, " and ", $b, "\n";
$b = ++$a * 2;
print "Now, we have ", $a, " and ", $b, "\n";
$a = --$b + 4;
print "Finally, we have ", $a, " and ", $b, "\n";
```

You should see the following output:

```
$ perl auto1.pl
Our variables are 4 and 10
After incrementing, we have 5 and 4
Now, we have 6 and 12
Finally, we have 15 and 11
$
```

Let's work this through a piece at a time. First we set up our variables, giving the values 4 and 10 to $a and $b respectively:

```
$a = 4;
$b = 10;
print "Our variables are ", $a, " and ", $b, "\n";
```

In the following line, the assignment happens before the increment—this is known as a *post-increment*. So $b is set to $a's current value, 4, and then $a is autoincremented, becoming 5.

```
$b = $a++;
print "After incrementing, we have ", $a, " and ", $b, "\n";
```

In the next line however, the incrementing takes place first—this is known as a *pre-increment*. $a is now 6, and $b is set to twice that, 12.

```
$b= ++$a * 2;
print "Now, we have ", $a, " and ", $b, "\n";
```

Finally, $b is decremented first (a *pre-decrement*), and becomes 11. $a is set to $b plus 4, which is 15.

```
$a= --$b + 4;
print "Finally, we have ", $a, " and ", $b, "\n";
```

The autoincrement operator actually does something interesting if the variable contains a string of only alphabetic characters, followed optionally by numeric characters. Instead of converting to a number, Perl "advances" the variable along the ranges a–z, A–Z, and 0–9. This is more easily understood from a few examples:

```
#!/usr/bin/perl
# auto2.pl

use warnings;

$a = "A9"; print ++$a, "\n";
$a = "bz"; print ++$a, "\n";
$a = "Zz"; print ++$a, "\n";
$a = "z9"; print ++$a, "\n";
$a = "9z"; print ++$a, "\n";
```

should produce

```
$ perl auto2.pl
B0
ca
AAa
aa0
10
$
```

This example shows that a 9 turns into a 0 and increments the next digit left. A z turns into an a and increments the next digit left, and if there are no more digits to the left, either an a or an A is created depending on the case of the current leftmost alpha character.

Multiple Assignments

We've said that = is an operator, but does that mean it returns a value? Well, actually it does; it returns whatever was assigned. This allows us to set several variables up at once. Here's a simple example; read it from right to left:

```
$d = $c = $b = $a = 1;
```

First we set $a to 1, and the result of this is 1. $b is set with that, the result of which is 1. And so it goes on.

Scoping

All the variables we've seen so far have been *global* variables. That is, they can be seen and changed from anywhere in the program. For the moment, that's fine, since our programs are very small and we can easily understand where things get assigned and used. However, when we start writing larger programs, it does become a problem.

Why? Well, suppose one part of your program uses a variable, $counter. If another part of your program wants a counter, it can't call it $counter as well for fear of clobbering the old value. This becomes more of an issue when you begin to use *subroutines*, which are little sections of code you can temporarily call upon to accomplish something before returning to what you were previously doing. As things stand now, we'd have to make sure all the variables in our program had different names, and with a large program that's not desirable. It's much easier to restrict the life of a variable to a certain area of the program.

To achieve this, Perl provides another type of variable, called a *lexical* variable. These variables are constrained to the enclosing block and all blocks inside it. If they're not currently inside a block, they are constrained to the current file. To tell Perl that a variable is *lexical*, we say my $variable;. This creates a brand-new lexical variable for the current block, and sets it to the undefined value. Here's an example:

```
#!/usr/bin/perl
# scope1.pl

use warnings;

$record = 4;
print "We're at record ", $record, "\n";

{
    my $record;
    $record = 7;
    print "Inside the block, we're at record ", $record, "\n";
}

print "Outside, we're still at record ", $record, "\n";
```

And this should tell you

```
$ perl scope1.pl
We're at record 4
Inside the block, we're at record 7
```

```
Outside we're still at record 4
$
```

Let's look at how this program works. First, we set our global variable $record to 4.

```
$record = 4;
print "We're at record ", $record, "\n";
```

Now we enter a new block, and create a new lexical variable. Important! This is completely and utterly unrelated to the global variable $record, because my() creates a *new* lexical variable that exists only for the duration of the block, and has the undefined value until it is assigned.

```
{
    my $record;
```

Next, the lexical variable is set to 7, and printed out. The global $record is unchanged.

```
    $record = 7;
    print "Inside the block, we're at record ", $record, "\n";
```

Finally, the block ends, and the lexical copy ends with it. We say that it has gone *out of scope*. The global variable remains however, and so $record has the value 4.

```
}

print "Outside, we're still at record ", $record, "\n";
```

In order to make us think clearly about our programming, we will ask Perl to be strict about our variable use. The statement use strict; checks that, among other things, we've declared all our variables. We declare lexicals with the my() function. Here's what happens if we change our program to use strict format:

```
#!/usr/bin/perl
# scope2.pl

use warnings;
use strict;

$record = 4;
print "We're at record ", $record, "\n";

{
    my $record;
    $record = 7;
    print "Inside the block, we're at record ", $record, "\n";
}

print "Outside, we're still at record ", $record, "\n";
```

Now, the global $record is not declared, so sure enough, Perl complains about it, generating this output:

```
$ perl scope2.pl
Global symbol "$record" requires explicit package name at scope2.pl line 7.
Global symbol "$record" requires explicit package name at scope2.pl line 8.
Global symbol "$record" requires explicit package name at scope2.pl line 16.
Execution of scope2.pl aborted due to compilation errors.
$
```

We'll see exactly what this means in later chapters, but for now it suffices to declare $record as a my() variable:

```
#!/usr/bin/perl
# scope3.pl

use warnings;
use strict;

my $record;
$record = 4;
print "We're at record ", $record, "\n";

{
    # can use my() and assign on the same line
    my $record = 7;
    print "Inside the block, we're at record ", $record, "\n";
}

print "Outside, we're still at record ", $record, "\n";
```

Now Perl is happy, and we get the same output as before. You should almost always start your programs with a use strict. Of course, nobody's going to force you, but it will help you avoid a lot of mistakes and will certainly give other people who have to look at your code more confidence in it.

One of the big mistakes that use strict; will catch is when you accidentally misspell a variable name (hey, it happens!). For instance, in one line of code you might refer to the variable by the right name:

```
$foo = 4;
```

And in another line, you misspell it as:

```
$ofo = 7;
```

use strict; will catch this mistake because if $ofo has not been declared with a my().

▓ **Note** Because use strict; will catch mistakes like this, and more, we highly recommend that use strict; always be used.

And notice that we can either use my() and assign in two statements:

```
my $record;
$record = 4;
```

Or do both in one statement:

```
my $record = 4;
```

Variable Names

We've not yet really examined the rules regarding what we can call our variables. We know that scalar variables have to start with a dollar sign, but what else? The next character must be a letter (uppercase or lowercase) or an underscore, and after that, any combination of numbers, letters, and underscores is permissible.

Note that Perl's variable names, like the rest of Perl, are case-sensitive, so $user is different from $User, and both are different from $USER.

The following are legal variable names: $I_am_a_long_variable_name, $simple, $box56, $__hidden, $B1.

The following are not legal variable names: $10c (doesn't start with letter or underscore), $mail-alias (- is not allowed), $your name (spaces not allowed).

The Special Variable $_

There are certain variables, called *special variables*, which Perl provides internally that you either are not allowed to or do not want to overwrite. An example is $_, a very special variable indeed. $_ is the *default variable* that a lot of functions and operators read from, write to, and operate upon if no other variable is given. We'll see plenty of examples of it throughout the book. For a complete list of all the special variables that Perl uses and what they do, type perldoc perlvar at the command line.

Variable Interpolation

We said earlier that double-quoted strings interpolate variables. What does this mean? Well, if you include a variable, say $name, in the middle of a double-quoted string, you get the value of the variable, rather than the actual characters in the variable name. As an example, see what Perl does to this:

```
#!/usr/bin/perl
# varint1.pl

use warnings;
use strict;

my $name = "fred";
print "My name is $name\n";
```

This produces

```
$ perl varint1.pl
My name is fred
$
```

Perl interpolates the value of $name into the string. Note that this doesn't happen with single-quoted strings, just like escape sequence interpolation:

```
#!/usr/bin/perl
# varint2.pl

use warnings;
use strict;

my $name = "fred";
print 'My name is $name\n';
```

Here we get

```
$ perl varint2.pl
My name is $name\n$
```

Notice that the system prompt is printed at the end of that line because \n is not a newline character within the single quotes (unless you are in the Windows shell, because then you'll only see the magically-added-by-the-shell blank line). This doesn't just happen in things you print, it happens every time you construct a string. So let's construct a string that includes a variable name:

```
#!/usr/bin/perl
# varint3.pl

use warnings;
use strict;

my $name = "fred";
my $salutation = "Dear $name,";
print $salutation, "\n";
```

This gives us

```
$ perl varint3.pl
Dear fred,
$
```

This has exactly the same effect as

```
my $salutation = "Dear " . $name . ",";
```

but is more concise and easier to understand.

If you need to place text immediately after the variable, you can use curly braces to delimit the name of the variable. Take this example:

```
#!/usr/bin/perl
# varint4.pl

use warnings;
use strict;
```

```
my $times = 8;
print "This is the $timesth time.\n";
```

This is syntactically incorrect, because Perl looks for a variable $timesth, which hasn't been declared. In this case, we have to change the last line by wrapping the variable name in curly braces to this:

```
print "This is the ${times}th time.\n";
```

Now we get the right result:

```
$ perl varint4.pl
This is the 8th time.
$
```

Currency Converter

Let's begin to wind up this chapter with a real example—a program to convert between currencies. This is our very first version, so we won't make it do anything too clever. As we get more and more advanced, we'll be able to hone and refine it.

```
#!/usr/bin/perl
# currency1.pl

use warnings;
use strict;

my $yen = 90.45;   # as of 13 November 2009
print "49518 Yen is ", (49_518/$yen), " dollars\n";
print "360 Yen is   ", (  360/$yen), " dollars\n";
print "30510 Yen is ", (30_510/$yen), " dollars\n";
```

Save this, and run it through Perl. You should see something like this:

```
$ perl currency1.pl
49518 Yen is 547.462686567164 dollars
360 Yen is   3.98009950248756 dollars
30510 Yen is 337.313432835821 dollars
$
```

First, we declare the exchange rate to be a lexical variable and set it to 90.45.

```
my $yen = 90.45;
```

Notice that we can declare and assign a variable at the same time. Now we do some calculations based on that exchange rate:

```
print "49518 Yen is ", (49_518/$yen), " dollars\n";
print "360 Yen is   ", (  360/$yen), " dollars\n";
print "30510 Yen is ", (30_510/$yen), " dollars\n";
```

Of course, this is currently of limited use, because the exchange rate changes and because we might want to use some different amounts at times. To account for both of these possibilities, we need to be able to ask the user for additional data when we run the program.

Introducing <STDIN>

Perl reads from *standard input* (the keyboard) with <STDIN>. It reads *up to and including* the newline character, so the newline is part of the string read in. To read a single line of input from the user, we can say something like

```
print "Please enter something interesting\n";
$comment = <STDIN>;
```

This code will read one line from the user, including the newline character, and assign the string to the variable $comment. Let's use this to get the exchange rate from the user when the program is run. This example will read the exchange rate from the user's keyboard and store it in $yen:

```
#!/usr/bin/perl
# currency2.pl

use warnings;
use strict;

print "Currency converter\n\nPlease enter the exchange rate: ";
my $yen = <STDIN>;
print "49518 Yen is ", (49_518/$yen), " dollars\n";
print "360 Yen is   ", (  360/$yen), " dollars\n";
print "30510 Yen is ", (30_510/$yen), " dollars\n";
```

Now when you run the program, you'll be asked for the exchange rate. The currency values will be calculated using the rate you entered:

```
$ perl currency2.pl
Currency converter

Please enter the exchange rate: 90
49518 Yen is 550.2 dollars
360 Yen is   4 dollars
30510 Yen is 339 dollars
$
```

Note that this time we read the exchange rate from the user's keyboard and it was read in as a string. Perl converts the string to a number in order to perform the calculation.

So far, we haven't done any checking to make sure that the exchange rate given makes sense; this is something we'll need to think about in the future.

The chomp() and chop() Functions

<STDIN> reads up to and including the newline character. Sometimes we don't want to include the newline in the text we have read, so we can chomp() the newline off the string.

The chomp()function removes the last character of a string if and only if it is the newline character. For instance:

```
$string = "testing 1, 2, 3\n";
chomp($string);                    # $string is now "testing 1, 2, 3"
```

Since <STDIN> reads up to and including the newline character, this code reads and then removes the newline:

```
my $input = <STDIN>;
chomp($input);
```

Those two statements can be combined into one:

```
chomp(my $input = <STDIN>);
```

A related function is chop(), which removes the last character of a string, regardless of what character it is. Here is an example:

```
$string = "testing, 1, 2, 3";
chop($string);                     # $string is now "testing 1, 2, "
```

Two Miscellaneous Functions

Before we end our discussion of scalars, we should discuss two functions that are often used to terminate Perl programs: exit() and die().

The exit() Function

The exit() function exits the program. If an argument is provided, it returns that value back to the calling program (or shell). If no argument is provided, it returns the value 0. In the shell, the value 0 means that the program terminated normally, so we can report that all is well with

```
exit(0);
```

or

```
exit;
```

If the program exits abnormally due to some error condition, simply return a nonzero value to tell the calling program that all is not well:

```
exit(1);
```

Here is an example of using the exit() function:

```
#!/usr/bin/perl
# exit.pl

use warnings;
use strict;

print "enter value to return back to the calling program: ";
```

```
chomp(my $value = <STDIN>);

exit($value);
```

In Unix, you can echo the value $? to see the return value of the most recent command:

```
$ perl exit.pl
enter value to return back to the calling program: 0
$ echo $?
0
$ perl exit.pl
enter value to return back to the calling program: 255
$ echo $?
255
$
```

The die() Function

The die() function is how we handle severe errors in Perl. It takes a character string argument and prints it to standard error output (this normally prints to the screen like standard output does). If the argument string does not end in a newline, the \n character, die() automatically appends to the output string the name of the Perl program and the line number of the program where the die() was executed; this is very helpful—it tells us right where the error took place. Then die() cleans up the program and exits with a non-0 exit status. Therefore, die() is a permanent solution—the program terminates:

```
die "there was an error";
```

Here is an example of using die().

```
#!/usr/bin/perl
# die.pl

use warnings;
use strict;

print "please enter a string to pass to die: ";
chomp(my $string = <STDIN>);

die($string);
print "didn't make it this far...\n";
```

Executing this code would produce something like:

```
$ perl die.pl
please enter a string to pass to die: this is the end
this is the end at die.pl line 10, <STDIN> line 1.
$
```

Notice that the name of the script and the line number are automatically added to the output of die() because the argument to die() did not end in the newline character (good thing we chomp()ed it off). Also notice that the last print() is not executed because the program terminated when die() executed.

Summary

Perl's basic data type is a scalar. A scalar can be an integer, a floating-point number, or a string. Perl converts between these three automatically when necessary.

Double- and single-quoted strings differ in the way they process the text inside them. Single-quoted strings do little or no processing, while double-quoted strings interpolate escape sequences and variables.

We can operate on these scalars in a number of ways—ordinary arithmetic, bitwise arithmetic, string manipulation, and logical comparison. We can also combine logical comparisons with Boolean operators. These operators vary in precedence, which is to say that some take effect before others, and as a result we must use parentheses to enforce the precedence we want.

Scalar variables are a way of storing scalars so that we can get at them and change their values. Scalar variable names begin with a dollar sign ($) and are followed by one or more alphanumeric characters or underscores. There are two types of variables—lexical and global. Globals exist throughout the entire program, and so can be troublesome if we don't keep very good track of where they are being used. Lexicals have a life span of only the current block, and so we can use them safely without worrying about clobbering similarly named variables elsewhere in the program.

`<STDIN>` reads in from standard input, which is normally the user's keyboard. We can store this input in a variable and then operate upon it, making our programs more flexible. `<STDIN>` reads up to and including the newline character, and we normally `chomp()` off the newline.

Two ways to terminate our programs are by using `exit()` and `die()`. `die()` is useful because it prints its argument, and if that argument does not end in `\n`, it obligingly adds the script name and line number to the output, which helps us locate the error.

Exercises

1. Change the currency conversion program so that it asks for an exchange rate and three prices to convert.

2. Write a program that asks for a hexadecimal number and converts it to decimal. Then change it to convert an octal number to decimal.

3. Write a program that asks for a decimal number less than 256 and converts it to binary. (Hint: You may want to use the bitwise and operator 8 times.)

4. Without the aid of the computer, work out the order in which each of the following expressions would be computed, and their value. Put the appropriate parentheses in to reflect the normal precedence:

   - `2+6/4-3*5+1`

   - `17+-3**3/2`

   - `26+3^4*2`

   - `4+3>=7||2&4*2<4`

CHAPTER 3

■ ■ ■

Control Flow Constructs

Most of the programs we've seen so far have had a very simple structure—they've done one statement after another in turn. If we use boxes to represent statements, our programs would look like this:

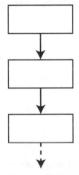

This sort of diagram is called a *flow chart*, and programmers have used them for a long time to help design their programs. They're considered a bit passé these days, but they're still useful. The path Perl (or any other language) takes when it follows the arrows is called the *flow of execution* of the program. Boxes denote statements (or a single group of statements), and diamonds denote tests. There are also a whole host of other symbols for magnetic tapes, drum storage, and all sorts of wonderful devices, now happily lost in the mists of time.

We can choose the path our program takes depending on certain things. For instance, we'll do something *if* two strings are equal:

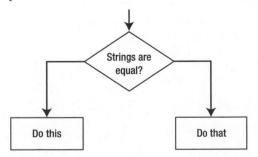

We can also iterate, or loop, through a number of items by executing a block of statements again and again for each element of the list:

We'll take a look at the other sorts of control structures we have in Perl, such as structures that do things *if* or *unless* something is true. We'll see structures that do things *while* something is true, or *until* it is true, and structures that loop *for* a certain number of times, or *foreach* element in a list. Each of the words in italic in this paragraph is a Perl keyword, and we'll examine them in this chapter.

The if Statement

In programming, we often need to test a condition, and if that condition is true, take some action. This can be performed using an *if statement*, which has the general syntax:

```
if ( condition ) {
    statements
}
```

Don't type this in and try to make it run—it is meant to be just the general structure of the construct. Note that those curly braces—{ … }—around the body (the *statements*) are *required*. You must use them, even if the body is one line of code.

Keep in mind that the `condition` is tested to be true or false, so the `if` test ultimately comes down to a Boolean test. For instance, let's say you want to divide by a number unless that number is 0. You can first check to see if the number is not 0, and if it is not, perform the division.

```
if ($number != 0) {
    $result = 100 / $number;
}
```

Let's create a program to use the `if` statement. It will prompt the user to enter a number. If the number is not 0, then 100 is divided by that number and the result is stored in `$result`. If the number is 0, the result will remain the default value of 0:

```
#!/usr/bin/perl
# if.pl

use warnings;
use strict;

print "please enter a number: ";
chomp(my $number = <STDIN>);
```

```
my $result = 0;
if ($number != 0) {
    $result = 100 / $number;
}

print "the result is: $result\n";
```

Recall that the statement

```
chomp(my $number = <STDIN>);
```

is shorthand for the two statements that read from standard input and then remove the newline:

```
my $number = <STDIN>;
chomp $number;
```

Now let's execute the program, once with a nonzero value and once with 0:

```
$ perl if.pl
please enter a number: 8
the result is: 12.5
$ perl if.pl
please enter a number: 0
the result is: 0
$
```

Operators Revisited

The if statement, and all the other control structures we're going to visit in this chapter, test to see whether a condition is true or false. They do this using the Boolean logic mentioned in Chapter 2, together with Perl's ideas of true and false. To remind you of these:

- An empty string, "", is false.

- The number 0 and the string "0" are both false.

- An empty list, (), is false.

- The undefined value is false.

- Everything else is true.

However, you need to be careful of a few traps here. A string containing invisible characters, like spaces or newlines, is true. A string that isn't "0" is true, even if its numerical value is 0, so "0.0" for instance, is true.

Larry Wall has said that programming Perl is an empirical science—you learn things about it by trying them out. Is (()) a true value? You can look it up in books and the online documentation, or you can spend a few seconds writing a program like this:

```
#!/usr/bin/perl
# emptylist.pl

use warnings;
```

```
use strict;

if ( (()) ) {
    print "Yes, it is.\n";
}
```

This way you get the answer straight away, with a minimum of fuss. (If you're interested, it isn't a true value.) We've also seen that conditional operators can test things out, returning **1** if the test was successful and empty string if it was not. Let's see what else we can test.

Comparing Numbers

We can test whether one number is bigger, smaller, or the same as another. Suppose we have two numbers stored in the variables $x and $y; Table 3-1 shows the operators we can use for testing.

Table 3-1. *Numeric Comparison Operators*

Operator	Description
$x > $y	$x is greater than $y.
$x < $y	$x is less than $y.
$x >= $y	$x is greater than or equal to $y.
$x <= $y	$x is less than or equal to $y.
$x == $y	$x has the same numeric value as $y.
$x != $y	$x does not have the same numeric value as $y.

Don't forget that the numeric comparison needs a doubled equal sign (==) so that Perl doesn't think you're trying to set $x to the value of $y.

And remember that Perl converts $x and $y to numbers in the usual way. It reads numbers or decimal points from the left for as long as possible, ignoring initial spaces, and then drops the rest of the string. If no numbers are found, the value is set to 0.

■ **Note** Be careful with the == operator when comparing strings. The expression:

```
"Pink Floyd" == "Captain and Tennille"
```

evaluates to true (and we all know there is no way those two are equal). Why? Because both strings, since they are not numeric, evaluate to 0. So, when comparing strings, don't use numeric comparison operators. Instead, use string comparison operators (discussed later in this chapter).

Let's see an example—a very simple guessing game. The computer has a number and the user has to guess what it is. If the user doesn't guess correctly, the computer gives a hint. As we learn more about Perl, we'll add the ability to give more than one try, and to pick a different number each game.

```perl
#!/usr/bin/perl
# guessnum1.pl

use warnings;
use strict;

my $target = 12;
print "Guess my number!\n";
print "Enter your guess: ";
my $guess = <STDIN>;

if ($target == $guess) {
    print "That's it! You guessed correctly!\n";
    exit;
}
if ($guess > $target) {
    print "Your number is more than my number\n";
    exit;
}
if ($guess < $target){
    print "Your number is less than my number\n";
    exit;
}
```

Let's have a few tries:

```
$ perl guessnum1.pl
Guess my number!
Enter your guess: 3
Your number is less than my number
$ perl guessnum1.pl
Guess my number!
Enter your guess: 15
Your number is more than my number
$ perl guessnum1.pl
Guess my number!
Enter your guess: 12
That's it! You guessed correctly!
$
```

The first thing we do in this program is set up our secret number. (OK, at the moment it's not exactly secret since it's right there in the source code, but we can improve on this later.) Next, we get a number from the user:

```perl
my $guess = <STDIN>;
```

Then we do three sorts of comparisons with the numeric operators we've just seen. We use the basic pattern of the if statement again: if (condition) { action }.

```perl
if ($target == $guess) {
    print "That's it! You guessed correctly!\n";
    exit;
}
```

Since only one of the tests can be true—the user's number can't be both smaller than our number and the same as it—we may as well stop work after a test was successful. The exit() function tells Perl to stop the program completely.

Comparing Strings

When we're comparing strings, we use a different set of operators to do the comparisons, as listed in Table 3-2.

Table 3-2. *String Comparison Operators*

Operator	Description
$x gt $y	$x is string greater than $y.
$x lt $y	$x is string less than $y.
$x ge $y	$x is string greater than or equal to $y.
$x le $y	$x is string less than or equal to $y.
$x eq $y	$x is the same as $y.
$x ne $y	$x is not the same as $y.

Here's a very simple way of testing if a user knows a password. (Don't use a good password in this program since the user can just read the source code to find it!)

```perl
#!/usr/bin/perl
# password.pl

use warnings;
use strict;

my $password = "foxtrot";
print "Enter the password: ";
my $guess = <STDIN>;
chomp $guess;
if ($password eq $guess) {
    print "Pass, friend.\n";
}
```

```
if ($password ne $guess) {
    die "Go away, imposter!\n";
}
```

Here's our security system in action:

```
$ perl password.pl
Enter the password: abracadabra
Go away, imposter!
$ perl password.pl
Enter the password: foxtrot
Pass, friend.
$
```

This program starts by asking the user for input:

```
my $guess = <STDIN>;
```

Please note: this is a horrendously bad way of asking for a password, since it's echoed to the screen and anyone looking at the user's computer would be able to read it. If you ever do need to get a password from the user, the Perl FAQ provides a better method in perlfaq8. Type `perldoc -q password` to find it.

```
chomp $guess;
```

This statement chomps the newline off of $guess. Never forget that a newline exists at the end of the user's data. Otherwise, even if the user enters the right password, it will be rejected. Perl would try to compare "foxtrot" with "foxtrot\n" and, of course, these are not the same. (We didn't need to chomp the newline for numeric comparison because Perl would remove it for us anyway during conversion to a number.)

```
if ($password ne $guess) {
    die "Go away, imposter!\n";
}
```

If the password we have isn't the same as the user's input, we send out a rude message and terminate the program.

Other Tests

What other tests can we perform? We can test if a variable is defined (it must contain something other than the undefined value) using `defined()`.

A variable that has not yet been assigned a value is considered undefined, or `undef` for short. Undefined means "lack of value" or "no value". When used as a string, an undefined variable is considered the empty string; as a number, it is considered 0. However, when an undefined variable is evaluated, Perl complains with a warning message. Warning messages are useful—they alert us to possible problems, after all—but it is usually desirable to resolve all warnings. So, if a program is warning that you are evaluating an undefined variable, you should check to see if it undefined and if so, define it. This example checks to see if variables are undefined:

```
#!/usr/bin/perl
# defined.pl
```

```
use warnings;
use strict;

my ($var1, $var2);
$var2 = 10;

if (defined $var1) {
   print "\$var1 has a value.\n";
}
if (defined $var2) {
   print "\$var2 has a value.\n";
}
```

Not surprisingly, the result we get is this:

```
$ perl defined.pl
$var2 has a value.
$
```

You can use this to avoid the warnings engendered when you try to use a variable that doesn't have a value. If we had tried to say

```
if ($var1 == $var2)
```

Perl would have said

```
Use of uninitialized value in numeric eq (==)
```

So we have our basic comparisons. Don't forget that some functions will return a true value if they were successful and false if they were not. You will often want to check whether the return value of an operation (particularly one that relates to the operating system) is true or not.

Logical Operators

We also saw in Chapter 2 that we can combine several tests into one using the logical operators. Table 3-3 summarizes these operators.

Table 3-3. *Logical Operators*

Operator	Description
$x and $y $x && $y	True if both $x and $y are true
$x or $y $x || $y	True if either of $x or $y, or both are true
not $x ! $x	True if $x is not true

The operators and, or, and not are usually used instead of &&, ||, and ! mainly due to their readability. The operator not means not, after all. Don't forget there is a difference in precedence between the two—and, or, and not all have lower precedence than their symbolic representations.

Multiple Choice: if . . . else

Consider these two if statements:

```
if ($password eq $guess) {
    print "Pass, friend.\n";
}
if ($password ne $guess) {
    die "Go away, imposter!\n";
}
```

We know that if the first test condition is true, then the second one will not be—we're asking exactly opposite questions: Are these the same? Are they not the same?

In which case, it seems wasteful to do two tests. It'd be much nicer to be able to say, "If the strings are the same, do this. Otherwise, do that." And in fact we can do exactly that, although the keyword is not *otherwise* but *else*:

```
if ($password eq $guess) {
    print "Pass, friend.\n";
} else {
    die "Go away, imposter!\n";
}
```

That's

```
if ( condition ) { action } else { alternative action }
```

As with the if statement, those curly braces are *required* in the else part.

Even More Choices: if . . . elsif . . . else

Some things in life aren't clear-cut. In some cases, we'll want to test more than one condition. When looking at several related possibilities, we'll want to ask questions like "Is this true? If this isn't true, is that true? If that's not true, how about the other?" Note that this is different from asking three independent questions; whether we ask the second depends on whether or not the first was true. In Perl, we could very easily write something like this:

```
if ( condition1 ) {
    action1
} else {
    if ( condition2 ) {
        action2
    } else {
        if ( condition3 ) {
            action3
        } else {
```

```
        action4
      }
    }
}
```

You might agree that this looks pretty messy. To make it nicer, we can combine the else and the next if into a single word, elsif. Here's what the preceding would look like when rephrased in this way:

```
if ( condition1) {
   action1
} elsif ( condition2 ) {
   action2
} elsif ( condition3 ) {
   action3
} else {
   action4
}
```

Much neater! We don't have an awful cascade of closing curly braces at the end, and it's easier to see what we're testing and when we're testing it.

Let's look at an example. Most of us will not go outside if it's raining, but we will always go out for a walk in the snow. We will not go outside if it's less than 18 degrees Celsius. Otherwise, we'll probably go out unless we've got too much work to do. Do we want to go for a walk?

```
#!/usr/bin/perl
# walking.pl

use warnings;
use strict;

print "What's the weather like outside? ";
chomp(my $weather = <STDIN>);
print "How hot is it, in degrees? ";
chomp(my $temperature = <STDIN>);
print "And how many emails left to reply to? ";
chomp(my $work = <STDIN>);

if ($weather eq "snowing") {
    print "It's snowing, let's go!\n";
} elsif ($weather eq "raining") {
    print "No way, sorry, it's raining so I'm staying in.\n";
} elsif ($temperature  < 18) {
    print "Too cold for me!\n";
} elsif ($work > 30) {
    print "Sorry - just too busy.\n";
} else {
    print "Well, why not?\n";
}
```

Let's say it is 20[1] degrees, we've got 27 e-mails to reply to, and it's cloudy out there:

```
$ perl walking.pl
What's the weather like outside? cloudy
How hot is it, in degrees? 20
And how many emails left to reply to? 27
Well, why not?
$
```

Looks like we can fit a walk in after all.

The point of this rather silly little program is that once it has gathered the information it needs, it runs through a series of tests, each of which could cause it to finish. First, we check to see if it's snowing:

```
if ($weather eq "snowing") {
    print "It's snowing, let's go!\n";
```

If so, then we print our message and, this is the important part, do no more tests. If not, we move on to the next test:

```
} elsif ($weather eq "raining") {
    print "No way, sorry, it's raining so I'm staying in.\n";
```

Again, if this is true, we stop testing; otherwise, we move on. Finally, if none of the tests are true, we get to the else:

```
} else {
    print "Well, why not?\n";
}
```

Please remember that this is very different from what would happen if we used four separate if statements. The tests overlap, so it is possible for more than one condition to be true at once. For example, if it was snowing and we had over 30 emails to reply to, we'd get two conflicting answers. elsif tests should be read as "Well, how about if . . . ?"

Now let's update the program we saw earlier, guessnum1.pl, to use if/elsif/else. The decision we made in the first version was implemented with three if statements:

```
if ($target == $guess) {
    print "That's it! You guessed correctly!\n";
    exit;
}
if ($guess > $target) {
    print "Your number is more than my number\n";
    exit;
}
if ($guess < $target){
    print "Your number is less than my number\n";
```

---

[1] Celsius, that is.

```
exit;
}
```

Notice that in each `if` statement we execute the `exit()` function since, if the condition is true, there is no reason to check any of the following conditions. Instead of using the `exit()` function in each of the `if` blocks, this would be better written with an `if/elsif/else,` as shown in `guessnum2.pl`:

```
#!/usr/bin/perl
# guessnum2.pl

use warnings;
use strict;

my $target = 12;
print "Guess my number!\n";
print "Enter your guess: ";
my $guess = <STDIN>;

if ($target == $guess) {
    print "That's it! You guessed correctly!\n";
} elsif ($guess > $target) {
    print "Your number is more than my number\n";
} elsif ($guess < $target) {
    print "Your number is less than my number\n";
}
```

The unless Statement

There's another way of saying `if (not $a)`. As always in Perl, there's more than one way to do it.[2] Some people prefer to think "If this is not true, then { ... }," but other people like to think "Unless this is true, then { ... }." Perl caters to both thought patterns, and we could just as easily have written:

```
unless ($a) {
    print "\$a is not true\n";
}
```

The psychology is different, but the effect is the same. We'll see later how Perl provides a few alternatives for these control structures to help them more effectively fit the way you think.

---

[2] TMTOWTDI-our favorite acronym!

Expression Modifiers

When we talk in English, it's quite normal to say

- If this is not true, then this happens, or
- Unless this is true, this happens.

And it's also quite natural to reverse the two phrases

- This happens if this is not true, or
- This happens unless this is true.

In Perl-speak, we can take this if statement:

```
if ($number == 0) {
    die "can't divide by 0";
}
```

and rewrite it as follows:

```
die "can't divide by 0" if $number == 0;
```

Notice how the syntax here is slightly different, it's *action if condition*. There is no need for parentheses around the condition, and there are no curly braces around the action. Indeed, the indentation isn't part of the syntax, so we can even put the whole statement on one line. Only a single statement will be covered by the condition. This form of the if statement is called an *expression modifier*.

We can turn unless into an expression modifier too, so, instead of this:

```
if (not $name) {
    die "\$name has a false value";
}
```

you may find it more natural to write this:

```
die "\$name has a false value" unless $name;
```

Using Short-Circuited Evaluation

There is yet another way to do something if a condition is true. By using the fact that Perl stops processing a logical operator when it knows the answer, we can create a sort of unless conditional:

```
$name or die "\$name has a false value";
```

How does this work? Well, it relies on the fact that Perl uses short-circuited, or lazy, evaluation to give a logical operator its value. If we have the statement X or Y, then if X is true, it doesn't matter what Y is, so Perl doesn't look at it. If X isn't true, Perl has to look at Y to see whether or not that's true. So if

$name has a true value, then the die() function will not be executed. Instead, Perl will do nothing and continue on to execute the next statement.

This form of conditional is most often used when checking that something we did succeeded or returned a true value. We will see it often when we're handling files.

To create a positive if conditional this way, use and instead of or. For example, to add one to a counter if a test is successful, you can say

```perl
$success and $counter++;
```

As you'll recall, and statements require both substatements to be true. So, if $success is not true, Perl won't bother evaluating $counter++ and upping its value by 1. If $success is true, then it would.

Looping Constructs

Now we know how to do everything once. What about if we need to repeat an operation or series of operations? Of course, there are constructs available in Perl to do this, too.

In programming, there are various types of loops. Some loop forever, and are called *infinite loops*, while most, in contrast, are *finite loops*. We say that a program "gets into" or "enters" a loop, and then "exits" or "falls out" when finished. Infinite loops may not sound very useful, but they certainly can be—particularly because most languages, Perl included, provide a way to exit the loop. They are useful when you want the program to continue running until the user stops it manually, the computer powers down, or the heat death of the universe occurs, whichever comes first.

There's also a difference between *definite loops* and *indefinite loops*. In a definite loop, you know in advance how many times the block will be repeated. An indefinite loop will check a condition in each iteration to determine whether it should loop again.

There's also a difference between an indefinite loop that checks before the iteration, and one that checks afterward. The latter will always go through at least one iteration, in order to get to the check, whereas the former checks first and so may not go through any iterations at all.

Perl supports ways of expressing all of these types of loops. First, let's examine the while loop.

The while Loop

Let's start with indefinite loops. These check a condition, then do an action, then go back and check the condition again. We'll look first at the while loop. As you might guess from the name, this type of loop keeps doing something while a condition is true. The syntax of while is much like the syntax of if:

```perl
while ( condition ) { action }
```

Once again, those curly braces are required. Here's a very simple while loop:

```perl
#!/usr/bin/perl
# while1.pl

use warnings;
use strict;

my $countdown = 5;

while ($countdown > 0) {
```

```
    print "Counting down: $countdown\n";
    $countdown--;
}
```

And here's what it produces:

```
$ perl while1.pl
Counting down: 5
Counting down: 4
Counting down: 3
Counting down: 2
Counting down: 1
$
```

Let's see a flow chart for this program. While there's still a value greater than 0 in the $counter variable, we do these two statements:

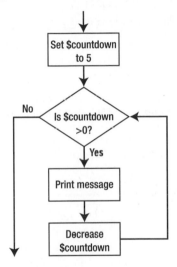

```
    print "Counting down: $countdown\n";
    $countdown--;
```

Perl goes through the loop a first time when $countdown is 5; the condition is met, so a message is printed and $countdown gets decreased to 4. Then, as the flow chart illustrates, back we go to the top of the loop. We test again: $countdown is still more than 0, so off we go again. Eventually, $countdown is 1, we print our message, $countdown is decreased, and now it's 0. This time around, the test fails, and we exit the loop.

while (<STDIN>)

Recall that we talked about using <STDIN> to read from standard input (normally the keyboard). This statement reads the next line of standard input, up to and including the newline character:

```
$line_in = <STDIN>;
```

We can put this assignment within a while loop that will read from standard input until end of file (in Unix a ^D, or the Ctrl and D keys pressed at the same time; in Windows a ^Z<enter>). This loop reads a line at a time into $line_in and then prints that line:

```perl
while ($line_in = <STDIN>) {
    print $line_in;
}
```

This behavior, reading from standard input until end of file, is so common that if <STDIN> is by itself within the while loop parentheses (and only within the while loop parentheses), then the line of standard input is magically assigned to the special variable $_. This loop reads each line into $_, and then the line is printed:

```perl
while (<STDIN>) {
    print $_;
}
```

This is so common that print() defaults to printing $_:

```perl
while (<STDIN>) {
    print;
}
```

Let's look at an example of using this magic variable $_. This program will loop through standard input one line at a time until end of file, and for each line it will print a message followed by the line entered:

```perl
#!/usr/bin/perl
# while2.pl

use warnings;
use strict;

while (<STDIN>) {
    print "You entered: ";
    print;
}
```

Here is an example of running this program in Unix:

```
$ perl while2.pl
Perl
You entered: Perl
is
You entered: is
cool
You entered: cool
^D
$
```

■ **Note** In Unix, end of file is ^D (Control-D). In Windows, end of file is ^Z<ret> (yes, you have to type the return key). You will have to adjust the example above if you are working in Windows.

The `$_` variable is very useful—it is the default argument for many different functions, such as the `chomp()` function. The statement

```perl
chomp $_;
```

could have been written as

```perl
chomp;
```

Many Perl programmers find it convenient and readable to write a loop like this one:

```perl
while ($line = <STDIN>) {
    chomp $line;
    ...
}
```

using the default nature of `$_`:

```perl
while (<STDIN>) {
    chomp;
    ...
}
```

Whether or not you write code to take advantage of the magic nature of `$_` is up to you, but we suggest you practice with it enough to be able to read code that others have written using `$_`.

Infinite Loops

The obvious but important point is that what we're testing gets changed inside the loop. If our condition is always going to give a true result, we have an infinite loop. Let's just remove the second of those two statements:

```perl
#!/usr/bin/perl
# while3.pl

use warnings;
use strict;

my $countdown = 5;

while ($countdown > 0) {
    print "Counting down: $countdown\n";
}
```

$countdown never changes. It's always going to be 5, and 5 is, we hope, always going to be more than 0. So this program will keep printing its message until you interrupt it by holding down Ctrl and D. Hopefully, you can see why you need to ensure that what you do in your loop affects the condition.

Should we actually want an infinite loop, there's a fairly standard way to do it. Just put a true value—typically 1—as the condition:

```
while (1) {
    print "Bored yet?\n";
}
```

The converse, of course, is to say while (0) in the loop's declaration, but nothing will ever happen because this condition is tested before any of the commands in the loop are executed. A bit silly really.

Looping Until

In the same sense that the opposite of if is unless, the opposite of while is until. The until loop is exactly the same as while (not condition) { ... }. Using the condition in the program while1.pl shown previously:

```
while ($countdown > 0) {
```

Its logical negation would be

```
until ($countdown <= 0) {
```

Therefore, we can write while1.pl as

```
#!/usr/bin/perl
# until.pl

use warnings;
use strict;

my $countdown = 5;

until ($countdown <= 0) {
    print "Counting down: $countdown\n";
    $countdown--;
}
```

And here's what it produces:

```
$ perl until.pl
Counting down: 5
Counting down: 4
Counting down: 3
Counting down: 2
Counting down: 1
$
```

■ **Note** The negation of `>` is `<=`, not `<`. Yes, we have made the same mistake many times....

The for Loop

Perl has a `for` loop, similar to the one found in C, C++, and Java. Its syntax is

```
for (init_expression; test_expression; step_expression) {
    action
}
```

The `init_expr` is done first and once. Then the `test_expr` is tested to be true or false. If true, the `action` is executed, then the `step_expr` is executed. Then the `test_expr` is tested to be true or false, and so on.

The most common use of a `for` loop is as an alternative way of writing a `while` loop that might resemble this one:

```
$i = 1;
while ($i <= 5) {
    # do something important
    $i++;
}
```

This can be written in a `for` loop as

```
for ($i = 1; $i <= 5; $i++) {
    # do something important
}
```

The foreach Loop

Perl has another loop called the `foreach` loop. It is used to loop through lists and arrays. We will talk about arrays in the next chapter, but since we have seen examples of a list, we can look at the `foreach` loop processing a list of numbers:

```
#!/usr/bin/perl
# foreach.pl

use warnings;
use strict;

my $number;

foreach $number (1 .. 10) {
    print "the number is: $number\n";
}
```

The foreach loop executes the body of the loop (the print() function in this example) for each number in the list. $number is called the *loop control variable*, and it takes on the values in the list, one at a time. Recall that (1 .. 10) is shorthand for (1, 2, 3, 4, 5, 6, 7, 8, 9, 10). The following code produces this result:

```
$ perl foreach.pl
the number is: 1
the number is: 2
the number is: 3
the number is: 4
the number is: 5
the number is: 6
the number is: 7
the number is: 8
the number is: 9
the number is: 10
$
```

■ **Note** The control variable in the foreach loop can be declared with my() right in the looping construct like this:

```
foreach my $number (1 .. 10) {
    print "the number is: $number\n";
}
```

This accomplishes two things: first, it satisfies use strict; since $number gets declared with my(), and second, it lexically scopes $number to the body of the foreach (it is not available outside the looping construct).

A note about the keywords for and foreach: they are synonyms for each other. In other words, we can say

```
foreach ($i = 1; $i <= 10; $i++)_ { .. }
```

and

```
for $number (1..10) { .. }
```

foreach is rarely used in place of for, but for is often used instead of foreach. In the spirit of minimal confusion, we will spell out foreach when we have a foreach loop.

We will talk more about foreach in the next chapter when we discuss the array data type.

do .. while and do .. until

When we were categorizing our lists, we divided indefinite loops into those that execute at least once and those that may execute zero times. The while loop we've seen so far tests the condition first and so, if the condition isn't true the first time around, the "body" of the loop never gets executed. There are two other ways to write our loop to ensure that the body is always executed at least once:

```
do { action } while ( condition );
do { action } until ( condition );
```

Now we do the test after the block. This is equivalent to moving the diamond in our flow chart from the top to the bottom.

Here is an example:

```perl
#!/usr/bin/perl
# dowhiledountil.pl

use warnings;
use strict;

my $i = 1;

print "starting do...while:\n";
do {
    print "    the value of \$i: $i\n";
    $i++;
} while ($i < 6);

$i = 1;

print "starting do...until\n";
do {
    print "    the value of \$i: $i\n";
    $i++;
} until ($i >= 6);
```

Executing this program produces the following:

```
$ perl dowhiledountil.pl
starting do...while:
    the value of $i: 1
    the value of $i: 2
    the value of $i: 3
    the value of $i: 4
    the value of $i: 5
starting do...until
    the value of $i: 1
    the value of $i: 2
    the value of $i: 3
    the value of $i: 4
    the value of $i: 5
$
```

The importance of the do..while and do..until loops is that the body of the loop is always executed at least once.

Expression Modifying

As before, you can use `while` and `until` as statement modifiers. Following the pattern for `if`, here's what you'd do with `while`:

```
while ( condition ) { statement }
```

becomes

```
statement while condition;
```

Similarly:

```
until ( condition ) { statement }
```

becomes

```
statement until condition;
```

Therefore, this loop:

```
while (<STDIN>) {
    print "You entered: $_";
}
```

can be written as

```
print "You entered: $_" while <STDIN>;
```

Loop Control Constructs

Perl provides constructs that let us control the flow of our loops. They allow us to break out of a loop, go to the next iteration of the loop, or reexecute the loop. We'll start with breaking out of a loop.

Breaking Out

The keyword `last`, in the body of a loop, will make Perl immediately exit, or "break out of" that loop (you can also last out of a block, but not out of a conditional statement (`if` or `unless`)). The remaining statements in the loop are not executed, and you end up at the executable statement following the loop. Here is an example of a program that breaks out of the loop when the user enters the text "done":

```
#!/usr/bin/perl
# last1.pl

use warnings;
use strict;

while (<STDIN>) {
    if ($_ eq "done\n") {
        last;
    }
    print "You entered: $_";
```

```
}

print "All done!\n";
```

```
$ perl last1.pl
Songs
You entered: Songs
from
You entered: from
the
You entered: the
Wood
You entered: Wood
done
All done!
$
```

You can use a last in any looping construct (while, until, for, and foreach). However, last does not work with do {} while or do {} until loops.

Note that last1.pl could have been written using an expression modifier. It can be argued that this code is a bit more readable:

```perl
#!/usr/bin/perl
# last2.pl

use warnings;
use strict;

while (<STDIN>) {
    last if $_ eq "done\n";
    print "You entered: $_";
}

print "All done!\n";
```

Going On to the Next

If you want to skip the rest of the processing of the body on the current iteration, but don't want to exit the loop, you can use next to immediately go execute the next iteration of the loop by testing the expression. Here is an example of a program that reads input from the user, and if the line of input is not blank, the line is printed. It the line is blank, the program immediately goes back to read the next line:

```perl
#!/usr/bin/perl
# next1.pl

use warnings;
use strict;

print "Please enter some text:\n";
while (<STDIN>) {
```

```perl
    if ($_ eq "\n") {
        next;
    }
    chomp;
    print "You entered: [$_]\n";
}
```

Here is an example of running this program in Windows:

```
$ perl next1.pl
Please enter some text:
testing
You entered: [testing]
one
You entered: [one]
two three
You entered: [two three]
^Z<enter>
$
```

Notice that when the user entered a blank line, the program immediately read the next line of input. This program could have been written with an expression modifier:

```perl
#!/usr/bin/perl
# next2.pl

use warnings;
use strict;

print "Please enter some text:\n";
while (<STDIN>) {
    next if $_ eq "\n";
    chomp;
    print "You entered: [$_]\n";
}
```

Reexecuting the Loop

On rare occasions, you'll want to go back to the top of the loop, but without testing the condition (in the case of a for or while loop) or getting the next element in the list (as in a for or while loop). If you feel you need to do this, the keyword to use is redo, as illustrated in this example:

```perl
#!/usr/bin/perl
# redo.pl

use warnings;
use strict;

my $number = 10;

while (<STDIN>) {
```

```
    chomp;
    print "You entered: $_\n";
    if ($_ == $number) {
        $_++;
        redo;
    }
    print "Going to read the next number now...\n";
}
```

If the user enters the value 10, then the input is incremented to 11 and we jump to the beginning of the block, at which point the value will be chomped (which has no effect on the value since it does not end in newline) and then the value 11 is reported. Executing this program in Windows would look like the following:

```
$ perl redo.pl
5
You entered: 5
Going to read the next number now...
20
You entered: 20
Going to read the next number now...
10
You entered: 10
You entered: 11
Going to read the next number now...
^Z<enter>
$
```

Loop Labels

By default, last, next, and redo operate on the innermost looping construct only. For instance, in this code:

```
#!/usr/bin/perl
# looplabel1.pl

use warnings;
use strict;

my $i = 1;

while ($i <= 5) {
    my $j = 1;
    while ($j <= 5) {
        last if $j == 3;
        print "$i ** $j = ", $i ** $j, "\n";
        $j++;
    }
    $i++;
}
```

the last statement within the innermost loop construct (while ($j <= 5)) will last out of the innermost looping construct only. Therefore, each time $j reaches 3 within the inner loop, we last out of the inner loop and increment $i, then go back up to test the expression for the outer while loop. This generates the following output:

```
$ perl looplabel1.pl
1 ** 1 = 1
1 ** 1 = 1
2 ** 1 = 2
2 ** 2 = 4
3 ** 1 = 3
3 ** 2 = 9
4 ** 1 = 4
4 ** 2 = 16
5 ** 1 = 5
5 ** 2 = 25
$
```

To make the last statement last out of the outer looping construct, we must label the outer looping construct with a *loop label*. A loop label is a variable that the programmer creates (it is recommended that you use all uppercase names) followed by a colon, preceding the looping construct. This is illustrated in looplabel2.pl:

```
#!/usr/bin/perl
# looplabel2.pl

use warnings;
use strict;

my $i = 1;

OUTER: while ($i <= 5) {
    my $j = 1;
    while ($j <= 5) {
        last OUTER if $j == 3;
        print "$i ** $j = ", $i ** $j, "\n";
        $j++;
    }
    $i++;
}
```

Now, when the last statement is executed, the code jumps out of the outer loop named OUTER:

```
$ perl looplabel2.pl
1 ** 1 = 1
1 ** 2 = 2
$
```

goto

As a matter of fact, you can put a label before any statement whatsoever. If you want to really mess around with the structure of your programs, you can use goto LABEL to jump anywhere in your program. It is highly recommended that you don't use this construct. Really, we mean it. Don't use it. Caveat emptor.

We're telling you about it for the simple reason that if you see it in anyone else's Perl, you can laugh heartily at them. goto with a label is to be avoided like the plague.

Why? Because not only does it turn the clock back 30 years (the structured programming movement started with the publication of a paper called "Go To Statement Considered Harmful"), but it tends to make your programs incredibly hard to follow. The flow of control can shoot off in any direction at any time, into any part of the file, maybe into a different file. You can even find yourself jumping into the middle of loops, which really doesn't bear thinking about. Don't use it unless you really, really, really understand why you shouldn't. And even then, don't use it. Larry Wall has never used goto with a label in Perl, and he created Perl.

Summary

Before this chapter, our programs plodded along in a straight line, one statement followed by another. We've now seen how we can react to different circumstances in our programs, which is the start of flexible and powerful programming. We can test whether something is true or false using if and unless, and take appropriate action.

We've also examined how to test multiple related conditions using elsif. We can repeat areas of a program, in several different ways, using while, until, for, and foreach. Finally, we've examined some ways to alter the flow of Perl's execution through these loops. We can break out of a loop with last, skip to the next element with next, and start processing the current element again with redo.

Exercises

1. Modify the number-guessing program guessnum2.pl so that it loops until the correct answer is entered.

2. Write a program that prints the squares of the numbers between 1 and 10.

3. Write a program to print all the numbers between 1 and 50 that are evenly divisible by 5. Loop by 1, not by 5!

CHAPTER 4

■ ■ ■

Lists and Arrays

In Chapter 2 we introduced the idea of a scalar, which is a single value—a number or string. Having the ability to work with numbers and strings, and having scalar variables into which we can store numbers and strings is nice—this allows us to write programs to manipulate data. However, because they can contain only a single value, scalars are somewhat limited.

There are times we want to group information together or express correspondences between information. Just like the ingredients in a recipe or the pieces in a jigsaw, some things belong together in a natural sequence: for example, individual lines in a file, or the names of players in a volleyball tournament. In Perl, we represent these relationships in *lists*—series of scalars. Lists can be stored in another type of variable called an *array*, and we call each piece of data in the list an *element*.

In this chapter, we'll see how to create and work with lists. We'll also take another look at the foreach loop, which enables us to step through lists and arrays.

Lists

We're all familiar with lists from everyday life. Think about a grocery store shopping list: what properties does it have? First of all, it's a single entity, one piece of paper. Second, it's made up of a number of values. In the case of a shopping list, you might want to say that these values are actually strings—"potato chips", "Guinness", "cheese", and so on. Finally, it's also ordered, which means that there's a first item and a last item.

Lists in Perl aren't actually much different; they're counted as a single unit, though they're made up of a number of values. In Perl, these values are scalars, rather than purely strings, and they're stored in the order they appear in the list.

We'll specify lists in our program code as literals, just like we did with strings and numbers. And we'll be able to perform certain operations on them. Let's begin by looking at a few simple lists and how to create them.

Simple Lists

The simplest shopping list is one that contains nothing at all[1]. Similarly, the simplest list in Perl has no elements in it, and it is called the *empty list*. Here's what it looks like:

```
()
```

A simple pair of parentheses—that's how we denote a list. However, the empty list is not very interesting. Let's try putting in some values:

```
(42)
("cheese")
```

As you can see, we have created two lists, one containing a number, and one containing a string—so far so good. Remember the `print()` function? It treats its arguments as lists, and the magic about functions like `print()` that treat their arguments as lists is that you can omit the parentheses. Saying `print "cheese"` is just the same as saying `print("cheese")`. So now we know that what we give to `print()` is really a list, and we're allowed to leave out the parentheses if we wish.

From this, we should be able to work out how to put multiple values into a list. When we said

```
print("Hello, ", "world", "\n");
```

we were actually passing the following list to the `print()` function:

```
("Hello ", "world", "\n")
```

As you can see, this is a three-element list, and the elements are separated with commas. Perl, like most modern programming languages, starts counting from 0, so here's your chance to practice. The zeroth element is `"Hello "`, the first is `"world"`, and the second is `"\n"`. Now, let's do that again with numbers instead of strings:

```
(123, 456, 789)
```

This is exactly the same as before, and if we were to print this new list, this is what would happen:

```
#!/usr/bin/perl
# numberlist.pl

use warnings;
use strict;

print(123, 456, 789);
```

```
$ perl numberlist.pl
123456789$
```

---

[1] Ah, the cupboards are full!

As before, Perl doesn't automatically put spaces between list elements for us when it prints them out, it just prints them as it sees them. Similarly, it doesn't put a newline on the end for us[2]. There's nothing special about lists from that point of view; if we want to add spaces and newlines, we need to put them into the list ourselves.

More Complex Lists

We can also mix strings, numbers, and variables in our lists. Let's see an example of a list with several different types of data. Although this isn't very different from what we were doing with print() in Chapter 2, this example reinforces the idea that lists can contain any scalar literals and scalar variables. So, type this in, and save it as mixedlist.pl:

```
#!/usr/bin/perl
# mixedlist.pl

use warnings;
use strict;

my $test = 30;

print
    "Here is a list containing strings, (this one) ",
    "numbers (",
    3.6,
    ") and variables: ",
    $test,
    "\n"
;
```

When you run that, here's what you should see:

```
$ perl mixedlist.pl
Here is a list containing strings, (this one) numbers (3.6) and variables: 30
$
```

Notice that the print() function prints a list of six elements, including literal strings, literal numbers, and a scalar variable for good measure.

```
print
    "Here is a list containing strings, (this one) ",
    "numbers (",
    3.6,
    ") and variables: ",
    $test,
```

---

[2] Unless, of course, you are using Windows…

```
    "\n"
;
```

Since variables interpolate in double-quoted strings inside lists just as well as at any other time, we could have done this all as one long single-element list:

```
print ("Here is a list containing strings, (this one) numbers (3.6) and
variables: $test\n");
```

There is a disadvantage to writing your code this way. Newlines in your string literals will turn into newlines in your output. So, if you keep the maximum length of the lines in your source code to about 80 columns (it's a good idea to keep your programs readable), one long string will wrap over and you'll see this sort of thing:

```
$ perl mixedlist.pl
Here is a list containing strings, (this one) numbers (3.6) and
variables: 30
$
```

So if you're ever printing long strings, consider splitting them up into a list of smaller strings on separate lines as we have done previously.

In the same way, single-quoted strings act no differently when they're list elements: ('A number:', '$test') will actually give you two strings, and if you print out that list, you will see this:

```
A number:$test
```

One last thing to note is that Perl automatically *flattens* lists. That is, if you try putting a list inside another list, the internal list loses its identity. In effect, Perl removes all the parentheses apart from the outermost pair. There's no difference at all between any of these three lists:

```
(3, 8, 5, 15)
((3, 8), (5, 15))
(3, (8, 5), 15)
```

Similarly, Perl sees each of these lists exactly the same as the others:

```
('one', 'two', 'three', 'four')
(('one', 'two', 'three', 'four'))
('one', ('two', 'three'), 'four')
(('one','two'), ('three', 'four'))
```

So we can say that in Perl all lists (and all arrays) are *one-dimensional*.

Creating Lists Easily with qw//

Perl provides a useful operator that lets us easily create lists of one-word strings. The operator is qw//, which stands for *quote words*. It is related to the other "q" operators we saw in Chapter 2: q// and qq//. The qw// operator takes all the items within the slashes that are separated by whitespace characters and creates a single-quoted list of them. For instance, this code:

```
qw/hello world good bye/
```

creates the following list:

```
('hello', 'world', 'good', 'bye')
```

The slashes that are part of `qw//` are called the *delimiters*—the elements that begin and end the operator. Any nonalphanumeric character can be used. So the preceding could have been written as either of these:

```
qw#hello world good bye#
qw|hello world good bye|
```

If the opening delimiter is the open angle bracket, square bracket, parenthesis, or curly brace, the closing delimiter is the matching close character. Therefore, you could write the preceding as

```
qw<hello world good bye>
qw[hello world good bye]
qw(hello world good bye)
qw{hello world good bye}
```

Ranges

Sometimes our lists can be a lot simpler than a group of different values. We may want to talk about "the numbers 1 to 10" or "the letters a–z." We don't have to write each one out longhand, though. Instead, Perl lets us specify a range of numbers or letters. Instead of this:

```
(1, 2, 3, 4, 5, 6)
```

we can say

```
(1 .. 6)
```

This shorthand can really save time when you're dealing with a few hundred elements, but note that it only works for integers. Fractional values in a list are rounded toward 0, so

```
(1.4 .. 6.9)
```

would produce `(1, 2, 3, 4, 5, 6)`. There's no problem with using negative numbers in ranges. For example,

```
(-6 .. 3)
```

produces the list `(-6, -5, -4, -3, -2, -1, 0, 1, 2, 3)`.

The right-hand number must, however, be higher than the left-hand one, so you can't use this technique to count down. Instead, you can reverse any list using the `reverse()` function, as we'll see very shortly.

We can do the same for letters as well:

```
('a'..'k')
```

This will give us an 11-element list, consisting of each letter from "a" to "k" inclusive. Note that we can't mix letters and numbers within a range. If we try, Perl interprets the string as a number and treats it as 0.

Here's a demonstration of all the things we can do with ranges:

```
#!/usr/bin/perl
# ranges.pl

use warnings;
use strict;

print "Counting up: ", (1 .. 6), "\n";
print "Counting down: ", (6 .. 1), "\n";
print "Counting down  (properly this time) : ", reverse(1 .. 6), "\n";

print "Half the alphabet: ", ('a' .. 'm'), "\n";
print "The other half (backward): ", reverse('n' .. 'z'), "\n";

print "Going from 3 to z: ", (3 .. 'z'), "\n";
print "Going from z to 3: ", ('z' .. 3), "\n";
```

Which of those will work and which won't? Let's find out . . .

```
$ perl ranges.pl
Argument "z" isn't numeric in range (or flop) at ranges.pl line 14.
Argument "z" isn't numeric in range (or flop) at ranges.pl line 15.
Counting up: 123456
Counting down:
Counting down  (properly this time): 654321
Half the alphabet: abcdefghijklm
The other half (backwards): zyxwvutsrqpon
Going from 3 to z:
Going from z to 3: 0123
$
```

After the usual opening, we first count upward with a range.

```
print "Counting up: ", (1 .. 6), "\n";
```

We've seen the range in action before, and we know this produces (1, 2, 3, 4, 5, 6). We pass print() a list containing the string "Counting up: ", the six elements, and a newline. Because a list inside a list gets flattened, we're actually just passing an eight-element list. It's the same as if we'd done the following:

```
print "Counting up: ", 1, 2, 3, 4, 5, 6, "\n";
```

And we get the expected result:

```
Counting up: 123456
```

Next, we try and count down:

```
print "Counting down: ", (6 .. 1), "\n";
```

This doesn't work because the right-hand side must be bigger than the left, so all that's produced is the empty list, (). To count down properly, we need to make a list using (1 .. 6) as before, and turn it around. The reverse() function reverses a list. For example:

```
reverse (qw(The cat sat on the mat))
```

produces the same as

```
qw(mat the on sat cat The)
```

In this case, reverse(1..6) produces (1, 2, 3, 4, 5, 6) and then reverses it to become (6, 5, 4, 3, 2, 1), and we see the list appear in that order:

```
Counting down (properly this time): 654321
```

Next we demonstrate a simple alphabetic range:

```
print "Half the alphabet: ", ('a' .. 'm'), "\n";
```

This range expands to the values "a", "b", "c", and so on all the way to "m". Doing that backward is easy:

```
print "The other half (backward): ", reverse('n' .. 'z'), "\n";
```

Now we come to the statements that produce the warnings:

```
Argument "z" isn't numeric in range (or flop) at ranges.pl line 13.
Argument "z" isn't numeric in range (or flop) at ranges.pl line 14.
```

The lines in question are

```
print "Going from 3 to z: ", (3 .. 'z'), "\n";
print "Going from z to 3: ", ('z' .. 3), "\n";
```

What does the error message mean? Pretty much what it says: we gave an argument of "z" to a range when it was expecting a number instead. The interpreter converted the "z" to a number as per the rules in Chapter 2, and got a 0. It's equivalent to this:

```
print "Going from 3 to z: ", (3 .. 0), "\n";
print "Going from z to 3: ", (0 .. 3), "\n";
```

The first one produces an empty list, and the second one counts up from 0 to 3.

Accessing List Values

We've now seen most of the ways of building up lists in Perl, and we can pass lists to functions like print(). But another thing we need to be able to do with lists is access a specific element or set of elements within them. The way to do this is to place the number of the elements we want in square brackets after a list, like this:

```
#!/usr/bin/perl
# access.pl
```

```
use warnings;
use strict;

print(('salt', 'vinegar', 'mustard', 'pepper')[2]);
print "\n";
```

Before you run this, though, see if you can work out which word will be printed.

```
$ perl access.pl
mustard
$
```

Did you think it was going to be "vinegar"? Don't forget that Perl starts counting things from 0!

You should also notice that we had to put parentheses around the arguments passed to print(); this is because the precedence of print() is extremely high. Without the parentheses, Perl groups the statement in two parts like this:

```
print('salt', 'vinegar', 'mustard', 'pepper')    [2];
```

This means the whole of the list is passed to print(), after which Perl attempts to retrieve the second element of print(). The problem is, you can only take an element from a list, and as we already know, print() isn't a list.

So, since print() needs to be passed a list, we make a list out of the element we want:

```
print (
    ('salt', 'vinegar', 'mustard', 'pepper')[2]
);
```

The element you want doesn't have to be given as a literal—variables work just as well. Here's an example of accessing an element of a list of months:

```
#!/usr/bin/perl
# months.pl

use warnings;
use strict;

my $month = 3;

print qw(
    January     February    March
    April       May         June
    July        August      September
    October     November    December
)[$month];
```

When this is run, you should now expect it to give you "April", and it does:

```
$ perl months.pl
April$
```

The key piece of code for this example is the last statement:

```
print qw(
    January     February    March
    April       May         June
    July        August      September
    October     November    December
)[$month];
```

We have set $month to 3, so we are telling Perl to print out the third element of the list, starting from 0. Because we're using qw//, we can use arbitrary whitespace, tabs, and newlines to separate each list element, which allows us to present the months in a neat table.

This is exactly the sort of situation for which qw// was created; we have a list composed completely of single words, and we want to represent that to Perl in a readable way in our source code. It's far easier to read than spelling the list out longhand, even though the preceding print() statement is equivalent to

```
print (('January','February', 'March', 'April', 'May',
        'June', 'July', 'August', 'September', 'October',
        'November', 'December')[$month]);
```

What do you think would happen if we chose a noninteger value for our element? Let's use a value with a fractional part. Change the preceding file so that line 7 reads

```
my $month = 2.2;
```

Perl will round the number in this case, and you should get the answer "March". In fact, Perl always rounds towards 0, so anything between 2 and 3 will get you March.

What about negative numbers? Actually, something interesting happens here—Perl starts counting backward from the end of the list. So element –1 is the last one, –2 the second to last one, and so on.

```
#!/usr/bin/perl
# backwards.pl

use warnings;
use strict;

print qw(
    January     February    March
    April       May         June
    July        August      September
    October     November    December
)[-1];
```

And, true to form, we'll get the last element of the array when we run the program.

```
$ perl backwards.pl
December$
```

List Slices

So much for getting a single element out of a list. What if we want to get several? Instead of putting a number or a scalar variable inside those square brackets, you can actually put a list. For example, this:

```
(19, 68, 47, 60, 53, 51, 58, 55, 47)[(4, 5, 6)]
```

returns another list consisting of the fourth, fifth, and sixth 0-based elements: (53, 51, 58). Actually, inside the square brackets we don't need the additional set of parentheses, so you might as well say

```
(19, 68, 47, 60, 53, 51, 58, 55, 47)[4, 5, 6]
```

We call this a *list slice*, and the same methods work with lists of strings, illustrated in the program multilist.pl. Just as in the preceding examples, we're taking several elements from a list.

```
#!/usr/bin/perl
# multilist.pl

use warnings;
use strict;

my $mone;
my $mtwo;
($mone, $mtwo) = (1, 3);

print(("heads ", "shoulders ", "knees ", "toes ")[$mone, $mtwo]);
print "\n";
```

Try to think what it's going to produce before you run it. Here's what happens:

```
$ perl multilist.pl
shoulders toes
$
```

As you may have realized, we simply printed out the first and the third elements from the list, if you start counting from 0.

There are two key tricks in this example. The first is on line 9:

```
($mone, $mtwo) = (1, 3);
```

You might be able to see what this line does from how the rest of the program runs. The value of $mone is set to 1, and $mtwo to 3. But how does this work?

Perl allows lists on the left-hand side of an assignment operator. When we assign one list to another, the right-hand list is built up first, and then Perl assigns each element in turn from the right-hand side of the statement to the left. So 1 is assigned to $mone, and then 3 is assigned to $mtwo. This is called an *assignable list*.

If you're okay with that, now is a good time for a quick quiz. Suppose we've done the preceding: $mone is 1 and $mtwo is 3. What do you think would happen if we said this?

```
($mone, $mtwo) = ($mtwo, $mone);
```

The right-hand list is built up first, so Perl looks at the values of the variables and constructs the list (3, 1). Then the 3 is assigned to $mone, and the 1 assigned to $mtwo. In effect, we've swapped the values of the variables around—a handy trick to learn and remember. Chances are it's something you'll need to do from time to time.

Back to our example! Once we've set `$mone` to 1 and `$mtwo` to 3, we can pick out these elements from a list. There's nothing that says that we have to use literals to access the elements we want. This:

```
print(("heads ", "shoulders ", "knees ", "toes ")[$mone, $mtwo]);
```

is interpreted by Perl just the same as this:

```
print(("heads ", "shoulders ", "knees ", "toes ")[1, 3]);
```

Indeed, both statements equate to the same thing—creating a list that consists of the first and third elements of our original list and printing them. In effect, we call

```
print("shoulders ", "toes ");
```

which is indeed what happens.

Combining Ranges and Slices

We can, of course, use ranges in our list slices. This gets March through September:

```
(qw(Jan Feb Mar Apr May Jun Jul Aug Sep Oct Nov Dec)[2..8])
```

And this gets November through February via December and January (remember that –2 is the second to last element and –1 the last element):

```
(qw(Jan Feb Mar Apr May Jun Jul Aug Sep Oct Nov Dec)[-2..1])
```

We can also use a mixture of ranges and literals in our slice. This gives us January, April, and August to December:

```
(qw(Jan Feb Mar Apr May Jun Jul Aug Sep Oct Nov Dec)[0,3,7..11])
```

It may be a bit confusing, but have a go at slicing your own arrays and you'll get the hang of it in no time.

Arrays

Just as with scalar literals, there's only so much you can do with list literals. Literal lists get cumbersome to repeat, and don't allow us to manipulate them at all. As with scalars, we need to find a way to store them in a variable.

The variable storage we use for lists is called an *array*. Whereas the name of a scalar variable starts with a dollar sign, arrays start with an at sign (@). The same rules for naming arrays apply as for any other variables: start with an alphabetic character or underscore, followed by zero or more alphabetic characters, underscores, or numbers.

Assigning Arrays

We store a list in an array just like we store a scalar literal into a scalar variable, by assigning it with =, as in:

```
@array = (1,2,3);
```

Once we've assigned our array, we can use it wherever we would use a list:

```
#!/usr/bin/perl
# dayarray.pl

use warnings;
use strict;

my @days;
@days = qw(Monday Tuesday Wednesday Thursday Friday Saturday Sunday);
print @days, "\n";
```

This prints

```
$ perl dayarray.pl
MondayTuesdayWednesdayThursdayFridaySaturdaySunday
$
```

Like scalars, arrays must be declared with my() if you use strict.

Note that $days is a completely different variable from @days—setting one does nothing to the other. In fact, if you were to do this:

```
#!/usr/bin/perl
# baddayarray1.pl

use warnings;
use strict;

my @days;
@days = qw(Monday Tuesday Wednesday Thursday Friday Saturday Sunday);
$days = 31;
```

you would get the following error:

```
Global symbol "$days" requires explicit package name at dayarray.pl line 9.
```

This is because you have declared @days to be a lexical variable, but not $days. Even when you declare them both, setting one has no effect on the other.

```
#!/usr/bin/perl
# baddayarray2.pl

use warnings;
use strict;

my @days;
my $days;
@days = qw(Monday Tuesday Wednesday Thursday Friday Saturday Sunday);
$days = 31;
print @days, "\n";
```

```
print $days, "\n";
```

prints

```
MondayTuesdayWednesdayThursdayFridaySaturdaySunday
31
```

What would happen if you assigned an array to a scalar variable? To find out, take a look at the following example of two arrays assigned to two different scalar variables:

```
#!/usr/bin/perl
# arraylen.pl

use warnings;
use strict;

my @array1;
my $scalar1;
@array1 = qw(Monday Tuesday Wednesday Thursday Friday Saturday Sunday);
$scalar1 = @array1;

print "Array 1 is @array1\nScalar 1 is $scalar1\n";

my @array2;
my $scalar2;
@array2 = qw(Winter Spring Summer Fall);
$scalar2 = @array2;
print "Array 2 is @array2\nScalar 2 is $scalar2\n";
```

Executing this program gives this result:

```
$ perl arraylen.pl
Array 1 is Monday Tuesday Wednesday Thursday Friday Saturday Sunday
Scalar 1 is 7
Array 2 is Winter Spring Summer Fall
Scalar 2 is 4
$
```

Hmm . . . the first array has seven elements, and the scalar value is 7. The second has four elements, and the scalar value is 4.

There are two things to note in this program. The first is how array variables interpolate in a double-quoted string. We've seen that if you put a scalar variable name inside a string, Perl fills in the value of the variable. Now we've put an array variable in a string and Perl has filled it in, but it has placed spaces between the elements. Look at the following two print() statements:

```
@array = (4, 6, 3, 9, 12, 10);
print @array, "\n";
print "@array\n";
```

The first one does exactly what we've seen with lists, printing all the elements next to each other. The second statement, however, inserts a space between each element:

```
46391210
4 6 3 9 12 10
```

This adding of spaces between elements is what happens when an array is interpolated in a double-quoted string. As with scalars, interpolation is not confined to `print()`. For example:

```
$scalar =  "@array\n";
```

is the same as

```
$scalar = "4 6 3 9 12 10\n";
```

Forcing variables to make sense in a string is called *stringifying* them.

Scalar vs. List Context

What happens when we assign an array to a scalar variable? One key point to remember is that Perl knows exactly what type of value you want, whether a scalar or an array, at any stage in an operation, and will do its best to make sure you get it.

For example, if we're looking to assign to a scalar variable, we need to have a scalar value—the assignment is taking place in *scalar context*. On the other hand, for example, `print()` expects to see a list of arguments. Those arguments are in *list context*. However, some operations may return different values depending on which context they are called. That's what's happening in this case:

```
print @array1;
$scalar1 = @array1;
```

The first line is in list context. In list context, an array evaluates to the list of its elements. In the second line, however, the assignment wants to see a single result, or scalar value, and therefore we're in scalar context. In scalar context, an array evaluates to the number of its elements, in our case, seven for the days and four for the seasons.

If we were to do this:

```
@array2 = @array1;
```

we would be assigning to an array. So we're looking for a *list* of values to fill @array2. Here, we're back in list context, and so @array2 gets filled with all of the values of @array1.

We can force something to be in scalar context when it expects to be in list context by using the `scalar()` function. Compare these two statements:

```
print @array1;
print scalar @array1;
```

As we've explained before, `print()` usually wants a list, so Perl evaluates `print()`'s arguments in list context. In the preceding example, `print()` is looking to get a list from each of its arguments. That's why the first statement prints the contents of @array1. If we force @array1 into scalar context, then the number of elements in the array is passed to `print()`, and not the contents of the array.

■ **Note** Perl distinguishes between operations that want a list and operations that want a scalar. Those that want a list, such as `print()` or assigning to an array, are said to be in list context. Those that want a scalar are said to be in scalar context. The value of an array in list context is the list of its elements—the value of an array in scalar context is the number of its elements.

Adding to an Array

How do we add elements to an array? One way to do it is by using the "list flattening" principle and treating arrays as lists. This isn't a particularly good way to do it, but it works:

```
#!/usr/bin/perl
# addelem.pl

use warnings;
use strict;

my @array1 = (1, 2, 3);
my @array2;
@array2 = (@array1, 4, 5, 6);
print "@array2\n";

@array2 = (3, 5, 7, 9);
@array2 = (1, @array2, 11);
print "@array2\n";

$ perl addelem.pl
1 2 3 4 5 6
1 3 5 7 9 11
$
```

It's far better, however, to use the functions we're going to see later on— `push()`, `pop()`, `shift()`, and `unshift()`.

Accessing an Array

Once we've got our list of scalars into an array, it would be nice to be able to access individual elements in them. We do this slightly differently from the way we get values out of lists.

Accessing Single Elements

We can now put elements into an array:

```
my @array = (10, 20, 30);
```

If we look at the array in scalar context, we get the number of elements in it. So

```
print scalar @array;
```

will print the value 3. But how do we get at one of those elements? We could use the list assignment we looked at earlier:

```
#!/usr/bin/perl
# assignlist.pl

use warnings;
use strict;

my $scalar0;
my $scalar1;
my $scalar2;
my @array = (10, 20, 30);

($scalar0, $scalar1, $scalar2) = @array;

print "Scalar zero is $scalar0\n";
print "Scalar one is $scalar1\n";
print "Scalar two is $scalar2\n";
```

This will print out each of the elements:

```
$ perl assignlist.pl
Scalar zero is 10
Scalar one is 20
Scalar two is 30
$
```

There is a better way to access a single element of an array using something quite similar to what we used with a list. To get a single element from a list, if you remember, we put the number we wanted in square brackets after it.

```
$a = (10, 20, 30)[0];
```

This sets $a to the zeroth element, 10. We could do this:

```
$a = (@array)[0];
```

in exactly the same way. However, it's more usual to write that as follows:

```
$a = $array[0];
```

Look carefully at this statement. Even though **@array** and **$array** are different variables, we use the **$array[ ]** form. Why?

■ **Note** The rule is this: the prefix represents what you want to get, not what you've got. So @ represents a list of values, and $ represents a single scalar. Hence, when we're getting a single scalar from an array, we never prefix the variable with @—that would mean a list. A single scalar is always prefixed with a $.

`$array[0]` can only refer to an element of the `@array` array. If you use the wrong prefix, Perl will complain with a warning.

```
#!/usr/bin/perl
# badprefix.pl

use warnings;
use strict;

my @array = (1, 3, 5, 7, 9);
print @array[1];
```

will print

```
$ perl badprefix.pl
Scalar value @array[1] better written as $array[1] at badprefix.pl line 8.
3$
```

We call the number in the square brackets the *array index* or *array subscript*. The array index is the number of the element that we want to access.

Just like extracting elements from lists, we can use a scalar variable as our subscript:

```
#!/usr/bin/perl
# scalarsub.pl

use warnings;
use strict;

my @array = (1, 3, 5, 7, 9);
my $subscript = 3;
print $array[$subscript], "\n";
$array[$subscript] = 12;

print $array[$subscript], "\n";
```

This prints the third element from zero, which has the value 7. It then changes that 7 to a 12 and prints the value of that element. Negative subscripts work from the right-hand side; as before, `$array[-1]` will give you the last element in the array. Executing this program produces the following:

```
$ perl scalarsub.pl
7
12
$
```

Now let's look at a program to extract a given element from an array. We'll use arrays to write a program to tell us some (really bad) jokes. We actually set up two arrays—one containing the question, and one containing the answer.

```perl
#!/usr/bin/perl
# joke1.pl

use strict;
use strict;

my @questions = qw(Java Python Perl C);
my @punchlines = (
    "None. Change it once, and it's the same everywhere.",
    "One. He just stands below the socket and the world revolves around him.",
    "A million. One to change it, the rest to try and do it in one line of code.",
    '"CHANGE?!!"'
);

print "Please enter a number between 1 and 4: ";
my $selection = <STDIN>;
$selection -= 1;
print "How many $questions[$selection] ";
print "programmers does it take to change a lightbulb?\n\n";
sleep 2;
print $punchlines[$selection], "\n";
```

Here is an example of running this program:

```
$.perl joke1.pl
Please enter a number between 1 and 4: 3
How many Perl programmers does it take to change a lightbulb?

A million. One to change it, the rest to try and do it in one line of code.
$
```

In this program, we first set up our arrays; one is a list of words, so we can use qw// to specify it. The other is a list of strings containing whitespace characters, so we have to quote them using the ordinary list style.

```perl
my @questions = qw(Java Python Perl C);
my @punchlines = (
    "None. Change it once, and it's the same everywhere.",
    "One. He just stands below the socket and the world revolves around him.",
    "A million. One to change it, the rest to try and do it in one line of code.",
    '"CHANGE?!!"'
);
```

We now ask the user to choose a joke:

```perl
print "Please enter a number between 1 and 4: ";
```

```
my $selection = <STDIN>;
$selection -= 1;
```

Why subtract 1 from $selection? We've asked for a number between 1 and 4, and our array subscripts go from 0 to 3.

Next we display the setup line:

```
print "How many $questions[$selection] ";
print "programmers does it take to change a lightbulb?\n\n";
```

From the first line we see that array elements stringify just like scalar variables. Next, this new sleep() function:

```
sleep 2;
```

What sleep() does, as you'll know if you've run the program, is pause the program's operation for a number of seconds. In this case, we're telling it to sleep for two seconds.

After the user has had time to think about it, we display the punchline:

```
print $punchlines[$selection], "\n";
```

$#array

For any given array, for example @array, there is an easy way to obtain the value of its last index: $#array. Therefore, for the array @a, its last index is $#a. For @b, its last index is $#b. Note that this syntax gives us the last *index* of the array, not its last *value*. The last value of @a can be accessed by indexing with $#a into @a with the syntax $a[$#a]. Yes, it looks a little weird, but it does work! This is illustrated in the following example:

```
#!/usr/bin/perl
# lastindex.pl

use warnings;
use strict;

my @array = (2, 4, 6, 8);

print "the last index is:   ", $#array, "\n";
print "the last element is: ", $array[$#array], "\n";
```

Executing this code produces

```
$ perl lastindex.pl
the last index is:   3
the last element is: 8
$
```

The last index will assist us in looping through an array with indexes.

Looping Through an Array with Indexes

Since we can access an individual element of an array with the syntax

```
$array[$index]
```

and we know the first index of the array is 0 and the last index is $#array, we can loop through an array with a loop that resembles

```
my $i = 0;
while ($i <= $#array) {
    # process array element using the syntax $array[$i]
    $i++;
}
```

Most Perl programmers would implement this using a for loop:

```
for (my $i = 0; $i <= $#array; $i++) {
    # process array element using the syntax $array[$i]
}
```

Here is an example of using both the while loop and the for loop to process an array. The code will loop left to right through an array named @names, accessing each element with $names[$i].

```
#!/usr/bin/perl
# whilefor.pl

use warnings;
use strict;

my @names = qw(John Joe Mary Sue);

print "processing using a while loop:\n";

my $i = 0;
while ($i <= $#names) {
    print "    Hello $names[$i]!\n";
    $i++;
}

print "processing using a for loop:\n";

for (my $i = 0; $i <= $#names; $i++) {
    print "    Hello $names[$i]!\n";
}
```

Executing this code results in the following:

```
$ perl whilefor.pl
processing using a while loop:
    Hello John!
    Hello Joe!
```

```
    Hello Mary!
    Hello Sue!
processing using a for loop:
    Hello John!
    Hello Joe!
    Hello Mary!
    Hello Sue!
$
```

■ **Note** Most often, when we process an array variable from left to right, we will use the `foreach` loop instead of the `for` loop. However, the `for` loop comes in handy sometimes, especially if we want to access all the even elements of an array:

```
for ($i = 0; $i <= $#a; $i+=2) {
    # process element
}
```

or all the odd elements of an array:

```
for ($1 = 1; $i <= $#a; $i+=2) {
    # process element
}
```

We'll see the use of the `foreach` loop later in this chapter.

Hopefully, you're starting to see alternative ways you can use arrays. Of course, we've only been pulling single values from arrays so far. The next logical step is to start working with multiple array elements.

Accessing Multiple Elements

If you'll recall, we created and used a list slice by putting ranges or several numbers in brackets to get multiple elements from a list. If we want to get multiple elements from an array, we can use the analogous concept, an *array slice*.

List slices, if you remember, looked like this:

```
(qw(Jan Feb Mar Apr May Jun Jul Aug Sep Oct Nov Dec))[3,5,7..9]
```

Can you work out which elements the preceding slice consists of? If not, write a short Perl program to print them out, and see if you can get it to separate them with spaces. (Hint: only arrays stringify with spaces, so you'll need to use one.)

Array slices look very similar. However, now that we are accessing multiple elements and expecting a list, we no longer want to use $ as the prefix—now we need to use @.

We can get the same list as the preceding one like this:

```
my @array = qw(Jan Feb Mar Apr May Jun Jul Aug Sep Oct Nov Dec);
print @array[3,5,7..9];
```

Array slices act like any normal list, and so can be assigned to. Here's a program that uses a bunch of slices, aslice.pl, implementing a year's sales results for a fictitious bathroom tile shop:

```
#!/usr/bin/perl
# aslice.pl

use warnings;
use strict;

my @sales = (69, 118, 97, 110, 103, 101, 108, 105, 76, 111, 118, 101);
my @months = qw(Jan Feb Mar Apr May Jun Jul Aug Sep Oct Nov Dec);

print "Second quarter sales:\n";
print "@months[3..5]\n@sales[3..5]\n";
my @q2 = @sales[3..5];

# Incorrect results in May, Aug, Oct, Nov and Dec!
@sales[4, 7, 9..11] = (68, 101, 114, 111, 117);

# Swap Apr and May
@months[3,4] = @months[4,3];
```

Most of the work is behind the scenes, but this is what you'd see if you run the code:

```
$ perl aslice.pl
Second quarter sales:
Apr May Jun
110 103 101
```

Let's take a look at what's actually going on. We set up our two arrays, one holding the sales figures, and the other holding the names of the months:

```
my @sales = (69, 118, 97, 110, 103, 101, 108, 105, 76, 111, 118, 101);
my @months = qw(Jan Feb Mar Apr May Jun Jul Aug Sep Oct Nov Dec);
```

To extract the information about the second quarter, we use an array slice for the months in question:

```
print "Second quarter sales:\n";
print "@months[3..5]\n@sales[3..5]\n";
my @q2 = @sales[3..5];
```

102

As well as saving the relevant elements to another array, we can print out the slice and it will be stringified. We can also assign values to an array slice as well as getting data from it:

```
@sales[4, 7, 9..11] = (68, 101, 114, 111, 117);
```

This sets new values for $sales[4], $sales[7], $sales[9], $sales[10], and $sales[11].

Finally, we can use something similar to the ($a, $b) = ($b, $a) list trick to swap two array elements:

```
@months[3,4] = @months[4,3];
```

This is exactly the same as the following statement:

```
($months[3], $months[4]) = ($months[4], $months[3]);
```

As you can see, this isn't all that far from the list assignment to swap two variables:

```
($mone, $mtwo) = ($mtwo, $mone);
```

Processing Arrays with the foreach Loop

One thing we'll want to do quite often is process each of the elements in an array or list in order. If we want to double every value in an array, then *for each* element we come across, we multiply by 2. The keyword to use here is *foreach*. The foreach loop has the following syntax:

```
foreach scalar_variable ( list_or_array ) {
    body
}
```

The block must start with an opening curly brace and end with a closing curly brace, and the list or array that we're processing must be surrounded by parentheses.

This loop executes the body for each item in the list or array. As it passes through the list or array, the scalar variable (called the *control variable*, or *iterator variable*) is the element of the list or array. Here is a simple example:

```
#!/usr/bin/perl
# foreach1.pl

use warnings;
use strict;

my $element;

foreach $element ('zero', 'one', 'two') {
    print "the element is: $element\n";
}
```

This program first declares $element. This variable will be used to pass through the list. Then the body is executed three times—once for each element in the list— producing the following output:

```
$ perl foreach1.pl
the element is: zero
```

103

```
the element is: one
the element is: two
$
```

The `foreach` loop can also process array variables. Here is an example that prints each element of an array followed by a newline:

```
#!/usr/bin/perl
# foreach2.pl

use warnings;
use strict;

my @array = qw(Australia Asia Europe Africa);
my $element;

foreach $element (@array) {
    print $element, "\n";
}
```

In this program, we set up an array and we declare a scalar variable, `$element`. What we then say is "Set each element of `@array` to `$element` in turn, and then do all the statements in the following block." So, on our first iteration, `$element` is set to `Australia`, and then the `print()` statement is executed. Next, `$element` is set to `Asia`, and the `print()` statement runs again. This continues until the end of the array is reached.

This should print the following:

```
$ perl foreach2.pl
Australia
Asia
Europe
Africa
$
```

Choosing an Iterator

We can specify the iterator variable ourselves, as we did in the preceding examples, or we can use the default one, `$_`. Furthermore, if we're being good and using `strict`, we can make our iterator variable a lexical `my()` variable as we go along. That is, we could write a program like this—note how `$i` is declared:

```
#!/usr/bin/perl
# foreach3.pl

use warnings;
use strict;

my @array = (1, 3, 5, 7, 9);
foreach my $i (@array) {
    print "This element: $i\n";
}
```

There's actually a very subtle difference between declaring your iterator inside and outside of the loop. If you declare your iterator outside the loop, any value it had then will be restored afterwards. We can check this out by setting the variable and testing it afterwards:

```
#!/usr/bin/perl
# foreach4.pl

use warnings;
use strict;

my @array = (1, 3, 5, 7, 9);
my $i = "Hello there";
foreach $i (@array) {
    print "This element: $i\n";
}
print "All done: $i\n";
```

This will produce the following output:

```
$ perl foreach4.pl
This element: 1
This element: 3
This element: 5
This element: 7
This element: 9
All done: Hello there
$
```

Declaring the iterator within the loop, as in foreach3.pl, creates a new variable $i each time, which exists only for the duration of the loop.

As a matter of style, it's usual to keep the names of iterator variables very short; the traditional iterator is $i as we've used here. The length of a variable name should be related to the importance of the variable—iterators are usually throwaway variables that exist only for one block, so they typically are not prominently named.

Modifying the Value of an Iterator

When processing a foreach loop, Perl makes the iterator refer to each element of the list or array in turn, and then executes the block. If the block happens to change the value of the iterator, the corresponding array element changes as well. We can double each element of an array like this:

```
#!/usr/bin/perl
# foreach5.pl

use warnings;
use strict;

my @array = (10, 20, 30, 40);

print "Before: @array\n";
```

```
foreach (@array) {
    $_ *= 2;
}

print "After: @array\n";
```

This prints as follows:

```
$ perl foreach5.pl
Before: 10 20 30 40
After: 20 40 60 80
$
```

Notice that in the `foreach` loop in `foreach5.pl,` there is no explicit control variable indicated:

```
foreach (@array) {
    $_ *= 2;
}
```

If the control variable is omitted, `$_` is used by default.

If you need to know the number of the element you're currently processing, it's usually best to have the iterator as the range of numbers you're processing—from 0 up to the highest element number in the array. Let's rewrite the joke machine so that it tells *all* the bad jokes, without prompting:

```
#!/usr/bin/perl
# joke2.pl

use warnings;
use strict;

my @questions = qw(Java Python Perl C);
my @punchlines = (
    "None. Change it once, and it's the same everywhere.",
    "One. He just stands below the socket and the world revolves around him.",
    "A million. One to change it, the rest to try and do it in one line of code.",
    '"CHANGE?!!"'
);

foreach (0..$#questions) {
    print "How many $questions[$_] ";
    print "programmers does it take to change a lightbulb?\n";
    sleep 2;
    print $punchlines[$_], "\n\n";
    sleep 1;
}
```

The changes to our old `joke1.pl` program produce this result:

```
$ perl joke2.pl
How many Java programmers does it take to change a lightbulb?
```

```
None. Change it once, and it's the same everywhere.

How many Python programmers does it take to change a lightbulb?
One. He just stands below the socket and the world revolves around him.

How many Perl programmers does it take to change a lightbulb?
A million. One to change it, the rest to try and do it in one line of code.

How many C programmers does it take to change a lightbulb?
"CHANGE?!!"

$
```

In this version of the joke program, the foreach loop is now the main part of our program. Let's have a look at it again:

```
foreach (0..$#questions) {
    print "How many $questions[$_] ";
    print "programmers does it take to change a lightbulb?\n";
    sleep 2;
    print $punchlines[$_], "\n\n";
    sleep 1;
}
```

The key point about this example is that we need to match the questions to the punchlines. This means we can't just go through one or the other of the arrays, but have to go through them both together. We do this by using a list, which counts up from 0 to the highest element of one of the arrays. Since the arrays are both the same size, it doesn't matter which one. The line that does this is

```
foreach (0..$#questions) {
```

$#questions is the index of the last element in the @questions array. That's different from the value we get when we look at @questions in a scalar context:

```
#!/usr/bin/perl
# elems.pl

use warnings;
use strict;

my @array = qw(alpha bravo charlie delta);

print "Scalar value : ", scalar(@array), "\n";
print "Highest index: ", $#array, "\n";

$ perl elems.pl
Scalar value : 4
Highest index: 3
$
```

Why? There are four elements in the array—so that's the scalar value. Their indices are 0, 1, 2, and 3. Since we're starting at 0, the highest index (`$#array`) will always be one less than the number of elements in the array.

So, we count up from 0 to the last index of `@questions`, which happens to be 3. We set the iterator to each number in turn. Where's the iterator? Since we didn't give one, Perl will use `$_`. Now we do the block four times, once when `$_` is 0, once when it is 1, and so on.

```
print "How many $questions[$_] ";
```

This line prints the zeroth element of `@questions` the first time around, then the first, then the second, third, and fourth.

```
print $punchlines[$_], "\n\n";
```

And so it is with the punchlines. If we'd just said

```
foreach (@questions) {
```

`$_` would have been set to each question in turn, but we would not have advanced our way through the answers.

A quick note: recall that the keywords `for` and `foreach` are synonyms for each other. We will stick to the style of calling a `foreach` a `foreach`, but some Perl programmers call the `foreach` a `for`. This also applies to the expression modifier form of the `foreach`.

Expression Modifier for the foreach Loop

Just as there was an expression modifier form of `if`, like this:

```
die "Something wicked happened" if $error;
```

there's also an expression modifier form of `foreach`. This means you can iterate an array, executing a single expression every time. Here, however, you don't get to choose your own iterator variable: it's always `$_`. It has this form:

```
statement foreach list_or_array;
```

Here is a quick example:

```
#!/usr/bin/perl
# foreach6.pl

use warnings;
use strict;

my @a = qw(John Paul George Ringo);

print "[$_]\n" foreach @a;
```

Running this code produces the following:

```
$ perl foreach6.pl
[John]
[Paul]
[George]
```

```
[Ringo]
$
```

Array Functions

It's time we met some more of the operations we can perform with arrays. These are called *array functions*. We've already met one of them: reverse(), which we used to count down ranges instead of counting up. We can use reverse() on arrays as well as lists:

```perl
#!/usr/bin/perl
# countdown.pl

use warnings;
use strict;

my @count = (1..5);

foreach (reverse(@count)) {
    print "$_...\n";
    sleep 1;
}

print "BLAST OFF!\n";
```

Hopefully, at this point, you have a good idea of what this will print out before you run it.

```
$ perl countdown.pl
5...
4...
3...
2...
1...
BLAST OFF!
$
```

There are some very useful functions for adding elements to arrays. Here they are now along with a couple of other useful tips and tricks.

pop() and push()

We've already seen a simple way to add elements to an array: @array = (@array, $scalar).

One of the original metaphors that computer programmers like to use to analyze arrays is a *stack* of spring-loaded plates in a cafeteria. You push down when you put another plate on the top, and the stack pops up when a plate is taken away:

Following this metaphor, `push()` is the function that adds an element, or list of elements, to the end of an array. Similarly, to remove the top element—the element with the highest index—we use the `pop()` function. These are illustrated in the following example.

Stacks are all around us. Many times, they're stacks of paper. We can manipulate arrays just as we can manipulate these stacks of paper:

```perl
#!/usr/bin/perl
# stacks.pl

use warnings;
use strict;

my $hand;
my @pileofpaper = ("letter", "newspaper", "gas bill", "notepad");

print "Here's what's on the desk: @pileofpaper\n";

print "You pick up something off the top of the pile.\n";
$hand = pop @pileofpaper;
print "You have now a $hand in your hand.\n";

print "You put the $hand away, and pick up something else.\n";
$hand = pop @pileofpaper;
print "You picked up a $hand.\n";

print "Left on the desk is: @pileofpaper\n";

print "You pick up the next thing, and throw it away.\n";
pop @pileofpaper;

print "You put the $hand back on the pile.\n";
push @pileofpaper, $hand;

print "You also put a leaflet and a bank statement on the pile.\n";
push @pileofpaper, "leaflet", "bank statement";

print "Left on the desk is: @pileofpaper\n";
```

Watch what happens:

```
$ perl stacks.pl
Here's what's on the desk: letter newspaper gas bill notepad
You pick up something off the top of the pile.
You have now a notepad in your hand.
You put the notepad away, and pick up something else.
You picked up a gas bill.
Left on the desk is: letter newspaper
You pick up the next thing, and throw it away.
You put the gas bill back on the pile.
You also put a leaflet and a bank statement on the pile.
Left on the desk is: letter gas bill leaflet bank statement
$
```

To see how this program works, let's talk about it line by line. First, we initialize our $hand and our @pileofpaper. Since the pile of paper is a stack, the zeroth element (the letter) is at the bottom, and the notepad is at the top.

```
my $hand;
my @pileofpaper = ("letter", "newspaper", "gas bill", "notepad");
```

We use pop @pileofpaper to remove the top, or rightmost, element from the array and it returns that element, which we store in $hand. So, we take the notepad from the stack and put it into our hand. What's left? The letter at the bottom of the stack, then the newspaper and gas bill.

```
print "You pick up something off the top of the pile.\n";
$hand = pop @pileofpaper;
print "You have now a $hand in your hand.\n";
```

As we pop() again, we take the next element (the gas bill) off the top of the stack, or the right-hand side of the array, and store it again in $hand. Since we didn't save the notepad from last time, it's lost forever now.

```
print "You put the $hand away, and pick up something else.\n";
$hand = pop @pileofpaper;
print "You picked up a $hand.\n";
```

The next item is the newspaper. We pop() this as before, but we never store it anywhere.

```
print "You pick up the next thing, and throw it away.\n";
pop @pileofpaper;
```

We've still got the gas bill in $hand from previously. push @array, $scalar will add the scalar onto the top of the stack. In our case, we're putting the gas bill on top of the letter.

```
print "You put the $hand back on the pile.\n";
push @pileofpaper, $hand;
```

push() can also be used to add a list of scalars onto the stack—in this case, we've added two more strings. We could add the contents of an array to the top of the stack with @array1, @array2. So we now know that we can replace a list with an array.

111

```
print "You also put a leaflet and a bank statement on the pile.\n";
push @pileofpaper, "leaflet", "bank statement";
```

As you might suspect, you can also push lists of lists onto an array—they simply get flattened first into a single list and then added.

shift() and unshift()

While the functions push() and pop() deal with the "top end," or right-hand side, of the stack, adding and taking away elements from the highest index of the array, the functions unshift() and shift() do the corresponding jobs for the bottom end, or left side, of the array:

```
#!/usr/bin/perl
# shift.pl

use warnings;
use strict;

my @array = ();
unshift @array, "first";
print "Array is now: @array\n";
unshift @array, "second", "third";
print "Array is now: @array\n";
shift @array ;
print "Array is now: @array\n";
```

```
$ perl shift.pl
Array is now: first
Array is now: second third first
Array is now: third first
$
```

First we unshift() an element onto the array, and the element appears at the beginning of the list. It's not easy to see this since there are no other elements, but it does. We then unshift() two more elements. Notice that the entire list is added to the beginning of the array all at once, not one element at a time. We then use shift() to take off the first element, ignoring what it was.

sort()

One last thing you may want to do while processing data is put it in alphabetical or numeric order. The sort() function takes a list and returns a sorted version.

```
#!/usr/bin/perl
# sort1.pl

use warnings;
use strict;

my @unsorted = qw(Cohen Clapton Costello Cream Cocteau);
print "Unsorted: @unsorted\n";
```

```
my @sorted = sort @unsorted;
print "Sorted:   @sorted\n";
```

```
$ perl sort1.pl
Unsorted: Cohen Clapton Costello Cream Cocteau
Sorted:     Clapton Cocteau Cohen Costello Cream
$
```

This is only good for strings and alphabetic sorting. If you're sorting numbers, there is a problem. Can you guess what it is? This may help:

```
#!/usr/bin/perl
# sort2.pl

use warnings;
use strict;

my @unsorted = (1, 2, 11, 24, 3, 36, 40, 4);
my @sorted = sort @unsorted;
print "Sorted:   @sorted\n";
```

```
$ perl sort2.pl
Sorted:   1 11 2 24 3 36 4 40
$
```

What?? 11 doesn't come between 1 and 2! It does when it is an ASCII sort, which is Perl's default. What we need to do is compare the numeric values instead of the string ones. Cast your mind back to Chapter 2 and recall how to compare two numeric variables, $a and $b. Here, we're going to use the <=> operator. sort() allows us to give it a block to describe how two values should be ordered, and we do this by comparing $a and $b. These two variables are given to us by the sort() function:

```
#!/usr/bin/perl
# sort3.pl

use warnings;
use strict;

my @unsorted = (1, 2, 11, 24, 3, 36, 40, 4);

my @string = sort { $a cmp $b } @unsorted;
print "String sort:  @string\n";

my @number = sort { $a <=> $b } @unsorted;
print "Numeric sort:  @number\n";
```

```
$ perl sort3.pl
String sort:  1 11 2 24 3 36 4 40
Numeric sort:  1 2 3 4 11 24 36 40
$
```

Another good reason for using string comparison operators for strings and numeric comparison operators for numbers!

Summary

Lists are a series of scalars in order. Arrays are variable incarnations of lists. Both lists and arrays are flattened, so we can't yet have a distinct list inside another list. We get at both lists and arrays with square-bracket subscripts; these can be single numbers or a list of elements. If we're looking up a single scalar in an array, we need to remember to use the syntax `$array[$element]` because the variable prefix always refers to what we want, not what we have. We can also use ranges to save time and to specify list and array slices.

Perl differentiates between scalar and list context, and returns different values depending on what the statement is expecting to see. For instance, the scalar context value of an array is the number of elements in it, and the list context value is, of course, the list of the elements themselves.

Exercises

1. Write a program that assigns an array the value (2, 4, 6, 8) and uses two loops to output

    - $2 ** 2 = 4$

    - $4 ** 2 = 16$

    - $6 ** 2 = 36$

    - $8 ** 2 = 64$

    - $8 ** 2 = 64$

    - $6 ** 2 = 36$

    - $4 ** 2 = 16$

    - $2 ** 2 = 4$

2. When you assign to a list, the elements are copied over from the right to the left.

    ```
    ($a, $b) = ( 10, 20 );
    ```

    will make `$a` become 10 and `$b` become 20. Investigate what happens when

    - There are more elements on the right than on the left.

    - There are more elements on the left than on the right.

    - There is a list on the left but a single scalar on the right.

    - There is a single scalar on the left but a list on the right.

3. What elements make up the range (`'aa'` .. `'bb'`)? What about (`'a0'` .. `'b9'`)?

CHAPTER 5

■ ■ ■

Hashes

We have talked about two types of data: scalars and arrays. Scalars are single pieces of information, while arrays are single variables containing many different values.

However, some items are better expressed as a set of one-to-one correspondences. A phone book, for example, is a set of correspondences between names and phone numbers. In Perl, structures like phone books are represented as a *hash*. Some people call them *associative arrays* because they look a bit like arrays where each element is associated with another value. Most Perl programmers find that a bit too long-winded, and end up just calling them *hashes*.

Comparing a hash to a phone book is helpful, but there is a difference in that a phone book is normally ordered—the names are sorted alphabetically. In a hash, the data is totally unsorted and has no intrinsic order. In fact, it's more like directory inquiries than a phone book, in that you can easily find out what the number is if you have the name. Someone else keeps the order for you, and you needn't ask what the first entry is.

Here's where a diagram helps:

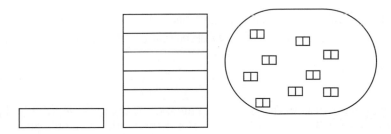

A scalar is one piece of data. It's like a single block. An array or a list is like a tower of blocks; it's kept in order, and it's kept together as a single unit. A hash, in contrast, is more like the right-most illustration above. It contains several pairs of data. The pairs are in no particular order, no pair is first or top, and they're all scattered around the hash.

Creating a Hash

Just like scalar variables have a $ prefix and arrays have a @ prefix, hashes have their own prefix—a percent sign. Again, the same naming rules apply, and the variables %hash, $hash, and @hash are all different.

One way of creating a hash variable is to assign it a list that is treated as a collection of key/value pairs:

```
%where = (
        "Gary"     , "Dallas",
        "Lucy"     , "Exeter",
        "Ian"      , "Reading",
        "Samantha" , "Portland"
);
```

In this case, the hash could be saying that "Gary's location is Dallas," "Lucy lives in Exeter," and so forth. All it really does is pair Gary and Dallas, Lucy and Exeter, and so on. How the pairing is interpreted is up to you.

If we want to make the relationship, and the fact that we're dealing with a hash, a little clearer, we can use the => operator. That's not >=, which is greater-than-or-equal-to; the => operator acts like a "quoting comma." That is, it's a comma, but whatever appears on the left-hand side of it—and only the left—is treated as a double-quoted string.

```
%where = (
        Gary     => "Dallas",
        Lucy     => "Exeter",
        Ian      => "Reading",
        Samantha => "Portland"
);
```

The scalars on the left of the arrow are called the *hash keys*, the scalars on the right are the values. We use the keys to look up the values.

■ **Note** Hash keys must be unique. You cannot have more than one entry for the same name, and if you try to add a new entry with the same key as an existing entry, the old one will be overwritten. Hash values, though, need not be unique.

Key uniqueness is more of an advantage than a limitation. Every time the word "unique" comes into a problem, like counting the unique elements of an array, your mind should immediately echo "Use a hash!"

Because hashes and arrays are both built from structures that look like lists, you can convert between them, from array to hash, like this:

```
@array = qw(Gary Dallas Lucy Exeter Ian Reading Samantha Portland);
%where = @array;
```

Assigning an array to a hash works properly only when there is an even number of elements in the array.

The hash can then be assigned back to an array like so:

```
@array = %where;
```

However, you need to be careful when converting back from a hash to an array. Hashes do not have a guaranteed order; although values will always follow keys, you can't tell what order the keys will come in. Since hash keys are unique, however, you can be sure that %hash1 = %hash2 is guaranteed to copy a hash accurately.

Working with Hash Values

To look up a value in a hash, we use something similar to the index notation for arrays. However, instead of locating elements by number, we locate them by name, and instead of using square brackets, we use curly braces.

Here's a simple example of looking up details in a hash:

```
#!/usr/bin/perl
# hash.pl

use warnings;
use strict;

my $who = "Ian";

my %where = (
        Gary     => "Dallas",
        Lucy     => "Exeter",
        Ian      => "Reading",
        Samantha => "Portland"
);

print "Gary lives in ", $where{Gary}, "\n";
print "$who lives in $where{$who}\n";
```

```
$ perl hash.pl
Gary lives in Dallas
Ian lives in Reading
$
```

The first thing we do in this program is set up our main hash, which tells us where people live.

```
my %where = (
        Gary     => "Dallas",
        Lucy     => "Exeter",
        Ian      => "Reading",
        Samantha => "Portland"
);
```

Like scalars and arrays, hash variables must be declared with my() when using strict.
Now we can look up an entry in our hash—we'll ask "Where does Gary live?"

```
print "Gary lives in ", $where{Gary}, "\n";
```

This is almost identical to looking up an array element, except for using curly braces instead of square brackets, and except for the fact that we are now allowed to use strings to index our elements. Notice that the key Gary is not quoted within the curly braces. If the key contains no whitespace characters, it is assumed to be quoted within the curly braces. If the key does contain whitespace characters, then we have to quote it.

The next line is

```perl
print "$who lives in $where{$who}\n";
```

Just as with array elements, we need not use a literal to index the element—we can look up using a variable as well.

Adding, Changing, and Removing Elements

Hash entries are very much like ordinary scalar variables, except that you need not declare an individual hash key before assigning to it or using it. You can add a new person to your hash just by assigning to her hash key:

```perl
$where{Eva} = "Uxbridge";
print "Eva lives in $where{Eva}\n";
```

A new entry springs into existence, without any problems. You can also change the entries in a hash just by reassigning to them. Let's move people around a little:

```perl
$where{Eva}      = "Denver";
$where{Samantha} = "San Francisco";
$where{Lucy}     = "Tokyo";
$where{Gary}     = "Las Vegas";
$where{Ian}      = "Southampton";

print "Gary lives in $where{Gary}\n";
```

To remove an entry from a hash, you use the delete() function, as in this little variant on hash.pl:

```perl
#!/usr/bin/perl
# badhash.pl

use warnings;
use strict;

my %where = (
        Gary     => "Dallas",
        Lucy     => "Exeter",
        Ian      => "Reading",
        Samantha => "Portland"
);

delete $where{Lucy};
print "Lucy lives in $where{Lucy}\n";
```

You can see that here we delete Lucy's entry in %where before we access it, so executing this program should produce a warning. Sure enough, we get

```
$ perl badhash.pl
Use of uninitialized value in concatenation (.) at badhash.pl line 15
Lucy lives in
$
```

It's not that we haven't initialized poor Lucy, but rather that we've decided to get rid of her.

Hash in List Context

When we discussed lists and arrays, we spent a lot of time talking about the difference between list and scalar context. Let's look at what happens when we evaluate a hash in list context. This is demonstrated with the following program:

```
#!/usr/bin/perl
# listcontext.pl

use warnings;
use strict;

my %person = (
    name  => 'John Doe',
    age   => 39,
    phone => '555-1212',
    city  => 'Chicago'
);

my @data = %person;

print "list context: ", join("|", @data), "\n";
print "another way: ", %person, "\n";
```

This program takes the hash in list context in two ways. First, it assigns the hash to an array:

```
my @data = %person;
```

then the array is printed by joining its contents with the string "|" (more on the join() function in Chapter 7):

```
print "list context: ", join("|", @data), "\n";
```

The second way is to simply print it:

```
print "another way: ", %person, "\n";
```

Recall that all arguments to the print() function are treated in list context.

When the program is executed, we can see that a hash variable in list context is a list of the key/value pairs in the order stored in memory (not necessarily in the order in which the hash was created):

```
$ perl listcontext.pl
list context: age|39|city|Chicago|phone|555-1212|name|John Doe
another way: phone555-1212age39cityChicagonameJohn Doe
$
```

We see a key (**phone**), followed by its value (**555-1212**), followed by a key (**age**), followed by its value (**39**), etc.

Hash in Scalar Context

A hash in scalar context is shown in this example:

```
#!/usr/bin/perl
# scalarcontext.pl

use warnings;
use strict;

my %person = (
    name  => 'John Doe',
    age   => 39,
    phone => '555-1212',
    city  => 'Chicago'
);

my $scalar = %person;

print "scalar context: $scalar\n";

if (%person) {
    print "%person has at least one key/value pair\n";
} else {
    print "%person is empty!\n";
}
```

Executing this program produces the following:

```
$ perl scalarcontext.pl
scalar context: 3/8
%person has at least one key/value pair
$
```

This code produces an unexpected result. The following code:

```
my $scalar = %person;

print "scalar context: $scalar\n";
```

prints the string "scalar context: 3/8". Therefore, this hash in scalar context is "3/8", which means we are using three buckets, or memory locations, out of eight buckets allocated.

This string is not so interesting unless we notice that the string "3/8" is a true value in Perl. Also, if our hash was empty, its value in scalar context would be the empty string, "". So a hash in scalar context is normally treated as a true/false value—true if there is anything in it, false if empty:

```
if (%person) {
    print "%person has at least one key/value pair\n";
} else {
    print "%person is empty!\n";
}
```

Hash Functions

Since hashes in list context are apparently random collections of key/value pairs, we can't really use foreach loops on them directly. If we did, we would get a list of key/value pairs in no apparent order. To help us, Perl provides three functions for iterating over hashes: keys(), values(), and each().

In addition, Perl provides functions to remove elements (delete(),seen previously), and to check whether a key exists in the hash (exists()).

The keys() Function

First, there is keys(%hash), which gives us a list of the keys (all of the scalars on the left-hand side). This is usually what we want when we visit each hash entry in turn, as in this example:

```
#!/usr/bin/perl
# keys.pl

use warnings;
use strict;

my %where = (
        Gary     => "Dallas",
        Lucy     => "Exeter",
        Ian      => "Reading",
        Samantha => "Portland"
);

foreach (keys %where) {
    print "$_ lives in $where{$_}\n";
}
```

Currently, this tells us

```
$ perl keys.pl
Lucy lives in Exeter
Samantha lives in Portland
Gary lives in Dallas
Ian lives in Reading
$
```

You may find that the output appears in a different order on your machine.[1] Don't worry. As mentioned before, hashes are unordered and there's no guarantee that the keys will appear in the same order each time. It really depends on the particular version of Perl you are using.

Let's look at the part of the program that does all the work:

```perl
foreach (keys %where) {
    print "$_ lives in $where{$_}\n";
}
```

keys() is a function that, like sort() and reverse(), returns a list. The list in this case is qw(Lucy Samantha Gary Ian), and the foreach loop visited each of those values in turn. As $_ was set to each one, we could print the name and look up that entry in the hash.

The values() Function

The counterpart to keys() is values(), which returns a list of all of the values in the hash. This is somewhat less useful, since you can always find the value if you have the key, but you can't easily find the key if you just have the value. It's almost always advantageous to use keys() instead.

Here is an example using the values() function:

```perl
#!/usr/bin/perl
# values.pl

use warnings;
use strict;

my %where = (
        Gary     => "Dallas",
        Lucy     => "Exeter",
        Ian      => "Reading",
        Samantha => "Portland"
);

foreach (values %where) {
    print "someone lives in $_\n";
}
```

Executing this program produces the following:

```
$ perl values.pl
someone lives in Exeter
someone lives in Portland
```

---

[1] Or even different every time that you run it! Some 5.10.x Perl installations have hash order randomization turned on by default.

```
someone lives in Dallas
someone lives in Reading
$
```

Once again the output appears to be in a random order, but the values, like the keys, are returned by `values()` in the order stored in memory.

The each() Function

The next hash function is `each()`. It returns *each* hash entry as a key/value pair. Normally, the values returned are copied into an assignable list like this:

```
($k, $v) = each %where;
```

This is illustrated in `each.pl`:

```perl
#!/usr/bin/perl
# each.pl

use warnings;
use strict;

my %where = (
        Gary     => "Dallas",
        Lucy     => "Exeter",
        Ian      => "Reading",
        Samantha => "Portland"
);

my($k, $v);
while (($k, $v) = each %where) {
    print "$k lives in $v\n";
}
```

Here is an example of this program executing:

```
$ perl each.pl
Lucy lives in Exeter
Samantha lives in Portland
Gary lives in Dallas
Ian lives in Reading
$
```

The delete() Function

You have already seen the `delete()` function. It removes a key/value pair from a hash. This statement from `badhash.pl` removes the pair Lucy/Exeter from `%where`:

```
delete $where{Lucy};
```

Since we are on the subject, we should mention that the delete() function also deletes array elements. The following code would remove element 3 from the array @array. Note that the element returns to an uninitialized state:

```
delete $array[3];
```

The exists() Function

The last hash function we will look at is exists(). This function returns true if the key exists in the hash, false if not. Here is an example:

```perl
#!/usr/bin/perl
# exists.pl

use warnings;
use strict;

my %where = (
        Gary     => "Dallas",
        Lucy     => "Exeter",
        Ian      => "Reading",
        Samantha => "Portland"
);

print "Gary exists in the hash!\n"  if exists $where{Gary};
print "Larry exists in the hash!\n" if exists $where{Larry};
```

Running this program results in the following:

```
$ perl exists.pl
Gary exists in the hash!
$
```

■ **Note** exists() returns 1 when true, an empty string when false.

The exists() function also works for array elements. This code checks to see if element 3 exists in @array:

```perl
if (exists $array[3]) {
    print "element 3 exists!\n";
}
```

Hash Examples

Hashes are very handy variables and there are many uses for them. Here are a few examples of using hashes to solve common problems.

Creating Readable Variables

The most basic use of a hash is to be able to index into a variable to obtain information using a readable string, which is far more user-friendly than using a numeric index as we would with an array. For instance, this program shows that we can create a record of strings representing RGB colors you might find in an HTML page:

```perl
#!/usr/bin/perl
# colors.pl

use warnings;
use strict;

my %colors = (
    red    => '#FF0000',
    green  => '#00FF00',
    blue   => '#0000FF',
    white  => '#FFFFFF',
    black  => '#000000',
    purple => '#520063'
);

print "Red is:    $colors{red}\n";
print "Blue is:   $colors{blue}\n";
print "Purple is: $colors{purple}\n";
```

Notice how the information in the hash is laid out in such a way that it is readable by human beings. It is easy to see that the RGB string for "red" is "#FF0000", and indexing into the hash is the human-friendly $colors{red}.

Executing this code produces the following:

```
$ perl colors.pl
Red is:    #FF0000
Blue is:   #0000FF
Purple is: #520063
$
```

"Reversing" Information

Recall the hash we created earlier in this chapter that was a collection of people and where they lived:

```perl
%where = (
        Gary      => "Dallas",
```

```
            Lucy     => "Exeter",
            Ian      => "Reading",
            Samantha => "Portland"
);
```

If you need to turn this hash around to look up people by where they live, you can use a hash in list context that produces a list of key/value pairs, reverse the list with the **reverse()** function, and then assign it to a new hash.

```
%who = reverse %where;
```

Be careful, though—if you have two values that are the same, then converting them to keys means that one will be lost. Remember that keys must be unique.

Here is a program that illustrates reversing a hash:

```
#!/usr/bin/perl
# reverse.pl

use warnings;
use strict;

my %where = (
    Gary     => "Dallas",
    Lucy     => "Exeter",
    Ian      => "Reading",
    Samantha => "Portland"
);

my %who = reverse %where;

foreach (keys %who) {
    print "in $_ lives $who{$_}\n";
}
```

Executing this code produces the following:

```
$ perl reverse.pl
in Portland lives Samantha
in Exeter lives Lucy
in Reading lives Ian
in Dallas lives Gary
$
```

After we assigned to %who, we created a hash indexed by the location producing the name that is the direct opposite of %where, which was indexed by name to produce the location.

Counting Things

A very common use of a hash variable is to count things. For instance, we can count the number of characters in a string or the items in an array. Let's look at counting items in an array.

We will create an array of names, then we will count the number of times each name occurs in the array. For instance, for this array:

```
my @names = qw(
    John    Sue     Larry
    Mary    John    Mary
    Larry   John    Joe
    Lisa    John    Mary
);
```

we see that @names is a collection of 12 names. Upon close inspection, we see that "John" occurs four times, "Sue" occurs once, and so on.

We can use a hash to keep a count of the number of times a name occurs in @names by creating a hash that has the names as its keys, and the number of occurrences of the name as the value associated with the key. For instance, when all the names in @names are processed, we will end up with a hash that resembles

```
John  => 4,
Sue   => 1,
Larry => 2,
Mary  => 3,
Joe   => 1,
Lisa  => 1
```

Here is a program illustrating this concept:

```
#!/usr/bin/perl
# count1.pl

use warnings;
use strict;

my @names = qw(
    John    Sue     Larry
    Mary    John    Mary
    Larry   John    Joe
    Lisa    John    Mary
);

my %count;

foreach (@names) {
    if (exists $count{$_}) {
        $count{$_}++;
    } else {
        $count{$_} = 1;
    }
}

foreach (keys %count) {
```

```
    print "$_ \toccurs $count{$_} time(s)\n";
}
```

Executing this code produces the following result:

```
$ perl count1.pl
Joe      occurs 1 time(s)
Lisa     occurs 1 time(s)
John     occurs 4 time(s)
Mary     occurs 3 time(s)
Sue      occurs 1 time(s)
Larry    occurs 2 time(s)
$
```

The most important part of this program is when we loop through the array and keep count:

```
foreach (@names) {
    if (exists $count{$_}) {
        $count{$_}++;
    } else {
        $count{$_} = 1;
    }
}
```

This code implements the logic "For each name in the array, if the name already exists in the hash, then increment the value by 1 (incrementing the count); else if it does not exist in the hash, then add the name to the hash with the initial value of 1." After all the names are processed, the hash will contain all the names and the number of times each name is present in @names.

For minimalists, the if statement can be shortened because this logic:

```
if (exists $count{$_}) {
    $count{$_}++;
} else {
    $count{$_} = 1;
}
```

is built into the statement

```
$count{$_}++;
```

Therefore, our foreach loop could be changed to

```
foreach (@names) {
    $count{$_}++;
}
```

or even more simply

```
$count{$_}++ foreach @names;
```

We can also write the foreach loop printing out the data as a one-line expression modifier. So, let's look at our more compact code in count2.pl:

128

```perl
#!/usr/bin/perl
# count2.pl

use warnings;
use strict;

my @names = qw(
    John    Sue     Larry
    Mary    John    Mary
    Larry   John    Joe
    Lisa    John    Mary
);

my %count;

$count{$_}++ foreach @names;

print "$_ \toccurs $count{$_} time(s)\n" foreach keys %count;
```

Summary

Hashes are unordered structures made up of pairs. Each pair consists of a key and a value, and given the key, we can look up the value. Generally, $hash{$key} = $value. We can loop over all the elements of a hash by processing the keys using a foreach loop to go through the keys.

Hashes are very useful variables that allow us to create data that is human-readable, reversible, and often used for counting things.

Exercises

1. Create this hash variable:

    ```perl
    scalar => 'dollar sign',
    array  => 'at sign',
    hash   => 'percent sign'
    ```

    Process it with a foreach loop that prints the key/value pairs so that the keys are printed in sorted order:

    ```
    array: at sign
    hash: percent sign
    scalar: dollar sign
    ```

2. Store your important phone numbers in a hash. Write a program to look up numbers by the person's name.

3. Turn the joke machine program in Chapter 4 from two arrays into one hash. While doing so, write some better lightbulb jokes.

CHAPTER 6

■ ■ ■

Subroutines/Functions

When programming, naturally there are activities we want to do again and again: adding up the values in an array, stripping extraneous blank spaces from a string, getting information into a hash in a particular format, and so on. It would be tedious to write out the code for each of these little processes every time we need to use it, and maintaining each code segment would be horrific: if there's a bug in the way we've coded the activity, we have to go through and find it each time and fix it. Wouldn't it be better if we could define a particular process just once, and then be able to call on it whenever we need to, just like we call on Perl's built-in functions?

This is exactly what *subroutines* allow us to do. Subroutines (or *functions*, or simply *subs*) enable us to give a name to a section of code. Then, when we need to use that code in our program, we just call it by name.

Functions help our programming in two ways. First, they let us reuse code, as described previously. This makes it easier to find and fix bugs, and it helps us write programs faster. Second, they allow us to chunk our code into organizational sections. Each subroutine can, for example, be responsible for a particular task.

So, when is it appropriate to use subroutines in Perl? There are two cases. You'll want to put code in a subroutine when you know it will be used to perform a calculation or action that's going to happen more than once, for instance, putting a string into a specific format, printing the header or footer of a report, turning an incoming data record into a hash, and so on.

You should also use subroutines if you want to break up your program into logical units to make it easier to understand. There is nothing worse than debugging several thousand lines of code that are not broken up in any way. Well, maybe one or two things. As an extreme example, sometimes—and only sometimes—it is desirable to have a "main program" that consists entirely of calls to subroutines, like this:

```
#!/usr/bin/perl

use warnings;
use strict;

setup();
get_input();
process_input();
output();
```

This immediately shows the structure of the program. Each of those four subroutines would, of course, have to be defined, and they'd probably call on other subroutines themselves. This kind of structure lets us partition our programs to change a single, monolithic piece of code into manageable chunks for ease of understanding, ease of debugging, and ease of maintaining the program.

One note about the terminology: in Perl, the words subroutine and function are synonyms—they both mean the same thing. We will use them interchangeably in this book.

Understanding Subroutines

Now that we know what subroutines are, let's look at how to define and use them. First, let's see how to create subroutines.

Defining a Subroutine

We can give Perl some code, and we can give the code a name, and that's our subroutine. Here's how we do this:

```
sub example_subroutine {
    ...
}
```

There are three sections to this declaration:

- The keyword sub.

- The name we're going to give the subroutine. The rules for naming a subroutine are exactly those for naming variables: names must begin with an alphabetic character or an underscore and must be followed by zero or more alphanumerics or underscores. Uppercase letters are allowed, but we tend to reserve all-uppercase names for special subroutines. And again, as with variables, you can have a scalar $fred, an array @fred, a hash %fred, and a subroutine fred(), and they'll all be distinct.

- A block of code delimited by curly braces, just as we used for constructs like while and if. Notice that we don't need a semicolon after the closing curly brace.

After we've set up the subroutine, we can use it.

Before we go any further, it's worth taking a quick time-out to consider the naming of subroutines. You can convey a lot about a subroutine's purpose with its name, much like that of a variable. Here are some guidelines—not hard-and-fast rules—about how you should name subroutines:

- If they're primarily about doing something, name them with a verb—for example, summarize() or download().

- If they're primarily about returning something, name them after what they return—for example, greeting() or header().

- If they're about testing whether something is true, give them a name that makes sense in an if statement; starting with is_... or can_... helps, or if that isn't appropriate, name them with an adjective: for example, is_available(), valid(), or readable().

- If you're converting between one thing and another, try to convey both things— traditionally this is done with a 2 or _to_ in the middle: text2html(), meters_to_feet(). That way you can tell easily what's expected and what's being produced.

Invoking a Subroutine

The conventional way to invoke a function is to follow the function name with parentheses. This invokes the example_subroutine() function:

```
example_subroutine();
```

If the function takes arguments (more on passing arguments later in this chapter), then drop them within the parentheses:

```
example_subroutine('Perl is', 'my favorite', $language);
```

Let's look at a complete example. It's traditional for programs to tell you their version and name either when they start up or when you ask them with a special option. It's also convenient to put the code that prints this information into a subroutine to get it out of the way. Let's take a familiar program and update it for this traditional practice.

Here's version 1:

```perl
#!/usr/bin/perl
# hello1.pl

use warnings;

print "Hello, world!\n";
```

And here it is with strict mode turned on and version information:

```perl
#!/usr/bin/perl
# hello2.pl

use warnings;
use strict;

sub version {
    print "Beginning Perl's \"Hello, world.\" version 2.0\n";
}

my $option = shift;    # defaults to shifting @ARGV

version() if $option eq "-v" or $option eq "--version";

print "Hello, world.\n";
```

Now, we're starting to look like a real utility:

```
$ perl hello2.pl -v
Beginning Perl's "Hello, world." version 2.0
Hello, world.
$
```

The first thing we see in `hello2.pl` is the definition of the `version()` function:

```
sub version {
    print "Beginning Perl's \"Hello, world.\" version 2.0\n";
}
```

It's a simple block of code that calls the `print()` function. It didn't have to—it could have done anything. Any code that's valid in the main program is valid inside a subroutine, including calling other functions.

We call this block the *body* of the subroutine, just like the body of a loop; similarly, it stretches from the open curly brace after the subroutine name to the matching closing curly brace.

Now that we've defined it, we can use it. We invoke the function with `version()`, and Perl runs that block of code, assuming we've added the right flag on the command line.

```
version() if $option eq "-v" or $option eq "--version";
```

When Perl finishes executing `version()`, it comes back and carries on with the next statement:

```
print "Hello, world.\n";
```

No doubt version 3 will address the warnings that Perl gives if you call this program without appending `-v` or `--version` to its name.

Order of Declaration and Invoking Functions

Normally, functions are called using parentheses as in the preceding program:

```
version()
```

We can also call them without the parentheses if the function is defined before it is invoked:

```
version
```

If we just call subroutines by name, without parentheses, we need to declare them before using them. This may not sound like much of a limitation, but there are times when you want to declare a subroutine after the main part of the program; in fact, that's the usual way to structure a program. This is because when you open up the file in your editor, you can see what's going on right there at the top of the file, without having to scroll through a bunch of definitions first. Take the extreme example shown at the beginning of this chapter:

```
#!/usr/bin/perl

use warnings;
use strict;
```

```
setup();
get_input();
process_input();
output();
```

This would be followed, presumably, by something like this:

```
sub setup {
    print "This is some program, version 0.1\n";
    print "Opening files...\n";
    open_files();
    print "Opening network connections...\n";
    open_network();
    print "Ready!\n";
}

sub open_files {
    ...
}
```

■ **Tip** This structure makes it far easier to understand the program than if we had to trawl through a pile of subroutines before getting to the four lines that constitute our main program.

In order to get this to work, we need to provide hints to Perl as to what we're doing: that's why the preceding calls to subroutines include parentheses: setup(), open_files(), and so on.

This tells Perl that it should be looking for a subroutine somewhere instead of referring to another type of variable. What happens if we don't do this?

```
#!/usr/bin/perl
# subdecl.pl

use warnings;
use strict;

setup;

sub setup {
    print "This is some program, version 0.1\n";
}
```

```
$ perl subdecl.pl
Bareword "setup" not allowed while "strict subs" in use at subdecl.pl line 7.
Execution of subdecl.pl aborted due to compilation errors.
$
```

135

Perl didn't know what we meant at the time and complained. So, to tell it we want to execute a subroutine, we use parentheses, just like when we want to disambiguate the parameters to a function like print().

There's another way we can tell Perl we're going to refer to a subroutine, and that's by providing a *forward definition*—also known as *predeclaring* the subroutine. This means "We're not going to define this right now, but look out for it later."

We do this by just saying sub *NAME*;, and note that this does require a semicolon at the end. Here's another way of writing the preceding example:

```
#!/usr/bin/perl

use warnings;
use strict;

sub setup;
sub get_input;
sub process_input;
sub output;
sub open_files;
sub open_network;
...
```

From now on, we can happily use the subroutines without the parentheses:

```
setup;
get_input;
process_input;
output;

sub setup {
    print "This is some program, version 0.1\n";
    print "Opening files...\n";
    open_files;
    print "Opening network connections...\n";
    open_network;
    print "Ready!\n";
}

sub open_files {
    ...
}
```

Alternatively, you can ask Perl to provide the forward declarations for you. If you say use subs (...), you can provide a list of subroutine names to be predeclared:

```
#!/usr/bin/perl

use warnings;
use strict;
```

```
use subs qw(setup get_input process_input output pen_files open_network);

...
```

And here's yet another way of calling subroutines:

```
&setup;
&get_input;
&process_input;
&output;
```

This was popular in the days of Perl 4, and we'll see later why the ampersand is important. For the time being, think of the ampersand as being the "type symbol" for subroutines.

In this book we will stick to calling functions with parentheses to clearly indicate that we are invoking a function. As a rule of thumb, the more clarity, the better.

■ **Tip** Here is a suggestion about the order of declaration: pick one and stick with it. If you prefer functions defined before the main code, do that consistently. If you prefer functions defined after the main code, again, be consistent.

Passing Arguments into Functions

As well as being set pieces of code to be executed whenever we need them, we can also use our user-defined functions just like Perl's built-in functions—we can pass *arguments* (aka *parameters*) to them

Just as with Perl's built-ins, we pass parameters by placing them between the parentheses:

```
my_sub(10,15);
```

Function arguments are passed in through one of Perl's special variables, the array @_, and from there they can be accessed within the function. We'll illustrate this with a subroutine that takes a list of values, adds them up, and prints the total. This example, `total1.pl`, contains a function named `total()` that loops through the argument list @_ and sums the arguments passed in:

```
#!/usr/bin/perl
# total1.pl

use warnings;
use strict;

total(111, 107, 105, 114, 69);
total(1...100);

sub total {
   my $total = 0;
```

```
    $total += $_ foreach @_;
    print "The total is $total\n";
}
```

And to see it in action:

```
$ perl total1.pl
The total is 506
The total is 5050
$
```

This program illustrates that you can pass any list to a subroutine, just as you can to `print()`. When you do, the list ends up in `@_`, where it's up to you to do something with it. Here, we go through each element and add them up:

```
    $total += $_ foreach @_;
```

This is a little cryptic, but it's how you're likely to see it if written by an experienced Perl programmer. You could write this a little less tersely, like this:

```
my @args = @_;
foreach my $element (@args) {
    $total = $total + $element;
}
```

In the first example, `@_` would contain (111, 107, 105, 114, 69), and we'd add each value to `$total` in turn.

When we pass arguments into functions, we often treat the arguments as individual values instead of treating `@_` as a single variable. To grab each value passed in to the function, there are two common options: shifting the arguments or using an assignable list.

Let's look at a simple program that grabs two arguments passed to the function `add()` and prints their sum. This example will `shift()` the arguments out of `@_` (recall that `shift()` removes the left-most element of an array, and note that within a function, it defaults to shifting `@_`):

```
#!/usr/bin/perl
# add1.pl

use warnings;
use strict;

add(10, 2);

sub add {
    my $arg1 = shift @_;
    my $arg2 = shift;      # defaults to shifting @_

    print "sum is: ", $arg1 + $arg2, "\n";
}
```

Executing this example:

```
$ perl add1.pl
```

```
sum is: 12
$
```

An alternative approach is to assign @_ to an assignable list as shown in add2.pl:

```
#!/usr/bin/perl
# add2.pl

use warnings;
use strict;

add(10, 2);

sub add {
    my($arg1, $arg2) = @_;

    print "sum is: ", $arg1 + $arg2, "\n";
}
```

Recall that an assignable list takes the list or array on the right of the assignment operator and copies it memberwise into the list on the left side of the assignment operator. This line of code copies the two function operators member-wise into the variables $arg1 and $arg2:

```
my($arg1, $arg2) = @_;
```

■ **Note** Make sure that parentheses are used even if there is only one argument assigned to a variable:

```
my($arg) = @_;
```
and not:
```
my $arg = @_;
```
Using parentheses creates a list so that the 0th element of @_ is copied. If the parentheses are dropped, then @_ is taken in scalar context, which is its size, in this case 1.

Return Values

Back to our example of summing the contents of @_. Sometimes we don't want to perform an action like printing out the total, but instead we want to return the total. We may also want to return a result to indicate whether what we were doing succeeded, allowing us to say things like

```
$sum_of_100 = total(1..100);
```

There are two ways to do this: implicitly or explicitly. The implicit way is nice and easy—we just make the value we want to return the last item in our subroutine:

```
#!/usr/bin/perl
# total2.pl

use warnings;
use strict;

my $total = total(111, 107, 105, 114, 69);
print "the total is: $total\n";

my $sum_of_100 = total(1..100);
print "the sum of 100 is: $sum_of_100\n";

sub total {
    my $total = 0;
    $total += $_ foreach @_;
    $total;
}
```

Running this code results in the following:

```
$ perl total2.pl
the total is: 506
the sum of 100 is: 5050
$
```

The last expression in the function doesn't need to be a variable: you could use any expression. You can also return a list instead of a single scalar.

Here is an example of returning a list from a function. Let's convert a number of seconds to hours, minutes, and seconds. We pass the time in seconds into the subroutine, and the subroutine returns a three-element list with the hours, minutes, and remaining seconds.

```
#!/usr/bin/perl
# seconds1.pl

use warnings;
use strict;

my ($hours, $minutes, $seconds) = secs2hms(3723);
print "3723 seconds is $hours hours, $minutes minutes and $seconds seconds";
print "\n";

sub secs2hms {
    my ($h,$m);
    my $seconds = shift;      # defaults to shifting @_
    $h = int($seconds/(60*60));
    $seconds %= 60*60;
    $m = int($seconds/60);
    $seconds %= 60;
    ($h,$m,$seconds);
}
```

This tells us that

```
$ perl seconds1.pl
3723 seconds is 1 hours, 2 minutes and 3 seconds
$
```

This program illustrates that just as with a built-in function, when you're expecting a subroutine to return a list, you can use an array or list of variables to collect the return values:

```
my ($hours, $minutes, $seconds) = secs2hms(3723);
```

When `secs2hms()` returns, this will be equivalent to

```
my ($hours, $minutes, $seconds) = (1,2,3);
```

And now let's look at how the subroutine works. We start in the usual way: `sub`, the name of the function, and a block.

```
sub secs2hms {
```

We have two variables to represent hours and minutes, and we read the parameters in from `@_`. As we mentioned before, if you don't tell `shift()` which array to take data from, it'll read from `@_` if you're in a subroutine or (`@ARGV` if you're not in a subroutine. Therefore, the first argument to `secs2hms()`, 3723, is shifted into `$seconds`:

```
  my ($h,$m);
  my $seconds = shift;
```

Then the actual conversion: there are 3600 (60*60) seconds in an hour, and so the number of hours is the number of seconds divided by 3600. However, that'll give us a floating point number—if we divided 3660 by 3600, we'd get 1.0341666. We'd rather have "one and a bit," so we use `int()` to get the integer value, the "1" part of the division, and use the modulus operator to get the remainder; having dealt with the first 3600 seconds, we want to carry on looking at the next 123.

```
  $h = int($seconds/(60*60));
  $seconds %= 60*60;
```

The second statement sets `$seconds` to `$seconds % (60*60)`—if it was 3723 before, it'll be 123 now.
The same goes for minutes: we divide to get "two and a bit," and getting the remainder tells us that there are 3 seconds outstanding. Hence, our values are 1 hour, 2 minutes, and 3 seconds.

```
  $m = int($seconds/60);
  $seconds %= 60;
```

We return this just by leaving a list of the values as the last item in the subroutine.

```
  ($h,$m,$seconds);
```

The return Statement

The explicit method of returning something from a subroutine is to say `return(...)`. The first `return` statement the program comes across will immediately return to the caller. For example:

```
sub secs2hms {

    ...

    return ($h,$m,$seconds);
    print "This statement is never reached.";
}
```

This means we can have more than one `return` statement, and it's often useful to do so. So the `seconds1.pl` program is better written as `seconds2.pl`:

```
#!/usr/bin/perl
# seconds2.pl

use warnings;
use strict;

my ($hours, $minutes, $seconds) = secs2hms(3723);
print "3723 seconds is $hours hours, $minutes minutes and $seconds seconds";
print "\n";

sub secs2hms {
    my ($h,$m);
    my $seconds = shift;     # defaults to shifting @_
    $h = int($seconds/(60*60));
    $seconds %= 60*60;
    $m = int($seconds/60);
    $seconds %= 60;
    return($h,$m,$seconds);
}
```

Understanding Scope

Now it's time to have a look at what we're doing when we declare a variable with `my()`. The truth, as we've briefly glimpsed, is that Perl has two types of variables, the *global* or *package* variable, which can be accessed anywhere in the program, and the *lexical* or *local* variable, which we declare with `my()` and which can be accessed only within the block where it is declared.

Global Variables

All variables in the program are global by default. Consider this code:

```
#!/usr/bin/perl

use warnings;

$x = 10;
```

$x is a global variable. It is available in every subroutine in the program. For instance, here is a program that accesses a global variable:

```
#!/usr/bin/perl
# global1.pl

use warnings;

$x = 10;

access_global();

sub access_global {
    print "value of \$x: $x\n";
}
```

Executing this code shows that $x is accessible in access_global():

```
$ perl global1.pl
value of $x: 10
$
```

Since variables within functions are global by default, functions can modify variables as shown in this program:

```
#!/usr/bin/perl
# global2.pl

use warnings;

$x = 10;

print "before: $x\n";
change_global();
print "after:  $x\n";

sub change_global {
    $x = 20;
    print "in change_global(): $x\n";
}
```

This program assigns the global variable $x the value 10 and then prints that value. Then, change_global() is invoked. It assigns $x the value 20—this accesses the global variable $x, then prints its value. Then in the main part of the code, after the function is called, the global $x is printed with its new value—20, as we can see:

```
$ perl global2.pl
before: 10
in change_global(): 20
after:  20
$
```

143

The fact that Perl function variables are global by default is not a bad thing, unless of course you are not expecting it. If you are not expecting it, accidentally overwriting global variables can cause hard-to-find bugs. Once you know that the variables are global by default, you will probably want to make function arguments local.

Introduction to Packages

When you start programming, you're in a *package* called main. A package is a collection of variables that is separate from other packages. Let's say you have two packages: A and B. Each package can have its own variable named $x, and those two $x variables are completely distinct.

If you assign $x, as in the previous global2.pl program, you create a package variable $x in package main (the main package is the default package). Perl knows it by its full name, $main::x—the variable $x in the main package—but because you're in the main package when you make the assignment, you can just call it by its short name, $x. It's like the phone system—you don't have to dial the area code when you call someone in the same area as you.[1]

You can create a variable in another package by using a fully qualified name. Suppose instead of the main package, we have a package called Fred where we store all of Fred's variables and subroutines. To get at the $name variable in package Fred, we say $Fred::name, like this:

```
$x = 10;
$Fred::name = "Fred Flintstone";
```

The fact that the variable is in a different package doesn't mean we can't get at it. Remember that these are global variables, available from anywhere in our program. All packages do is give us a way of subdividing the namespace.

What do we mean by "subdividing the namespace"? Well, the namespace is the set of names we can give our variables. Without packages, you could only have one $name. What packages do is help us make $name in package Fred different to $name in package Barney and $name in package main.

```
#!/usr/bin/perl
# globals1.pl

use warnings;

$main::name   = "Your Name Here";
$Fred::name   = "Fred Flintstone";
$Barney::name = "Barney Rubble";

print "\$name in package main   is $name\n";
print "\$name in package Fred   is $Fred::name\n";
print "\$name in package Barney is $Barney::name\n";
```

---

[1] Depending on your location, of course. Nowadays, with so many area codes in a metropolitan area, to call across the street often requires dialing 10 digits . . .

```
$ perl globals1.pl
$name in package main    is Your Name Here
$name in package Fred    is Fred Flintstone
$name in package Barney is Barney Rubble
$
```

You can change what package you're working in with the aptly named `package` operator. We could write the preceding like this:

```
#!/usr/bin/perl
# globals2.pl

use warnings;

$main::name   = "Your Name Here";
$Fred::name   = "Fred Flintstone";
$Barney::name = "Barney Rubble";

print "\$name in package main    is $name\n";
package Fred;
print "\$name in package Fred    is $name\n";
package Barney;
print "\$name in package Barney is $name\n";
package main;
```

When `use strict` is in force, we have to use the full names of our package variables. If we try to say this:

```
#!/usr/bin/perl
# strict1.pl

use warnings;
use strict;

$x = 10;
print $x;
```

Perl will give us an error—global symbol $x requires an explicit package name. The package name it's looking for is main, and it wants us to say `$main::x`.

```
#!/usr/bin/perl
# strict2.pl

use warnings;
use strict;

$main::x = 10;
print $main::x, "\n";
```

Global variables can be accessed and altered at any time by any subroutine or assignment you care to apply to them. Of course, this is handy if you want to store a value—for instance, the user's name—and be able to get it anywhere.

It's also an absolute pain in the neck when it comes to subroutines. Here's why:

```
$foo = 25;
$bar = some_sub(10);
print $foo;
```

Looks innocent, doesn't it? Looks like we should see the answer 25. But what happens if some_sub() uses and changes the global $foo? Any variable anywhere in your program can be wiped out by another part of your program—we call this *action at a distance*, and it can be difficult to debug. Packages alleviate the problem, but to make sure we never get into this mess, we have to ensure that every variable in our program has a different name. In small programs, that's feasible, but in huge team efforts, it's a nightmare. It's far clearer to be able to restrict the possible effect of a variable to a certain area of code, and that's exactly what lexical variables do.

Lexical Variables (aka Local Variables)

The range of effect that a variable has is called its *scope*, and lexical variables declared with my() are said to have *lexical* or *local scope*. That is, they exist from the point where they're declared until the end of the enclosing block. The name "lexical" comes from the fact that they're confined to a well-defined chunk of text.

```
my $x;
$x = 30;
{
    my $x; # new $x
    $x = 50;
    # we can't see the old $x, even if we want to
}
print $x;   # this $x is, and always has been, 30
```

Great. We can now use variables in our subroutines with the knowledge that we're not going to upset any behavior outside of them. Let's modify global2.pl by adding my() in the function (now called change_global_not()):

```
#!/usr/bin/perl
# my.pl

use warnings;

$x = 10;

print "before: $x\n";
change_global_not();
print "after:  $x\n";

sub change_global_not {
    my $x = 20;
```

```
        print "in change_global_not(): $x\n";
}
```

This gives us the output we expect:

```
$ perl my.pl
before: 10
in change_global_not(): 20
after:  10
$
```

Some Important Notes on Passing Arguments

Sometimes we want to pass things other than an ordinary list of scalars, so it's important to understand how passing arguments works.

Function Arguments Passed by Reference

It's important to know that in Perl, arguments are passed into functions by reference, not by value. This is illustrated in the following example:

```
#!/usr/bin/perl
# byref1.pl

use warnings;
use strict;

my $var = 10;
print "before: $var\n";
change_var($var);
print "after:  $var\n";

sub change_var {
    print "in change_var() before: $_[0]\n";
    ++$_[0];
    print "in change_var() after:  $_[0]\n";
}
```

First, $var is assigned 10 and then printed. Then, $var is passed into the function change_var(). This function prints the value of $_[0], increments it, then prints it again. The important line of code in this function is

```
++$_[0];
```

Since the arguments to the function are passed in through the array @_, to access the zeroth argument of the array we use the syntax $_[0]—this function prints $var, increments it, then prints it again. The important thing to note about this code is that since $var is passed into the function by reference, when $_[0] is incremented, Perl actually increments the argument passed in, $var, from 10 to 11. After the function call, the program then prints the resulting value of $var, which is now 11. Executing the code proves this:

```
$ perl byref1.pl
before: 10
in change_var() before: 10
in change_var() after:  11
after:  11
$
```

The fact that Perl passes arguments by reference is not in itself a bad thing, but it can be if you are not expecting it. Having functions modify arguments when you don't want them to can create hard-to-find bugs. There is a very simple way to ensure that your functions don't modify their arguments—simply copy them into my() variables as shown in this example:

```
#!/usr/bin/perl
# byref2.pl

use warnings;
use strict;

my $var = 10;
print "before: $var\n";
change_var($var);
print "after:  $var\n";

sub change_var {
    my($v) = @_;
    # or: my $v = shift;

    print "in change_var() before: $v\n";
    ++$v;
    print "in change_var() after:  $v\n";
}
```

The big change here is the first line of change_var():

```
my($v) = @_;
```

This copies the zeroth element of @_, or $_[0], into $v. As mentioned before and as indicated by the comment, we could have written this as

```
my $v = shift;
```

since the shift() function shifts @_ by default if invoked within a function (recall also that if shift() is invoked outside a function it shifts @ARGV by default). Now, since the argument is copied into $v, when we increment it with

```
++$v;
```

the copy within the function is incremented, not $var. Executing the program proves this:

```
$ perl byref2.pl
before: 10
in change_var() before: 10
in change_var() after:  11
after:  10
$
```

Lists Are One-Dimensional

Recall that all lists and all arrays are one-dimensional. If we have this list:

(@a, @b)

it becomes a one-dimensional list containing the contents of @a followed by the contents of @b. This is an important rule when it comes to passing arrays into functions, since they will be passed in as a one-dimensional list. This is illustrated in the following example:

```
#!/usr/bin/perl
# passarrays.pl

use warnings;
use strict;

my(@nums1, @nums2);

@nums1 = (2, 4, 6);
@nums2 = (8, 10, 12);

process_arrays(@nums1, @nums2);

sub process_arrays {
    my(@a, @b) = @_;

    print "contents of \@a\n";
    print "[$_] " foreach @a;
    print "\n\n";

    print "contents of \@b\n";
    print "[$_] " foreach @b;
    print "\n";
}
```

This program creates two 3-element arrays, @nums1 and @nums2. These arrays are then passed into process_arrays() and are immediately copied into two arrays, @a and @b. We might think that @a receives the contents of @nums1 and @b receives the contents of @nums2, but that is not what happens. Since the arguments are passed in as

process_arrays(@nums1, @nums2);

the elements are flattened into this one-dimensional list:

(2, 4, 6, 8, 10, 12)

and this list is passed in and assigned to the assignable list:

```
my(@a, @b) = @_;
```

Since this assignable list contains an array, @a, it will consume all the elements that are assigned to it. Therefore, @b will be empty because there are no elements remaining to assign to it. So, when we execute this program, we will see that @a contains all the elements passed in and @b contains no elements:

```
$ perl passarrays.pl
contents of @a
[2] [4] [6] [8] [10] [12]

contents of @b

$
```

Later, when we discuss references in Chapter 11, you will see how to pass two arrays (or hashes) into a function and treat them as two separate variables.

Default Argument Values

It can be useful at times to give the arguments for your subroutine a default value. That is, supply the argument with a value to use in the subroutine if one is not specified when the subroutine is called. This is very easily done with the || operator (the logical *or* operator).

|| has a very special feature: it returns the last thing it evaluates. So, for instance, if we say $a = 3 || 5, then $a will be set to 3. Because 3 is a true value, the *or* operator has no need to examine anything else, and so 3 is the last value || evaluates. If, however, we say $a = 0 || 5, then $a will be set to 5; 0 is not a true value, so the operator looks at the next operand, 5, which is the last thing it evaluates. This behavior is called *short circuiting*.

Hence, anything we get from @_ that doesn't have a true value can be given a default with the || operator. We can create subroutines with a flexible number of parameters and have Perl fill in the blanks for us:

```
#!/usr/bin/perl
# defaults.pl

use warnings;
use strict;

log_warning("Klingons on the starboard bow", "Stardate 60030.2");
log_warning("/earth is 99% full, please delete more people");
log_warning();

sub log_warning {
   my $message = shift || "Something's wrong";
   my $time    = shift || localtime; # Default to now.
   print "[$time] $message\n";
}
```

```
$ perl defaults.pl
[Stardate 60030.2] Klingons on the starboard bow
[Wed Nov 18 09:18:50 2009] /earth is 99% full, please delete more people

[Wed Nov 18 09:18:50 2009] Something's wrong
$
```

One by-product of specifying defaults for parameters is the opportunity to use those parameters as flags. Your subroutine can then alter its functionality based on the number of arguments passed to it.

Named Parameters

One of the more irritating aspects of calling subroutines is that you have to remember the order of the parameters. Was it username first and then password, or host first and then username, or . . . ?

Named parameters are a readable way of solving this. What we'd rather say is something like this:

```
logon(username => $name, password => $pass, host => $hostname);
```

and then give the parameters in any order. Now, Perl makes this really, really easy because that set of parameters can be thought of as a hash:

```
sub logon {
    die "Parameters to logon should be even" if @_ % 2;
    my %args = @_;
    print "Logging on to host $args{hostname}\n";
    ...
}
```

Whether and how often you use named parameters is a matter of style; for subroutines that take lots of parameters, some of which may be optional, it's an excellent idea. For those that take two or three parameters, it's probably not worth the hassle.

Named parameters also help when you want to provide default values to your arguments. For instance, let's say we write a function named college_degree() and it expects three arguments: university, degree, year. We could call the function with all three arguments:

```
college_degree(
    university => 'Illinois',
    degree     => 'MSEE',
    year       => 2000
);
```

Since we are using named parameters, the order of those three argument pairs is not important—they could be in any order. We could also call the function with only two pair, as in

```
college_degree(
    degree     => 'MSEE',
    year       => 2000
);
```

provided our function defaults the arguments. This implementation of `college_degree()` ensures that the three arguments have default values:

```
sub college_degree {
    my %args = @_;

    $args{university} = 'Northwestern' unless exists $args{university};
    $args{degree}     = 'BSCS'         unless exists $args{degree};
    $args{year}       = 2010           unless exists $args{year};

    ...
}
```

Summary

Subroutines are a bit of code with a name, and they allow us to do two things: chunk our program into organizational units, and perform calculations and operations on pieces of data, possibly returning some more data. The basic format of a subroutine definition is

`sub name BLOCK`

We can call a subroutine by just saying `name` if we've had the definition beforehand. If the definition's lower down in the program, we can say `name()`, and you may see `&name` used in older programs. Otherwise, we can use a forward definition to tell Perl that `name` should be interpreted as the name of a subroutine. The conventional notation is `name()`.

When we pass arguments into a subroutine, they end up in the special array `@_`, which contains aliases of the data that was passed so data is passed in by reference. We discussed ways of passing variables in by value (copying the arguments into `my()` variables) and also how to implement default argument values and named parameters.

Exercises

1. Write a program that computes the factorial of a number. Just to remind you, the factorial of a number is that number times that number minus 1 and so on, stopping at 1. For instance, the factorial of 5 is

    `5! = 5 * 4 * 3 * 2 * 1`

    The factorial of 0 is 1.

2. If you know about recursion, implement the `factorial()` function as a recursive function.

3. Modify the `seconds.pl` program shown earlier in the chapter so that it contains a second subroutine that asks the user for a number, puts the number into a global variable, and converts that into hours, minutes, and seconds.

CHAPTER 7

■ ■ ■

Regular Expressions

11:15 Restate my assumptions:

1. *Mathematics is the language of nature.*
2. *Everything around us can be represented and understood through numbers.*
3. *If you graph these numbers, patterns emerge. Therefore: There are patterns everywhere in nature.*

—Max Cohen in π *(Pi, 1998)*

Whether you agree that Max's assumptions should give rise to his conclusion is up to you, but his case is much easier to support in the field of computers—there are patterns everywhere in programming.

Regular expressions allow us to look for patterns in our data. So far we've been limited to checking a single value against that of a scalar variable or the contents of an array or hash. With the rules outlined in this chapter, we can use that one single value (or pattern) to describe what we're looking for in more general terms: we can check that every sentence in a file begins with a capital letter and ends with a period, find out how many times James Bond's name is mentioned in *Goldfinger,* or even if there are any repeated sequences of numbers in the decimal representation of greater than five in length.

Regular expressions, however, are a huge topic. They're among the most powerful features of Perl, and so our examination of them will be divided up into six sections:

- Basic patterns

- Special characters to use

- Quantifiers, anchors, and memorizing patterns

- Matching, substituting, and transforming text using patterns

- Backtracking

- A quick look at some simple pitfalls

Generally speaking, if you want to ask Perl something about a piece of text, regular expressions are going to be your first port of call. First, however, there's probably one simple question burning in your mind . . .

What Are They?

The term *regular expression* (now commonly abbreviated to *regex* or even *RE*) simply refers to a pattern that follows particular rules of syntax—for Perl, those outlined in the rest of this chapter. Regular expressions are not limited to Perl—Unix utilities such as **sed** and **egrep** use the same notation for finding patterns in text (well, not exactly the same since Perl regexes are an extension of **egrep**'s regexes). So why aren't they just called "search patterns" or something less obscure?

The actual phrase itself originates from the mid-fifties when a mathematician named Stephen Kleene developed a notation for manipulating *regular sets*. Perl's regular expressions have grown far beyond the original notation and have significantly extended the original system, but some of Kleene's notation remains and the name has stuck.

Patterns

History lesson aside, regular expressions are all about identifying patterns in text. So what constitutes a pattern? And how do you compare it against something?

The simplest pattern is a word—a simple sequence of characters—and we may, for example, want to ask Perl whether a certain string contains that word. We can split the string into separate words, and then test to see if each word is the one we're looking for. Here's how we might do that:

```perl
#!/usr/bin/perl
# match1.pl

use warnings;
use strict;

my $found = 0;
$_ = "Nobody wants to hurt you... 'cept, I do hurt people sometimes, Case.";

my $sought = "people";

foreach my $word (split) {
    if ($word eq $sought) {
        $found = 1;
        last;
    }
}

if ($found) {
    print "Hooray! Found the word 'people'\n";
}
```

Sure enough the program returns success . . .

```
$ perl match1.pl
Hooray! Found the word 'people'
$
```

But oh, that's messy! It's complicated, and it's slow to boot! Worse still, the **split()** function, which breaks up each line into a list of "words," actually *keeps* all the punctuation. (We'll see more about **split()** later in the chapter.) So the string "you" wouldn't be found in the preceding example, but "you . . ." would. This is looking like a hard problem, but it should be easy. Perl was designed to make easy things easy and hard things possible, so there should be a better way to do this. Let's see how it looks using a regular expression:

```perl
#!/usr/bin/perl
# match2.pl

use warnings;
use strict;

$_ = "Nobody wants to hurt you... 'cept, I do hurt people sometimes, Case.";
```

```
if ($_ =~ /people/) {
    print "Hooray! Found the word 'people'\n";
}
```

Much, much easier, and the same result. We place the text we want to find between forward slashes—that's the regular expression part; that's our pattern, what we're trying to match. We also need to tell Perl in which particular string to look for that pattern, and we do so with the =~ operator. This operator returns 1 if the pattern match was successful (in our case, whether the character sequence "people" was found in the string) and the empty string if it wasn't.

Before we move on to more complicated patterns, let's just have a quick look at that syntax. As we have noted previously, a lot of Perl's operations take $_ as a default argument, and regular expressions are among those operations. Since we have the text we want to test in $_, we don't need to use the =~ operator to "bind" the pattern to another string. We could write the code even more simply:

```
$_ = "Nobody wants to hurt you... 'cept, I do hurt people sometimes, Case.";

if (/people/) {
    print "Hooray! Found the word 'people'\n";
}
```

Alternatively, we might want to test for the pattern not matching—for the word *not* being found. Obviously, we could say unless (/people/), but if the text we're looking at isn't in $_, we can also use the negative form of that =~ operator, which is !~. For example:

```
#!/usr/bin/perl
# nomatch.pl

use warnings;
use strict;

my $gibson =
    "Nobody wants to hurt you... 'cept, I do hurt people sometimes, Case.";

if ($gibson !~ /fish/) {
    print "There are no fish in William Gibson.\n";
}
```

True to form, as cyberpunk books don't regularly involve fish, we get the result:

```
$ perl nomatch.pl
There are no fish in William Gibson.
$
```

Literal text is the simplest regular expression to look for, but we needn't look for just the one word—we could look for any particular phrase. However, we have to make sure that we exactly match *all* the characters—words (with correct capitalization), numbers, punctuation, and even whitespace.

```
#!/usr/bin/perl
# match3.pl

use warnings;
use strict;

$_ = "Nobody wants to hurt you... 'cept, I do hurt people sometimes, Case.";

if (/I do/) {
    print "'I do' is in that string.\n";
}
```

```
if (/sometimes Case/) {
    print "'sometimes Case' matched.\n";
}
```

Let's run this program and see what happens:

```
$ perl match3.pl
'I do' is in that string.
$
```

The other string didn't match, even though the two words are there. This is because everything in a regular expression has to match the string, from start to finish: first "sometimes", then a space, then "Case". But in $_ there was a comma before the space, so it didn't match exactly. Similarly, spaces inside the pattern are significant:

```
#!/usr/bin/perl
# match4.pl

use warnings;
use strict;

my $test1 = "The dog is in the kennel";
my $test2 = "The sheepdog is in the field";

if ($test1 =~ / dog/) {
    print "This dog's at home.\n";
}

if ($test2 =~ / dog/) {
    print "This dog's at work.\n";
}
```

This will only find the first dog, as Perl is looking for a space followed by the three letters "dog":

```
$.perl match4.pl
This dog's at home.
$
```

So, for the moment, it looks like we have to specify our patterns with absolute precision. As another example, look at this:

```
#!/usr/bin/perl
# match5.pl

use warnings;
use strict;

$_ = "Nobody wants to hurt you... 'cept, I do hurt people sometimes, Case.";

if (/case/) {
    print "I guess it's just the way I'm made.\n";
} else {
    print "Case? Where are you, Case?\n";
}
```

```
$ perl match5.pl
Case? Where are you, Case?
$
```

Hmm, no match. Why not? Because we asked for a lowercase "c" when the string has an uppercase "C"—regexes are (if you'll pardon the pun) case-sensitive. We can get around this by asking Perl to compare insensitively, and we do this by putting an "i" (for "insensitive") after the closing slash. If we alter the preceding code as follows:

```
if (/case/i) {
    print "I guess it's just the way I'm made.\n";
} else {
    print "Case? Where are you, Case?\n";
}
```

Then we find him:

```
$ perl match5.pl
I guess it's just the way I'm made.
$
```

This "i" is one of several *modifiers* we can append to the end of a regular expression to change its behavior slightly. We'll see more of them later.

Interpolation

Regular expressions work a little like double-quoted strings—variables and metacharacters are interpolated. This means we can store patterns or parts of patterns in variables. Exactly what gets matched will be determined when the program is run—patterns need not be hard-coded.

The following program illustrates this concept. It asks the user for a pattern, then tests to see if the pattern matches our string. We can use this program throughout the chapter to help test the various styles of pattern we'll be looking at.

```
#!/usr/bin/perl
# matchtest.pl

use warnings;
use strict;

$_ = q("I wonder what the Entish is for 'yes' and 'no'," he thought.);
# Tolkien, Lord of the Rings

print "Enter some text to find: ";
my $pattern = <STDIN>;
chomp($pattern);

if (/$pattern/) {
    print "The text matches the pattern '$pattern'.\n";
} else {
    print "'$pattern' was not found.\n";
}
```

Now we can test a few things:

```
$ perl matchtest.pl
Enter some text to find: wonder
The text matches the pattern 'wonder'.

$ perl matchtest.pl
Enter some text to find: entish
```

'entish' was not found.

```
$ perl matchtest.pl
Enter some text to find: hough
The text matches the pattern 'hough'.

$ perl matchtest.pl
Enter some text to find: and 'no',
The text matches the pattern 'and 'no''.
```

matchtest.pl has its basis in these three lines:

```
my $pattern = <STDIN>;
chomp($pattern);

if (/$pattern/) {
```

First we take a line of text from the user. Since it will end in a newline and we don't necessarily want to find a newline in our pattern, we chomp() it off. Then we do our test.

Since we're not using the =~ operator, the test will be looking at the variable $_. The regular expression is /$pattern/; the variable $pattern is interpolated into the regex, just as it would be in the double-quoted string "$pattern". Hence, the regular expression is purely and simply whatever the user typed in, once we have removed the newline.

Metacharacters and Escaping

Of course, regular expressions can be more than just words and spaces. The rest of this chapter will discuss the various ways we can specify more advanced matches—where portions of the match are allowed to be any one of a set of characters, for instance, or where the match must occur at a certain position in the string. To do this, we'll describe the special meanings given to certain characters—called *metacharacters*—looking at what these meanings are and what sort of things we can express with them.

At this stage, though, we might not want to use their special meanings; we may want to literally match the characters themselves. As you've already seen with double-quoted strings, we can use a backslash to escape these characters' special meanings. So, if you want to match ... in the preceding text, your pattern needs to say \.\.\.. For example:

```
$ perl matchtest.pl
Enter some text to find: Ent+
The text matches the pattern 'Ent+'.

$ perl matchtest.pl
Enter some text to find: Ent\+
'Ent\+' was not found.
```

We'll see later why the first one matched—due to the special meaning of +.

■ **Note** The following characters have special meaning within a regular expression. You therefore need to backslash these characters whenever you want to use them literally.

. * ? + [( ) { ^ $ | \

All other characters automatically assume their literal meanings.

You can also turn off the special meanings using the escape sequence \Q. After Perl sees \Q, the 12 special characters shown in the preceding note will automatically assume their ordinary, literal meanings. This remains the case until Perl sees either \E or the end of the pattern.

For instance, if we wanted to adapt our matchtest.pl program to look for just literal strings instead of regular expressions, we could change it to look like this:

```
if (/\Q$pattern\E/) {
```

Now the meaning of + is turned off:

```
$ perl matchtest.pl
Enter some text to find: Ent+
'Ent+' was not found.
$
```

Note in particular that all \Q does is turn off the regular expression magic of those 12 characters shown earlier—it doesn't stop, for example, variable interpolation.

■ **Tip** Don't forget to change this back again: we'll be using matchtest.pl throughout this chapter to demonstrate the regular expressions we look at, so we'll need the normal metacharacter behavior!

Anchors

So far, our patterns have tried to find a match anywhere in the string. The first way we'll extend our regular expressions is by telling Perl where the match must occur. We can say "These characters must match the beginning of the string" or "This text must be at the end of the string." We do this by *anchoring* the match to either end.

The two anchors we use are ^, which appears at the beginning of the pattern, anchoring a match to the beginning of the string; and $, which comes at the end of the pattern, anchoring it to the end of the string. So, to see if our quotation ends in a period—and remember that the period is a metacharacter—we say something like this:

```
$ perl matchtest.pl
Enter some text to find: \.$
The text matches the pattern '\.$'.
```

That's a period (which we've escaped to prevent it from being treated as a metacharacter) and a dollar sign at the end of our pattern—to show that the pattern must match the end of the string.

■ **Note** We suggest that you to get into the habit of reading out regular expressions in English—break them into pieces and say what each piece does. Remember to say that each piece must immediately follow the other in the string in order to match. For instance, the preceding regex could be read "Match a period immediately followed by the end of the string." Similarly, the regex "Ent" is read as "Match an uppercase 'E' immediately followed by a lowercase 'n' immediately followed by a lowercase 't'."

If you can get into this habit, you'll find that reading and understanding regular expressions becomes a lot easier, and that you'll be able to "translate" back into Perl more naturally as well.

Here's another example: do we have a capital "I" at the beginning of the string?

```
$ perl matchtest.pl
Enter some text to find: ^I
'^I' was not found.
$
```

We use ^ to mean "beginning of the string," followed by an "I". In our case, though, the character at the beginning of the string is a ", so our pattern does not match. If you know that what you're looking for can only occur at the beginning or the end of the string, it's far more efficient to use anchors; instead of searching through the entire string to see whether the match succeeded, Perl needs to look at only a small portion, and can give up immediately if the match fails on the very first character.

Let's see if we can match "I at the beginning of the string:

```
$ perl matchtest.pl
Enter some text to find: ^"I
The text matches the pattern '^"I'.
$
```

Let's see one more example of this, where we'll combine looking for matches with looking through the lines in a file.

Imagine yourself as a poor poet. In fact, not just poor, but downright bad—so bad you can't even think of a rhyme for "pink." So, what do you do? You do what every sensible poet does in this situation, and you write the following Perl program:

```
#!/usr/bin/perl
# rhyming.pl

use warnings;
use strict;

my $syllable = "ink";

while (<>) {
    print if /$syllable$/;
}
```

We can now feed it a file of words, and find those that end in "ink":

```
$ perl rhyming.pl wordlist.txt
bethink
blink
bobolink
brink
clink
$
```

■ **Tip** For a really thorough result, you would need to use a file containing every word in the dictionary. Be prepared for a bit of a wait if you do this, though! For this example, however, any text-based file will do (though it will help if it is in English). A bobolink, in case you're wondering, is a migratory American songbird, otherwise known as a ricebird or reedbird.

Let's look at this code in detail. First, we see the following:

```
while (<>) {
    print if /$syllable$/;
}
```

The first thing to note are the <> characters within the `while` loop parentheses. We will talk about the <> in detail in the next chapter, but briefly, <> reads from either of two places: from one or more files specified on the command line (here `wordlist.txt`) or from standard input if there are no files on the command line. The data is read into `$_` one line at a time, and this continues by default until all input has been read. We test each line of the file read into `$_` to see if it matches the pattern, which is our syllable, "ink", anchored to the end of the line (with $). If so, we print it out. Recall that `print()` defaults to printing `$_`.

The important thing to note here is that Perl treats the "ink" as the last thing on the line, even though there is a newline at the end of `$_`. Regular expressions typically ignore the last newline in a string—we'll look at this behavior in more detail later.

Shortcuts and Options

This is all very well if you know exactly what it is you're trying to find, but matching patterns means more than just locating exact strings of text—you may want to find a three-digit number, the first word on the line, four or more letters all in capitals, and so on.

You can do this using *character classes*—these aren't just individual characters, but a pattern that signifies that any one of a *set* of characters is acceptable. To specify such a pattern, you put the characters you consider acceptable inside square brackets. Let's go back to our `matchtest.pl` program, using the same test string:

```
$_ = q("I wonder what the Entish is for 'yes' and 'no'," he thought.);
```

```
$ perl matchtest.pl
Enter some text to find: w[aoi]nder
The text matches the pattern 'w[aoi]nder'.
$
```

What have we done? We've tested whether the string contains a "w", followed by either an "a", an "o", or an "i", followed by "nder"; in effect, we're looking for either of "wander", "wonder", or "winder". Since the string contains "wonder", the pattern is matched.

Conversely, we can say that all characters are acceptable *except* a given sequence of characters—we can "negate the character class." To do this, the first character inside the square brackets should be a ^, like so:

```
$ perl matchtest.pl
Enter some text to find: th[^eo]
'th[^eo]' was not found.
$
```

So, we're looking for "th" followed by any character that is neither an "e" nor an "o". But all we have is "the" and "thought", so this pattern does not match.

If the characters you wish to match form a sequence in the character set you're using, you can use a hyphen to specify a range of characters rather than spelling out the entire range. For instance, the numerals can be represented by the character class [0-9]. A lowercase letter can be matched with [a-z]. Let's see if there are any numeric characters in our quote:

```
$ perl matchtest.pl
Enter some text to find: [0-9]
'[0-9]' was not found.
$
```

You can use one or more of these ranges alongside other characters in a character class, so long as they stay inside the brackets. If you want to match a digit followed immediately by a letter from A through F, you would say [0-9][A-F]. However, to match a single hexadecimal digit, you'd write [0-9A-F], or [0-9A-Fa-f] if you wished to include lowercase letters. (You could also accomplish that by using the /i case-insensitive regexp modifier discussed earlier

161

in this chapter.) Finally, if you want a hyphen to itself be one of the matchable characters of the set, you should specify it as the very first character inside the square brackets (or the first character following an initial ^ negator). This will prevent Perl from interpreting the hyphen as indicating a character range.

Some character classes are going to come up again and again: digits, word characters, and the various types of whitespace. Perl provides some neat shortcuts for these. Table 7-1 lists the most common shortcuts and what they represent, and Table 7-2 lists the corresponding negative forms of the shortcuts.

Table 7-1. *Predefined Character Classes*

Shortcut	Expansion	Description
\d	[0-9]	Digits 0 to 9
\w	[0-9A-Za-z_]	A "word" character (allowable, for example, in a Perl variable name)
\s	[\t\n\r\f]	A whitespace character—that is, a space, tab, newline, carriage return, or formfeed

Table 7-2. *Negative Predefined Character Classes*

Shortcut	Expansion	Description
\D	[^0-9]	Any nondigit
\W	[^0-9A-Za-z_]	Any non"word" character
\S	[^ \t\n\r\f]	Any non-whitespace character

So, if we wanted to see if there was a five-letter word in the sentence, you might think we could do this:

```
$ perl matchtest.pl
Enter some text to find: \w\w\w\w\w
The text matches the pattern '\w\w\w\w\w'.
$
```

But that isn't correct—there are no five-letter words in the sentence! The problem is that we've asked for five letters in a row, and any word with *at least* five letters in a row will match that pattern. We actually matched "wonde", which was the first possible series of five letters in a row. To actually get a five-letter word, we might consider deciding that the word must appear in the middle of the sentence—that is, in between two spaces:

```
$ perl matchtest.pl
Enter some text to find: \s\w\w\w\w\w\s
'\s\w\w\w\w\w\s' was not found.
$
```

Word Boundaries

The problem with that is, when we're looking at text, words aren't always between two spaces. They can be followed by or preceded by punctuation, or appear at the beginning or end of a string, or otherwise next to nonword characters. To help us properly search for words in these cases, Perl provides the special \b metacharacter. The interesting thing about \b is that it doesn't match any actual character—rather, it matches the point between something that isn't a word character (either \W or one of the ends of the string) and something that is a word character—hence \b for boundary. So, for example, to look for one-letter words:

```
$ perl matchtest.pl
Enter some text to find: \s\w\s
'\s\w\s' was not found.
```

```
$ perl matchtest.pl
Enter some text to find: \b\w\b
The text matches the pattern '\b\w\b'.
```

As the "I" was preceded by a quotation mark, a space wouldn't match it—but a word boundary does the job. Later, we'll see how to tell Perl how many repetitions of a character or group of characters we want to match without spelling it out directly.

What, then, if we wanted to match anything at all? You might consider something like [\w\W] or [\s\S], for instance. Actually, matching any character is quite a common operation, so Perl provides an easy way to specify it: the period metacharacter, which by default matches any character except \n. What if we want to match an "r" followed by two characters—any two characters—followed by an "h"?

```
$ perl matchtest.pl
Enter some text to find: r..h
The text matches the pattern 'r..h'.
$
```

Is there anything after the period?

```
$ perl matchtest.pl
Enter some text to find: \..
'\..' was not found.
$
```

What's that? One backslashed period to match an actual period character, followed by an unescaped period to mean "match any character but \n."

Alternatives

Instead of specifying a set of acceptable individual characters, you may want to say "Match either this or that multi-character sequence." The *either-or* operator | within a regular expression behaves like Perl's bitwise *or* operator, |. So, to match either "yes" or "maybe" in our example, we could say this:

```
$ perl matchtest.pl
Enter some text to find: yes|maybe
The text matches the pattern 'yes|maybe'.
$
```

That's either "yes" or "maybe"—but what if we wanted either "yes" or "yet"? To get alternatives for part of an expression, we need to group the options. In a regular expression, grouping is always done with parentheses:

```
$ perl matchtest.pl
Enter some text to find: ye(s|t)
The text matches the pattern 'ye(s|t)'.
$
```

If we had forgotten the parentheses and written `yes|t`, Perl would have tried to match either "yes" or "t". In this case, we'd still get a positive match, but it wouldn't be what we want—we'd get a match for "yes" and also for any string with a "t" in it, whether the word "yes" or "yet" was there or not.

You can match either "this" or "that" or "the other" by adding more alternatives:

```
$ perl matchtest.pl
Enter some text to find: this|that|the other
'this|that|the other' was not found.
$
```

However, in this case, it's more efficient to separate out the common elements:

```
$ perl matchtest.pl
Enter some text to find: th(is|at|e other)
'th(is|at|e other)' was not found.
$
```

You can also nest alternatives. Suppose you want to match either of the following patterns:

- "the" followed by whitespace or a lowercase letter

- "or"

You might include something like this:

```
$ perl matchtest.pl
Enter some text to find: (the(\s|[a-z]))|or
The text matches the pattern '(the(\s|[a-z]))|or'.
$
```

It looks fearsome, but let's break it down into its components: our two alternatives are

- the(\s|[a-z])

- or

The second part is easy, while the first contains "the" followed by two alternatives: `\s` and `[a-z]`. That is, "the" followed by either a whitespace or a lowercase letter, or "or". We can, in fact, tidy this up a little by replacing (`\s|[a-z]`) with the less cluttered [`\sa-z`]. We thus eliminate the need for the nested grouping.

```
$ perl matchtest.pl
Enter some text to find: (the[\sa-z])|or
The text matches the pattern '(the[\sa-z])|or'.
$
```

Repetition with Quantifiers

We've already moved from matching a specific character to matching a more general *type* of character—when we don't know (or don't care) exactly what the character will be. Now we're going to see what happens when we want to match a more general *quantity* of characters: four or more consecutive digits, for example, or two to four capital letters, and so on. The metacharacters that we use in a Perl regexp to match zero or more repeating characters (or other sequences) are called *quantifiers*.

Indefinite Repetition

The simplest of these is the question mark. It should suggest uncertainty—something may be there, or it may not. And that's exactly what it does: stating that the immediately preceding character(s)—or metacharacter(s)—may appear once, or not at all. It's a good way of saying that a particular character or group is optional. To match the words "he" or "she", you can use the following:

```
$ perl matchtest.pl
Enter some text to find: \bs?he\b
The text matches the pattern '\bs?he\b'.
$
```

■ **Note** A quantifier modifies the character or group immediately to its left. Therefore, in the preceding example the ? applies only to the preceding "s".

To make not just one character but an entire series of characters (or metacharacters) optional, group them in parentheses as before. Did he say "what the Entish is" or "what the Entish word is"? Either will do:

```
$ perl matchtest.pl
Enter some text to find: what the Entish (word )?is
The text matches the pattern 'what the Entish (word )?is'.
$
```

Notice that we had to put the space inside the group; otherwise we end up trying to match two mandatory spaces between "Entish" and "is", and our text only has one:

```
$ perl matchtest.pl
Enter some text to find: what the Entish (word)? is
'what the Entish (word)? is' was not found.
$
```

As well as matching something one or zero times, you can also match something one or more times. We do this with the plus sign. To match an entire word without specifying how long it should be, you can say:

```
$ perl matchtest.pl
Enter some text to find: \b\w+\b
The text matches the pattern '\b\w+\b'.
$
```

In this case, we match the first available word—"I".

If, on the other hand, you have something that may be there any number of times but also might not be there at all—zero or one or many—you need what's called *Kleene's star*: the * quantifier. So, how would you find a capital letter after any number of spaces (even no spaces) at the start of the string? Specify your regex as the start of the string, followed by any number of whitespace characters, followed by an uppercase letter:

```
$ perl matchtest.pl
Enter some text to find: ^\s*[A-Z]
'^\s*[A-Z]' was not found.
$
```

Of course, our test string begins with a quotation mark, so the preceding pattern won't match; but, sure enough, if you take away that first quote, the pattern will match fine.

Table 7-3 summarizes the three quantifiers just covered.

Table 7-3. Quantifier Examples

Quantifier	Description
/bea?t/	0 or 1 times, matches either "beat" or "bet"
/bea+t/	1 or more times, matches "beat", "beaat", "beaaat" . . .
/bea*t/	0 or more times, matches "bet", "beat", "beaat" . . .

Novice Perl programmers tend to go to town on combinations of dot and star and the results often surprise them, particularly when it comes to search-and-replace operations (to be discussed soon). We'll explain the rules of the regular expression engine shortly.

You should also consider the fact that .* and .+ within a regular expression will match as much of your string as they possibly can. We'll look more at this "greedy" behavior later on.

Well-Defined Repetition

If you want to be more precise about how many times a character or groups of characters might be repeated, you can specify the maximum and minimum number of repeats in curly braces. For example, "match 2 or 3 white space characters" can be written as follows:

```
$ perl matchtest.pl
Enter some text to find: \s{2,3}
'\s{2,3}' was not found.
$
```

So there are no doubled or tripled white space characters in our string. Notice how we construct that—the minimum, a comma, and the maximum, all inside curly braces. Omitting the maximum signifies "or more." For example, {2,} denotes "2 or more." In these cases, the same warnings apply as for the star operator.

Finally, you can specify a precise number of repetitions simply by putting that number inside the curly braces. Here's the five-letter-word example tidied up a bit:

```
$ perl matchtest.pl
Enter some text to find: \b\w{5}\b
'\b\w{5}\b' was not found.
$
```

Summary Table

To refresh your memory, Table 7-4 lists the various metacharacters we've seen so far.

Table 7-4. Metacharacter Summary

Metacharacter	Meaning
[abc]	Any one of the characters a, b, or c
[^abc]	Any one character other than a, b, or c
[a-z]	Any one ASCII lowercase character between a and z
\d \D	A digit; a nondigit
\w \W	A "word" character; a non"word" character
\s \S	A whitespace character; a non-whitespace character
\b	The boundary between a \w character and a \W character
.	Any character (except newline)
(abc)	The phrase abc as a group
?	Preceding character or group may be present 0 or 1 times
+	Preceding character or group is present 1 or more times
*	Preceding character or group may be present 0 or more times
{x,y}	Preceding character or group is present between x and y times
{x,}	Preceding character or group is present at least x times
{x}	Preceding character or group is present x times

Memory and Backreferences

What if we want to know what a certain regular expression matched? It was easy when we were matching literal strings: we knew that "Case" was going to match those four letters and nothing else—but now, what's matching? If we have /\w{3}/, which three word characters are getting matched?

Perl has a series of special variables in which it stores anything that's matched within a group in parentheses. Each time it sees a set of parentheses, it *triggers memory* and copies the matched text inside into a numbered variable—the first matched group is stored in $1, the second group in $2, and so on. By looking at these variables, which we call the *backreference* variables, we can see what triggered various parts of our match, and we can also extract portions of the data for later use.

First, though, let's rewrite our test program so that we can see what's in those variables.

```
#!/usr/bin/perl
# matchtest2.pl

use warnings;
use strict;

$_ = '1: A silly sentence (495,a) *BUT* one which will be useful. (3)';

print "Enter a regular expression: ";
my $pattern = <STDIN>;
chomp($pattern);

if (/$pattern/) {
    print "The text matches the pattern '$pattern'.\n";
    print "\$1 is '$1'\n" if defined $1;
    print "\$2 is '$2'\n" if defined $2;
    print "\$3 is '$3'\n" if defined $3;
    print "\$4 is '$4'\n" if defined $4;
    print "\$5 is '$5'\n" if defined $5;
} else {
    print "'$pattern' was not found.\n";
}
```

■ **Tip** Note that we use a backslash to escape the first "dollar" symbol in each print() statement—thus displaying the actual $ character—while leaving the second dollar symbol in each line unescaped, to display the contents of the corresponding variable.

We have our special variables in place, and we have a new sentence on which to do our matching. Let's see what's been happening:

```
$ perl matchtest2.pl
Enter a regular expression: ([a-z]+)
The text matches the pattern '([a-z]+)'.
$1 is 'silly'

$ perl matchtest2.pl
Enter a regular expression: (\w+)
The text matches the pattern '(\w+)'.
$1 is '1'

$ perl matchtest2.pl
Enter a regular expression: ([a-z]+)(.*)([a-z]+)
The text matches the pattern '([a-z]+)(.*)([a-z]+)'.
$1 is 'silly'
$2 is ' sentence (495,a) *BUT* one which will be usefu'
$3 is 'l'

$ perl matchtest2.pl
Enter a regular expression: e(\w|n\w+)
The text matches the pattern 'e(\w|n\w+)'.
$1 is 'n'
```

By printing out what's in each of the groups, we can see exactly what caused Perl to start and stop matching, and when. If you look carefully at these results, you'll find they can tell you a great deal about how Perl goes about handling regular expressions.

How the Regular Expression Engine Works

We've seen most of the syntax behind regular expression matching, and plenty of examples of it in action. The code that does all the regex work is called Perl's *regular expression engine*. You might be wondering about the exact rules applied by this engine when determining whether or not a piece of text matches, and how much of it matches. From what the examples have shown, let's make some deductions about the engine's operation.

Our first expression, ([a-z]+), plucked out a set of one or more lowercase letters. The first such set that Perl came across was "silly". The next character after "y" was a space, and so no longer matched the expression.

- *Rule 1*: Once the engine starts matching, it will keep matching a character at a time for as long as it can. As soon as it sees something that doesn't match, however, it has to stop. In this example, it can never get beyond a character that is not a lowercase letter. It musts stop as soon as it encounters one.

Next, we looked for a series of word characters using (\w+). The engine started looking at the beginning of the string, and found one, "1". The next character was not a word character (it was a colon), and so the engine had to stop.

- *Rule 2*: The engine is *eager*. It's eager to start work and eager to finish, and it starts matching as soon as possible in the string; if the first character doesn't match, it tries to start matching from the second. Then, it takes every opportunity to finish as quickly as possible.

Then we tried this: ([a-z]+)(.*)([a-z]+). The result we got with this was a little strange. Let's look at it again:

```
$ perl matchtest2.pl
Enter a regular expression: ([a-z]+)(.*)([a-z]+)
The text matches the pattern '([a-z]+)(.*)([a-z]+)'.
$1 is 'silly'
$2 is ' sentence (495,a) *BUT* one which will be usefu'
$3 is 'l'
$
```

Our first group was the same as what matched before—nothing new there. When we could no longer match lowercase letters, we switched to matching anything we could. Now, this *could* take up the rest of the string, but that wouldn't allow a match for the third group—we have to leave at least one lowercase letter.

So, the engine started to backtrack along the string, giving up characters one by one. It gave up the closing parenthesis, the 3, then the opening parenthesis, and so on, until we got to the first thing that would satisfy all the groups and let the match go ahead—namely a lowercase letter: the "l" at the end of "useful".

From this, we can draw up the third rule:

- *Rule 3*: The engine is *greedy*. If you use the +, *, or ? operators, they will try and consume as much of the string as possible. If the rest of the expression does not match, it grudgingly gives up a character at a time and tries to match again, in order to find the longest possible match.

We can turn a greedy match into a non-greedy match by putting the ? operator after either the plus, star, or question mark. For instance, let's turn this example into a non-greedy version: ([a-z]+)(.*?)([a-z]+). This gives us an entirely different result:

```
$ perl matchtest2.pl
Enter a regular expression: ([a-z]+)(.*?)([a-z]+)
The text matches the pattern '([a-z]+)(.*?)([a-z]+)'.
$1 is 'silly'
$2 is ' '
```

```
$3 is 'sentence'
$
```

Now that we've shut off rule 3, rule 2 takes over: the smallest possible match for the second group was a single space. First, it tried to match nothing at all, but then the third group would be faced with a space—this wouldn't match. So, the regex engine grudgingly accepts the space and again tries to finish—this time the third group has some lowercase letters, and that can match as well.

Now suppose we turn off greediness in all three groups, and say this: ([a-z]+?)(.*?)([a-z]+?):

```
$ perl matchtest2.pl
Enter a regular expression: ([a-z]+?)(.*?)([a-z]+?)
The text matches the pattern '([a-z]+?)(.*?)([a-z]+?)'.
$1 is 's'
$2 is ''
$3 is 'i'
$
```

What about this? The smallest possible match for the first group is the "s" of "silly"—we asked it to find one character or more, and so the smallest it could find was one. The second group actually matched no characters at all. This left the third group facing an "i", which it accepted to complete the match.

Our last example included an alternation:

```
$ perl matchtest2.pl
Enter a regular expression: e(\w|n\w+)
The text matches the pattern 'e(\w|n\w+)'.
$1 is 'n'
$
```

The engine took the first branch of the alternation and matched a single character, even though the second branch would actually satisfy greed. This leads us to the fourth rule:

- *Rule 4*: The regular expression engine *hates decisions*. If there are two branches, it will always choose the first one, even though the second one might allow it to gain a longer match.

To summarize: the regular expression engine starts as soon as it can, grabs as much as it can, then tries to finish as soon as it can, while always taking the first decision available to it.

Working with Regexes

Now that we've matched a string, what do we do with it? Sometimes it's useful just to know whether or not a string matches a given pattern. On the other hand, we often want to perform search-and-replace operations on text, and we'll explain how to do that here. We'll also cover some of the more advanced features of regular expression processing.

Substitution

Now that we know all about matching text, substitution is very easy. Why? Because all of the cleverness is in the search part, rather than the replace—all the character classes, quantifiers, and so on only make sense when matching. You can't substitute, say, a word with any number of digits. So, all we need to do is take the "old" text—our match— and tell Perl the text that we want to replace it. This we do with the s/// operator.

The s stands for "substitute." Between the first two slashes, we put our regular expression as before. Before the final slash, we put our replacement text. Just as with matching, we can perform the substitution on an explicitly specified string by using the =~ operator . Otherwise, the substitution is performed on the default variable $_.

```
#!/usr/bin/perl
# subst1.pl
```

```
use warnings;
use strict;
s
$_ = "Awake! Awake! Fear, Fire, Foes! Awake! Fire, Foes! Awake!";
# Tolkien, Lord of the Rings

s/Foes/Flee/;
print $_,"\n";
```

```
$ perl subst1.pl
Awake! Awake! Fear, Fire, Flee! Awake! Fire, Foes! Awake!
$
```

Here we have replaced the first occurrence of "Foes" with the word "Flee". Had we wanted instead to change *every* occurrence, we would have needed to use a regex modifier. Just as the /i modifier we saw earlier matches upper and lower case, the /g modifier on a substitution acts globally:

```
#!/usr/bin/perl
# subst2.pl

use warnings;
use strict;

$_ = "Awake! Awake! Fear, Fire, Foes! Awake! Fire, Foes! Awake!";
# Tolkien, Lord of the Rings

s/Foes/Flee/g;
print $_,"\n";
```

```
$ perl subst2.pl
Awake! Awake! Fear, Fire, Flee! Awake! Fire, Flee! Awake!
$
```

Like the left-hand side of the substitution, the right-hand side behaves like a double-quoted string in that it, too, is subject to variable interpolation. Especially useful is that we can use the backreference variables we collected during the match on the right-hand side. So, for instance, to swap the first two words in a string, we would say something like this:

```
#!/usr/bin/perl
# subst3.pl

use warnings;
use strict;

$_ = "there are two major products that come out of Berkeley: LSD and UNIX";
# Jeremy Anderson

s/(\w+)\s+(\w+)/$2 $1/;
print $_, "?\n";
```

```
$ perl subst3.pl
are there two major products that come out of Berkeley: LSD and UNIX?
$
```

What would happen if we tried doing that globally? Let's do it and see:

```
#!/usr/bin/perl
# subst4.pl
```

```
use warnings;
use strict;

$_ = "there are two major products that come out of Berkeley: LSD and UNIX";
# Jeremy Anderson

s/(\w+)\s+(\w+)/$2 $1/g;
print $_, "?\n";
```

```
$ perl subst4.pl
are there major two that products out come Berkeley of: and LSD UNIX?
$
```

Here, every word in a pair is swapped with its neighbor—when processing a global match, Perl always starts where the previous match left off.

Changing Delimiters

You may have noticed that // and s/// resemble the operators q// and qq//. Just as with q// and qq//, we can change the delimiters when matching and substituting to increase the readability of our regular expressions. The same rules apply: any nonword character can be the delimiter, and paired delimiters such as <>, (), {}, and [] may be used—with two provisos.

First, if you change the delimiters on //, you must put an m in front of it ("m" for "match"). This is so that Perl can still recognize it as a regular expression, rather than a block or comment or anything else. Thus,

```
/^\s*[A-Z]/;
```

can be written as follows, explicitly including the m operator

```
m/^\s*[A-Z]/;
```

and using alternative delimiters, can be written as

```
m#^\s*[A-Z]#;
```

Second, if you use paired delimiters with the substitution operator, you must use two pairs.

```
s/old text/new text/g;
```

becomes

```
s{old text}{new text}g;
```

You may, however, leave spaces or newlines between the pairs for the sake of clarity:

```
s{old text}
 {new text}g;
```

Also, they can be different pairs:

```
s{old text}(new text)g;
```

The prime example of when you would want to do this is when you are dealing with file paths, which contain a lot of slashes. For instance, if you are moving files on your Unix system from /usr/local/share/ to /usr/share/, you may want to munge[1] the filenames like this:

```
s/\/usr\/local\/share\//\/usr\/share\//g;
```

However, the substitution is far easier to read if alternative delimiters are used in this case:

```
s#/usr/local/share/#/usr/share/#g;
```

Modifiers

We've already seen the /i modifier being used to indicate that the match should be case insensitive. We've also seen the /g modifier applied to a substitution to make it global. What other modifiers are there?

- /m: Treats the string as multiple lines. Normally, ^ and $ will match only the very start and very end of a string. But if the /m modifier is specified, then ^ and $ will match the start and end of each individual line in the string (separated by \n). For example, given the string "one\ntwo", the pattern /^two$/ will not match, but /^two$/m will.

- /s: Treats the string as a single line. Normally, . does not match a newline character. But when /s is given, it will.

- /g: In addition to making a substitution global, this modifier allows us to match multiple times. When using this modifier, placing the \G anchor at the beginning of the regex will anchor it to the end point of the last match.

- /x: Allows the use of whitespace and comments inside a match.

Regular expressions can get quite difficult to read. The /x modifier helps make the regex more readable. For instance, if you're matching a string in a log file that contains a time followed by a computer name in square brackets and then a message, the expression you'll create to extract the information could easily end up looking like this:

```
# Time in $1, machine name in $2, text in $3
/^([0-2]\d:[0-5]\d:[0-5]\d)\s+\[([^\]]+)\]\s+(.*)$/
```

However, if you use the /x modifier, you can stretch it out as follows:

```
/
^              # Match at the beginning of the string
(              # First group: time
   [0-2]\d
   :
   [0-5]\d
   :
   [0-5]\d
   )
   \s+
   \[          # Square bracket
   (           # Second group: machine name
   [^\]]+      # Anything that isn't a square bracket
```

_____

[1] Most dictionaries define munge to be a derogatory term for imperfectly transforming data. But in the Perl culture, munge is not derogatory—being able to transform data, even if imperfectly, is one thing that Perl programmers aspire to.

```
    )
    \]          # End square bracket

    \s+
    (           # Third group: everything else
    .*
    )
    $           # Finally, match the end of the string
/x
```

Another way to tidy this up is to put each of the groups into variables and interpolate them:

```
my $time_re = '([0-2]\d:[0-5]\d:[0-5]\d)';
my $host_re = '\[([^\]]+)\]';
my $mess_re = '(.*)';

/^$time_re\s+$host_re\s+$mess_re$/;
```

The split() Function

We briefly saw `split()` earlier in this chapter, where we used it to break up a string into a list of words. In fact, we saw it only in its simplest form, and strictly speaking, it was a bit of a cheat to use it—we didn't see it then, but behind the scenes `split()` was actually using a regular expression to do its work.

Using `split()` without arguments is equivalent to saying

```
split /\s+/, $_
```

which breaks the default string `$_` into a list of substrings using one or more whitespace characters as the delimiter. However, you can also specify your own regular expression: Perl advances through the string, breaking it at each point where the regex matches. The text matching the delimiter is thrown away.

For example, configuration files on the Unix operating system often consist of lines of colon-separated text fields. A sample line from the `/etc/passwd` file might look like this:

```
kake:x:10018:10020::/home/kake:/bin/bash
```

To get at each field, we can split the line on its colons:

```
#!/usr/bin/perl
# split.pl

use warnings;
use strict;

my $passwd = "kake:x:10018:10020::/home/kake:/bin/bash";
my @fields = split /:/, $passwd;
print "Login name : $fields[0]\n";
print "User ID : $fields[2]\n";
print "Home directory : $fields[5]\n";
```

```
$ perl split.pl
Login name : kake
User ID : 10018
```

```
Home directory : /home/kake
$
```

Note that the fifth field, stored in $fields[4] (zero-based indexing), is the empty string, because Perl recognized that there were two adjacent delimiter characters (colons). The field is empty, and the array element is thus the empty string. Therefore, $fields[5] contains /home/kake. Be careful though—if the line you are splitting contains trailing empty fields on the *right*, they will be dropped; no empty array elements will be created for them by split().

The join() Function

To perform the reverse operation, we can use the join() function, which takes a specified delimiter and "glues" it between the elements of a list. For example:

```
#!/usr/bin/perl
# join.pl

use warnings;
use strict;

my $passwd = "kake:x:10018:10020::/home/kake:/bin/bash";
my @fields = split /:/, $passwd;
print "Login name : $fields[0]\n";
print "User ID : $fields[2]\n";
print "Home directory : $fields[5]\n";

my $passwd2 = join "#", @fields;
print "Original password : $passwd\n";
print "New password :      $passwd2\n";
```

```
$ perl join.pl
Login name : kake
User ID : 10018
Home directory : /home/kake
Original password : kake:x:10018:10020::/home/kake:/bin/bash
New password :      kake#x#10018#10020##/home/kake#/bin/bash
$
```

Common Blunders

There are a few common mistakes people tend to make when writing regular expressions—for instance, /a*b*c*/ will happily match any string at all, since it matches each letter zero times. What else can go wrong?

- Forgetting to group:

  /Bam{2}/ will match "Bamm", while /(Bam){2}/ will match "BamBam", so be careful when choosing which one to use. The same goes for alternation: /Simple|on/ will match "Simple" and "on", while /Sim(ple|on)/ will match both "Simple" and "Simon"—group each option separately.

- Getting the anchors wrong:

  ^ goes at the beginning, $ goes at the end. A dollar sign anywhere else in the string makes Perl try to interpolate a variable.

175

- Forgetting to escape metacharacters:

    If you want a special character to simply represent itself instead of acting as a metacharacter, you must escape it with a backslash. Beware the following characters: . * ? + [( ) { ^ $ | and, of course, \ itself.

- Indexing from 1 instead of from 0:

    The first element in an array is assigned the index 0, while index 1 refers to the second element.

- Counting from 0 instead of from 1:

    Yes, all along we've been telling you that computers start counting from 0. (See the previous item in this list.) Nevertheless, there's always the odd exception—the first backreference is $1, while $0 has another special use—a string containing the way in which the program was executed.

Backreferences (Again)

Finally, in our tour of regular expressions, let's look again at backreferences. Suppose you want to find any repeated words in a string—how would you do it? You might want to try this:

```
if (/\b(\w+) $1\b/) {
    print "Repeated word: $1\n";
}
```

But that doesn't work, because $1 is set only after the match is complete. In fact, if you have Perl warnings turned on, you'll be alerted to the fact that $1 is undefined every time. To use a backreference while still inside the regular expression, you need to use the following syntax:

```
if (/\b(\w+) \1\b/) {
    print "Repeated word: $1\n";
}
```

However, when you're replacing, you'll get a warning if you try to use the \number syntax on the right side of a substitution. It will work, but you'll be told that \1 is better written as $1.

Summary

Regular expressions are quite possibly the most powerful means at your disposal for searching for patterns in text, extracting subpatterns, and replacing portions of text. They're at the heart of any text shuffling you do in Perl, and they should be your first port of call when you need to do string manipulation.

In this chapter, we've seen how to match simple text, different classes of text, and different amounts of text. We've also seen how to provide alternative matches, how to refer back to portions of the match, and how to substitute text.

The key to learning and understanding regular expressions is breaking them down into their component parts and unraveling the language, translating it piecewise into English. Once you can fluently read out the intention of a complex regular expression, you're well on your way to creating powerful matches of your own.

We have only scratched the surface of regular expressions in this chapter. There are so many features and so much power in regular expressions that an entire book could be written on the subject. As a matter of fact, that has already happened—*Regular Expression Recipes: A Problem-Solution Approach* by Nathan Good (Apress, 2004) and *Mastering Regular Expressions, Second Edition* by Jeffrey Friedl (O'Reilly & Associates, 2002). We suggest you check out these books for everything you need to know about regular expressions, and then some.

Exercises

1. Translate each of the following regular expressions into English:

   `/hello.*world/`

   `/^\d+\s\w*$/`

   `/\b[A-Z][a-z]*\b/`

   `/(.).*\1/`

2. Translate each of the following English statements into a regular expression:

   A digit at the beginning of the string and a digit at the end of the string

   A string that contains only whitespace characters or word characters

   A string containing no whitespace characters

3. Write a program that loops through the lines of a file or standard input (where each line contains a single word) and prints all words containing two adjacent vowels.

   Modify the preceding to instead match all words with exactly two vowels appearing anywhere within the word.

CHAPTER 8

■ ■ ■

Files and Data

We're starting to write real programs now, and real programs need to be able to read and write files from and to your hard drive. At the moment, all we can do is ask the user for input using <STDIN> and print data on the screen using print(). Pretty simple stuff, yes—but these two ideas actually form the basis of a great deal of the file handling you'll do in Perl.

What we want to do in this chapter is extend these techniques into reading from and writing to files using *filehandles*, and we'll also look at the other techniques we have for handling files and data, including the very useful diamond (<>).

Filehandles

A *filehandle* is a variable that you associate with a file, which allows you to then either read from the file or write to the file, depending on how the file was opened.

We've already seen a filehandle: the STDIN of <STDIN>. This is a filehandle for the special input stream *standard input*, and whenever we've used the idiom <STDIN> to read a line, we've been reading from standard input via the STDIN filehandle. Standard input is the input a user provides either directly by typing on the keyboard, or indirectly through the use of a "pipe" that, as we'll see later, pumps input into a program.

As a counterpart to standard input, there's also standard output: STDOUT. This is the exact opposite—it's the output we provide to a user, which we've been doing so far by writing to the screen; every time we've used the print() function so far, we've been implicitly using STDOUT. The line

```
print STDOUT "Hello, world!\n";
```

is just the same as our original example in Chapter 1. There's one more "standard" filehandle: standard error, or STDERR, which is where we write the error messages when we die().

The open() Function

The open() function opens files. The preferred way of executing open() is with three arguments: the filehandle we choose to associate with the file, the mode in which we are opening the file (read, write, or append), and the file name:

```
open(filehandle, mode, filename)
```

An example would be:

```
open(FH, '<', 'input.txt')
```

The left angle bracket indicates *read mode*. (We'll look at all the modes in more detail later.) It is also common to call the function with two arguments by combining the mode in the string that contains the file name:

```
open(filehandle, filename_with_mode)
```

Opening `input.txt` in this form would look like the following:

```
open(FH, '< input.txt')
```

This function returns true on success, false on failure. You should always handle a file-opening failure. Failing to open a file you expect to open is usually considered a severe error. We handle such errors by `die()`ing when the open fails. Recall from Chapter 2 that `die()` sends its argument (typically an error message explaining what went wrong) to standard error and then exits the program. Here's an example:

```
open(FH, $mode, $filename) or die $!;
```

What's `$!`? This is one of Perl's *special variables*, variables that have a special use or meaning within Perl. In the case of `$!`, Perl is passing on an error message from the system, and this error message should tell you why the `open()` failed: it's usually something like "No such file or directory" or "Permission denied." See `perldoc perlvar` for a complete list of all the special variables.

Filehandles are slightly different from the other variables we've seen, and they do not need to be declared with `my()`, even if you're using `strict` (as you should). It's traditional to use all capitals for filehandles to distinguish them from keywords.

You can provide the second and third arguments as variables or as string literals, like this:

```
open(FH, $mode, $file)    or die $!;
open(FH, '<', 'output.log') or die $!;
```

You can specify a full path to a file, but don't forget that if you're on Windows, a backslash in a double-quoted string introduces an escape character. So, for instance, you should say this:

```
open(FH, '<', 'c:\test\news.txt') or die $!;
```

rather than this:

```
open(FH, '<', "c:\test\news.txt") or die $!;
```

as `\t` in a double-quoted string is a tab, and `\n` is a newline. You could also say `"c:\\test\\news.txt"`, but that's a little hard to read. Recall that Windows allows forward slashes internally, and forward slashes do not need to be escaped, so `"c:/test/news.txt"` should work perfectly fine.

We will look at three different ways to open a file in just a couple of pages.

The close() Function

When you finish reading from or writing to a file, the filehandle should be closed. This is done with the `close()` function:

```
close(filehandle)
```

If you don't explicitly close a filehandle, it is not the end of the world. Perl will autoclose it for you. But it is considered good programming style to close files when you are finished with them.

Here is an example of opening and closing a file successfully:

```perl
#!/usr/bin/perl
# goodopen.pl

use warnings;
use strict;

open(FH, '<', 'goodopen.dat') or die $!;

print "goodopen.dat opened successfully\n";

close FH;
```

This example assumes, of course, that the file goodopen.dat exists in the current directory. If that is the case, here is the output of this program:

```
$ perl goodopen.pl
goodopen.dat opened successfully
$
```

Here is an example of opening a file that does not exist (assuming, of course, that badopen.dat does in fact not exist). Note the value of $!.

```perl
#!/usr/bin/perl
# badopen.pl

use warnings;
use strict;

open(FH, '<', 'badopen.dat') or die "We have a problem: $!";

print "Did we make it here?  Nope...\n";

close FH;
```

This is what happens when we attempt to execute this program:

```
$ perl badopen.pl
We have a problem: No such file or directory at badopen.pl line 7.
$
```

Recall that if the argument you give to die() does not end with a newline, Perl automatically adds the name of the program and the line number that had the problem. If you want to avoid this, remember to put newlines on the end of the string you pass to the die() function.

Three Ways to Open a File

In the sections below, we will discuss three ways of opening a file: read mode, write mode, and append mode. To start, here is a quick summary:

Opening a file in *read mode* provides read access only. You can read the contents of the file, but you can't change those file contents in any way.

Opening a file in *write mode* creates the file from scratch if it did not previously exist. If it did exist, the existing file is opened and truncated (emptied out). In either case, the only thing you can do is write entirely new contents to the file.

Opening a file in *append mode* also means that the file is opened for writing, but in this case, any previous file contents are preserved (not truncated), and you can then write new content to the end of the file. However, you can't change any of the file contents that were there already.

Read Mode

We often write programs that read input data from an external site, such as a file on disk. This can be any data that our program needs, such as a list of addresses or information to send out in an e-mail. When it's time to read that data in from a file, the file must first be opened in *read mode*, which means we can only read in from the file; we can't modify the contents of the file. In Perl, read mode is the default mode for opening a file.

If you attempt to open a file in read mode, the open() function will fail if the file does not exist or if you do not have permission to read it. Because read is the default mode, this example opens as read only:

```
open(FH, 'data.txt') or die $!;
```

You can explicitly open in read mode by using the left angle bracket (<) as the first character in the string that contains the file name:

```
open(FH, '<data.txt') or die $!;
```

Or, better yet, use the preferred three-argument syntax:

```
open(FH, '<', 'data.txt') or die $!;
```

If you attempt to open a file in read mode and the file does not exist, or if you don't have permission to read the file, the open() will fail. The file will not be opened, and the program will not have any access to the file whatsoever through the given filehandle.

Write Mode

Up to this point, our programs have printed text to standard output—the user's terminal. This is fine for some programs, but the data that is printed out is lost as soon as it is printed. Sometimes we want our program to generate output that can last beyond the execution of the program. If we want the output data to be accessible later, we can write the data out to a file that will be saved on disk. To do this, we open the file in *write mode*.

An important note: write mode will overwrite the file if it already exists. This means that the entire contents of the file will be lost and the file will start as empty. If you want to retain the contents of the file and add to them, the file should be opened in *append mode*, discussed in the next section.

You can open a file in write mode by using the right angle bracket (>) as the second argument to open() or as the first character of the string that contains the file name if you are using two-argument invocation. As noted, if you open a file in write mode and the file exists, the file will be overwritten and the contents lost. If you open a file in write mode and the file does not exist, it will be created. The open()

function will fail if you open in write mode and you don't have permission to create the file or write to it. Here is an example:

```
open(FH, '>', 'data.txt') or die $!;
```

Here is the same example using the two-argument version:

```
open(FH, '>data.txt') or die $!;
```

Append Mode

To write to the file and keep its current contents intact, open it in *append mode.* In append mode, the file is opened and *not* overwritten, and any output written to the file will be added to the bottom of the file.

A file can be opened in append mode by using two right angle brackets (>>) as the second argument (or in the string that contains the file name if you use the two-argument invocation). If you open a file in append mode and the file exists, you will add to the bottom of the file. If the file does not exist, it will be created. The open() function will fail if you do not have permission to create the file or if you do not have write permission to the file. Here is an example:

```
open(FH, '>>', 'data.txt') or die $!;
```

Or, using the two-argument version:

```
open(FH, '>>data.txt') or die $!;
```

Reading in Scalar Context

To read from a file opened in read mode, simply wrap the filehandle in angle brackets:

```
<FH>
```

We did this before when we read from standard input: <STDIN>. Just as with reading from standard input, there are two ways to read from any filehandle: scalar context and list context.

Scalar context reads the next line of the file, newline included:

```
$line = <FH>;
```

Here is an example of reading line by line through a file until end of file. Notice that <FH> is not assigned to a variable within the while loop parentheses; like <STDIN>, it is automatically assigned to $_:

```
while (<FH>) {
    # process the line
}
```

Now create this program, which reads through a file and prints each line of the file with the line number prepended:

```
#!/usr/bin/perl
# nl1.pl

use warnings;
use strict;
```

```perl
open(FILE, '<', 'nlexample.txt') or die $!;
my $lineno = 1;

while (<FILE>) {
    print $lineno++;
    print ": $_";
}

close FILE;
```

Next, create the file nlexample.txt with the following contents:

```
One day you're going to have to face
    A deep dark truthful mirror,
And it's gonna tell you things that I still
    Love you too much to say.
####### Elvis Costello, Spike, 1988 #######
```

This is what you should see when you run the program:

```
$ perl nl1.pl
1: One day you're going to have to face
2:     A deep dark truthful mirror,
3: And it's gonna tell you things that I still
4:     Love you too much to say.
5. ####### Elvis Costello, Spike, 1988 #######
$
```

Let's look at this program in detail. We begin by opening our file, making sure it was opened correctly.

```perl
open(FILE, '<', 'nlexample.txt') or die $!;
```

Since we expect the line numbers to start at 1, we initialize our counter as follows:

```perl
my $lineno = 1;
```

Now we read each line from the file in turn:

```perl
while (<FILE>) {
```

Recall that this syntax is actually equivalent to the following:

```perl
while (defined ($_ = <FILE>)) {
```

That is, we read a line from a file and assign it to $_, and we see whether it is defined. If it is, we do whatever's in the loop; if not, we are at the end of the file so we fall out of the loop. This gives us a nice, easy way of setting $_ to each line in turn.

As we have a new line of text, we print out its line number and advance the counter.

```perl
print $lineno++;
```

Finally, we print out the line in question:

```perl
print ": $_";
```

There's no need to add a newline since we didn't bother **chomp()**ing the incoming line. Of course, by using a statement modifier, we can make this program even more concise:

```
open(FILE, '<', 'nlexample.txt') or die $!;
my $lineno = 1;

print $lineno++, ": $_" while <FILE>;

close FILE;
```

But since we're going to want to expand the capabilities of our program—adding more operations to the body of the loop—we're probably better off with the original format.

Reading with the Diamond

Most of us who come from the Unix world have used the **sort** command (those of us in the Windows world have probably used its version of **sort** as well). If invoked with a command-line argument, **sort** treats the argument as a file name and reads from that file, sorting the content and printing the sorted content to standard output:

```
$ sort nlexample.txt
    A deep dark truthful mirror,
    Love you too much to say.
####### Elvis Costello, Spike, 1988 #######
And it's gonna tell you things that I still
One day you're going to have to face
$
```

The reason the first two lines are printed first is that they begin with a space character which is a string less than "#", which in turn is a string less than "A" and "O".

Ever wonder what happens if **sort** is invoked with no command-line arguments? It reads from standard input until end of file (^D is end-of-file for Unix standard input and ^Z<enter> is end-of-file in Windows). Here's an example:

```
$ sort
the
power
to
believe
^D
believe
power
the
to
$
```

This important behavior is evident in many different Unix (and Windows) commands:

- If the program is invoked with command-line arguments, treat the arguments as file names and read from them.

- If the program is invoked with no command-line arguments, read from standard input.

If Perl is to be indeed practical, there should be a way to model this behavior, and it should be easy—and it is, with the *diamond*.

The diamond (<>) operator checks to see if the program was invoked with command-line arguments. If so, it reads from them in scalar context one file at a time, one line at a time; in list context it reads all content of all files in order. If it is invoked with no command-line arguments, it reads from standard input just like <STDIN>.

Here is a program called diamond1.pl:

```
#!/usr/bin/perl
# diamond1.pl

use warnings;
use strict;

while (<>) {
    print "text read: $_"
}
```

Let's see what happens when we invoke this program with command-line arguments. Given the file file1.dat:

```
this is file1.dat
it is not too exciting...
```

and file2.dat:

```
this is file2.dat
equally unexciting...
```

Here is what the program generates when executed with these two file names:

```
$ perl diamond1.pl file1.dat file2.dat
text read: this is file1.dat
text read: it is not too exciting...
text read: this is file2.dat
text read: equally unexciting...
$
```

As you can see, file1.dat is opened and read first. The first line is read and processed, then the second line. When the entire contents of file1.dat are read, the program opens file2.dat and reads each line until end of file.

Now let's run the same program with no command-line arguments. Notice it reads from standard input.

```
$ perl diamond1.pl
I
```

186

```
text read: I
Don't
text read: Don't
Want
text read: Want
to
text read: to
Be
text read: Be
a
text read: a
Star
text read: Star
^D
$
```

Here we see the practical nature of Perl—being able to mimic this important behavior and able to do so easily.

Let's modify nl1.pl to read from the file on the command line. Notice we don't need to explicitly open and close the file now.

```perl
#!/usr/bin/perl
# nl2.pl

use warnings;
use strict;

my $lineno = 1;

while (<>) {
    print $lineno++;
    print ": $_";
}
```

When we execute the program, we provide the data file on the command line. This invocation produces the same output as nl1.pl:

```
$ perl nl2.pl nlexample.txt
1: One day you're going to have to face
2:    A deep dark truthful mirror,
3: And it's gonna tell you things that I still
4:    Love you too much to say.
5: ####### Elvis Costello, Spike, 1988 #######
$
```

@ARGV: The Command-Line Arguments

There is some behind-the-scenes work that is going on with the diamond. When a program is invoked, all the command-line arguments—the text after the program name—are stored in the special array variable @ARGV Let's write a program that will display this array's contents:

```
#!/usr/bin/perl
# argv1.pl

use warnings;
use strict;

print "[$_]\n" foreach @ARGV;
```

This program simply loops through all the elements of @ARGV, printing them to standard output. Note that since @ARGV is a special array variable, it does not need to be declared with my() even though we are using strict. As a matter of fact, don't declare it with my()—if you do, you will break its magic.

If the program is invoked with no arguments after the program name, @ARGV is empty:

```
$ perl argv1.pl
$
```

If invoked with arguments, it is a bit more interesting:

```
$ perl argv1.pl king crimson rocks
[king]
[crimson]
[rocks]
$
```

Notice that text after the program name is treated as a whitespace-separated list of terms, and each is its own element of @ARGV. One more invocation shows that the contents of @ARGV are entirely dependent on the command-line arguments:

```
$ perl argv1.pl It was the best of times,
[It]
[was]
[the]
[best]
[of]
[times,]
$
```

The command-line arguments can be stored into variables for later use by simply accessing the elements of @ARGV.

```
my $zeroth_arg = $ARGV[0];
my $first_arg  = $ARGV[1];
```

It is common to do this in a different way (TIMTOWTDI) by shifting @ARGV.

```
my $zeroth_arg = shift @ARGV;
my $first_arg  = shift @ARGV;
```

And because we can, we might want to shorten this code a bit by taking advantage of the fact that the shift() function, outside the body of a function definition, shifts @ARGV by default. So this code produces the same result as the preceding code:

```
my $zeroth_arg = shift;
```

```perl
my $first_arg  = shift;
```

@ARGV and <>

The diamond and @ARGV have a functional relationship (as opposed to a dysfunctional one). Here is how <> really works:

- If there are any elements in @ARGV, shift out the first one, treat it as a file, and read from it; repeat for each element in @ARGV until @ARGV is empty.

- If @ARGV is empty, read from standard input.

Here is a program that illustrates this relationship. In argv2.pl, @ARGV is assigned the value of three files. Then, when the <> reads from within the while loop parentheses, it will read from the files that were assigned to @ARGV.

```perl
#!/usr/bin/perl
# argv2.pl

use warnings;
use strict;

@ARGV = qw(file1.dat file2.dat file3.dat);

while (<>) {
    print "text read: $_";
}
```

Executing this program produces the following:

```
$ perl argv2.pl
text read: this is file1.dat
text read: it is not too exciting...
text read: this is file2.dat
text read: equally unexciting...
text read: this is file3.dat
text read: yep, you guessed it, not too exciting...
$
```

Note that in this program we assign to @ARGV, which overwrites its value. Thus, if we executed this program with command-line arguments, they would be immediately overwritten and lost. We could easily change the code to add the three files to the command-line arguments by using the push() function:

```perl
push @ARGV, qw(file1.dat file2.dat file3.dat);
```

$ARGV

As the <> reads through the files on the command line, the file that is being read is stored in the special variable $ARGV. You can use this variable to see the name of the file being read if you want. Here is a program that prints its value as it is reading:

```perl
#!/usr/bin/perl
# argv3.pl

use warnings;
use strict;

@ARGV = qw(file1.dat file2.dat file3.dat);

while (<>) {
    print "text read from $ARGV: $_";
}
```

Executing this code produces the following:

```
$ perl argv3.pl
text read from file1.dat: this is file1.dat
text read from file1.dat: it is not too exciting...
text read from file2.dat: this is file2.dat
text read from file2.dat: equally unexciting...
text read from file3.dat: this is file3.dat
text read from file3.dat: yep, you guessed it, not too exciting...
$
```

Like @ARGV, $ARGV does not need to be declared with my(). Moreover, it should not be declared or its magic will be broken.

Reading in List Context

Sometimes we want to read more than just one line at a time. When you read from a filehandle in scalar context, as we've been doing so far, it gives you the next line. However, in list context, it returns all of the remaining lines (newlines included). This is known as a *file slurp*. For instance, you can read in an entire file like this:

```perl
open(INPUT, '<', 'somefile.dat') or die $!;
my @data;
@data = <INPUT>;
close INPUT;
```

File slurps can be quite memory-intensive, however. Perl has to store every single line of the file into the array, even if you only want to deal with one or two of them. Usually, you'll want to step through a file with a while loop as before. Still, for some things, an array is the easiest way of processing data. For example, how do you print the last five lines in a file?

The problem with reading a line at a time is that you don't know how much you have left to read. You can only tell when you run out of data, so you'd have to keep an array of the last five lines read, and drop an old line when a new one comes in. You'd do it something like this:

```perl
#!/usr/bin/perl
# tail1.pl

use warnings;
use strict;

open(FILE, '<', 'gettysburg.txt') or die $!;
my @last5;

while (<FILE>) {
    push @last5, $_;             # add to the end
    shift @last5 if @last5 > 5; # take from the beginning
}

close FILE;

print "Last five lines:\n", @last5;
```

And that's exactly how you'd do it if you were concerned about memory use on big files. Given a suitably primed **gettysburg.txt**, this is what you'd get:

```
$ perl tail1.pl
Last five lines:
last full measure of devotion—that we here highly resolve
that these dead shall not have died in vain—that this
nation, under God, shall have a new birth of freedom—and
that government: of the people, by the people, for the
people, shall not perish from the earth.
$
```

However, if memory wasn't a problem or you knew you were going to be primarily dealing with small to medium-size files, this would be perfectly sufficient:

```perl
#!/usr/bin/perl
# tail2.pl

use warnings;
use strict;

open(FILE, '<', 'gettysburg.txt') or die $!;
my @speech = <FILE>;   # slurp the whole file into memory
close FILE;

print "Last five lines:\n", @speech[-5 .. -1];
```

Writing to Files

We're now ready to write to a file, which we'll do by using a form of the `print()` function. Normally, to print something to standard output, you say this:

```
print list;
```

When we want to write to a file associated with the filehandle `FH`, though, we use this instead:

```
print FH list;
```

That's `print`, followed by a space, followed by a filehandle, followed by a space (*not* a comma), followed by the stuff to print.

So, for instance, here's a program that demonstrates one way of copying a file. This program takes two command-line arguments: the first is the file to read, the second is the file to write.

```perl
#!/usr/bin/perl
# copy.pl

use warnings;
use strict;

my $source      = shift @ARGV;
my $destination = shift @ARGV;

open(IN, '<', $source)      or die "Can't read source file $source: $!\n";
open(OUT, '>', $destination) or die "Can't write to file $destination: $!\n";

print "Copying $source to $destination\n";

while (<IN>) {
   print OUT $_;
}

close IN;
close OUT;
```

Now there isn't much to see when we run this program, but let's run it anyway:

```
$ perl copy.pl gettysburg.txt speech.txt
Copying gettysburg.txt to speech.txt
$
```

Let's look at this program in detail. First, we get the name of the file to copy and the name of the destination file from the command line:

```perl
my $source      = shift @ARGV;
my $destination = shift @ARGV;
```

The command-line arguments to our program are in the `@ARGV` array, and we use `shift()` (which removes and returns the left-most element of an array) to get an element out. We could quite easily have said this:

```perl
my $source      = $ARGV[0];
my $destination = $ARGV[1];
```

However, **shift()** is a slightly more common way of grabbing the command-line argument. Next, we open our two files:

```perl
open(IN, '<', $source)      or die "Can't read source file $source: $!\n";
open(OUT, '>', $destination) or die "Can't write to file $destination: $!\n";
```

The first **open()** opens the source file in read mode and the second **open()** opens the destination file in write mode. Notice that we're taking care to check that the files can be opened for reading and writing. It is essential to let the user know if, for example, she does not have permission to access a certain file or the file does not exist. There is rarely a really good reason not to do this.

The copying procedure is simple enough: read a line from the source file, then write it to the destination.

```perl
while (<IN>) {
    print OUT $_;
}
```

The **while** loop is reading from **<IN>** in scalar context—one line at a time—until end of file. In list context **<IN>** returns a list of all the remaining lines in the file. So why don't we just say

```perl
print OUT <IN>;
```

The trouble is, that's not very memory-conscious; Perl would have to read in the *whole* file at once in order to construct the list, and only then pass it out to **print()**. For small files, this is fine. For large files, it is usually better to read line by line in scalar context.

Let's look at another example. This time, instead of immediately writing the file, we'll first sort the lines. In this case, we can't avoid reading every line into memory—we need to have all the lines in an array or something similar. Let's see how we'd go about doing this. This program will take two arguments—the input file to sort and the output file that will contain the sorted content.

If you've ever needed to sort the lines in a file, this is for you. The program works in three stages:

- First, open the input file and the output file that the user specifies.

- Then, read in the input file and sort its content.

- Finally, write out the sorted content.

Here's the full listing:

```perl
#!/usr/bin/perl
# sort1.pl

use warnings;
use strict;

my $input  = shift;
my $output = shift;

open(INPUT, '<', $input)   or die "Couldn't open file $input: $!\n";
```

```
open(OUTPUT, '>', $output) or die "Couldn't open file $output: $!\n";

my @file = <INPUT>;
@file = sort @file;

print OUTPUT @file;

close INPUT;
close OUTPUT;
```

Suppose we have the following file, sortme.txt:

```
Well, I finally found someone to turn me upside-down
And nail my feet up where my head should be
If they had a king of fools then I could wear that crown
And you can all die laughing, because I'd wear it proudly
```

We can run our program like this:

```
$ perl sort1.pl sortme.txt sorted.txt
$
```

And we'll end up with a file, sorted.txt:

```
And nail my feet up where my head should be
And you can all die laughing, because I'd wear it proudly
If they had a king of fools then I could wear that crown
Well, I finally found someone to turn me upside-down
```

The first stage of this program—opening the files—is very similar to what we did before, with one small change:

```
my $input  = shift;
my $output = shift;

open(INPUT, '<', $input)   or die "Couldn't open file $input: $!\n";
open(OUTPUT, '>', $output) or die "Couldn't open file $output: $!\n";
```

We don't tell Perl which array to shift(), so it assumes we want @ARGV, which is just as well, because in this case, we do!

Getting the file sorted is a simple matter of reading it into an array and calling sort(), passing in the array.

```
my @file = <INPUT>;
@file = sort @file;
```

In fact, we could just say my @file = sort <INPUT>; and that would be slightly more efficient—Perl would only have to store the lines of text in memory once.

Finally, we write out the sorted array:

```
print OUTPUT @file;
```

We could even do all this in one line, without using an array:

```
print OUTPUT sort <INPUT>;
```

This is arguably the most efficient solution, and you might think it's relatively easy to understand. What are we doing after all? Printing to the output file the sorted input file. But it's the least extensible way of writing it. We can't change any of the stages when it's written like that.

Buffering

Try this little program:

```
#!/usr/bin/perl
# time1.pl

use warnings;
use strict;

foreach (1..20) {
    print ".";
    sleep 1;
}
print "\n";
```

You'd probably expect it to print 20 dots, leaving a second's gap between each one, and on Windows with ActiveState Perl, that's exactly what it does. However, this is something of an exception; on most other operating systems, you'll have to wait for 20 seconds first, before it prints all 20 dots at once.

So what's going on? Operating systems often won't actually write something to (or read something from) a filehandle until the end-of-line character—this is to save doing a lot of short, repetitious read/write operations. Instead, they keep everything you've written queued up in a buffer and access the filehandle once only. This is called *buffering*.

However, you can tell Perl to stop the OS from doing this by modifying the special variable $|. If this variable is set to 0, which it usually is, Perl will tell the operating system to use standard output buffering if possible. If it's set to 1, Perl turns off standard output buffering.

So, to make the program steadily print out dots—as you might to show progress on a long operation—we just need to set $| to 1 before we do our printing:

```
#!/usr/bin/perl
# time2.pl

use warnings;
use strict;

$| = 1;
foreach (1..20) {
    print ".";
    sleep 1;
}
print "\n";
```

Opening Pipes

The open() function can be used for more than just plain old files—you can read data from and send data to programs as well. Anything that can read from standard input or write to standard output can talk directly to Perl via a *pipe*.

Pipes were invented by Doug McIlroy for the Unix operating system, and were soon carried over to other operating systems. They're one of those things that sound amazingly obvious once someone else has thought of it.

■ **Note** A pipe is something that connects two filehandles together.

That's it. Usually you'll be connecting the standard output of one program to the standard input of another. Unix users are probably quite familiar with pipes. Here is a command that will list all the nonhidden files in a directory (ls) and then page through the output (more):

```
$ ls | more
```

The vertical bar character (|) connects the standard output of the ls command to the standard input of the more command. This causes the file listing output to be sent into the more command, whose job it is to page through it.

The Windows version of this command is

```
$ dir | more
```

We can write Perl programs that pipe into programs (our Perl program will write into the pipe) or pipe from programs (our Perl program will read from the pipe).

Receiving Piped Data from a Process

To read the output of a program, simply use open(), with '-|' as the second argument and the name of the program (and any command-line arguments you want to give it) as the third argument. For instance, let's write a program to sort either the file on the command line or standard input (sort2.pl):

```perl
#!/usr/bin/perl
# sort2.pl

use warnings;
use strict;

my @text = <>;

print sort @text;
```

Recall that the <> reads from either the file or files on the command line, or from standard input if there are no command-line arguments. Reading from <> into @text will read in list context, slurping the contents into the array. We then print the sorted array. Here's how you would execute this program:

$ **perl sort2.pl gettysburg.txt**

This invocation would produce the contents of gettysburg.txt in sorted order.

Let's write a program that will execute this program and print every third line of the output. We'll call it sortslash3.pl.

```
#!/usr/bin/perl
# sortslash3.pl

use warnings;
use strict;

open(FH, '-|', 'perl sort2.pl gettysburg.txt');

my $i = 1;

while (<FH>) {
    if ($i % 3 == 0) {
        print;
    }
    $i++;
}

close FH;
```

The important line in this program is

```
open(FH, '-|', 'perl sort2.pl gettysburg.txt');
```

This line starts a process that executes the sort2.pl program, passing the argument gettysburg.txt. The dash-vertical bar as the second argument means "Pipe from this program's standard output into our program." Since this standard output is coming into our program, we can read from the pipe by wrapping the filehandle variable in angle brackets.

```
<FH>
```

In the while loop, we are reading from the filehandle in scalar context, one line of output at a time. We then keep count of what line we are processing and if that line is divisible by 3 (which we determine by using the modulus operator %), we print that line to standard output.

Running this program produces the following:

```
$ perl sortslash3.pl
But, in a larger sense, we can not dedicate...we can not
can long endure. We are met on a great battle-field of that
equal.
increased devotion to that cause for which they gave the
living and dead, who struggled here, have consecrated it,
on this continent a new nation, conceived in Liberty, and
rather for us to be here dedicated to the great task
that government: of the people, by the people, for the
that these dead shall not have died in vain—that this
$
```

Sending Piped Data to Another Process

In addition to reading data in from external programs, we can write out to the standard input of another program. For instance, we could send mail out by writing to a program like sendmail,[1] or we could generate output that we'd like to have sorted before it gets to the user. We'll deal with the second example because, while it's easy enough to collect the data into an array and sort it ourselves before writing it out, we just happen to have a sorting program handy—we wrote one just a few pages ago. It is called sort2.pl.

Here is a program that will count things and then open a pipe into our sort2.pl program, displaying those things and their counts in sorted order. This program also illustrates a very common use of a hash variable—counting. (We talked about using a hash to count things at the end of Chapter 5.)

Things hide in the kitchen cabinet. Tins of tomatoes can lurk unseen for weeks and months, springing forth only after another can has been purchased. Every so often, then, we need to investigate the cabinets and take inventory to enumerate our baked beans and root out reticent ravioli. The following program can help us do that:

```perl
#!/usr/bin/perl
# inventory.pl

use warnings;
use strict;

my %inventory;
print "Enter individual items, followed by a new line.\n";
print "Enter a blank line to finish.\n";
while (<STDIN>) {
    chomp;
    last if $_ eq "";
    $inventory{lc $_}++;
}

open(SORT, '|-', 'perl sort2.pl');

while (my ($item, $quantity) = each %inventory) {
    if ($quantity > 1) {
        $item =~ s/^(\w+)\b/$1s/ unless $item =~ /^\w+s\b/;
    }
    print SORT "$item: $quantity\n";
}

close SORT;
```

Now let's take stock:

---

[1] sendmail is arguably the most ubiquitous Mail Transfer Agent (MTA) used on the Internet. See www.sendmail.org for more information.

```
$ perl inventory.pl
Enter individual items, followed by a new line.
Enter a blank line to finish.
jar of jam
loaf of bread
can of tuna
packet of pancake mix
can of tomatoes
can of tuna
packet of pasta
clove of garlic
packet of pasta

can of tomatoes: 1
cans of tuna: 2
clove of garlic: 1
jar of jam: 1
loaf of bread: 1
packet of pancake mix: 1
packets of pasta: 2
```

As you can see, we get a sorted list of totals back. Let's look at this code in more detail.

Whenever you're counting how many of each item you have in a list, you should immediately think about hashes. Here we use a hash to key each item to the quantity—each time we see another one of those items, we add to the quantity in the hash:

```perl
while (<STDIN>) {
    chomp;
    last unless $_ eq "";
    $inventory{lc $_}++;
}
```

This loop will end when we reach end of file or if $item contains nothing after having been chomped—it was nothing more than a newline.

To ensure that the capitalization of our item is not significant, we use the lc() function to return a lowercase version of the item. Otherwise, "Can of beans", "CAN OF BEANS", and "can of beans" would be treated as three totally separate items, instead of three examples of the same thing. By forcing them into lowercase, we remove the difference.

■ **Tip** The lc() function returns the string it was given, but with uppercase characters turned into lowercase, so print lc("FuNnY StRiNg"); should give you the output "funny string". There's also a uc() function that returns an uppercased version of the string, so print uc("FuNnY StRiNg"); will output "FUNNY STRING".

Next, we open our pipe. We're going to pass data from our program to another external program:

```
open(SORT, '|-', 'perl sort2.pl');
```

Now we can print the data out:

```
while (my ($item, $quantity) = each %inventory) {
```

We use each() to get each key/value pair from the hash, as explained in Chapter 5.

```
if ($quantity > 1) {
    $item =~ s/(\w+)/$1s/ unless $item =~ /\w+s\b/;
}
```

This makes the output a little more presentable. If there is more than one of the current item, the name should be pluralized unless it already ends in an "s". \w+ gets the first word in the string, the parentheses will store that word in $1, and we then add an "s" after it.

Last of all, we print this out by printing to the sort2.pl filehandle. That filehandle is in turn connected to the standard input of the sort2.pl program so the output is in sorted order.

Bidirectional Pipes

It is possible to pipe into the standard input of a process and then pipe the resulting standard output. The syntax to accomplish this is a bit beyond the scope of this book, but you can quench your curiosity by checking out perldoc IPC::Open2.

File Tests

So far, we've just been reading and writing files, and die()ing if anything bad happens. For small programs, this is usually adequate; but if we want to use files in the context of a larger application, we should really check their status before we try to open them and, if necessary, take preventive measures. For instance, we may want to warn the user if a file we're going to overwrite already exists, giving them a chance to specify a different file. We also want to ensure that, for instance, we're not trying to read a directory as if it were a file.

■ **Tip** This sort of programming—anticipating the consequences of future actions—is called *defensive programming*. Just like defensive driving, you assume that everything is out to get you. Just because this is paranoid behavior does not mean they are not out to get you—files will not exist or not be writable when you need them, users will specify things inaccurately, and so on. Properly anticipating, diagnosing, and working around such obstacles is the mark of a top-class programmer.

Perl provides us with *file tests*, which allow us to check various characteristics of files. Most of these tests act as logical operators and return a true or false value. For instance, to check if a file exists, we write this:

```
if (-e "somefile.dat") {...}
```

The test is -e and it takes a file name (or filehandle) as its argument. Just like open(), this file name can also be specified from a variable. You can just as validly say

```
if (-e $filename) {...}
```

where $filename contains the name of the file you want to check.

Table 8-1 shows the most common file tests. For a complete list of file tests, see perldoc perlfunc.

Table 8-1. File Test Operators

Test	Meaning
-e	True if the file exists
-f	True if the file is a plain file—not a directory
-d	True if the file is a directory
-z	True if the file has zero size
-s	True if the file has nonzero size—returns size of file in bytes
-r	True if the file is readable by you
-w	True if the file is writable by you
-x	True if the file is executable by you
-o	True if the file is owned by you

The last four tests will only make complete sense on operating systems for which files have meaningful permissions, such as Unix and Windows. If this isn't the case, they'll frequently *all* return true (assuming the file or directory exists). So, for instance, if we're going to write to a file, we should check to see whether the file already exists, and if so, what we should do about it.

■ **Tip** Note that on systems that don't use permissions comprehensively, -w is the most likely of the last four tests to have any significance, testing for read-only status.

This program does all it can to find a safe place to write a file:

```
#!/usr/bin/perl
# filetest.pl

use warnings;
```

```perl
use strict;

my $target;
while (1) {
    print "What file should I write to? ";
    $target = <STDIN>;
    chomp $target;
    if (-d $target) {
        print "No, $target is a directory.\n";
        next;
    }
    if (-e $target) {
        print "File already exists. What should I do?\n";
        print "(Enter 'r' to write to a different name, ";
        print "'o' to overwrite or\n";
        print "'b' to back up to $target.old)\n";
        my $choice = <STDIN>;
        chomp $choice;
        if ($choice eq "r") {
            next;
        } elsif ($choice eq "o") {
            unless (-o $target) {
                print "Can't overwrite $target, it's not yours.\n";
                next;
            }
            unless (-w $target) {
                print "Can't overwrite $target: $!\n";
                next;
            }
        } elsif ($choice eq "b") {
            if ( rename($target, $target.".old") ) {
                print "OK, moved $target to $target.old\n";
            } else {
                print "Couldn't rename file: $!\n";
                next;
            }
        } else {
            print "I didn't understand that answer.\n";
            next;
        }
    }
    last if open(OUTPUT, '>', $target);
    print "I couldn't write to $target: $!\n";
    # and round we go again.
}
print OUTPUT "Congratulations.\n";
print "Wrote to file $target\n";

close OUTPUT;
```

So, after all that, let's see how the program handles our input. First of all, what happens with a text file that doesn't exist?

```
$ perl filetest.pl
What file should I write to? test.txt
Wrote to file test.txt
$
```

Seems OK. What about if we "accidentally" give it the name of a directory? Or give it a file that already exists? Or give it a response it's not prepared for?

```
$ perl filetest.pl
What file should I write to? work
No, work is a directory.
What file should I write to? filetest.pl
File already exists. What should I do?
(Enter 'r' to write to a different name, 'o' to overwrite or
'b' to back up to filetest.pl.old)
r
What file should I write to? test.txt
File already exists. What should I do?
(Enter 'r' to write to a different name, 'o' to overwrite or
'b' to back up to test.txt.old)
g
I didn't understand that answer.
What file should I write to? test.txt
File already exists. What should I do?
(Enter 'r' to write to a different name, 'o' to overwrite or
'b' to back up to test.txt.old)
b
OK, moved test.txt to test.txt.old
Wrote to file test.txt
$
```

There is a lot going on with this program. Let's look at it in detail.

The main program takes place inside an infinite loop—the only way we can exit the loop is via the `last` statement at the bottom:

```
last if open(OUTPUT, '>', $target);
```

That `last` will happen only if we're happy with the file name and we can successfully open the file. In order to be happy with the file name, though, we have a gauntlet of tests to run:

```
if (-d $target) {
```

We need to first see whether what has been specified is actually a directory. If it is, we don't want to go any further, so we go back and get another file name from the user:

```
print "No, $target is a directory.\n";
next;
```

We print a message and then use `next` to take us back to the top of the loop.

Next, we check to see whether the file already exists. If so, we ask the user what we should do about this.

```
if (-e $target) {
    print "File already exists. What should I do?\n";
    print "(Enter 'r' to write to a different name, ";
    print "'o' to overwrite or\n";
    print "'b' to back up to $target.old\n";
    my $choice = <STDIN>;
    chomp $choice;
```

If he wants a different file, we merely go back to the top of the loop:

```
if ($choice eq "r") {
        next;
```

If he wants us to overwrite the file, we see if this is possible:

```
} elsif ($choice eq "o") {
```

First, we see if the user actually owns the file: it's unlikely he'll be allowed to overwrite a file he doesn't own.

```
unless (-o $target) {
        print "Can't overwrite $target, it's not yours.\n";
        next;
    }
```

Next we check to see if there are any other reasons we can't write to the file; if there are, we report them and go around for another file name:

```
unless (-w $target) {
        print "Can't overwrite $target: $!\n";
        next;
    }
```

If the user wants to back up the file—that is, rename the existing file to a new name—we see if this is possible:

```
} elsif ($choice eq "b") {
```

The `rename()` function renames a file; it takes two arguments: the current file name, and the new name.

```
if ( rename($target, $target.".old") ) {
        print "OK, moved $target to $target.old\n";
    } else {
```

If we couldn't rename the file, we explain why and start from the beginning again:

```
        print "Couldn't rename file: $!\n";
        next;
```

```
        }
```

Otherwise, if the user said something we weren't prepared for, we say:

```
} else {
        print "I didn't understand that answer.\n";
        next;
    }
```

You may think this program is excessively paranoid—after all, it's 50 lines just to print a message to a file. In fact, it isn't paranoid enough: it doesn't check to see whether the backup file already exists before renaming the currently existing file. This just goes to show you can never be too careful when dealing with the operating system. Later, we'll see how to turn big blocks of code like this into reusable elements so we don't have to reinvent the wheel every time we want to safely write to a file.

Summary

Files give our data permanence by allowing us to store the data on disk. It's no good having the best accounting program in the world, say, if it loses all your accounts every time the computer is switched off. What we've seen here are the fundamentals of getting data in and out of Perl.

Files are accessed through filehandles. Perl gives us three filehandles when our program executes: standard input (STDIN), standard output (STDOUT), and standard error (STDERR). We can open other filehandles, either for reading or for writing, with the open() function, and we should always remember to check the return value of the open() function.

Wrapping the filehandle in angle brackets, <FILEHANDLE>, reads from the specified filehandle. We can read in scalar context (one line at a time) or list context (all remaining lines until end of file).

Writing to a file is done with the print() function. By default, this writes to standard output, so the filehandle must be specified.

The diamond, <>, allows us to write programs that read from the files provided on the command line, or from STDIN if no files are given.

Pipes can be used to talk to programs outside of Perl. We can read in and write out data to them as if we were looking at the screen or typing on the keyboard. We can also use them as filters to modify our data on the way in or out of a program.

File test operators can be used to check the status of a file in various ways, and we've seen an example of using file test operators to ensure that there are no surprises when we're reading or writing a file.

Exercises

1. Read each line of gettysburg.txt. Ignore all blank lines in the file. For all other lines, break the line into all the text separated by whitespace (keeping all punctuation) and write each piece of text to the output file ex1out.txt on its own line.

2. Write a program that, when given files as command-line arguments, displays their contents. For instance, if the program is invoked as

```
$ perl ex2.pl file1.dat
```

it displays the contents of file1.dat. If invoked as

```
$ perl ex2.pl file2.dat file3.dat
```

it displays the contents of `file2.dat` followed by `file3.dat`. However, if invoked with no arguments like so:

```
$ perl ex2.pl
```

it always displays the contents of `file1.dat` followed by `file2.dat` followed by `file3.dat`.

3. Modify the file backup facility in `filetest1.pl` so that it checks to see if a backup already exists before renaming the currently existing file. When a backup does exist, the user should be asked to confirm that she wants to overwrite it. If not, she should be returned to the original query.

CHAPTER 9

■ ■ ■

String Processing

Perl was created to be a text processing language, and it is arguably the most powerful text processing language around. As discussed in Chapter 7, one way that Perl displays its power in processing text is through its built-in regular expression support. Perl also has many built-in string operators (such as the string concatenation operator • and the string replication operator x) and string functions. In this chapter you will explore several string functions and one very helpful string operator.

Character Position

Before getting started with some of Perl's built-in functions, let's talk about the ability to access characters in a string by *indexing* into the string. The numeric position of a character in a string is known as its *index*. Recall that Perl is 0-based—it starts counting things from 0, and this applies to character indexing as well. So, for this string:

```
"Wish You Were Here"
```

here are the characters of the string and their indexes:

```
character 0:   W
character 1:   i
character 2:   s
character 3:   h
character 4:   <space>
character 5:   Y
...
character 17:  e
```

You can also index characters by beginning at the rightmost character and starting from index –1. Therefore, the characters in the preceding example string can also be accessed using the following *negative* indices:

```
character -1:  e
character -2:  r
character -3:  e
character -4:  H
character -5:  <space>
```

```
character -6:  e
...
character -18: W
```

String Functions

Perl has many string functions built into the language. This section will discuss several of the most common built-in functions used to process text.

The length() Function

To determine the length of a string, you can use the length() function.

length(*string*)

This function returns the number of characters in its argument. If no argument is given, length() returns the number of characters in Perl's default variable $_. An example of the code follows:

```
#!/usr/bin/perl
# length.pl

use warnings;
use strict;

my $song = 'The Great Gig in the Sky';
print 'length of $song: ', length($song), "\n";
# the *real* length is 4:44

$_ = 'Us and Them';
print 'length of $_: ', length, "\n";
# this one is 7:40
```

Running the code produces this result:

```
$ perl length.pl
length of $song: 24
length of $_: 11
$
```

The index() Function

The index()function locates substrings in strings. Its syntax is

index(*string, substring*)

It returns the starting index (0-based) of where the substring is located in the string. If the substring is not found, it returns –1. This invocation:

index('Larry Wall', 'Wall')

would return 6 since the substring "Wall" is contained within the string "Larry Wall" starting at position 6 (0-based, remember?). This invocation:

```
index('Pink Floyd', 'ink');
```

would return 1.

The `index()` function has an optional third argument that indicates the starting position from which it should start looking. For instance, this invocation:

```
index('Roger Waters', 'er', 0)
```

tells `index()` to try to locate the substring "er" in "Roger Waters" (`http://en.wikipedia.org/wiki/Roger_Waters`) and to start looking from position 0. Position 0 is the default, so it is not necessary to include it, but it is OK if you do. This function returns 3. If you provide another starting position as in

```
index('Roger Waters', 'er', 5)
```

it tells `index()` to search for the substring "er" in "Roger Waters" but to start searching from index 5. This returns 9 because it finds the "er" in Roger's last name.

The following is an example illustrating the use of the `index()` function. It prompts the user for a string and then a substring and determines if the string contains any instance of the substring. If so, `index()` returns something other than –1, so you print that result to the user. Otherwise, you inform the user that the substring was not found.

```perl
#! /usr/bin/perl
# index.pl

use warnings;
use strict;

print "Enter a string:    ";
chomp(my $string = <STDIN>);

print "Enter a substring: ";
chomp(my $substring = <STDIN>);

my $result = index($string, $substring);

if ($result != -1) {
    print "the substring was found at index: $result\n";
} else {
    print "the substring was not found\n";
}
```

Here is an example of running this program:

```
$ perl index.pl
Enter a string:    Perl is cool!
Enter a substring: cool
the substring was found at index: 8
$ perl index.pl
Enter a string:    hello, world!
Enter a substring: cool
```

```
the substring was not found
$
```

The rindex() Function

The **rindex()** function is similar to **index()** except that it searches the string from right to left (instead of left to right). Except for the name of the function itself, the syntax for calling **rindex()** is exactly the same as for **index()**:

```
rindex(string, substring)
```

This function searches right-to-left through the string searching for the substring. It returns the 0-based index of where the substring is in the string or –1 if the substring is not found.

An important note: even though this function searches through the string from right to left, the 0th character of the string is still the leftmost character.

This invocation:

```
rindex('David Gilmour', 'i')
```

searches from the right-hand side of "David Gilmour" looking for the substring "i". It finds it at position 7 (the "i" in "Gilmour").

This function also has an optional third argument that is the character position from which it begins looking for the substring. This invocation:

```
rindex('David Gilmour', 'i', 6)
```

starts at position 6 (the "G" in "Gilmour") and looks right to left for an "i" and finds it at position 3.

The substr() Function

When processing text, you often have the situation where a string follows a specific column layout. For example, a string that contains a customer's last name in columns 1–20, the last name in columns 21–40, and address in columns 40–70. You can use the **substr()** function to extract these fields out of the string. Its syntax is

```
substr(string, starting_index, length)
```

It returns *length* number of characters starting from *starting_index* in *string*. If the number of characters extends beyond the length of the string, then it returns all the characters of the string from *starting_index* to the end. For example, let's say you have read a fixed-length record from a file, and you know that from column 24 (0-based) to column 53 is the job title for that record. Here is an example line from the file:

```
'John A.    Smith        Perl programmer'
```

If this record was read into the variable **$record**, this invocation would access John's job:

```
$s = substr($record, 24, 30);
```

Since there is more than one way to do it in Perl (TMTOWTDI), this invocation of **substr()** can be performed with a regular expression:

```
($s) = $record =~ /^.{24}(.{1,30})/;
```

This statement matches the string literal **$record** against a regex that translates to "Match 24 of any character but '\n' at the beginning of the string followed between 1 and 30 of any character but '\n'". The parentheses around .{1,30} store those characters in **$1**. Then an assignment is made to the list (**$s**) that copies over **$1** and stores it into **$s**. As a result, **$s** is the string "Perl programmer".

An interesting feature of the **substr()** function is that it can be on the left-hand side of an assignment. For instance, this code:

```
substr($record, 24, 30) = 'Technical manager';
```

would overwrite the substring of **$record** starting from position 24 length 30 (John's job, "Perl programmer") with the string "Technical manager". This results in **$record** being modified to be

```
'John A.    Smith        Technical manager'
```

Is this a promotion or a demotion?

Here is an example of using **substr()**. It prompts the user for a string, a starting index, and a length and then prints the substring to the user. It then overwrites the first five characters of the string the user enters with the string "hello, world!" and prints the result:

```
#!/usr/bin/perl
# substr.pl

use warnings;
use strict;

print "Enter a string:        ";
chomp(my $string = <STDIN>);

print "Enter starting index: ";
chomp(my $index = <STDIN>);

print "Enter length:          ";
chomp(my $length = <STDIN>);

my $s = substr($string, $index, $length);

print "result: $s\n";

# now, overwrite $string
substr($string, 0, 5) = 'hello, world!';

print "string is now: $string\n";
```

Here is an example of executing this code:

```
$ perl substr.pl
Enter a string:        practical extraction and report language
Enter starting index: 10
Enter length:          8
result: extracti
string is now: hello, world!ical extraction and report language
$
```

Transliteration

Now let's look at another text processing operator—the transliteration operator. Its syntax is

`tr/old/new/.`

This operator resembles the substitute operator, `s///`, which you saw in Chapter 7 when I discussed regular expressions. While the `tr///` operator resembles `s///`, the only thing it has in common with the substitute is that both operators operate on `$_` by default. The `tr///` operator has nothing to do with regular expressions.

This operator correlates the characters in its two arguments, one by one, and uses these pairings to substitute individual characters in the referenced string. The code `tr/one/two/` replaces all instances of "o" in the referenced string with "t", all instances of "n" with "w", and all instances of "e" with "o".

This operator translates the characters in `$_` by default. To translate a string other than `$_`, use the `=~` operator as in

`$string =~ tr/old/new/;`

Let's say you wanted to replace, for some reason, all the numbers in a string with letters. You might write something like this:

`$string =~ tr/0123456789/abcdefghij/;`

This would turn, say, "2011064" into "cabbage". You can use ranges in transliteration, but not any of the character classes. You could write the preceding as

`$string =~ tr/0-9/a-j/;`

The return value of this operator is, by default, the number of characters transliterated. You can therefore use the transliteration operator to count the number of occurrences of certain characters. For example, to count the number of vowels in a string, you can use

`my $vowels = $string =~ tr/aeiou//;`

Note that this will not actually change any of the vowels in the variable `$string`. As the second group is blank, it is exactly the same as the first group. However, the transliteration operator can take the `/d` modifier, which *will* delete occurrences on the left that do not have a correlating character on the right. To get rid of all spaces in a string quickly, you could use this line:

`$string =~ tr/ //d;`

The following is an example program that loops through the diamond operator, reading line by line through either the file or files on the command line or standard input. For each line, the `tr///` operator is used to uppercase the lowercase letters in `$_`:

```perl
#!/usr/bin/perl
# tr.pl

use warnings;

while (<>) {
    tr/a-z/A-Z/;
    print;
}
```

Here is an example of executing this program. You invoke it with no command line arguments so it reads though your standard input until end of file (^D in Unix, ^Z<enter> in Windows):

```
$ perl tr.pl
And
AND
she's
SHE'S
buying
BUYING
a
A
stairway
STAIRWAY
^D
$
```

Summary

In this chapter I have discussed some very useful functions and operators to help you process text files. You determined the length of a string with length(). You worked with string indices and substrings with the functions index(), rindex(), and substr(). Finally, you looked at the transliteration operator, tr///, which translates characters in a string.

Exercises

1. Open ex1.dat in read mode. Each line of the file is a string with customer information. The information in the line is based on the following character positions:

1–24	Customer name
25–52	Address
53–72	City
73–74	State
76–80	Zip code

Print the information for each line so that it resembles

```
Record:
name    : John Q Public
address : 23 Main St.
city    : Des Moines
```

```
state    : IA
zip      : 50309
```

2. Write a program to perform the rot13 encoding algorithm. Rot13 is a simple encoding
    algorithm with the purpose of making text temporarily unreadable. It is called rot13 because
    it rotates alpha characters 13 positions in the alphabet. For instance, "a" is the first character
    of the alphabet and it is rotated 13 positions to the 14th character, "n". The second character,
    "b", is rotated to the 15th character "o" and so on through "m", the 13th character rotated to
    "z", the 26th character. When the 14th character, "n", is rotated 13 positions, it rotates back
    around to "a", "o" to "b", and so on through "z" to "m":

```
a -> n          A -> N
b -> o          B -> O
...             ...
m -> z          M -> Z
n -> a          N -> A
o -> b          O -> B
...             ...
z -> m          Z -> M
```

This program will read with the diamond. Execute the program like this:

```
$ perl ex2.pl ex2.dat
```

To double-check your work, take the standard output from the program and pipe it back into
the standard input of the same program:

```
$ perl ex2.pl ex2.dat | perl ex2.pl
```

## CHAPTER 10

Interfacing to the Operating System

Perl is a popular language for system administrators and programmers who have to work with files and directories due to the fact that there are many built-in functions to perform sys admin activities. These activities include creating directories, changing the names of files, creating links, and executing programs in the operating system.

In this chapter you will look at several functions that make working with files and directories easy. Also, you will look at two ways of executing operating system commands or other applications such as system() and backquotes.

The %ENV Hash

When a Perl program starts executing, it inherits from the shell all of the shell's exported environment variables. If you are curious about what environment variables are defined in your shell, try this command in Unix:

```
$ env
```

Depending on what shell you are using, you might need to execute

```
$ printenv
```

In Windows try

```
c:\> set
```

All of the environment variables that the Perl program inherits are stored in the special hash %ENV. Here are a few possible examples:

```
$ENV{HOME}
$ENV{PATH}
$ENV{USER}
```

These environment variables can be assigned. If you want to change the path for the current execution of the program, simply assign to $ENV{PATH} (note that this will not change the path for the shell that is invoking this program).

```perl
$ENV{PATH} = '/bin:/usr/bin:/usr/local/bin';
```

The following program whereis.pl is an example of reading from %ENV. It will implement the whereis command, a useful program found in Unix that reports to the user the location of a program within the PATH environment variable. Here is the code:

```perl
#!/usr/bin/perl
# whereis.pl

use warnings;
use strict;

my $prog = shift @ARGV;
die "usage: perl whereis.pl <file>" unless defined $prog;

my $found = 0;

foreach my $dir (split /:/, $ENV{PATH}) {
    if (-x "$dir/$prog") {
        print "$dir/$prog\n";
        $found = 1;
        last;
    }
}

print "$prog not found in PATH\n" unless $found;
```

First, you grab the command line argument and place it in $prog. This argument is the program that you are trying to locate. If the argument is not provided, you complain:

```perl
my $prog = shift @ARGV;
die "usage: perl whereis.pl <file>" unless defined $prog;
```

Then you see the following:

```perl
my $found = 0;

foreach my $dir (split /:/, $ENV{PATH}) {
    if (-x "$dir/$prog") {
        print "$dir/$prog\n";
        $found = 1;
        last;
    }
}
```

First, assume you won't find the program and you assign $found the value 0, or false. You'll check this variable at the end of the program and print a message, if necessary. The foreach loop loops through each directory listed in $ENV{PATH}, a colon—separated list of filenames. For each of these directories, you test to see if the program you are looking for is an executable file in that directory:

```
if (-x "$dir/$prog") {
```

If so, you print the directory/filename, set $found to true since you found the program, and then last out of the foreach loop.

Finally, if you did not find the program, the program says so:

```
print "$prog not found in PATH\n" unless $found;
```

Executing this code produces the following:

```
$ perl whereis.pl sort
/usr/bin/sort
$ perl whereis.pl noprogram
noprogram not found in PATH
$
```

Working with Files and Directories

Perl provides various mechanisms to work with files and directories. In this section, you will explore the concept of file globbing, directory streams, and several built-in functions that allow you to perform operating system actions. I'll first cover file globbing.

File Globbing with glob()

Those of us who are Unix users know that this command lists all the files in the current directory that end with the .pl extension:

```
$ ls *.pl
```

A similar command in Windows would be

```
c:\> dir *.pl
```

The part of these commands that indicates which files you want to list is *.pl. This is known as a *file glob*—it globs, or collects together, all the filenames that end in .pl. Those filenames are then listed.

The glob() function does this for us in Perl:

```
glob('*.pl')
```

■ **Note** You can perform the same action in Perl by taking the glob pattern and, like reading from a filehandle, wrap it in angle brackets. Therefore, this glob() invocation:

```
glob('*.pl')
```

can be written as:

```
<*.pl>
```

There are two ways of reading from a file glob—scalar context or list context. In scalar context, it returns back the next filename that ends in .pl:

```perl
$nextperlfilename = glob('*.pl');
```

In list context, it returns back all the filenames that end in .pl:

```perl
@alltheperlfilenames = glob('*.pl');
```

Like using the ls or dir commands, you can indicate more than one pattern to glob. These patterns can be absolute or relative paths. For instance, this example globs all the filenames in the current directory that end in .pl and all the filenames that end in .dat:

```perl
glob('*.pl *.dat')
```

This example lists all the .c and .h files in specific directories:

```perl
glob('/usr/src/*.c /usr/include/*.h')
```

Like reading from a filehandle, if you read from glob() within a while loop, and the function return value is not explicitly assigned to a variable, it is assigned to $_ by default:

```perl
while (glob('*.dat')) {
    print "found a data file: $_\n";
}
```

This program lists the contents of the current directory and uses file tests to examine each file:

```perl
#!/usr/bin/perl
# directory-glob.pl

use warnings;
use strict;

print "Contents of the current directory:\n";
foreach (glob<'*'>) {
    next if $_ eq "." or $_ eq "..";
    print $_, " " x (30 - length($_));
    print "d" if -d $_;
    print "r" if -r _;
    print "w" if -w _;
    print "x" if -x _;
    print "o" if -o _;
    print "\t";
    print -s _ if -r _ and -f _;
    print "\n";
}
```

After the code does a friendly print() is

```perl
foreach (glob('*')) {
```

This loops `foreach` filename returned by `glob('*')`, or all files in the current directory. The filename is read into `$_`. Then you check to see if it is either `.` or `..`, special directories in DOS and Unix that refer to the current and parent directories, respectively. You skip these in your program:

```
next if $_ eq "." or $_ eq "..";
```

You then print out the name of each file, followed by some spaces. The length of the filename plus the number of spaces will always add up to 30, so you have nicely arranged columns.

```
print $_, " " x (30 - length($_));
```

First you test to see if the file is a directory using the `-d` file test covered in Chapter 8:

```
print "d" if -d $_;
```

Then you test to see if the file is readable, writable, executable, and that you are the owner:

```
    print "r" if -r _;
    print "w" if -w _;
    print "x" if -x _;
    print "o" if -o _;
```

No, this isn't a typo: I do mean `_` and not `$_` here. Just as `$_` is the default value for some operations, such as `print()`, `_` is the default filehandle for Perl's file tests. It actually refers to the last file explicitly tested. Since you tested `$_` previously, you can use `_` for as long as you're referring to the same file.

■ **Note** When Perl does a file test, it actually looks up all the data at once—ownership, readability, writability, and so on; this is called a *stat* of the file. `_` tells Perl not to do another stat, but to use the data from the previous one. As such, it's more efficient than stating the file each time.

Finally, you print out the file's size—this is only possible if you can read the file, and only useful if it is a regular file:

```
print -s _ if -r _ and -f _;
```

Executing this code produces the following:

```
$ perl directory-glob.pl
Contents of the current directory:
a.dat                         rwo      20
addsizes.pl                   rwo      242
b.dat                         rwo      20
backquote.pl                  rwo      297
dir1                          drwxo
directory-dir.pl              rwo      460
directory-glob.pl             rwo      371
links.pl                      rwo      316
os.pl                         rwo      1049
```

```
system.pl                        rwo         132
whereis.pl                       rwo         334
$
```

The number at the end of the line is the size of the file in bytes; as for the letters, "d" shows that this is a directory, "r" stands for readable, "w" for writable, "x" for executable, and "o" shows that the user that is running the program is the owner.

Reading Directories

Directories can be treated kind of like files—you can open them and read from them. Instead of using open() and a filehandle, which are used with files, you use opendir() and a *directory handle*:

```
opendir DH, "." or die "Couldn't open the current directory: $!";
```

To read each file in the directory, you use readdir() on the directory handle.

Previously, you saw directory-glob.pl, a program to perform file tests on files that you obtained from a glob. In the spirit of TMTOWTDI, let's do the same action using a directory handle instead of a file glob:

```perl
#!/usr/bin/perl
# directory-dir.pl

use warnings;
use strict;

print "Contents of the current directory:\n";
opendir DH, "." or die "Couldn't open the current directory: $!";
while ($_ = readdir(DH)) {
    next if $_ eq "." or $_ eq "..";
    print $_, " " x (30 - length($_));
    print "d" if -d $_;
    print "r" if -r _;
    print "w" if -w _;
    print "x" if -x _;
    print "o" if -o _;
    print "\t";
    print -s _ if -r _ and -f _;
    print "\n";
}
closedir DH;
```

The only changes from the previous program are these two lines:

```perl
opendir DH, "." or die "Couldn't open the current directory: $!";
while ($_ = readdir(DH)) {
```

and this line:

```perl
closedir DH;
```

The current directory, ., is opened. Then you read from the directory with `readdir()`, and as long as you have a filename, you perform the same tests as before. After we are all finished with the files, we close the directory handle. This program produces the same result as `directory-glob.pl`:

```
$ perl directory-dir.pl
Contents of the current directory:
a.dat                    rwo         20
addsizes.pl              rwo         242
b.dat                    rwo         20
backquote.pl             rwo         297
dir1                     drwxo
directory-dir.pl         rwo         460
directory-glob.pl        rwo         371
links.pl                 rwo         316
os.pl                    rwo         1049
system.pl                rwo         132
whereis.pl               rwo         334
$
```

■ **Note** Well, it produces almost the same results. Reading from the glob pattern '*' returns all non-hidden files in the current directory, whereas reading from a directory handle will also return hidden files. But, since you don't have any hidden files in this directory, none are displayed, so the output is the same as before.

Functions to Work with Files and Directories

Perl provides many built--in functions to perform operating system actions on files and directories. Let's look at a few of them.

The chdir() Function

To change directories within a Perl script, use the `chdir()` function. Its syntax is

`chdir(directory)`

This function attempts to change directories to the directory passed as its argument (defaulting to $ENV{HOME}). If it successfully changed directories, it returns true, otherwise false.

■ **Note** `chdir()` changes the working directory in the script. This has no effect on the shell in which the script is invoked—when the script exits the user will be in whatever directory they were in when they executed the program.

The fact that this function returns true on success or false on failure can be very helpful. You should always check the return value and respond appropriately if the directory change failed. For instance, this code attempts to change directory and die()s if you couldn't make the change:

```
chdir '/usr/local/src' or die "Can't change directory to /usr/local/src: $!";
```

Recall that $! is a variable that contains the error string of whatever just went wrong.

The unlink() Function

The unlink() function deletes files from disk. Its syntax is

unlink(*list_of_files*)

This function removes the files from disk. It returns true if successful, false if not. This function acts like the Unix rm command and the Windows del command. Here is an example in the following code:

```
unlink 'file1.txt', 'file2.txt' or warn "Can't remove files: $!";
```

The rename() Function

The rename() function renames one file to a new name. Its syntax is

rename(*old_file_name*, *new_file_name*)

This function renames the old file to the new name. It returns true if successful, false if not. This function acts like the Unix mv command and the Windows ren command. Here is an example in the following code:

```
rename 'old.txt', 'new.txt' or warn "Can't rename file: $!";
```

Note that you can also move a file with this function (like the mv command in Unix and move command in Windows):

```
rename 'oldir/old.txt', 'newdir/new.txt' or warn "Can't move file: $!";
```

The link(), symlink(), and readlink() Functions

These functions allow us to work with hard and soft links. These functions are Unix-centric—they don't function the same in the Windows world, so it is suggested you avoid using them there.

The link() function creates a hard link. Its syntax is

link(*file_to_link_to*, *link_name*)

The symlink() function creates a symbolic link. Its syntax is

symlink(file_to_link_to, sym_link_name)

To find out what file a symbolic link points to, use the readlink() function:

readlink(*sym_link_name*)

Here is an example of creating a soft link in Perl and finding out the name of the file to which it links:

```
#!/usr/bin/perl
# links.pl

use warnings;
use strict;

my $filetolink = 'links.pl';
my $linkname   = 'linktolinks.pl';

symlink($filetolink, $linkname) or die "link creation failed: $!";

print "link created ok!\n";

my $readlinkresult = readlink($linkname);
print "$linkname is a sym link to $readlinkresult\n";
```

Here is an example of executing this code. Note that the link doesn't exist before the code is executed:

```
$ ls -l link*
-rw-r--r-- 1 jdoe    users  349 22 Apr 14:05 links.pl
$ perl links.pl
link created ok!
linktolinks.pl is a sym link to links.pl
$ ls -l link*
-rw-r--r-- 1 jdoe    users  349 22 Apr 14:05 links.pl
lrwxr-xr-x 1 jdoe    users    8 22 Apr 14:06 linktolinks.pl -> links.pl
$
```

The mkdir() and rmdir() Functions

The mkdir() function makes a directory. Its syntax is

mkdir(*directory_name*, mode)

This function creates *directory_name*. It returns true on success, false on failure. The mode, or permissions, is applied to the directory (possibly modified by the umask). Note that the mode should be represented as an octal number by preceding it with a 0 since Unix interprets the number representation of the mode as an octal value.

Here is an example of mkdir() that creates the directory newdir in the current directory with the permissions of 751 (in the Unix world, this looks like rwxr-x--x):

mkdir('newdir', 0751) or die $!;

As usual, you are handling the failure of this function—in this case you are die()ing.

The rmdir() removes an empty directory. It returns true on success, false on failure. Its syntax is

rmdir(*directory_name*)

The chmod() Function

Speaking of permissions, the chmod() function changes the mode, or permissions, on a file or directory. Its syntax is

chmod(*file_or_directory_name*, *mode*)

Again, the mode should be represented as an octal number since that is how Unix interprets it. This changes the mode of the file resume.txt to be readable only by the owner of the file, die()ing if the chmod fails:

```
chmod('resume.txt', 0600) or die $!;
```

An Example

Here is an example program using a bunch of these functions. The comments describe what is going on:

```perl
#!/usr/bin/perl
# os.pl

use warnings;
use strict;

# first prompt the user for a directory name and attempt
# to create the directory in the current directory
print "please enter a directory name: ";
chomp(my $dir = <STDIN>);

mkdir $dir, 0777 or die "failed to make directory $dir: $!\n";
print "made the directory $dir ok!\n";

# so far so good - now, change directory into the
# directory
chdir $dir or die "failed to change into $dir: $!\n";
print "changed into $dir ok!\n";

# ok, now move the file ../a.dat into this new directory
# giving it a new name
print "enter new file name: ";
chomp(my $newname = <STDIN>);
rename "../a.dat", $newname or die "rename failed: $!\n";
print "file moved successfully!\n";

# list the contents of the directory
# using a directory handle
print "contents of the new directory:\n";
opendir DH, '.' or die "opendir failed: $!";
my $filename;
while ($filename = readdir(DH)) {
    print "    $filename\n";
}
```

```
close DH;

# that's it, say goodbye
print "we are all done... goodbye!\n";
```

Here is what happens when it is executed on a Unix system:

```
$ perl os.pl
please enter a directory name: newdir
made the directory newdir ok!
changed into newdir ok!
enter new file name: new.dat
file moved successfully!
contents of the new directory:
    .
    ..
    new.dat
we are all done... goodbye!
$
```

Executing External Programs

There are times when you want your Perl program to execute external programs such as another Perl script, shell commands (like ls and dir), or other programs or applications.

There are several ways to execute other programs from within a Perl script. You have already seen one way: opening pipes with the open() function discussed in Chapter 8. In this chapter I will discuss two other ways: the system() function and backquotes.

The system() Function

The system() function takes an argument and executes that argument as if it were entered into a shell. If the command produces any standard output, system() allows it to go to standard output. Its syntax is

system(*command*)

It returns the error status of command. In Unix and Windows, the error status is a way for a program to report back to whoever invoked it, informing the calling program or shell whether or not the program executed correctly. By convention, when all is well, the error status is 0. If there was a problem, the program will return a non-0 value (such as 1 or 255).

THINK TWICE BEFORE YOU USE SYSTEM()

The `system()` function can perform all sorts of operating system commands such as making directories, copying files, moving files, etc. For instance, in Unix you could execute

```
system("rm a.dat"); # delete the file a.dat in Unix
```

instead of

```
unlink('a.dat');
```

There are two main reasons not to use the `system()` function instead of the `unlink()` function to remove a file. First, passing `"rm a.dat"` to the `system()` function as shown previously works fine in Unix, but not in Windows (in Windows you would use the `del` command). Therefore, in many cases, the `system()` function is not portable between operating systems, while the `unlink()` function is portable. Second, the `unlink()` function is named `unlink()` because it calls the low-level operating system library function named `unlink()`, immediately removing the file. The `system()` function, on the other hand, creates a shell. The shell is a big program that must start up, reading various configuration files. The shell is then passed the argument to the `system()`function as if a user typed it into the shell. The shell then parses the string, determines that the user wants to remove a file, and calls the low-level operating system function named `unlink()`. So, you can call the `unlink()` function yourself using the Perl function named `unlink()`, or you can start up a big program that does a lot of work before finally calling the low-level operating system `unlink()` function.

A shell is also created when using one of these two methods of executing an external program: backquotes, and opening pipes with `open()`, so keep this in mind when deciding between built-in functions such as `unlink()` and `rename()` and using another Perl mechanism to perform operating system actions.

Another important note: the program `system.pl` displayed the current date using the `system()` function:

```
 my $error_status = system 'date';
```

This created a shell, which is an inefficient way of determining the date on the machine. A better way is to use the `localtime()` function in scalar context:

```
print scalar(localtime), "\n";
```

A rule of thumb follows: Most actions that you want to take in Perl are implemented in the language in a way that does not require launching a shell. Mentioning every feature of Perl is not the intent of this book, so I will not discuss all the different ways of doing the same thing.[1] But a little bit of searching on your part may uncover an efficient, cool way of taking action in Perl without going out to the shell, so get in the habit of looking deeper into this language when you are trying to do something new.[2]

---

[1] Remember TMTOWTDI? Divining how many is left as an exercise to the reader.

[2] `www.perl.com`, `www.perlmonks.org`, `www.google.com`, and `perdoc` are our friends.

Here is an example program that executes the date command—its job is to print to standard output the date in a readable format. The return from system() is stored in a variable and then printed to standard output.

```
#!/usr/bin/perl
# system.pl

use warnings;
use strict;

my $error_status = system 'date';

print "system() returned: $error_status\n";
```

Executing this program might produce the following:

```
$ perl system.pl
Mon Dec 14 11:28:47 CST 2009
system() returned: 0
$
```

Backquotes

The system() function prints the output of its argument to the screen. Sometimes, however, you want to capture the output and bring it into your program. The backquotes allow us to do just that. Here is the syntax:

```
`command`
```

That is the backquote (aka the grave character), not the single quote character.

The backquotes execute the operating system command, capturing and returning its standard output, if any. The error status is available in the special variable $?. The backquotes can be read in either scalar context or in list context:

```
$output = `$command`;
@output = `$command`;
```

In scalar context, the entire output including newline characters is returned as a single string (here stored in $output). In list context, the entire output is returned as a list, newlines included; each line of output is a single element in the list (here stored in @output).

The following is an example that executes the program directory-dir.pl that I discussed earlier in this chapter and adds up all the sizes of the files:

```
#!/usr/bin/perl
# addsizes.pl

use warnings;
use strict;

my @result = `perl directory-dir.pl`;
```

```
my $size = 0;

foreach (@result) {
    if (/^.{30}[drwox]*\t(\d+)$/) {
        $size += $1;
    }
}

print "The total size of all files: $size\n";
```

First, you execute the script `directory-dir.pl` and capture the output of the backquotes in list context. This means that `@result` will be an array and each element is an individual line of output from the script:

```
my @result = `perl directory-dir.pl`;
```

Then, the size is initialized to 0:

```
my $size = 0;
```

Now it is time to examine the output:

```
foreach (@result) {
    if (/^.{30}[drwox]*\t(\d+)$/) {
        $size += $1;
    }
}
```

The `foreach` is looping though each line of output. If the line matches the pattern that includes a size (that is, the `\d+`), then you use the parentheses to extract the size into `$1`. The size is added to `$size`.

Executing this program produces the following:

```
$ perl addsizes.pl
The total size of all files: 3241
$
```

There's More

There are many other ways that Perl interfaces to the operating system—I've only covered the basics here. There are dozens of built-in functions available to do all sorts of system administration stuff (see `perldoc perlfunc` for a list). Other operating system things that Perl can do include create child processes (with `fork()`), send processes signals (with `kill()`), low-level file i/o (with `sysread()` and `syswrite()`), read password information (with `getpwent()` and others), and many more. . .

Summary

In this chapter, I have discussed several ways of performing operating system actions from within a Perl script. These include file globs, executing built-in functions such as `mkdir()` and `rename()`, and executing operating system commands with `system()` and backquotes.

Exercises

1. Write a program that takes two arguments: a directory and an integer. Change into the directory that is the first argument and list all the files that have a size greater than or equal to the second argument. First use a glob and then use a filehandle.
   Code your program twice, using two different methods: 1) File globbing. 2) Directory handles. Verify that the two methods yield equivalent results, or account for any valid differences between your two sets of output.

2. Use Perl to automate a task that you perform on a regular basis.

CHAPTER 11

■ ■ ■

References

When we discussed lists and arrays in Chapter 4, we learned that all lists and all arrays are one-dimensional collections of scalars. Similarly, when we looked at hashes in Chapter 5, we found that hash values are scalars as well. As a result, in our exploration of Perl so far, we have not yet been able to create arrays of arrays (also known as *multidimensional arrays*) or other, more complex data types.

However, being able to create more complex data types is something we will want to do from time to time. For instance, we might want to represent a chessboard as eight arrays of eight squares so that we can address each square by row and column (an array of arrays). We might also want to store a bunch of information about certain individuals—their addresses, phone numbers, and occupations—and key it to their name (a hash of hashes).

In this chapter, we will look at another form of scalar data that will allow us to create these and other more complex data types—*references*.

What Is a Reference?

Put at its very simplest, a reference is a piece of data that tells us the location of another piece of data—if we told you to "See the first paragraph on page 130," we'd effectively be giving you a reference to the text in that paragraph. The data we gave you wouldn't be the text itself, but it would tell you where to find the text. This would also let us talk about (refer to) the text right away, despite the fact that it's somewhere else in the book. That's why references are so useful—we can specify data once, and they let us access it from wherever we happen to be.

In Perl, a reference is always a scalar, although the data it refers to may not be: our cross-reference in the previous paragraph wasn't even a sentence, but it referred to an entire paragraph. Likewise, a reference, even though it's only a scalar, can talk about the data stored in an array or hash.

Languages like C and C++ have a feature that's similar to references, called *pointers*. They are like Perl references in that both point to locations in the computer's memory. However, C's pointers tend to leave the interpretation of what's there for the programmer to disentangle. Perl's references, on the other hand, only store memory locations for specific, clearly defined data structures—maybe not *pre*defined, but defined nevertheless. They allow you to leave the arrangement of computer memory to the computer itself, which can be a huge relief for us mere mortal programmers, as the machine is far better at that sort of thing than we are.

The main use for references is the one we previously mentioned—being able to treat arrays and hashes as single entities. We can now refer *unambiguously* to the contents of an array or a hash using a single scalar—so we're now in a position to do things like putting hashes inside hashes, arrays inside arrays, even hashes in arrays and vice versa. But that's not all . . .

231

Anonymity

We can also use references to create *anonymous data*. Anonymous data, as you might have guessed, is data that doesn't have a variable name attached to it. Instead, it's placed at a certain memory location, and we're given a simple reference to that location. Our array (or hash, or whatever) has no name to speak of, but we know exactly where to find it, should we need to use it.

For example, instead of creating an array (1,2,3) called @array and then creating a reference to @array, we can cut out the middleman by referencing (1,2,3) directly.

This allows us to create real scalars, arrays, and hashes containing data we can refer to and modify, just as if it were a normal variable. This doesn't mean we leave arrays and hashes floating about randomly in our program to be plucked out of the air whenever we need them; we know where to find this anonymous data (we have a reference that's telling us), and it exists only for as long as part of our program is using it.

The Life Cycle of a Reference

To understand how to deal with references, let's look at the three areas of a reference's life cycle—creation, use, and destruction. After that, we'll see how to put references to use to create more complicated data structures than simple arrays and hashes.

Reference Creation

There are two ways to create a reference, one for each of the following situations:

- You already have the data in an existing variable.

- You want to create anonymous data that is only available using a reference.

The simple rule for the first situation where the variable is already defined is as follows:

> You create a reference by putting a backslash in front of the variable.

That's it. Let's see some examples:

```
my @array   = (2, 4, 6, 8, 10);
my $array_r = \@array;
```

You create a perfectly normal array variable and then make a reference to it by putting a backslash before the variable's name—that's literally all there is to it. In the same way, you can create a reference to a hash:

```
my %hash   = ( apple => "pomme", pear => "poire" );
my $hash_r = \%hash;
```

or a scalar:

```
my $scalar   = 42;
my $scalar_r = \$scalar;
```

We can treat our references just like ordinary scalars—so we can put them in an array:

```
my $var1 = 10;
my $var2 = 20;
my $var3 = 30;
my @refs = (\$var1, \$var2, \$var3);
```

Since pictures help when trying to conceptualize this data structure, here's a diagram that illustrates what this code produces.

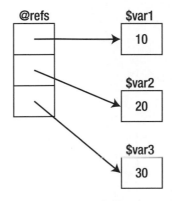

We can also put references in a hash, but only as values—Perl keys are simple strings. You can certainly do this, though:

```
my @english = qw(January February March April May June);
my @french = qw(Janvier Fevrier Mars Avril Mai Juin);
my %months = ( english => \@english, french => \@french );
```

So what does this give us? We have a hash with two keys, english and french. The english key contains a reference to an array of English month names, while the french key contains a reference to an array of French month names. With these references, we can access and modify the original data, which means that, in effect, we've stored two arrays inside a single hash.

Again, pictures help:

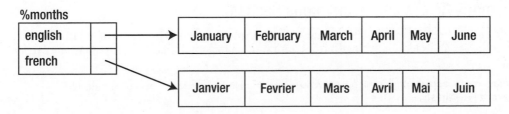

We can use the same trick to store arrays inside arrays:

```
my @array1 = (10, 20, 30, 40, 50);
my @array2 = ( 1, 2, \@array1, 3, 4);
```

Now @array2 is made up of five scalars, and the middle one is a reference to another array. We can do this over and over again if we want:

```
my @array3 = (2, 4, \@array2, 6, 8);
my @array4 = (100, 200, \@array3, 300, 400);
```

This gives us a very versatile way to store complex data structures; what we've just done is to store a structure that looks like this:

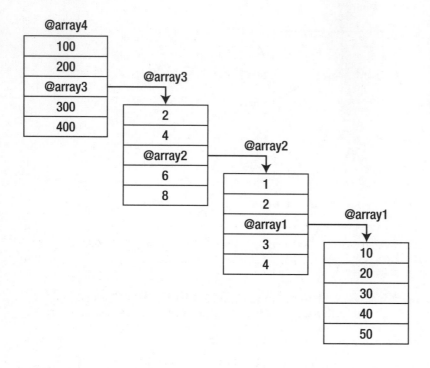

Anonymous Arrays and Anonymous Hashes

Our next step is to do all of this without having to go through the interim stages of creating the variables. Anonymous variables let us go straight from our raw data to a reference, and the rules here are just as simple:

- To get a reference to an anonymous array, use square brackets ([]) instead of parentheses.

- To get a reference to an anonymous hash, use curly braces ({}) instead of parentheses.

So, referring to our previous examples, instead of doing this:

```
my @array   = (1, 2, 3, 4, 5);
my $array_r = \@array;
```

we can create a reference to an anonymous array like this:

```
my $array_r = [1, 2, 3, 4, 5];
```

Likewise, to get a hash reference, instead of doing this:

```
my %hash   = ( apple => "pomme", pear => "poire" );
my $hash_r = \%hash;
```

we say

```
my $hash_r = { apple => "pomme", pear => "poire" };
```

Now we have two variables—the array with no name referred to only by **$array_r** and the hash with no name referred to by **$hash_r**.[1]

We can put anonymous variables inside hashes and arrays, just like references created from variables:

```
my %months  = (
    english => ["January", "February", "March", "April", ",May", ",June"],
    french  => ["Janvier", "Fevrier", "Mars", "Avril", "Mai", "Juin"]
);
```

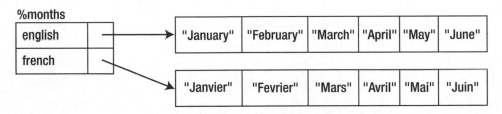

And we can put anonymous variables inside anonymous variables:

```
my @array = ( 100,200,[ 2,4,[ 1,2,[ 10,20,30,40,50 ],3,4 ],6,8 ],300,400 );
```

That's exactly the same structure shown in the earlier picture. Here it is again, with a lot more spacing added:

```
my @array = ( 100, 200,
                [ 2, 4,
                  [ 1, 2,
```

---

[1] Hmmm, variables with no names—now you see why they are called anonymous variables.

```
        [ 10, 20, 30, 40, 50 ],
      3, 4 ],
    6, 8 ],
   300, 400 );
```

Using References

Once we've created our references (whether to real variables or to anonymous data), we're going to want to use them—so how do we access the data? The operation used to get data back from a reference is called *dereferencing* and, once again, the rule is very simple.

> To dereference data, put the reference in curly braces wherever you would normally use a variable's name.

First, we'll see how to do this with arrays. Say we've got an array and a reference:

```perl
my @array   = (1, 2, 3, 4, 5);
my $array_r = \@array;
```

We can get at the array like this:

```perl
my @array2  = @{$array_r};
```

We put the reference, $array_r, inside curly braces and use that instead of our original array variable name **array**. We can use this dereferenced array, @{$array_r}, anywhere we might otherwise use an array.

Let's start with a simple example. We'll just create a reference to an array and then use it as we'd normally use an array.

```perl
#!/usr/bin/perl
# deref1.pl

use warnings;
use strict;

my @array   = (2, 4, 6, 8, 10);
my $array_r = \@array;

print "This is our dereferenced array: @{$array_r}\n";
foreach (@{$array_r}) {
    print "An element: $_\n";
}
print "The highest index is $#{$array_r}\n";
print "This is what our reference looks like: $array_r\n";
```

Let's run this:

```
$ perl deref1.pl
This is our dereferenced array: 2 4 6 8 10
```

236

```
An element: 2
An element: 4
An element: 6
An element: 8
An element: 10
The highest index is 4
This is what our reference looks like: ARRAY(0x806eb8)
$
```

Looking at this program in more detail, we first define an array variable and its contents, and then backslash it to create a reference to it.

```
my @array   = (2, 4, 6, 8, 10);
my $array_r = \@array;
```

Now we can use @{$array_r} instead of @array—both refer to exactly the same data, and both do exactly the same things. For instance, @{$array_r} will interpolate inside double quotes:

```
print "This is our dereferenced array: @{$array_r}\n";
```

Just as if we'd used the original @array, our dereferenced array prints out the contents of the array, separated by spaces:

```
This is our dereferenced array: 2 4 6 8 10
```

In the same way, we can use the array in a foreach loop, with no surprises:

```
foreach (@{$array_r}) {
    print "An element: $_\n";
}
```

Finally, we can also get the highest element number in the array, just as if we'd said $#array, like this (remember that Perl indexes 0-based, so the first index is 0):

```
print "The highest index is $#{$array_r}\n";
```

Now, we take a look at what the reference itself actually looks like. After all, it's a scalar, so it must have a value we can print out and look at. It does, and this is what we get if we print out the reference:

```
This is what our reference looks like: ARRAY(0x806eb8)
```

The ARRAY part obviously tells us that we have an array reference, but what about the part in parentheses? We know that a reference is a memory location, telling us where the data is stored in Perl's virtual memory. We generally don't need to worry about this actual value, as we can't do that much with it. Note also that it's unlikely you'll get exactly the same value as this example. It depends on what hardware your system has, what other software you're running, and what Perl is doing.

■ **Tip** There is one way you might want to make use of this value directly: to see if two references refer to the same piece of data, you can compare them as numbers using ==.

If you try to manipulate the reference, it ceases to be a reference and becomes an ordinary number—the value of the hexadecimal shown earlier. We can see that if we run the following program:

```
#!/usr/bin/perl
# noref.pl

use warnings;
use strict;

my $ref = [1, 2, 3];
print "Before: $ref\n";
print "@{$ref}\n";
$ref++;
print "After: $ref\n";
print "@{$ref}\n";
```

which will give us something like this:

```
$ perl noref.pl
Before: ARRAY(0x800368)
1 2 3
After: 8389481
Can't use string ("8389481") as an ARRAY ref while "strict refs" in use at noref.pl
 line 11.
$
```

When we tried to modify the reference, it degenerated to the ordinary number **8389480**, which is the equivalent of the hexadecimal number **0x800368** shown previously. Adding 1 to that number gave us the **8389481**, which is an ordinary string, rather than a reference. Perl then complains if we try and use it as a reference.

This is why you can't use references as hash keys—hash keys can only be strings, so your references will get stringified to something like the preceding form. Once that happens, you can't use them as references again.

Array Elements

What about the individual elements in an array—how do you access them? The rule is pretty much the same as for the array as a whole—just use the reference in curly braces in the same way you would the array name:

```
#!/usr/bin/perl
# deref2.pl

use warnings;
use strict;

my @band = qw(Crosby Stills Nash Young);
my $ref  = \@band;
foreach (0..$#band) {
   print "Array    : ", $band[$_]  , "\n";
```

```
    print "Reference: ", ${$ref}[$_], "\n";
}
```

As you can see, $band[$_] and ${$ref}[$_] refer to the same thing:

```
$ perl deref2.pl
Array    : Crosby
Reference: Crosby
Array    : Stills
Reference: Stills
Array    : Nash
Reference: Nash
Array    : Young
Reference: Young
$
```

The key point here is that these are not two different arrays—they are two ways of referring to the *same* piece of data—this is very important to remember when we start modifying references.

As we saw earlier, the last index of @band is $#band. We could have used the reference to obtain that value: $#{$ref}.

Reference Modification

If you want to modify the data pointed to by a reference, the same rule applies as before—replace the name of the array with the reference in curly braces. However, when you do this, the data in the original array will change, too.

```
#!/usr/bin/perl
# modify1.pl

use warnings;
use strict;

my @band = qw(Crosby Stills Nash Young);
my $ref  = \@band;
print "Band members before: @band\n";
pop @{$ref};
print "Band members after: @band\n";
```

```
$ perl modify1.pl
Band members before: Crosby Stills Nash Young
Band members after: Crosby Stills Nash
$
```

Now CSN&Y has changed forever.[2]

---

[2] For the worse?

We can still use push(), pop(), shift(), unshift(), and so on to manipulate the array using its reference. However, in doing so, we'll also be changing what's stored in @band.

It's quite possible to have multiple references to the same data and, just as before, if you use one to change the data, you change it for the others, too. This will give the same results as before:

```perl
my @band = qw(Crosby Stills Nash Young);
my $ref1 = \@band;
my $ref2 = \@band;
print "Band members before: @band\n";
pop @{$ref1};
print "Band members after: @{$ref2}\n";
```

and the same goes for anonymous arrays:

```perl
my $ref1 = [qw(Crosby Stills Nash Young)];
my $ref2 = $ref1;
print "Band members before: @{$ref2}\n";
pop @{$ref1};
print "Band members after: @{$ref2}\n";
```

Notice here that we're using [qw(...)], which is the same as saying

```perl
[('Crosby', 'Stills', 'Nash', 'Young')]
```

and the parentheses inside the square brackets get removed, just like when we said ((1,2,3)) back in Chapter 4.

You can also modify individual elements, using the syntax ${$reference}[$element]:

```perl
#!/usr/bin/perl
# modelem.pl

use warnings;
use strict;

my @array = (68, 101, 114, 111, 117);
my $ref = \@array;
${$ref}[0] = 100;
print "Array is now : @array\n";
```

```
$ perl modelem.pl
Array is now 100 101 114 111 117
$
```

And, again, you can do the same with anonymous data:

```perl
my $ref = [68, 101, 114, 111, 117];
${$ref}[0] = 100;
print "Array is now : @{$ref}\n";
```

Hash References

For references to hashes, the rule is exactly the same—replace the hash's name with the reference in curly braces. So, to access the hash pointed to by a reference, you use %{$hash_r}. If you want to get at a hash entry $hash{green}, you say ${$hash_r}{green}.

```
#!/usr/bin/perl
# hashref.pl

use warnings;
use strict;

my %hash = (
    1 => "January",    2 => "February", 3 => "March",      4 => "April",
    5 => "May",        6 => "June",     7 => "July",       8 => "August",
    9 => "September", 10 => "October", 11 => "November", 12 => "December"
);

my $href = \%hash;
foreach (keys %{$href}) {
    print "Key: ", $_, "\t";
    print "Hash: ", $hash{$_}, "\t";
    print "Ref: ", ${$href}{$_}, "\n";
}
```

As expected, we get the same data with the hash as when using the reference:

```
$ perl hashref.pl
Key: 6  Hash: June      Ref: June
Key: 11 Hash: November  Ref: November
Key: 3  Hash: March     Ref: March
Key: 7  Hash: July      Ref: July
Key: 9  Hash: September Ref: September
Key: 12 Hash: December  Ref: December
Key: 2  Hash: February  Ref: February
Key: 8  Hash: August    Ref: August
Key: 1  Hash: January   Ref: January
Key: 4  Hash: April     Ref: April
Key: 10 Hash: October   Ref: October
Key: 5  Hash: May       Ref: May
$
```

This should also help to remind you that Perl's hashes aren't ordered as you might expect!

Notation Shorthand Using ->

You can run into problems when you have one reference stored inside another. If you have the following array reference:

```
$ref = [ 1, 2, [ 10, 20 ] ];
```

241

you can get at the internal array reference by saying `${$ref[2]}`. But say we want to get at the first element (0-based) of that array—the one containing the value 20? We could store the reference inside another scalar and then dereference it, like this:

```
$inside  = ${$ref}[2];
$element = ${$inside}[1];
```

Or we could get the element directly, by repeatedly substituting references for array names:

```
$element = ${${ref}[2]}[1];
```

This gets very ugly very quickly, however, especially if you're dealing with hash references where it becomes hard to tell if the curly braces surround a reference or a hash key.

So, to help us clear it up again, we introduce this rule:

- Instead of `${$ref}`, we can say `$ref->`.

Let's demonstrate this by taking one of our previous examples, `modelem.pl`, and incorporating this into the code. Here's the relevant piece of the original:

```
my @array = (68, 101, 114, 111, 117);
my $ref = \@array;
${$ref}[0] = 100;
print "Array is now : @array\n";
```

and here it is rewritten:

```
my @array = (68, 101, 114, 111, 117);
my $ref = \@array;
$ref->[0] = 100;
print "Array is now : @array\n";
```

Likewise for hashes, we can use this arrow notation to make things a bit clearer. Recall `hashref.pl` from a little while ago:

```
foreach (keys %{$href}) {
    print "Key: ", $_, "\t";
    print "Hash: ", $hash{$_}, "\t";
    print "Ref: ", ${$href}{$_}, "\n";
}
```

Instead, we can write the following:

```
foreach (keys %{$href}) {
    print "Key: ", $_, "\t";
    print "Hash: ", $hash{$_}, "\t";
    print "Ref: ", $href->{$_}, "\n";
}
```

Now we can get at our array-in-an-array like this:

```
$ref = [ 1, 2, [ 10, 20 ] ];
$element = ${$ref->[2]}[1];
```

or more simply:

```
$element = $ref->[2]->[1];
```

However, we've got one more subrule that can simplify this even further:

- Between sets of square brackets, the arrow is optional.

We can therefore rewrite the preceding as

```
$element = $ref->[2][1];
```

Reference Counting and Destruction

We've seen the ways you can create and use references. Now we'll look at how you destroy them. Every piece of data in Perl has something called a *reference count* attached to it, which keeps track of the number of references that refer to that exact chunk of data.

When we create a reference to some data, the data's reference count goes up by 1. When we stop referring to it—we reassign the reference variable or "break" it (as when we modify its value)—the reference count goes down. When nobody's using the data and the reference count gets down to 0, the data is removed. Consider the following example:

```
#!/usr/bin/perl
# refcount.pl

use warnings;
use strict;

my $ref;
{
    my @array = (1, 2, 3);
    $ref = \@array;
    my $ref2 = \@array;
    $ref2 = "Hello!";
}
undef $ref;
```

Now, let's look at the references to the array (1, 2, 3) as we go through the program. To start with:

```
my $ref;
{
    my @array = (1, 2, 3);
```

the array is created, and the data (1, 2, 3) has one reference—it's in use by the array @array. Next we create another reference to it:

```
$ref = \@array;
```

and the reference count increases to 2. Once again we create a reference:

```
my $ref2 = \@array;
```

and the count goes up to 3. Next, we change that reference to be an ordinary string:

```
$ref2 = "Hello!";
```

$ref2 is not pointing at our array any more, so the reference count on (1, 2, 3) goes back down to 2. Note that changing $ref2 doesn't affect the original array—that only happens when we dereference. Now a block ends, and all the lexical variables—the my() variables—inside that block go out of scope:

```
}
```

That means that $ref2 and @array are destroyed. The reference count of the data (1, 2, 3) goes down again because @array is not referring to it. However, $ref still has a reference to it, so the reference count is still 1, and the data itself is not removed from memory. $ref still refers to (1, 2, 3) and can access and change this data as before. That is, of course, until we get rid of it:

```
undef $ref;
```

Now the final reference to the data (1, 2, 3) is removed and the memory for the array is finally freed.

Counting Anonymous References

Anonymous data works in the same way, though it doesn't get its initial reference count from being attached to a variable, but rather from when its first explicit reference is created:

```
my $ref = [1, 2, 3];
```

This data, therefore, has a reference count of 1, rather than

```
my @array = (1, 2, 3);
my $ref = \@array;
```

which has a count of 2.

Using References for Complex Data Structures

Now that we've looked at what references are, you might be asking, "Why on earth would we want to use them?" As noted in the introduction, we often want to create data structures that are more complex than simple arrays or hashes. We may need to store arrays inside arrays, or hashes inside hashes, and references help us do this.

So let's take a look at a few of the complex data structures we can create with references. This won't be exhaustive by any means, but it should give you some idea as to how complex data structures look and work in Perl, and it should help you to understand the most common data structures.

Matrices

What is a matrix? No, not the thing that Neo wants out of[3]. A *matrix* is simply an array of arrays. You can refer to any single element in a matrix with a combination of two subscripts, which you can think of as a row number and a column number; this harks back to the chessboard example we mentioned in the introduction.

If you use the arrow syntax, matrices are very easy to use. You get at an element by saying

```
$array[$row]->[$column]
```

which can be written as

```
$array[$row][$column]
```

`$array[$row]` is an array reference, and we're dereferencing the `$column`'th element in it. With a chessboard example, it would look like this:

So, `$array[0][0]` would be the bottom left-hand corner of our chessboard, and `$array[7][7]` would be the top right corner.

Autovivification

There's one last thing you need to know about references before we go on—if we assign values to a reference, Perl will automatically create all the appropriate references necessary to make it work. So, if we say this:

```
my $ref;
$ref->{UK}->{England}->{Oxford}->[1999]->{Population} = 500000;
```

Perl will automatically know that we need `$ref` to be a hash reference. So, it'll make us a nice new anonymous hash:

```
$ref = {};
```

---

[3] http://en.wikipedia.org/wiki/The_Matrix

Then we need `$ref->{UK}` to be a hash reference because we're looking for the hash key `England`; that hash entry needs to be an array reference, and so on. Perl effectively does this:

```
$ref = {};
$ref->{UK} = {};
$ref->{UK}->{England} = {};
$ref->{UK}->{England}->{Oxford} = [];
$ref->{UK}->{England}->{Oxford}->[1999] = {};
$ref->{UK}->{England}->{Oxford}->[1999]->{Population} = 500000;
```

What this means is that we don't have to worry about creating all the entries ourselves. We can just go ahead and write

```
my @chessboard;
$chessboard[0]->[0] = "WR";
```

This is called *autovivification*—things springing into existence. We can use autovivification to greatly simplify the way we use references.

Now that we can represent our chessboard, let's set up a chess game. This will consist of two stages: setting up the board, and making moves. The computer will have no idea of the rules, but will simply function as a board, allowing us to move pieces around. Here's our program:

```perl
#!/usr/bin/perl
# chess.pl

use warnings;
use strict;

my @chessboard;
my @back = qw(R N B Q K B N R);
foreach (0..7) {
    $chessboard[0][$_] = "W" . $back[$_]; # White Back Row
    $chessboard[1][$_] = "WP";            # White Pawns
    $chessboard[6][$_] = "BP";            # Black Pawns
    $chessboard[7][$_] = "B" . $back[$_]; # Black Back Row
}

while (1) {
    # Print board
    foreach my $i (reverse (0..7)) { # Row
        foreach my $j (0..7) {       # Column
            if (defined $chessboard[$i][$j]) {
                print $chessboard[$i][$j];
            } elsif ( ($i % 2) == ($j % 2) ) {
                print "..";
            } else {
                print "  ";
            }
            print " ";  # End of cell
        }
```

```perl
print "\n";      # End of row
   }

   print "\nStarting square [x,y]: ";
   my $move = <>;
   last unless ($move =~ /^\s*([1-8]),([1-8])/);
   my $startx = $1-1; my $starty = $2-1;

   unless (defined $chessboard[$starty][$startx]) {
      print "There's nothing on that square!\n";
      next;
   }
   print "\nEnding square [x,y]: ";
   $move = <>;
   last unless ($move =~ /([1-8]),([1-8])/);
   my $endx = $1-1; my $endy = $2-1;

   # Put starting square on ending square.
   $chessboard[$endy][$endx] = $chessboard[$starty][$startx];
   # Remove from old square
   undef $chessboard[$starty][$startx];
}
```

Now let's see the first part of a game in progress:

```
$ perl chess.pl
BR BN BB BQ BK BB BN BR
BP BP BP BP BP BP BP BP
   ..    ..    ..    ..
..    ..    ..    ..
   ..    ..    ..    ..
..    ..    ..    ..
WP WP WP WP WP WP WP WP
WR WN WB WQ WK WB WN WR

Starting square [x,y]: 4,2

Ending square [x,y]: 4,4
BR BN BB BQ BK BB BN BR
BP BP BP BP BP BP BP BP
   ..    ..    ..    ..
..    ..    ..    ..
   ..    WP    ..    ..
..    ..    ..    ..
WP WP WP .. WP WP WP WP
WR WN WB WQ WK WB WN WR

Starting square [x,y]: 4,7
```

247

```
Ending square [x,y]: 4,5
BR BN BB BQ BK BB BN BR
BP BP BP BP BP BP BP
   ..    ..    ..       ..
..    ..  BP    ..  ..
   ..    WP    ..    ..
..    ..       ..  ..
WP WP WP .. WP WP WP WP
WR WN WB WQ WK WB WN WR
```

Let's look at this program in detail. Our first task is to set up the chessboard with the pieces in their initial positions. Remember that we're assigning $chessboard[$row][$column] = $thing. First, we set up an array of pieces on the "back row." We'll use this to make it easier to put each piece in its appropriate column.

```
my @back = qw(R N B Q K B N R);
```

Now we'll go over each column.

```
foreach (0..7) {
```

In row 0, the back row for white, we want to place the appropriate piece from the array in each square.

```
$chessboard[0][$_] = "W" . $back[$_]; # White Back Row
```

In row 1 of each column, we want a white pawn, WP.

```
$chessboard[1][$_] = "WP";              # White Pawns
```

Now we do the same again for black's pieces on rows 6 and 7.

```
    $chessboard[6][$_] = "BP";           # Black Pawns
    $chessboard[7][$_] = "B" . $back[$_]; # Black Back Row
}
```

What about the rest of the squares on board? Well, they don't exist right now, but they will spring into existence when we try and read from them.

Next we go into our main loop, printing out the board and moving the pieces. To print the board, we obviously want to look at each piece—so we loop through each row and each column:

```
foreach my $i (reverse (0..7)) { # Row
     foreach my $j (0..7) {        # Column
```

If the element is defined, it's because we've put a piece there, so we print it out.

```
if (defined $chessboard[$i]->[$j]) {
          print $chessboard[$i]->[$j];
```

This next piece of prettiness prints out the "checkered" effect. On a checkerboard, dark squares come in odd rows in odd columns and even rows in even columns. $x % 2 tests whether $x divides equally by 2—whether it is odd or even. If the "oddness" (or "evenness") of the row and column is the same, we print a dark square.

```
} elsif ( ($i % 2) == ($j % 2) ) {
            print "..";
```

Otherwise, we print a blank square consisting of two spaces:

```
} else {
            print "  ";
        }
```

To separate the cells, we use a single space.

```
 print " ";  # End of cell
        }
```

And at the end of each row, we print a new line.

```
print "\n";      # End of row
    }
```

Now we ask for a square to move from:

```
print "\nStarting square [x,y]: ";
   my $move = <>;
```

We're looking for two digits with a comma in the middle:

```
last unless ($move =~ /([1-8]),([1-8])/);
```

Now we convert human-style coordinates (1 to 8) into computer-style coordinates (0 to 7):

```
my $startx = $1-1; my $starty = $2-1;
```

Next, we check if there's actually a chess piece there. Note that a y coordinate is a row, so it goes first—look back at the diagram if you're not sure how this works.

```
    unless (defined $chessboard[$starty][$startx]) {
        print "There's nothing on that square!\n";
        next;
    }
```

We do the same for the ending square, and then move the piece. We copy the piece to the new square:

```
$chessboard[$endy][$endx] = $chessboard[$starty]->[$startx];
```

And then we delete the old square:

```
undef $chessboard[$starty][$startx];
```

We've now used a matrix, a two-dimensional array. The nice thing about Perl's autovivification feature is that we didn't need to say explicitly that we were dealing with references—Perl takes care of all that behind the scenes, and we just assigned the relevant values to the right places. However, if we were to look at the contents of the @chessboard array, we'd see eight array references.

Trees

We're now going to build on the principle of matrices by introducing *tree*-like data structures, in which we use hashes as well as arrays. The classic example of one of these structures is an address book. Suppose we want to keep someone's address and phone number in a hash. We could say this:

```
%paddy = (
    address => "23 Blue Jay Way",
    phone   => "404-6599"
);
```

That's all very well, and it makes sense—the only problem is, you have to create a separate hash for each person in your address book, and put each one in a separate variable. This isn't easy at all at run time, and is very messy to write. Instead, you use references.

What you do is create a main "address book" hash, referenced as $addressbook, with everyone else's hashes as values off that:

```
$addressbook{"Paddy Malone"} = {
    address => "23 Blue Jay Way",
    phone   => "404-6599"
};
```

This creates a data structure that looks like:

■ **Note** Bear in mind that if you've included the use strict; pragma, you'll have to declare this hash explicitly as my %addressbook; before using it.

It's now very easy to take new entries from the user and add them to the address book:

```
print "Give me a name:"; chomp($name   = <>);
print "Address:";        chomp($address= <>);
print "Phone number:";   chomp($phone  = <>);
$addressbook{$name} = {
    address => $address,
    phone   => $phone
};
```

To print out a single person, we'd use this:

```
if (exists $addressbook{$who}) {
    print "$who\n";
```

```
   print "Address:  ", $addressbook{$who}{address}, "\n";
   print "Phone no: ", $addressbook{$who}{phone},   "\n";
}
```

And to print every address:

```
foreach $who (keys %addressbook) {
   print "$who\n";
   print "Address:  ", $addressbook{$who}{address}, "\n";
   print "Phone no: ", $addressbook{$who}{phone},   "\n";
}
```

Deleting an address is very simple:

```
delete $addressbook{$who};
```

How about adding another level to our tree? Can we have an array of "friends" for each person? No problem—we just use an anonymous array:

```
$addressbook{"Paddy Malone"} = {
   address => "23 Blue Jay Way",
   phone   => "404-6599",
   friends => [ "Baba O'Reilly", "Mick Flaherty" ]
};
```

This creates the structure:

We can get at each person's friends by saying `$addressbook{$who}{friends}`, and that'll give us an anonymous array. We can then dereference that to a real array and print it out:

```
foreach $who (keys %addressbook) {
   print "$who\n";
   print "Address:  ", $addressbook{$who}{address}, "\n";
   print "Phone no: ", $addressbook{$who}{phone},   "\n";
   my @friends = @{$addressbook{$who}{friends}};
   print "Friends:";
   foreach (@friends) {
      print "\t$_";
   }
```

251

```
print "\n\n";
}
```

This would now give us something like the following:

```
Paddy Malone
Address:  23 Blue Jay Way
Phone no: 404-6599
Friends:
        Baba O'Reilly
        Mick Flaherty
```

What we now have is one hash (address book), containing another hash (peoples' details), in turn containing an array (each person's friends).

We can quite easily *traverse* the tree structure—that is, move from person to person—by following links. We do this by visiting a link, and then adding all of that person's friends onto a "to do" array. We must be very careful here not to get stuck in a loop—if one person links to another, and the other links back again, we need to avoid bouncing about between them indefinitely. One simple way to keep track of the links we've already processed is to use a hash. Here's how:

```
$, = "\t";               # Set output field separator for tabulated display
my %added_to_todo = ();
my @todo = ("Paddy Malone"); # Start point
$added_to_todo{"Paddy Malone"}++;
while (@todo) {
    my $who = shift @todo; # Get person from the end
    my @friends = @{$addressbook{$who}{friends}};
    print "$who has friends: ", @friends, "\n";
    foreach (@friends) {
        # Visit unless they're already visited
        unless (exists $added_to_todo{$_}) {
            push @todo, $_;
            $added_to_todo{$_}++;         # Mark them as seen.
        }
    }
}
```

The hash `%added_to_todo` is used to build up a table of everyone whose name has been added to the array `@todo`. The `foreach` loop at the bottom only adds names to the `@todo` list if they're not defined in that hash—that is, if they've not been added already.

Let's put all these ideas together into a program. Notice in this example how all the data is assigned to %addressbook in one assignment:

```
#!/usr/bin/perl

use warnings;
use strict;

my %addressbook = (
    "Paddy Malone" => {
        address => "23 Blue Jay Way",
```

```
        phone   => "404-6599",
        friends => [ "Baba O'Reilly", "Mick Flaherty" ]
    },
    "Baba O'Reilly" => {
        address => "123 Main St.",
        phone   => "984-5912",
        friends => [ "Bob McDowell", "Mick Flaherty", "Andy Donahue" ]
    },
    "Mick Flaherty" => {
        address => "5983 2nd Ave.",
        phone   => "377-5885",
        friends => [ "Paddy Malone", "Timothy O'Leary" ]
    },
    "Bob McDowell" => {
        address => "6149 Oak St.",
        phone   => "299-3885",
        friends => [ "Andy Donahue", "Baba O'Reilly" ]
    },
    "Andy Donahue" => {
        address => "8712 Central St.",
        phone   => "598-2813",
        friends => [ "Jimmy Callahan", "Mick Flaherty" ]
    },
    "Timothy O'Leary" => {
        address => "3983 Green Bay Rd.",
        phone   => "944-3487",
        friends => [ "Bob McDowell", "Mick Flaherty", "Paddy Malone" ]
    },
    "Jimmy Callahan" => {
        address => "533 Ridge Rd.",
        phone   => "869-1298",
        friends => [ "Andy Donahue", "Baba O'Reilly", "Mick Flaherty" ]
    }
);

foreach my $who (keys %addressbook) {
    print "$who\n";
    print "Address:  ", $addressbook{$who}{address}, "\n";
    print "Phone no: ", $addressbook{$who}{phone},   "\n";
    my @friends = @{$addressbook{$who}{friends}};
    print "Friends:";
    foreach (@friends) {
        print "\t$_";
    }
    print "\n\n";
}

$, = "\t";           # Set output field separator for tabulated display
my %added_to_todo = ();
my @todo = ("Paddy Malone"); # Start point
$added_to_todo{"Paddy Malone"}++;
```

```
while (@todo) {
    my $who = shift @todo; # Get person from the end
    my @friends = @{$addressbook{$who}{friends}};
    print "$who has friends: ", @friends, "\n";
    foreach (@friends) {
        # Visit unless they're already visited
        unless (exists $added_to_todo{$_}) {
            push @todo, $_;
            $added_to_todo{$_}++;              # Mark them as seen.
        }
    }
}
```

Executing this code produces all of this output (it is a lot—whew!):

```
$ perl addressbook.pl
Andy Donahue
Address:  8712 Central St.
Phone no: 598-2813
Friends:        Jimmy Callahan  Mick Flaherty

Mick Flaherty
Address:  5983 2nd Ave.
Phone no: 377-5885
Friends:        Paddy Malone    Timothy O'Leary

Baba O'Reilly
Address:  123 Main St.
Phone no: 984-5912
Friends:        Bob McDowell    Mick Flaherty   Andy Donahue

Timothy O'Leary
Address:  3983 Green Bay Rd.
Phone no: 944-3487
Friends:        Bob McDowell    Mick Flaherty   Paddy Malone

Paddy Malone
Address:  23 Blue Jay Way
Phone no: 404-6599
Friends:        Baba O'Reilly   Mick Flaherty

Jimmy Callahan
Address:  533 Ridge Rd.
Phone no: 869-1298
Friends:        Andy Donahue    Baba O'Reilly   Mick Flaherty

Bob McDowell
Address:  6149 Oak St.
Phone no: 299-3885
Friends:        Andy Donahue    Baba O'Reilly
```

```
Paddy Malone has friends:        Baba O'Reilly     Mick Flaherty
Baba O'Reilly has friends:       Bob McDowell      Mick Flaherty    Andy Donahue
Mick Flaherty has friends:       Paddy Malone      Timothy O'Leary
Bob McDowell has friends:        Andy Donahue      Baba O'Reilly
Andy Donahue has friends:        Jimmy Callahan    Mick Flaherty
Timothy O'Leary has friends: Bob McDowell          Mick Flaherty    Paddy Malone
Jimmy Callahan has friends:      Andy Donahue      Baba O'Reilly    Mick Flaherty
```

Summary

We've looked at references, a way to put one type of data structure inside another. References work because they allow us to use a scalar to refer to another piece of data. They tell us where Perl stores the data, and give us a way to get at it with a scalar.

We can create a reference explicitly by putting a backslash in front of a variable's name: `\%hash` or `\@array`, for example. Alternatively, we can create an anonymous reference by using `{}` instead of `()` for a hash, and `[]` instead of `()` for an array. Finally, we can create a reference by creating a need for one—if a reference needs to exist for what we're doing, Perl will bring one into existence by autovivification.

We can use a reference by placing it in curly braces where a variable name should go. `@{$array_r}` can replace `@array` everywhere. We can then access elements of array or hash references using the arrow notation: `$array_ref->[$element]` for an array, and `$hash_ref->{$key}` for a hash.

We've also seen a few complex data structures: matrices, which are arrays of arrays; and trees, which may contain hashes or arrays. For more information on these kinds of data structures, consult the Perl "Data Structures Cookbook" documentation (`perldoc perldsc`) or the Perl "List of Lists" documentation (`perldoc perllol`).

If you're really interested in data structures from a computer science point of view, *Mastering Algorithms in Perl* by Orwant et al. (O'Reilly Media, 1999) has some chapters on these kinds of structures, primarily trees and tree traversal. The ultimate guide to data structures is still *The Art of Computer Programming, Volume 1*, by Donald Knuth (Addison-Wesley, 1997)—affectionately known as "The Bible."

Exercises

1. Modify the chessboard example to detect when a piece is taken. This occurs when a piece is sitting in a square that another piece moves into. The piece that was originally in the square is taken by the new piece and removed from the board.

2. Without being concerned with checks, checkmates, and castling, check to ensure that a move is valid. If you don't know the rules of chess, just check the following: no player may take either king (K), and no player may take their own pieces.

3. Turn the snippets of address book code into an address book management program. Allow the user to add, search for, and delete entries. See if you can think of a way to save the hash to disk and load it again.

CHAPTER 12

■■■

Modules

Now that we can write Perl functions to solve our problems, we can collect together functions into a *module*. A module is a collection of (hopefully) related functions and variables that can be used by any program.

Very simply, a module is a package within a file—a collection of subroutines and variables that all work together to perform some set of tasks that we can use to solve our programming problems.

There exists a large collection of prewritten Perl modules—we programmers can use these modules, free of charge, to solve our problems. The modules are available at CPAN, the Comprehensive Perl Archive Network (www.cpan.org and mirrors all over the world). There are modules available at CPAN that are easy-to-use solutions to many different problems—for example, modules to simplify network programming, process XML files, create web programs (CGI and others), connect to SQL databases, and do complex mathematics. This list could go on and on, but we suggest you visit http://search.cpan.org/, which offers both browsing and searching of the CPAN.

In this chapter you will start by creating your own module that can be used by your programs. Then you will look at several very useful prewritten modules that are released with the Perl distribution. This discussion is only meant to be a sample of what is available at CPAN; we suggest that you point your browser at CPAN and start installing and using modules—they will almost certainly make your programming life easier.

Why Do We Need Them?

Why should you use modules? The simple answer is that it saves time. If you need that program written yesterday, it's exceptionally handy to be able to download a bunch of modules that you know will do the job, and then simply glue them together.

The second answer is because most of us programmers are lazy—that's just a fact of life. Programmers are, on the whole, naturally lazy people and don't like reinventing the wheel. Now, don't get us wrong—there's good laziness and there's bad laziness. Bad laziness says "I should get someone else to do this for me," whereas good laziness says "Maybe someone's already done this." The good kind pays off. Most of the programming you'll be doing will, at some level, have been done before.

Modules that have been around on CPAN for a while will have been used by thousands of individuals, many of whom will have spent time fixing bugs and returning the results to the maintainer. Most of the borderline cases will have been worked out by now, and you can be pretty confident that the modules will do things right. When it comes to things like parsing HTML or processing CGI form data, we're perfectly willing to admit that the people who wrote `HTML::Parser` and the `CGI` modules have done more work on the subject than we have—so we use their code, instead of trying to work out our own.

In short: don't reinvent the wheel—use modules.

Creating a Module

Let's say you are working on a team that is developing software for the Acme webserver.[1] You have been assigned the role of developing an easy-to-use logging interface. It will utilize the idea of *log levels*, or logging at varying degrees of detail. Level 1 is the least detail, and higher values indicate more details.

You want to make your module easy to use and functional. What you need the module to do is to open and close the log file, write into the log file, and set the log level (which has the default value of 1, or the least level of detail).

To create your module, you will follow these five steps:

- Think of a good name for the module. Since you are creating a module to log information, you will call your module Logger.

- Put the source code into a file named *modulename*.pm (pm stands for "Perl module"), in this example, Logger.pm.

- Make the module a *package*, or namespace (more on packages later), by placing the line of code package Logger; at the top of the file.

- Define variables and function in the file.

- Have the file return a true value by ending in 1;.

Implementing step 4, let's define some functions. You want to provide the user a function to open the file. A good name for the function is open_log(), since it is opening the log file, and it might look like the following:

```
sub open_log {
    my $filename = shift;
    open(LOGFILE, '>>', $filename) or die "can't open $filename: $!";
    print LOGFILE "Log started: ", scalar(localtime), "\n";
}
```

This function grabs the first argument, which is the filename to open. Then, the log file is opened in append mode and a message is printed to the log file stating that the logging has begun. You also need a function to close the log file:

---

[1] This is probably not a good idea, since there is already a really good webserver available for free—httpd.apache.org.

```perl
sub close_log {
    close LOGFILE;
}
```

Next, you need a function to write into the log file:

```perl
sub write_log {
    my($level, $message) = @_;
    print LOGFILE "$message\n" if $level <= $LEVEL;
}
```

This function is expecting two arguments: the log message level and the message. The message is then printed if the level of the message is less than or equal to the level that is set for this logger.

Finally, you need a way to set the log level in case you want more (or less) detail. Here it is:

```perl
sub log_level {
    my $level = shift;
    $LEVEL = $level if $level =~ /^\d+$/;
}
```

The argument is assigned to $LEVEL if the argument is a positive integer.

■ **Note** You should probably add a lot more error checking to these functions to make them a bit harder to break. For instance, what if write_log() was called with no log level and message? The function would work (printing an empty string to the log file since it would treat the level as 0, less than your minimum level, and the message would be undef), but it would be polite to instead report to the user that they are using the function incorrectly. Also, any real logging module would lock the file with flock(). But if error checking and file locking were added to this example, it would be way too long and complicated for our purpose here.

Here is the whole module, including the initial value assigned to $LEVEL:

```perl
package Logger;
# Logger.pm

use strict;
use warnings;

my $LEVEL = 1;  # default level is 1

sub open_log {
    my $filename = shift;
    open(LOGFILE, '>>', $filename) or die "can't open $filename: $!";
    print LOGFILE "Log started: ", scalar(localtime), "\n";
}

sub close_log {
```

```
    close LOGFILE;
}

sub write_log {
    my($level, $message) = @_;
    print LOGFILE "$message\n" if $level <= $LEVEL;
}

sub log_level {
    my $level = shift;
    $LEVEL = $level if $level =~ /^\d+$/;
}

1;
```

■ **Note** A note about 1; at the end of the file. Earlier versions of Perl required that the module return a true value when it is used by a program. Since the module will return the last line of code in the file, most programmers simply put 1;, a true value, at the end of the module. Newer versions of Perl do not require the 1; at the end of the file, but for backward compatibility and historical reasons, programmers still put in that true value.

Including Other Files with use

Now that you have created a module, you will want to put it to use in your programs. Let's talk about several different ways for a Perl program to import a module and call that module's functions. You have three ways of doing this: do, require, and use.

do

This is the most difficult of the three to understand—the others are just slightly varied forms of do.

do will look for a file by searching the @INC path. If the file can't be found, it will silently move on. If it is found, it will run the file just as if it was placed in a block within your main program—but with one slight difference: you won't be able to see lexical variables from the main program once you're inside the additional code. So if you have a file dothis.pl:

```
#!/usr/bin/perl
# dothis.pl

use warnings;
use strict;

our $var = "Been there, done that, got the T-shirt";
do "printit.pl";
```

and a file printit.pl:

```
# printit.pl

use warnings;

print $a;
print "this should go to standard output...\n";
```

`dothis.pl` will do, or execute, the file `printit.pl`. This means that the contents of `printit.pl` are compiled and executed. Executing this code produces the following:

```
$ perl dothis.pl
Use of uninitialized value in print at printit.pl line 5.
this should go to standard output...
$
```

The first line of output is a warning that $var is undefined. The second line of output is a result of executing the second `print()` function.

This program shows that do can execute arbitrary code in another file. On the other hand, you can have subroutines in your included file and call them from the main file.

require

`require` is like do, but it'll only do it once. It'll record the fact that a file has been loaded, and will henceforth ignore further requests to `require` it again. It also fails with an error if it can't find the file you're loading.

```
#!/usr/bin/perl
# cantload.pl

use warnings;
use strict;

require "not_there.pl";
```

will `die()` with an error like this:

```
$ perl cantload.pl
Can't locate not_there.pl in @INC (@INC contains: /etc/perl /usr/local/lib/perl/5.10.0
/usr/local/share/perl/5.10.0 /usr/lib/perl5 /usr/share/perl5 /usr/lib/perl/5.10
/usr/share/perl/5.10 /usr/local/lib/site_perl .) at ./cantload.pl line 7.
$
```

This displays the contents @INC array, which contains a list of paths in which Perl looks for modules and other additional files. These paths include directories where the standard library are stored, "site" modules (third-party modules that are typically installed from CPAN) and the current directory.

Therefore, when Perl was looking for the file `not_there.pl`, it first looked in `/etc/perl`, then in `/usr/local/lib/perl/5.10.0` and so on until it finally looked in `.`, the current directory. Of course, Perl didn't find `not_there.pl` because it was, well, not there.

You can also invoke `require` like this:

```
require Wibble;
```

Using a bareword tells Perl to look for a file called `Wibble.pm` in the `@INC` path. It also converts any instance of `::` into a directory separator. For instance:

```
require Monty::Python;
```

will send Perl looking for `Python.pm` in a directory called `Monty`, which is itself in one of the directories given in `@INC`.

use

The way you normally use modules is, logically enough, with the **use** statement. This is like `require`, except that Perl applies it *before* anything else in the program starts—if Perl sees a **use** statement *anywhere* in your program, it'll include that module. So, for instance, you can't say this:

```
if ($graphical) {
    use MyProgram::Graphical;
} else {
    use MyProgram::Text;
}
```

because when Perl's reading your program, it will include *both* modules—the **use** takes place way before the value of `$graphical` is decided. You say that **use** takes place at compile time and not at run time.

Changing @INC

The default contents of the search path `@INC` are decided when Perl is compiled—if you move those directories elsewhere, you'll have to recompile Perl to get it working again. However, you can tell it to search in directories other than these. `@INC` is an ordinary array, so you might expect to be able to say

```
unshift @INC, "my/module/directory";
use Wibble;
```

However, this isn't going to work. Why not? Remember that the preceding statement will execute at run time. Unfortunately the **use** statement takes place at compile time, well before that. No problem! There's a special subroutine called `BEGIN` that is guaranteed execution at compile time, so you can put it there:

```
sub BEGIN {
    unshift @INC, "my/module/directory";
}
use Wibble;
```

Now that'll work just fine—however, it's a little messy, and what's more, there's an easier way to do it. You can use the `lib` pragma to add your directory to `@INC` before anything else gets a chance to look at it:

```
use lib "my/module/directory";
use Wibble;
```

The directory that is indicated is inserted into the front of `@INC` so that it is the first directory searched when Perl is looking for the module.

Ok, it is time to use your `Logger` module. Here is a program that uses `Logger.pm`. Notice how the functions are invoked with the package name preceding the function names.

```perl
#!/usr/bin/perl
# logtest1.pl

use warnings;
use strict;
use Logger;

Logger::open_log("webserver.log");

# this will go to the log file
Logger::write_log(1, "A basic message");

# this won't to the log file - the level is too high
Logger::write_log(10, "A debugging message");

# set the level so the debugging message will end up
# in the log file
Logger::log_level(10);
Logger::write_log(10, "Another debugging message");

Logger::close_log();
```

When executed, this program creates and adds text to the log file `webserver.log`.

$ perl logtest1.pl

Here is the content of the log file:

```
Log started: Fri Jul  2 11:42:12 2009
A basic message
Another debugging message
```

Now you can use this module in all of your Acme webserver programs to log information to a log file.

Package Hierarchies

Let's say the Acme Corporation is going to develop several different servers in addition to the webserver such as a DNS server, a DHCP server, and an FTP server. Each of these servers needs a way to log information to a log file, each in its own way. You would then need several modules:

- WebserverLogger
- DNSserverLogger

- DHCPserverLogger

- FTPserverLogger

These modules are, for now, all stored in the same directory (for us, the current directory). Storing them all in the same directory can become a problem if the number of modules continues to grow—imagine if the directory contains hundreds of modules. To combat the problem with having unique names for all the modules and the problem of having a lot of modules in the same directory, you can create *package hierarchies*.

Instead of naming your webserver logging module `WebserverLogger`, you can name it `Acme::Webserver::Logger`. This longer name shows the hierarchy of the module: under the overall name of `Acme`, you see the `Webserver` product, and under that the module named `Logger`. Therefore, instead of the module names shown previously, you would have:

- Acme::Webserver::Logger

- Acme::DNSserver::Logger

- Acme::DHCPserver::Logger

- Acme::FTPserver::Logger

A package name indicates the location of the module. For instance, the `Acme::Webserver::Logger` module will be stored in this file:
`Acme/Webserver/Logger.pm`

This file will be stored in the directory `Webserver` under the directory `Acme` in some location in the filesystem. For now, that location is the current directory (but we will soon show how to change that). Here is the content of `Acme/Webserver/Logger.pm`, a slight modification from the previous example. We just changed the name of the package in the first line and the comment showing the name of the file in the second line (and of course moved the file to the `Acme/Webserver` directory):

```perl
package Acme::Webserver::Logger;
# Acme::Webserver/Logger.pm

use warnings;
use strict;

my $LEVEL = 1;  # default level is 1

sub open_log {
    my $filename = shift;
    open(LOGFILE, '>>', $filename) or die "can't open $filename: $!";
    print LOGFILE "Log started: ", scalar(localtime), "\n";
}

sub close_log {
    close LOGFILE;
}

sub write_log {
    my($level, $message) = @_;
    print LOGFILE "$message\n" if $level <= $LEVEL;
```

```
}

sub log_level {
    my $level = shift;
    $LEVEL = $level if $level =~ /^\d+$/;
}

1;
```

To use this new module, you modify the use statement, and then adjust the function calls to use the full package name as showing in logtest2.pl:

```
#!/usr/bin/perl
# logtest2.pl

use warnings;
use strict;
use Acme::Webserver::Logger;

Acme::Webserver::Logger::open_log("webserver.log");

# this will go to the log file
Acme::Webserver::Logger::write_log(1, "A basic message");

# this won't - the level is too high
Acme::Webserver::Logger::write_log(10, "A debugging message");

# set the level so the debugging message will end up
# in the log file
Acme::Webserver::Logger::log_level(10);
Acme::Webserver::Logger::write_log(10, "Another debugging message");

Acme::Webserver::Logger::close_log();
```

The syntax for calling the functions in the module is way too long! We can shorten these lines by *exporting* the function names in the module.

Exporters

Let's say you try to call the open_log() function without the fully qualified name as in:

```
open_log("webserver.log");
```

When you run this code, Perl will be looking for a function named open_log() in the main package and since you have defined one, it will produce the following error message:

```
Undefined subroutine &main::open_log called at line 8.
```

If you want to call the open_log() function with the fully qualified package name, you need to make the Logger package an exporter. The module can then export to the calling package all the symbols function names the calling package will invoke. To make the module and exporter and to export the desired function names, you add these three lines of code:

```
use Exporter;
use base 'Exporter';
our @EXPORT = qw(open_log close_log write_log log_level);
```

The first line of new code uses the Exporter module which does some magic and allows you to use a variable in that package: @EXPORT.

The second line implements object-oriented inheritance (we will talk more about inheritance in Chapter 13).

The last line assigns to the array @EXPORT. Any symbol that you want to export to the calling package is assigned to this array, and you are exporting your four functions defined in the package. Since the function name open_log() is included in the assignment, you can call the function directly with no fully qualified package name. Nice!

Here is the new package converted to an exporter:

```
package Acme::Webserver::LoggerExporter;
# Acme/Webserver/LoggerExporter.pm

use strict;
use warnings;

# become an exporter and export the functions
use Exporter;
use base 'Exporter';
our @EXPORT = qw(open_log close_log write_log log_level);

my $LEVEL = 1;  # default level is 1

sub open_log {
    my $filename = shift;
    open(LOGFILE, '>>', $filename) or die "can't open $filename: $!";
    print LOGFILE "Log started: ", scalar(localtime), "\n";
}

sub close_log {
    close LOGFILE;
}

sub write_log {
    my($level, $message) = @_;
    print LOGFILE "$message\n" if $level <= $LEVEL;
}

sub log_level {
    my $level = shift;
    $LEVEL = $level if $level =~ /^\d+$/;
}

1;
```

The code to all these exported functions is much cleaner than the previous example:

```perl
#!/usr/bin/perl
# logtest3.pl

use warnings;
use strict;
use Acme::Webserver::LoggerExporter;

open_log("webserver.log");

# this will go to the log file
write_log(1, "A basic message");

# this won't - the level is too high
write_log(10, "A debugging message");

# set the level so the debugging message will end up
# in the log file
log_level(10);
write_log(10, "Another debugging message");

close_log();
```

Ah, much better! Executing this program will add to the log file:

```
$ perl logtest3.pl
```

so that its content is

```
Log started: Fri Jul  2 11:42:12 2004
A basic message
Another debugging message
Log started: Fri Jul  2 11:50:41 2004
A basic message
Another debugging message
```

The Perl Standard Modules

Not only can you create your own modules, you can also use modules that others have created and have made available at CPAN. When Perl is installed, there are many modules automatically installed. These are called the *standard modules*. You will look at a few of the more interesting ones here. For a complete list of all the modules in the Perl distribution, execute perldoc perlmodlib at a shell prompt.

Online Documentation

The perldoc program is a simple way to view the online documentation for a module. Simply provide the module name as its argument:

$ perldoc Data::Dumper

You can also check out www.perldoc.com and www.cpan.org for module documentation.

Data::Dumper

Data::Dumper stringifies data types in Perl syntax so a programmer can see a visual representation of the data structure. Here is a simple example:

```perl
#!/usr/bin/perl
# data1.pl

use warnings;
use strict;
use Data::Dumper qw(Dumper);   # import the Dumper() function

# create a complex data type

my @a = (
    'hello, world',
    1234.56,
    [ 2, 4, 6 ],
    { one => 'first', two => 'second' }
);

# create a reference to it

my $r = \@a;

# dump it out

print Dumper($r);
```

This program first uses Data::Dumper, importing the Dumper() function. It then creates a complex data type: an array that contains a string, a float, an anonymous array, and an anonymous hash. Then, a reference to the array is created. Finally, that reference is dumped out. This code produces

```
$ perl data1.pl
$VAR1 = [
          'hello, world',
          '1234.56',
          [
            2,
            4,
            6
          ],
```

```
    {
      'one' => 'first',
      'two' => 'second'
    }
  ];
```

This displays the complex data type so we programmers can read it and understand it. It appears that $VAR1 (a name chosen for us by Data::Dumper) is a reference to an array that contains a string, a float, an anonymous array, and an anonymous hash. Being able to view this output can assist in debugging your program.[2]

Data::Dumper chooses the variable name $VAR1 for you. Perhaps you want to name the variable yourself. A small change to data1.pl will do the trick:

```perl
#!/usr/bin/perl
# data2.pl

use warnings;
use strict;
use Data::Dumper;

# create a complex data type

my @a = (
    'hello, world',
    1234.56,
    [ 2, 4, 6 ],
    { one => 'first', two => 'second' }
);

# create a reference to it

my $r = \@a;

# dump it out
print Data::Dumper->Dump([$r], ['myvarname']);
```

This code produces the following:

```
$ perl data2.pl
$myvarname = [
              'hello, world',
              '1234.56',
```

---

[2] This output can also be stored for later use. If you store this output into a scalar variable, you can eval() that variable, which will reconstruct the data structure (for information on eval(), check out perldoc -f eval).

```
        [
          2,
          4,
          6
        ],
        {
          'one' => 'first',
          'two' => 'second'

        }
      ];
```

File::Find

`File::Find` is a module for traversing directory trees, visiting each file in turn and running a subroutine (the callback) on them. This module has a very useful method: `find()`. It does a depth-first search, visiting directories only after their files have been processed. This is useful if, for example, you want to delete entire directory trees, since you're not usually permitted to delete a directory until you've deleted all the files in it.

You call the subroutine with two parameters: the callback subroutine reference, and the directory (or a list of directories) from which to start:

```
find(\&wanted, "/home/simon/");
```

The subroutine `wanted()` is executed for every file that it finds in the directory. For each of the files, the following is true:

- You are moved into the same directory as the file under consideration.

- The current directory, relative to the top of the tree, is held in `$File::Find::dir`.

- `$_` contains the name of the current file.

- `$File::Find::name` is the name including the directory.

With that, you can do anything you want to do. Here is a program to delete useless files. The program is caller `hoover.pl`, but take care when you are executing it: it runs from the root directory; if used carelessly, it might delete a lot more than a few text files.

```perl
#!/usr/bin/perl
# hoover.pl

use warnings;
use strict;
use File::Find;

find(\&cleanup, "/");

sub cleanup {
    # Not been accessed in six months?
    if (-A > 180) {
        print "Deleting old file $_\n";
```

```
        unlink $_ or print "oops, couldn't delete $_: $!\n";
        return;
    }
    open FH, '<', $_ or warn "Couldn't open $_: $!\n";
    foreach (1..5) { # You've got five chances.
        my $line = <FH>;
        next unless defined $line;
        if ($line =~ /Perl|Camel|important/i) {
            # Spare it.
            return;
        }
    }
    print "Deleting unimportant file $_\n";
    unlink $_ or print "oops, couldn't delete $_: $!\n";
}
```

This code assumes, of course, that any file that contains "Perl," "Camel," or "important" in the first five lines is, well, important. You can alter this so it doesn't look for the words "Perl," "Camel," or "important" in the first five lines and indeed so it doesn't look through and delete files from your entire directory structure.

Getopt::Std

The Getopt::Long and Getopt::Std modules provide a flexible way to use command line arguments in your programs. Getopt::Std is the simpler of the two, providing you with a way to get single-letter switches with values and support for clustered flags (-a -l written as -al). You can also arrange to have the flags placed in a hash. For instance, to provide your wonderful "Hello World" program (from Chapter 1) with help, a version identifier, and internationalization, you could do this:

```
#!/usr/bin/perl
# hello3.pl
# Hello World (Deluxe)

use warnings;
use strict;
use Getopt::Std;

my %options;
getopts("vhl:", \%options);

if ($options{v}) {
    print "Hello World, version 3.\n";
    exit;
} elsif ($options{h}) {
    print <<EOF;

$0: Typical Hello World program

Syntax: $0 [-h|-v|-l <language>]
```

```
    -h : This help message
    -v : Print version on standard output and exit
    -l : Turn on international language support.
EOF
    exit;
} elsif ($options{l}) {
    if ($options{l} eq "french") {
        print "Bonjour, tout le monde.\n";
    } else {
        die "$0: unsupported language\n";
    }
} else {
    print "Hello, world.\n";
}
```

getopts() takes the following as its arguments: a specification (the letters for which you provide options) and a hash reference. If you follow a letter with a colon, you expect that a value will be stored in the hash. If you don't use a colon, then the hash value stored is just true or false depending on whether or not the option was given. You can now get output like this:

```
$ perl hello3.pl -l french
Bonjour, tout le monde.
$
```

Getopt::Std also produces a warning if it sees options it's not prepared for:

```
$ perl hello3.pl -f
Unknown option: f
Hello, world.
$
```

Getopt::Long

The Free Software Foundation, when they were developing the GNU project, decided that single-letter flags weren't friendly enough, so they invented "long" flags. These use a double minus sign followed by a word. To give a value for the option, you'd say something like --language=french. The equal sign is optional—a space character can be used instead.

The module Getopt::Long handles this style of option. Its documentation is extremely informative (perldoc Getopt::Long), but it's still useful to see an example. Let's convert the preceding program to GNU options:

```
#!/usr/bin/perl
# hellolong.pl
# Hello World (Deluxe) - with long flags

use warnings;
use strict;
use Getopt::Long;

my %options;
GetOptions(\%options, "language:s", "help", "version");
```

```
if ($options{version}) {
    print "Hello World, version 3.\n";
    exit;
} elsif ($options{help}) {
    print <<EOF;

$0: Typical Hello World program

Syntax: $0 [--help|--version|--language=<language>]

    --help     : This help message
    --version  : Print version on standard output and exit
    --language : Turn on international language support.
EOF
    exit;
} elsif ($options{language}) {
    if ($options{language} eq "french") {
        print "Bonjour, tout le monde.\n";
    } else {
        die "$0: unsupported language\n";
    }
} else {
    print "Hello, world.\n";
}
```

We can still use the previous syntax, but now we can also say

```
$ perl hellolong.pl --language=french
Bonjour, tout le monde.
$
```

File::Spec

If you want to write really portable programs in Perl, you have to be careful when doing things like dealing with filenames. File::Spec is a module for handling, constructing, and breaking apart filenames.

Normally it has an object-oriented interface, but it's much easier to use the subroutine interface, File::Spec::Functions. The following are some of the subroutines it provides.

Function and Syntax	Description
canonpath($path)	Cleans up $path to its simplest form
catdir($directory1, $directory2)	Concatenates the two directories together to form a new path to a directory, ensuring an appropriate separator in the middle, and removing the separator from the end
catfile($directory, $file)	Like catdir(), but the path will end with a filename

continued

273

continued

Function and Syntax	Description
tmpdir()	Finds a writable directory for temporary files (See the File::Temp module before working with temporary files!)
splitpath($path)	Splits up a path into volume (drive on Windows, nothing on Unix), directories, and filename
splitdir($path)	Splits a path into its constituent directories: the opposite of catdir()
path()	Returns the search path for executable files

Here is an example of locating a copy of the **sort** program:

```
#!/usr/bin/perl
# whereisit.pl

use warnings;
use strict;
use File::Spec::Functions;

foreach my $path (path()) {
    my $test = catfile($path, "sort");
    if (-e $test) {
        print "Yes, sort is in the $path directory.\n";
        exit;
    }
}
print "sort was not found here.\n";
```

Executing this code might produce the following:

```
$ perl whereisit.pl
Yes, sort is in the /usr/bin directory.
$
```

■ **Note** To read all the documentation for File::Spec, be sure to check out File::Spec::Unix or File::Spec:Win32, depending on your operating system.

Benchmark

There's More Than One Way To Do It—that's our motto (TMTOWTDI). However, some ways are always going to be faster than others. How can you tell? You could analyze each of the statements for efficiency, or you could simply roll up your sleeves and try it out.

The next module, Benchmark, provides many functions used for testing and timing code. Two of these functions are timethis() and timethese(). The first of these, timethis(), is quite easy to use:

```perl
#!/usr/bin/perl
# benchtest1.pl

use warnings;
use strict;
use Benchmark;

my $howmany = 200000;
my $what    = q/my $j=1; foreach (1..100) {$j *= $_}/;

timethis($howmany, $what);
```

This program provides timethis() some code and a number of times to run it. Make sure the code is in single quotes so that Perl doesn't attempt to interpolate it. You should, after a little while, see some output. This will, of course, vary depending on the speed of your CPU and how busy your computer is, but here is an example in the following code:

```
$ perl benchtest1.pl
timethis 200000:  3 wallclock secs ( 2.90 usr +  0.02 sys =  2.92 CPU) @ 68493.15/s (n=200000)

$
```

The results share that you ran something 200,000 times, and it took 3 seconds of real time. These seconds were 2.90spent in calculating ("usr" time) and 0 seconds interacting with the disk (or other noncalculating time). It also tells you that you ran through 68493.15iterations of the test code each second.

To test several things and compare them, you can use timethese(). This method takes as its second argument an anonymous hash. The values of the hash are strings (single quoted again) that will be executed $howmany number of times.

To check the fastest way to read a file from the disk, you could do the following:

```perl
#!/usr/bin/perl
# benchtest2.pl

use warnings;
use strict;
use Benchmark;

my $howmany = 1000;

timethese($howmany, {
    line => q{
        my $file;
        open TEST, "/usr/share/dict/words" or die $!;
```

```
        while (<TEST>) { $file .= $_ }
        close TEST;
    },
    slurp => q{
        my $file;
        local undef $/;
        open TEST, "/usr/share/dict/words" or die $!;
        $file = <TEST>;
        close TEST;
    },
    join => q{
        my $file;
        open TEST, "/usr/share/dict/words" or die $!;
        $file = join "", <TEST>;
        close TEST;
    }
});
```

One way reads the file in a line at a time, one slurps the whole file in at once, and one joins the lines together. As you might expect, the slurp method is considerably faster:

```
$ perl benchtest2.pl
Benchmark: timing 1000 iterations of join, line, slurp...
     join: 130 wallclock secs (121.24 usr +  5.10 sys = 126.34 CPU) @  7.92/s (n=1000)
     line: 69 wallclock secs (63.75 usr +  4.12 sys = 67.87 CPU) @ 14.73/s (n=1000)
    slurp:  6 wallclock secs ( 1.58 usr +  3.34 sys =  4.92 CPU) @ 203.25/s (n=1000)
$
```

Also, bear in mind that each benchmark will not only time differently between each machine and the next, but often between times you run the test—so *don't* base your life around benchmark tests. If a pretty way to do it is a thousandth of a second slower than an ugly way to do it, choose the pretty one.

Win32

Those familiar with Windows' labyrinthine Win32 APIs will probably want to examine the `libwin32` modules. These all live in the `Win32::` hierarchy and come as standard with Active-State Perl. If you've compiled another Perl yourself on Windows, you can get a copy of the modules from CPAN—you'll see how later in this chapter.

These modules, which give you access to such things as Semaphores, Services, OLE, the Clipboard, and a whole bunch of other things besides, will probably be of most interest to existing Windows programmers. For the rest of us though, there are two modules that will be of particular use.

Win32::Sound

The first, `Win32::Sound`, lets you play with the sound subsystem—you can play `.wav` files, set the speaker volume, and so on. You can also use it to play the standard system sounds.

The following program will play all the `.wav` files in the current directory:

```
#!/usr/bin/perl
# wavplay.pl
```

```
use strict;
use Win32::Sound;

Win32::Sound::Volume(65535);
while (<*.wav>) {
    Win32::Sound::Play($_);
}
```

You won't see any output, but if you're in a directory containing .wav files, you should certainly be able to hear some!

The Win32::Sound module provides us with a number of subroutines.

Function	Description
Win32::Sound::Volume($left, $right)	Sets the left and right speaker volumes to the requested amount. If only $left is given, both speakers are set to that volume. If neither is given, the current volume is returned. You can give the volume either as a percentage or a number from 0 to 65535.
Win32::Sound::Play($name)	Plays the named sound file, or the named system sound (for example, SystemStart).
Win32::Sound::Format($filename)	Returns information about the format of the given sound file.
Win32::Sound::Devices()	Lists all the available sound-related devices on the system.
Win32::Sound::DeviceInfo($device)	Provides information on the given sound device.

You can get a full list of the subroutines from the Win32::Sound documentation page if you have the module installed (perldoc Win32::Sound).

Win32::TieRegistry

Windows uses a centralized system database to store information about applications, users, and its own state. This is called the *registry*, and you can get at it by using Perl's Win32::TieRegistry module. This just provides a convenient layer around the Win32::Registry module, which is more technical in nature. Win32::TieRegistry transforms the Windows registry into a Perl hash.

The registry is a complicated beast, and revolves around a hierarchical tree structure—like a hash of hashes or a directory. For instance, information about users' software is stored under HKEY_CURRENT_USER\Microsoft\Windows\CurrentVersion\. Now you can get to this particular part of the hash by saying the following:

```
#!/usr/bin/perl
# registry.pl
```

```
use warnings;
use strict;
use Win32::TieRegistry (Delimiter => "/") ;
```

You load the module, and change the delimiter from a backslash to a forward slash so you don't end up drowning in a sea of backslashes.

```
my $users = $Registry->
  {HKEY_CURRENT_USER/Software/Microsoft/Windows/CurrentVersion/};
```

Now that you've got that key, you can dig further into the depths of the registry. This is where the Windows Explorer tips are stored:

```
my $tips = $users->{Explorer/Tips};
```

and from there you can add your own tips:

```
$tips->{/186} = "It's easy to use Perl as a Registry editor with the " .
                "Win32::TieRegistry module.";
```

You can always delete them again, using ordinary hash techniques.

```
delete $tips->{/186};
```

Again, if you're after more information, it's available in the `Win32::TieRegistry` documentation.

CPAN

So far you've been looking at standard modules provided with most Perl distributions. However, as was mentioned in the introduction, there's also a central repository for Perl modules—collections of code that will do virtually any kind of job: the Comprehensive Perl Archive Network, or CPAN, which you can find on the web at http://www.cpan.org. You can also find the standard Perl modules on CPAN and can read their documentation in web browser–friendly HTML by surfing http://search.cpan.org/.

So before you ask "How do I do . . . ?" or start plugging away at any long task, it's always worth taking a quick look here to see if it's already been done. CPAN is searchable in plenty of different ways—the most common are by keyword, by topic, or by module name. There are also a few CPAN search engines, but the easiest for browsing is probably the web-based CPAN search engine at http://search.cpan.org/.

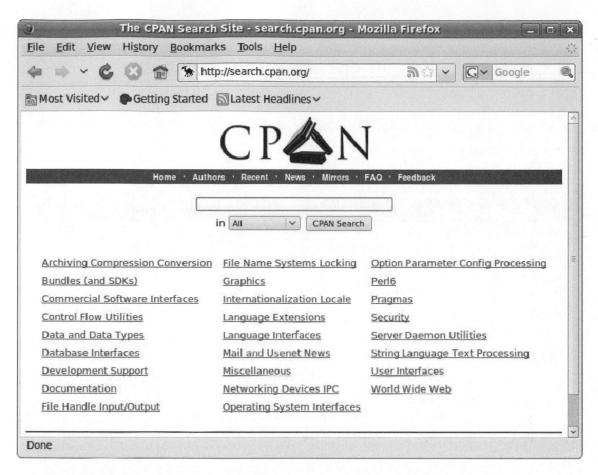

This lets us look up modules by category, as well as searching for words in the modules' documentation. Once you've found a module that might do what you want, you follow a link to get further information on it and get yourself a download. For example, this is what you get for the `Archive::Tar` module:

Now that you've seen how to find the modules you want, you're ready to look at the various ways in which you can install them.

Installing Modules with PPM

If you're using ActivePerl, module installation is made very simple by the Perl Package Manager (PPM). This is a useful little tool that's provided along with installations of ActivePerl, which allows you to install modules from the command line with the minimum of effort.

■ **Note** It is important to mention that PPM is not an interface to CPAN; it is a convenient program that allows you to install copies from CPAN, many of which are in some stage of being out-of-date. There is no guarantee that what is available on CPAN will be available with PPM. The rule of thumb is for the latest and greatest, visit CPAN.

So without further ado, let's install `Net::Telnet`—a module that allows you to automate a telnet session.

1. Type `ppm` at the command line; this will give you the PPM prompt: `PPM>`.

2. Now type `install Net::Telnet`—you may be asked to confirm your request, if so type `y`.

3. Exit the PPM prompt by typing `quit`, and now you have `Net::Telnet` installed.

Installing a Module Manually

You'll now take a look at what's involved in installing a module using CPAN. If you search CPAN for the module `Net::Telnet`, you should find yourself looking at the file `Net-Telnet-3.03.tar.gz` (unless there's a newer version out by the time you read this . . .) Download and unpack this file. On Unix systems, `gzip -dc Net-Telnet-3.03.tar.gz | tar -xvf` (or `tar xzvf Net-Telnet-3.03.tar.gz` if your version of `tar` also unzips) should do the trick, while you can use WinZip to extract these files on Windows.

Every module should contain a `Makefile.PL`, which can be used to generate the instructions to install the module. Let's run that file first:

```
$ perl Makefile.PL
```

If you can't install in Perl's site directories because you don't have the appropriate permissions, run

```
$ perl Makefile.PL PREFIX=/my/module/path
```

`Makefile.PL` first checks that you have all the modules it requires, and then that you've got everything you should have in the module archive itself—a file called `MANIFEST` contains a list of what should be in the archive.

Now you're ready to type `make`—assuming, of course, you have `make` on your system:

```
$ make
```

Once that's done, you check to see if your module's working:

```
$ make test
```

Finally, you actually install it, moving the files to the correct location:

```
$ make install
```

Hooray! The module's now installed. However, there's a much, much easier way of doing it.

The CPAN Module

Another easy way to navigate and install modules from CPAN is to use the standard module called `CPAN`. The "CPAN Shell" is an extremely powerful tool for finding, downloading, building, and installing modules.

To get into the CPAN shell, type

```
$ perl -MCPAN -e shell
```

This is actually just the same as saying

```
#!/usr/bin/perl
use CPAN;
shell();
```

The whole shell is actually a function in the (massively complex) CPAN module. The first time you run it, you'll see something like this:

```
CPAN is the world-wide archive of perl resources. It consists of about
300 sites that all replicate the same contents around the globe. Many
countries have at least one CPAN site already. The resources found on
CPAN are easily accessible with the CPAN.pm module. If you want to use
CPAN.pm, lots of things have to be configured. Fortunately, most of
them can be determined automatically. If you prefer the automatic
configuration, answer 'yes' below.

If you prefer to enter a dialog instead, you can answer 'no' to this
question and I'll let you configure in small steps one thing after the
other. (Note: you can revisit this dialog anytime later by typing 'o
conf init' at the cpan prompt.)
Would you like me to configure as much as possible automatically? [yes]
```

Press the Enter key and the CPAN module will configure itself. After a short amount of time, you'll end up at a prompt like this:

```
cpan shell -- CPAN exploration and modules installation (v1.9205)
ReadLine support available (maybe install Bundle::CPAN or Bundle::CPANxxl?)

cpan[1]>
```

Now we're ready to issue commands. The install command, as shown in the prompt, will download and install a module. For example, we could install the DBD::mysql module by simply saying

```
cpan[1]>install DBD::mysql
```

Alternatively, you could get information on a module with the i command. Let's get some information on the MLDBM module:

```
cpan[2]> i MLDBM
Strange distribution name [MLDBM]
Module id = MLDBM
    DESCRIPTION  Transparently store multi-level data in DBM
    CPAN_USERID  GSAR (Gurusamy Sarathy <gsar@cpan.org>)
    CPAN_VERSION 2.01
    CPAN_FILE    C/CH/CHAMAS/MLDBM-2.01.tar.gz
    DSLIP_STATUS RdpOp (released,developer,perl,object-oriented,Standard-Perl)
    MANPAGE      MLDBM - store multi-level hash structure in single level tied hash
    INST_FILE    /usr/share/perl5/MLDBM.pm
    INST_VERSION 2.01
```

This sares that the module is called MLDBM, and there's a description of it. It was written by the CPAN author GSAR, which translates to Gurusamy Sarathy in the real world. It's at version 2.01, and it's stored on CPAN in the directory C/CH/CHAMAS/MLDBM-2.01.tar.gz.

The funny little code thing is the CPAN classification. It tells you this module has been released (the implication being that it's been released for a while); that you should contact the developer if you need any support on it; that it's written purely in Perl without any extensions in C; that it's object oriented; and, finally, that you don't have it installed. So let's install it:

```
cpan[3]> install MLDBM
```

■ **Note** In fact, you don't even have to go into the shell to install a module. As well as exporting the shell subroutine, CPAN provides us with install, with which you can simply say perl -MCPAN -e 'install "MLDBM"' to produce the same results.

You'll then see a few lines that will be specific to your computer—different systems have different ways of downloading files, and depend on whether or not you have the external programs lynx, ftp, or ncftp, or the Perl Net::FTP module installed.

The CPAN module will download the file, and then, if you've got the Digest::MD5 module installed, download a special file called a *checksum*—it's like a summary of that file so you can make sure that what you've downloaded is what's on the server.

```
Checksum for /home/simon/.cpan/sources/authors/id/ C/CH/CHAMAS/MLDBM-2.01.tar.gz ok
```

You should then see tons of output: the tar file is unpacked, a Makefile is generated and executed, the module is tested, and then installed. Once all this takes place, you will see the CPAN prompt again:

```
cpan[4]>
```

Successfully installed, and with the minimum of effort!

How about if you don't actually know the name of the module you're looking for? CPAN lets you use a regular expression match to locate modules. For instance, if you're about to do some work involving MIDI electronic music files, you could search for "MIDI." Here is a portion of what you might see:

```
cpan[4]>i /MIDI/
Distribution     BMAMES/MIDI-XML-0.02.tar.gz
Distribution     BMAMES/MIDI-XML-0.03.tar.gz
Distribution     CBOURNE/MIDI-Praxis-Variation-0.05.tar.gz
Distribution     CHURCH/MIDI-Trans-0.15.zip
...
```

"Distributions" are archive files: zips or tar.gz files containing one or more Perl modules. We see that MIDI-Realtime contains just the MIDI::Realtime module.

Bundles

Some modules depend on other modules being installed. For instance, the `Win32::TieRegistry` module needs `Win32::Registry` to do the hard work of getting at the registry. If you're downloading packages from CPAN manually, you'll have to try each package, find out what's missing, and download another repeatedly until you've got everything you need. The `CPAN` module does a lot of this work for you—it can detect dependencies in packages and download and install everything that's missing.

This is fine for making sure that things work, but as well as *needing* other modules, some merely *suggest* other modules. For instance, the `CPAN` module itself works fine with nothing other than what's in the core, but if you have `Term::Readline` installed, it gives you a much more flexible prompt, with tab completion, a command history (meaning you can use the up and down arrows to scroll through previous commands), and other niceties.

Enter bundles—collections of packages that go well together. The CPAN bundle, `Bundle::CPAN`, for instance, contains various modules that make the CPAN shell easier to use: `Term::ReadLine` as mentioned previously, `Digest::MD5` for security checking the files downloaded, some `Net::` modules to make network communication with the CPAN servers nicer, and so on.

You'll now look at two particularly useful bundles, which contain modules that we personally wouldn't go *anywhere* without.

Bundle::LWP

`Bundle::LWP` contains modules for *everything* to do with the Web. It has modules for dealing with HTML, HTTP, MIME types, handling URLs, downloading and mirroring remote web sites, creating web spiders and robots, and so on.

The main chunk of the bundle is the `LWP` (`libwww-perl`) distribution, containing the modules for visiting remote web sites. Let's have a look at what it gives us.

This module will export five methods to your current package.

- The `get()` method fetches a web site and returns the underlying HTML. This subroutine knows all about proxies, error codes, and other things:

  ```
  $file = get("http://www.perl.com/");
  ```

- The `head()` method fetches the header of the site and returns a few headers: what type of document the page is (such as text/html), how big it is in bytes, when it was last modified, when it should be regarded as old (these are both Unix times suitable for feeding to `localtime()`), and what the server has to say about itself. Some servers may not return all these headers.

  ```
  ($content_type, $document_length, $modified_time, $expires, $server) =
   head("http://www.perl.com/");
  ```

The next three methods are all quite similar in that they all involve retrieving an HTML page.

- The first, `getprint()`, retrieves the HTML file and then prints it out to standard output—useful if you're redirecting to a file or using a filter as some sort of HTML formatter. You can copy a web page to a local file like this:

  ```
  getprint("http://www.perl.com/");
  ```

- Alternatively, you can use the `getstore()` subroutine to store it to a file.

  ```
  perl -MLWP::Simple -e
      'getstore("http://www.perl.com/", "perlpage.html")'
  ```

- Finally, `mirror()` is like `getstore()`, except it checks to see if the remote site's page is newer than the one you've already got.

  ```
  perl -MLWP::Simple -e
      'mirror("http://www.perl.com/","perlpage.html")'
  ```

Be sure to read the main `LWP` documentation and the `lwpcook` page, which contains a few ideas for things to do with `LWP`.

Bundle::libnet

Similarly, `Bundle::libnet` contains a bunch of stuff for dealing with the network, although it's not nearly as big as LWP. The modules in `Bundle::libnet` and its dependencies allow you to use FTP, telnet, SMTP mail, and other network protocols.

Submitting Your Own Module to CPAN

CPAN contains almost everything you'll ever need. Almost. There'll surely come a day when you're faced with a problem where no known module can help you. If you think it's a sufficiently general problem that other people are going to come across, why not consider making your solution into a module and submitting it to CPAN? Think of it as a way of giving something back to the community that gave you all this . . .

Seriously, if you do have something you think would be useful to others, there are a few things you need to do to get it to CPAN:

- Check to make sure it has not already been written. Search CPAN at http://search.cpan.org/.

- Read the `perlmod` and `perlmodlib` documentation pages until you really understand them.

- Learn about the Carp module, and use `carp()` and `croak()` instead of `warn()` and `die()`.

- Learn about the Test module and how to produce test suites for modules.

- Learn about documenting your modules in POD, Plain Old Documentation.

- Look at the source to a few simple modules like `Text::Wrap` and `Text::Tabs` to get a feel of how modules are written.

- Take a deep breath, and issue the following command:

  ```
  $ h2xs -AXn Your::Module::Name
  ```

- Edit the files produced, remembering to create a test suite and provide really good documentation.

- Run `perl Makefile.PL` and then `make`.

Your module's now ready to ship!

For more information, check out the excellent book *Writing Perl Modules for CPAN* by Sam Tregar (Apress, 2002). Also, be sure to read `perldoc perlnewmod`,.

Summary

Modules save you time. In essence, a module is just a package stored in a file, which you load with the `use` statement.

Perl provides a number of standard modules. You can get documentation on each and every one by running `perldoc`. You looked briefly at `Data::Dumper` (to print out data structures), `File::Find` (for examining files in directory trees), the `Getopt` modules (for reading options from the command line), the `File::Spec::Functions` module (for portable filename handling), the `Benchmark` module (for timing and testing code), and the `Win32` modules (for access to the Windows system and registry).

CPAN is the Comprehensive Perl Archive Network. It's a repository of free Perl code. You can search it from http://search.cpan.org/, or use the Perl module `CPAN` for easy searching and installation. The `CPAN` module has the advantage of knowing about file dependencies and can therefore download and install files in the correct order.

Bundles provide sets of related modules. You looked at `LWP::Simple` (from the `libwww` bundle) and the `libnet` bundle. Finally, you looked at some of what's involved in abstracting your code and putting it into a module.

CHAPTER 13

■ ■ ■

Object-Oriented Perl

There are two main schools of thought when approaching a solution to a problem in the programming world. The first school of thought is one that we have used in this book up to this point: *procedural programming*. This approach is based on what actions to take—*procedures*—and developing subroutines that carry out those actions. In procedural programming, you take the overall system and break it up into smaller and smaller pieces, code the steps for the individual pieces into functions, and then put the functions together to form the entire system.

The other school of thought is an approach that has been quite popular for a while: *object-oriented programming* (OOP, or simply OO for short). In the OO approach, you take a step back from what the program needs to do and instead look at the nature of the things with which you are working.

In this chapter, you'll learn how to start thinking in OO terms. OO involves a lot of jargon, so the first thing you'll do is look in some detail at all the new terms associated with OO and what they mean to a Perl programmer. After that, you'll see how to go about approaching a problem using this style of programming. You'll use a Perl module that involves creating an object, and you'll also construct some object-oriented modules of your own.

This chapter is meant only as a beginning in OO in Perl. For more details, I recommend the excellent book *Object Oriented Perl* by Damian Conway (Manning Publications, 2000).

OO Buzzwords

Object-oriented programming wouldn't be a good buzz phrase if it didn't use a lot of familiar words in unfamiliar contexts. Before going any further, let's investigate the jargon that you'll need in order to understand object-oriented Perl programming.

The first thing to note is that object-oriented programming is a concept, rather than a standard. There are a few things that object-oriented languages should do, a lot they can do, but nothing that they absolutely *have* to do. Other languages may implement more or less of these ideas than Perl does, and may well do so in a completely different way. We'll explain here the terms that are most commonly used by object-oriented programmers.

Objects

What is an object, anyway? An object is a chunk of data that has behaviors, but that's not all. To be honest, an object can be anything—it really depends on what your application is. For instance, if you're writing a contact management database, a single contact might be an object. If you're communicating with a remote computer via FTP, you could make each connection to the remote server an object.

An object can always be described in terms of two things:

- What it can do (*actions* or *methods*)

- What you know about it (*information* or *attributes*)

With a "contact record" object, you'd probably know the contact's name, date of birth, address, and so on. These are the object's *attributes*. You might also be able to ask it to do certain things: print an address label for this contact; work out how old they are; or send them an email—these are the object's *methods*.

In Perl, what you see as an object is simply a reference—in fact, you can convert any ordinary reference *into* an object simply by using the `bless()` function. You'll see later on how that happens. Typically, however, objects are represented as references to a hash, and that's the model we'll use in this chapter.

Attributes

An *attribute* is something you know about an object, its information. A contact database object will possess attributes such as date of birth, address, and name. An FTP session will possess attributes such as the name of the remote server you're connected to, the current directory, and so on. Two contacts will have different values for their name attribute, unless you have duplicates in the database, but they will both have the name attribute.

If you're using a reference to a hash, it's natural to have the attributes as hash entries. The person object then becomes a `bless`ed version of the following:

```
my $person = {
    lastname    => "Galilei",
    firstname   => "Galileo",
    address     => "9.81 Pisa Apts.",
    occupation  => "bombadier"
};
```

You can get to (and change) your attributes simply by accessing these hash values directly (that is, by saying something like `$person->{address}`—remember that you use this syntax because you're dealing with a reference), but this is generally regarded as a bad idea. For starters, it requires you to know the internal structure of the object and where and how the attributes are stored, which, as end users, we should have no need or desire to fiddle with. Secondly, it doesn't give the object a chance to examine the data you're giving it to make sure it makes sense. Instead, access to an attribute usually goes through a *method*.

Methods

A *method* is anything you can tell the object to do. It could be something complicated, such as printing out address labels and reports, or something simple such as accessing an attribute. Those methods directly related to attributes are called *get-set* methods, as they'll typically either *get* the current value of the attribute or *set* a new one.

The fact that methods are all about instructions for doing things may give you a clue as to how we represent them in Perl—methods in Perl are just subroutines. However, there is a special syntax called the *arrow operator* (->), which you use to call methods. So instead of getting the address attribute directly, as in the preceding example, you're more likely to say something like this:

```
print "Address: ", $person->get_address(), "\n";
```

You're also able to set an attribute (change its value) like this:

```
$person->set_address("Campus Mirabilis, Pisa, Italy");
```

Alternatively, you can call a method to produce an envelope for this object:

```
$person->print_envelope();
```

This syntax $object->method(@arguments) "invokes" the method, which just means that it calls the given subroutine. In our examples this is either get_address(), set_address() or print_envelope(). You'll see how it's done shortly.

Classes

Normally, objects of different types are very different things—they have different methods and attributes. For instance, your contact object is very different from an object created to perform FTP connections. While $person->date_of_birth() may make sense, you wouldn't expect $ftp_session->date_of_birth() to do anything sensible.

A *class* is the formal term for a *type* of object—it is a general description of a group of things. Classes define the methods an object can have and how those methods work. All objects in the Person class will have the same set of methods and possess the same attributes (although the values of these attributes will likely be different), and these will be different from the FTP class. An object is sometimes referred to as an *instance* of a class; this just means that it's a specific thing created from a general category.

In Perl's object–oriented philosophy, a class is an ordinary package. Let's start piecing this together:

- A method is a subroutine in a package. For instance, the date_of_birth() method in the Person class is merely the subroutine date_of_birth() in the Person package.

- Blessing a scalar just means telling it from what package to take its methods. At that point, it's more than just a complex data structure, or scalar reference. It has attributes—the data you've stored in the hash reference or elsewhere; and it has methods—the subroutines in its package; therefore it can be considered a full–fledged object.

Classes can also have what are known as *class methods* (some programming languages call these *static methods*). These are methods that do things relevant to the whole class rather than individual objects. Instead of acting on an object, as you would by saying $object->method(), you act on the class: Person->method(). An important thing to note is that Perl doesn't necessarily know whether a given subroutine is a class method, an object method, or just an ordinary subroutine. Therefore, programmers have to do the checking themselves.

Similarly, classes can have attributes that refer to the whole class—in Perl these are just package variables (some programming languages call these *static data*). For instance, you might have a population attribute in your Person class, which tells how many Person objects are currently in existence.

One final note: you'll probably have noticed that we capitalized Person. The Perl convention is to capitalize all class names, so as to help distinguish them from object names.

Polymorphism

The word *polymorphism* comes from the Greek πολυ μορφου, meaning "many forms." What it means in object–oriented programming is that a single method can do different things depending on the class of the object that calls it. For instance, `$person->address()` would return the person's address, but `$ftp_session->address()` might return the IP address of the remote server. On the other hand, `$object->address()` would *have* to do the right thing according to which class `$object` was in.

When you invoke `$person->address()`, you are calling the subroutine `Person::address()`, and when you invoke `$ftp_session->address()`, you are calling the subroutine `FTP::address()`. They're defined completely separately, in different packages, probably even in different files. Since Perl already knows what class each object belongs to, neither you nor Perl need to do anything special to make the distinction. Perl looks at the object, finds the class it is in, and calls the subroutine in the appropriate package. This brings us to . . .

Encapsulation

One of the nice things about object–oriented programming is that it hides complexity from the user. This is known as *encapsulation* (or *abstraction*). This means that users of the object need not care how the class is structured or how the attributes are represented in the object. Nor do users have to care how the methods work or where they come from—they can just use them.

This also means that the author of the class has complete freedom to change its internal workings at any time. As long as the methods have the same names and take the same arguments, all programs using the class should continue to work and produce the same results. That is as long as they use the method *interface*, or way of invoking the method, as they should, rather than trying to access or modify the data directly.

In this sense, working with objects is a little like driving a car. The object, the car, has a set of attributes, such as the model, current speed, and amount of fuel in the tank. You can't get at these directly, but some read–only methods like the speedometer and the fuel gauge expose them to us. It also provides us with some more methods and a well–defined interface to get it to do things.

You have a pedal to make it accelerate and one to make it brake, a stick to change gear, a hole to put fuel into the tank, and so on. You don't actually need to know how the engine works if you're prepared to stick to using these methods; of course, you do need to know what each of them does. You don't even need to know the whereabouts of the fuel tank, you just put fuel in the appropriate place. If you really want to, you can lift the hood, look inside it, and fiddle with it—but then you only have yourself to blame if it breaks!

Inheritance

Another property that makes object–oriented programming easy to use is its support for *inheritance*. Classes can be built quickly by specifying how they differ from other classes. For example, humans inherit attributes from their parents, such as hair color and height, while Perl's classes inherit methods. If a class inherits from another class, it receives the ability to call every method defined by the class from which it inherits. If the new class wants to implement a method differently, it defines the method in its own class. If it doesn't want its own version of the method, it will automatically get the method from the parent class. The parent class, which provides the new class with the methods, is called the *superclass* or *base class*, and the class which inherits from the superclass is known as a *subclass* or *derived class*.

The relationship between the classes can be described as an *IS-A* relationship. If you have a superclass `Animal`, you may create a subclass `Vertebrate`. You could then say that a `Vertebrate` IS-A

`Animal`. In fact, the classification system for animals can be thought of as a series of IS–A relationships, with more specific subclasses inheriting properties of their superclasses.

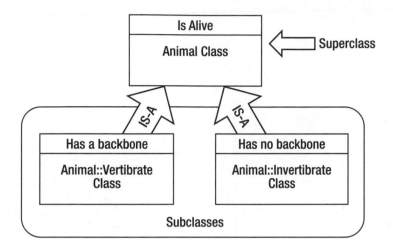

Here you see that vertebrates and invertebrates are both subclasses of a general animal class. They both inherit the fact that they are alive, and so you need not specify this in the subclass. Next, you could create an `Animal::Vertebrate::Mammal` class, which would be a subclass of `Animal::Vertebrate`. You wouldn't need to specify that the mammal had a backbone or was alive, because these characteristics would be inherited from the superclass.

We won't talk much about inheritance in this book. This topic is perhaps the most difficult topic in OO and deserves a chapter, if not several chapters, of its own. Once you grasp the basic concepts of OO, we recommend that you check out the book *Object Oriented Perl* for an excellent discussion of inheritance.

Constructors

Objects have to come from somewhere, and in keeping with the principles of encapsulation, users of a class shouldn't be expected to put together an object themselves. This would require knowledge of how the object is represented and what initialization is required. To take this responsibility away from the user, there's a class method that all classes should possess—it's called the *constructor*.

As the name implies, this constructs and returns a new object. For this reason, it's usually called `new()`.[1] You may pass arguments to the constructor, which it can then use to do the initial setup of the object. Sometimes these arguments are in the form of a hash, allowing you to create an object like this:

---

[1] This is also called `new()` so that your C++ brethren will feel a sense of familiarity when they create objects in Perl.

```
my $galileo = Person->new(
    lastname    => "Galilei",
    firstname   => "Galileo",
    address     => "9.81 Pisa Apts.",
    occupation  => "bombadier",
);
```

There's also another syntax for calling methods, which you'll particularly see used with the constructor:

```
my $galileo = new Person (...);
```

The constructor will now check that the arguments are acceptable, do any conversion it requires, and create a hash reference, bless() it, and return it to us. More on this later in this chapter.

Destructors

When the object is no longer in use—when it's a lexical variable that goes out of scope—Perl automatically destroys it. However, before doing so, Perl will attempt to call a method named DESTROY(). If the class provides this method, it should be responsible for any tasks that need to be performed before the object is disposed of. For instance, your FTP session object will want to ensure that it has closed the connection to the remote server.

An Example

It is now time for an example. Let's start off by using a class that is already created for us: Net::FTP.[2] This class (also known as a *module*) allows you to create objects that transfer files to and from an FTP server. The following example will connect to the CPAN—and download the README.html file. This example will illustrate some of the buzz words mentioned previously.

```
#!/usr/bin/perl
# ftp.pl

use strict;
use Net::FTP;

my $ftp = Net::FTP->new("ftp.cpan.org")
    or die "Couldn't connect: $@\n";

$ftp->login("anonymous");
$ftp->cwd("/pub/CPAN");
$ftp->get("README.html");
$ftp->close();
```

---

[2] This code was written by Graham Barr. Thanks, Graham!

Network and firewalls permitting, this should retrieve the file—although it may take some time. Here is the proof on a Windows machine:

```
$ perl ftp.pl
$ dir README.html
README~1 HTM              2,902         ...    ...           README.html
$
```

The first line of interest in this program is

```
use Net::FTP;
```

This line finds the file that contains the definition of the Net::FTP class (as you learned in Chapter 12, its name happens to be FTP.pm and it is located in a directory named Net) and compiles it for use with this program.

After loading the Net::FTP module, you create an object:

```
my $ftp = Net::FTP->new("ftp.cpan.org")
    or die "Couldn't connect: $@\n";
```

The class is called Net::FTP, the same as the module. This is because, as mentioned previously, a class is just an ordinary package.

You create the object by calling the constructor, which is the class method new(). This takes a number of arguments: a remote machine to which you want to connect and a hash specifying things like whether you have a firewall, which port to connect to, whether you want debugging information, and so on. These arguments will become the attributes of the object. If you don't specify them, the constructor comes up with some sensible defaults for you. In your case, the defaults are fine, so you just need to supply a remote machine—you'll use the CPAN server, ftp.cpan.org.

When you call the constructor, it takes your argument (the remote host), and stashes it away internally in the object—encapsulation means you don't need to know how or where. Then it takes a reference to that hash, blesses the reference, and returns it to you. That blessed reference is your new object (your FTP session), and you're now ready to do things with it..

Next, you see a call to the login() method:

```
$ftp->login("anonymous");
```

First of all, you have to log in to the server. The usual way of getting things from an FTP server is by logging in with a username of "anonymous" and your email address as the password. The login() method tells the object to issue the appropriate login commands.

How did Perl know that it should use Net::FTP::login() rather than any other login()? When your constructor blessed the reference, it gave the reference knowledge of where to find the methods. To quote from the perlobj documentation, "an object is just a reference that happens to know which class it belongs to."

Since Perl takes care of passing the object to the subroutine as the first parameter, the method automatically receives all the data it needs. This means you can easily have multiple objects doing different things.

```
my $ftp1 = Net::FTP->new("ftp.cpan.org");
my $ftp2 = Net::FTP->new("ftp.apress.com");
$ftp1->login("anonymous");
```

The object $ftp1 is just a blessed reference to a hash, and that hash contains all the data about the connection to CPAN, like the settings, the filehandles, and anything else that Net::FTP needs to store.

These are the object's attributes. Everything you know about the connection is bundled into that object. The important thing to note is that it's completely independent from `$ftp2`, which is another object containing another set of data about a different connection. Hence, the method call `$ftp1->login()` has no impact on the other connection at all.

After logging in, you change the working directory on the target machine and get the file.

```
$ftp->cwd("/pub/CPAN");
$ftp->get("README.html");
```

`cwd()` and `get()` are two more methods your object supplies. The object has a huge number of methods, due to the fact that it has a long chain of inheritance. However, there are some methods `Net::FTP` defines directly that you should know about. They mainly relate directly to FTP commands— Table 13-1 presents an incomplete list of them.

Table 13-1. *Net::FTP Methods*

Method Name	Behavior
`$ftp->login($login,$passwd)`	Log into the server with the given username and password.
`$ftp->type($type) $ftp->ascii()` `$ftp->binary()`	Set the transfer type to ASCII or binary; this is quite similar to Perl's `binmode` operator.
`$ftp->rename($old,$new)`	Rename a file.
`$ftp->delete($file)`	Delete a file.
`$ftp->cwd($directory)`	Change directory on the FTP server.
`$ftp->pwd()`	Give the name of the current directory.
`$ftp->ls()`	List the current directory on the FTP server.
`$ftp->get($remote, $local, $offset)`	Get a file from the remote server.
`$ftp->put($local, $remote)`	Put a file to the remote server.

There are also some get–set methods that will affect the object's attributes. For instance, the `$ftp->hash()` method controls an attribute that determines whether or not to print a # character after every 1024 bytes transferred.

After you've called the `get()` method to get your file, you'll call the `close()` method to shut down the connection to the server.

```
$ftp->close();
```

So, you've used your first class. Hopefully, you can see that using objects and classes in Perl is just as easy as calling functions. In fact, it's easier—Perl not only takes care of finding out where to find the subroutine you're trying to call, but it also takes care of passing a whole bunch of data to the subroutine for you.

Because this all goes on behind the scenes, you can happily pretend that an object contains a bunch of methods that act on it, and it alone. In fact, it doesn't—it only contains information regarding where to find methods that can act on any object in that class.

Rolling Your Own Classes

You've seen how to use a class and an object. Let's now see how to make your own classes. As an example, you'll implement the Person class we used in our definitions.

As mentioned previously, a class is just a package—nothing more, nothing less. So the simplest class looks like this:

```
package Person;
```

That's it. However, this class has nothing—no methods, no attributes, no constructor, nothing. It's a totally empty class. You will eventually want to add more stuff (attributes and methods) to this class.

Usually, you'll want to put your class into its own file. It's not necessary by any means, but it gets the implementation out of the way. So, let's create a module by putting the following in the file Person1.pm. The file must end in the .pm file extension because when you use this class you will say

```
use Person1;
```

and this looks for the file named Person1.pm. Here is its content:

```
package Person1;
# Person1.pm

# Class for storing data about a person

use strict;


1;
```

Normally, the name of the package is the same as the name of file (minus the .pm extension). So if the package name is Person1, the filename is Person1.pm. Likewise, if the filename is Person1.pm, the package name is Person1.

As we discuss the various features of OO in this chapter, you will develop a class that represents a person. You will start with package Person1, then enhance that package to be Person2, and so on. Keep in mind that these packages are representing an evolution of a definition.

As was mentioned in Chapter 12, that 1; at the end of the file looks weird, but it is necessary because Perl expects to see a true value as the last thing in the package; this tells Perl that everything went OK when loading the file. Now in a separate program, you can say use Person1; and start using the class, like this:

```
#!/usr/bin/perl
# person1.pl

use warnings;
use strict;
use Person1;
```

This program doesn't do anything except read in and compile the class you created, because you can't yet create any objects as you do not yet have a constructor. Therefore, the next step is to write a constructor.

What does your constructor create? It creates an object, which is a blessed reference. Before going any further, then, let's have a look at what bless() is and what it does.

Bless You, My Reference

The bless()function takes a reference and turns it into an object. The way it does that is simple: it changes the type of the reference. Instead of being an array reference or a hash reference, Perl now thinks of it as a Person1 reference (or whatever other class you bless() the reference into).

You can use the ref() function to tell what type of reference you have:

```
#!/usr/bin/perl
# reftypes.pl

use warnings;
use strict;

my $a = [];
my $b = {};
my $c = \1;
my $d = \$c;
print '$a is a ', ref($a), " reference\n";
print '$b is a ', ref($b), " reference\n";
print '$c is a ', ref($c), " reference\n";
print '$d is a ', ref($d), " reference\n";
```

```
$ perl reftypes.pl
$a is a ARRAY reference
$b is a HASH reference
$c is a SCALAR reference
$d is a REF reference
$
```

The syntax of bless() is

```
bless(reference, package);
```

If the package isn't given, the reference is blessed into the current package. Let's bless() a reference into the Person1 package.

```
#!/usr/bin/perl
# bless1.pl

use warnings;
use strict;

my $a = {};
```

```
print '$a is a ', ref($a), " reference\n";

bless($a, "Person1");

print '$a is a ', ref($a), " reference\n";
```

```
$ perl bless1.pl
$a is a HASH reference
$a is a Person1 reference
$
```

OK, so you've changed $a into a Person1 reference. What just happened?

Actually, nothing changed in the structure of $a at all. It's still a hash reference, and you can still dereference it—or add, access, and delete entries in the hash, and so on. It still has the same keys and values. Nothing magical has happened.

But $a is now a reference with knowledge of which package it belongs to, and if you try and call a method with it, Perl now knows that it should look in the Person1 package for a definition of that method. It has become an object.

What if you bless() it again? What happens then? Let's try it.

```
#!/usr/bin/perl
# bless2.pl

use warnings;
use strict;

my $a = {};

print '$a is a ', ref($a), " reference\n";

bless($a, "Person1");
print '$a is a ', ref($a), " reference\n";

bless($a, "Animal::Vertebrate::Mammal");
print '$a is a ', ref($a), " reference\n";
```

```
$ perl bless2.pl
$a is a HASH reference
$a is a Person1 reference
$a is a Animal::Vertebrate::Mammal reference
$
```

All that's happened is you've once again changed what type of reference it is. You've changed where Perl should look if any methods are called by the reference. Note that at this stage you haven't even *defined* an Animal::Vertebrate::Mammal package, but that's OK because you're not going to call any methods yet—if you did, they would surely fail.

Again, the internal structure of that reference hasn't changed. It's still a hash reference with the same keys and values. You usually don't want to bless() an object that's already been blessed. This is because something that was originally a Person1 may have different attributes to what the new class expects it to have when methods are called. Worse still, the program using the object could well try and call a method that was fine in the old class but doesn't exist in the new one—attempting to magically turn a person into an FTP session can only have undesirable (and pretty weird) results.

Storing Attributes

Before looking at methods, let's examine attributes. An attribute is, as defined at the start of this chapter, something you know about the object. In other words, it's a piece of data that belongs to this particular object. How do you store this data, then?

This is what the reference is for; if you store your data in the reference, your object carries around both a set of data unique to it and knowledge of where to find methods to act on that data. If you know that your object is only going to contain one attribute, one piece of data, you could conceivably use a scalar reference, like this:

```perl
my $attribute = "green";
my $object = \$attribute;
bless $object, "Simple";
```

Now you have a nice simple object that stores a single attribute contained in the Simple class. You can access and change the attribute just as we'd work with an ordinary scalar reference:

```perl
$var      = ${$object};
${$object} = "red";
```

This is nice and simple, but it's not very flexible. Similarly, you could have an array reference and bless() that to turn it into an object, which is slightly more flexible. You can access attributes as elements in the array, and you can add and delete attributes by using array operations. If you are storing a set of unnamed data, this is perfectly adequate.

However, for maximum flexibility, you can use a hash to give names to your attributes. Here is an example of creating a reference to an anonymous hash and then blessing it as an object of your class:

```perl
my $object = {
    lastname   => "Galilei",
    firstname  => "Galileo",
    address    => "9.81 Pisa Apts.",
    occupation => "bombadier",
};
bless $object, "Person1";
```

This allows easy access to the individual attributes, as if you were carrying a bunch of variables around with you. Therefore, you generally use an anonymous hash reference for any nontrivial class.

The Constructor

You're now ready to create objects. Let's put this knowledge into a constructor, and put a constructor into your currently empty Person1 class. As mentioned previously, your definition of a person is a work in progress, so you will call the next version Person2 and store it in Person2.pm.

To construct an object, you make a hash reference, and bless() it as an object of the class.

```
package Person2;
# Person2.pm

# Class for storing data about a person

use strict;

sub new {
    my $self = {};
    bless $self, "Person2";
    return $self;
}

1;
```

Now you can use your `Person2` class to create an object:

```
#!/usr/bin/perl
# person2.pl

use warnings;
use strict;
use Person2;

my $person = Person2->new();
```

which should execute without any errors.

Your constructor does a simple job, and does it well. First, you create your hash reference:

```
my $self = {};
```

`$self` is the traditional name for an object when it's being manipulated by methods inside the class. Now you'll turn it into an object by telling it which class it belongs to:

```
bless $self, "Person2";
```

Finally, you return the object:

```
return $self;
```

Excellent. Now let's see how you can improve this.

Considering Inheritance

It's possible that someone someday will want to inherit from this class, and you won't necessarily be told about it. If they don't provide their own constructor, they'll get yours, and as things stand, that'll produce an object `bless`ed into your class—not theirs.

You really need to remove the hard–wired `"Person2"` in your constructor and replace it with the called class. How do you know what the called class is though? Perl translates `Class->new()` into `new("Class")`. In other words, the class name is magically passed into the constructor as its first argument. Therefore, you know what class the user wants because it's the first argument to the constructor. All you need to do is take that argument and use that as the class to `bless()` into (the second argument to the bless() function). So here's a more general constructor that takes inheritance into account:

```
sub new {
    my $class = shift;
    my $self = {};
    bless $self, $class;
    return $self;
}
```

As usual, shift() without any arguments means shift @_—it takes the first element of the argument array. This gives us the first thing you were passed, the class name. You can therefore use this to bless our reference without needing to hard–code the name.

Providing Attributes

Now let's make one more enhancement. At the moment, you can create a completely anonymous Person2 with no attributes at all. You want to be able to give the end user of the class the opportunity to specify some attributes when the object is created. So let's take the next step in your evolution and define class Person3.

As before, you're going to store the data in a hash reference. The object's data will be provided to the constructor through its argument list. Ideally, you'll want the constructor to be called something along these lines:

```
my $object = Person3->new(
    lastname   => "Galii",
    firstname  => "Galileo",
    address    => "9.81 Pisa Apts.",
    occupation => "bombardier"
);
```

This is the easiest syntax for the user, because it allows them to specify the attributes in any order, and give as many or as few as they want. It's also a lot easier to use and remember than if you make them use a list like this:

```
my $object = Person3->new ("Galilei","Galileo","9.81 Pisa Apts.","bombardier");
```

In fact, it's the easiest syntax for us too. Since you want your attributes stored in a hash, and the key–value syntax you proposed previously *is* a hash, all you've got to do is place the arguments straight into your hash reference:

```
my $self = {@_};
```

Let's plug this into your package:

```
package Person3;

# Person3.pm

# Class for storing data about a person
```

```
use strict;

sub new {
    my $class = shift;
    my $self = {@_};
    bless $self, $class;
    return $self;
}

1;
```

What have you done? Since Perl magically passes in the class name as the first argument to the function, Perl sees something like this when you call the constructor:

```
@_ = (
    "Person3",
    "lastname",   "Galilei",
    "firstname",  "Galileo",
    "address",    "9.81 Pisa Apts.",
    "occupation", "bombardier"
);
```

The first line of the constructor grabs the class name as before.

```
my $class = shift;
```

Now what's left in the argument array @_ is

```
@_ = (
    "lastname",   "Galilei",
    "firstname",  "Galileo",
    "address",    "9.81 Pisa Apts.",
    "occupation", "bombardier"
);
```

This is what you put verbatim into your hash reference:

```
my $self = {@_};
```

Your hash now contains all the attributes you provided. As usual, it's blessed and returned to the caller.

You now have a full–featured constructor. You've taken some initial data and constructed an object out of it, storing the data as attributes in the object. Now it's time to add some methods so you can actually do something with it!

Creating Methods

Your constructor was a class method; creating an object method will be very similar. In the same way that a class method magically gets passed the name of the class as the first argument, an object method is just a subroutine that magically gets passed the object as the first argument.

Let's create a method to return the last name of the person. This directly accesses an attribute—sometimes called an *accessor method*. Remember that the `lastname` attribute is just an entry in the hash, referenced by the object. So what does this involve? You'll need to:

- Receive the object being passed to us.

- Extract the lastname entry from the hash.

- Pass it back to the caller.

Using the techniques you learned in Chapter 11 for directly accessing values in a hash reference, you can code the accessor and add it into your class creating the next iteration, `Person4`.

```perl
package Person4;

# Person4.pm

# Class for storing data about a person

use strict;

sub new {
    my $class = shift;
    my $self = {@_};
    bless $self, $class;
    return $self;
}

sub lastname {
    my $self = shift;
    return $self->{lastname};
}

1;
```

Now you can create an object with some attributes, and retrieve the attributes again.

```perl
#!/usr/bin/perl
# accessor1.pl

use warnings;
use strict;
use Person4;

my $object = Person4->new(
    lastname   => "Galilei",
    firstname  => "Galileo",
    address    => "9.81 Pisa Apts.",
    occupation => "bombadier"
```

```
);
```

```
print "This person's last name: ", $object->lastname(), "\n";
```

If all is well, you should be told the last name.

```
$ perl accessor1.pl
This person's last name: Galilei
$
```

Your accessor method is a very simple one—it takes an object, and extracts an attribute from it. First, you use shift() to get the object passed to you.

```
my $self = shift;
```

Then, you take out the relevant hash entry and pass it back.

```
return $self->{lastname};
```

Don't confuse the arrow used here for accessing parts of a reference with the arrow used as a method call. When accessing a reference, there will be either a curly brace or a square bracket at the end of the arrow.

```
$reference->{lastname}; # Accesses a hash reference
$reference->[3];         # Accesses an array reference
```

When calling a method, there will be a name following the arrow.

```
$reference->lastname();
```

So while your method is called with $object->lastname(), the last name entry in the hash is accessed with $self->{lastname}.

Get-Set Methods

As well as getting the value of an attribute, you may well want to set or change it. The syntax you'll use is as follows:

```
print "Old address: ", $object->address(), "\n";
$object->address("Campus Mirabilis, Pisa, Italy");
print "New address: ", $object->address(), "\n";
```

This kind of accessor is called a *get-set method* because you can use it to both get and set the attribute. Turning your current read–only accessors into accessors that can also set the value is simple. Let's create a get–set method for address():

```
sub address {
   my $self = shift;

   # Receive more data
   my $data = shift;
```

```
        # Set the address if there's any data there.
        $self->{address} = $data if defined $data;

        return $self->{address};
}
```

If you don't particularly want to trap calling the method as a class method (since it'll generate an error when we try to access the hash entry anyway), you can write really miniature get–set methods like the following:

```
sub address   { $_[0]->{address  } = $_[1] if defined $_[1]; $_[0]->{address  } }
sub lastname  { $_[0]->{lastname } = $_[1] if defined $_[1]; $_[0]->{lastname } }
sub firstname { $_[0]->{firstname} = $_[1] if defined $_[1]; $_[0]->{firstname} }
```

While that's fine for getting classes up and running quickly, writing out the get–set method in full as shown previously allows you to easily extend it in various ways, like testing the validity of the data, doing any notification you need to when the data changes, and so on.

Class Attributes

Classes can have attributes, too—instead of being entries in a hash, they're variables in a package. Just like object attributes, it's a really good idea to access them through get–set methods, but since they're ordinary variables, your methods are a lot simpler. Let's use a class attribute to keep score of how many times you've created a Person5 object (Person5 is your next step in creating your definition of a person). You'll call your attribute $Person5::Population, and you'll get the current value of it via the method headcount().

A class attribute is a package variable, and an accessor method just returns or sets the value of that variable. Here, you make your accessor method read–only to stop the end user changing it and confusing their own code:

```
package Person5;
# Person5.pm

# Class for storing data about a person

use strict;

my $Population = 0;

sub new {
    my $class = shift;
    my $self = {@_};
    bless $self, $class;
    $Population++;
    return $self;
}

# Object accessor methods
sub address   { $_[0]->{address  } = $_[1] if defined $_[1]; $_[0]->{address  } }
sub lastname  { $_[0]->{lastname } = $_[1] if defined $_[1]; $_[0]->{lastname } }
```

```perl
sub firstname { $_[0]->{firstname} = $_[1] if defined $_[1]; $_[0]->{firstname} }
sub phone_no  { $_[0]->{phone_no } = $_[1] if defined $_[1]; $_[0]->{phone_no } }
sub occupation  {
    $_[0]->{occupation}=$_[1] if defined $_[1]; $_[0]->{occupation}
}

# Class accessor methods
sub headcount { return $Population; }

1;
```

Now as you create new objects, the population increases:

```perl
#!/usr/bin/perl
# classattr1.pl

use warnings;
use strict;
use Person5;

print "In the beginning: ", Person5->headcount(), "\n";
my $object = Person5->new(
    lastname    => "Galilei",
    firstname   => "Galileo",
    address     => "9.81 Pisa Apts.",
    occupation  => "bombadier"
);
print "Population now: ", Person5->headcount(), "\n";

my $object2 = Person5->new(
    lastname    => "Einstein",
    firstname   => "Albert",
    address     => "9E16, Relativity Drive",
    occupation  => "Plumber"
);
print "Population now: ", Person5->headcount(), "\n";
```

```
$ perl classattr1.pl
In the beginning: 0
Population now: 1
Population now: 2
$
```

There's actually nothing object–oriented-specific about this example. All you're doing is taking advantage of the way Perl's scoping works. A lexical variable can be seen and used by anything in the current scope and inside any curly braces. So, naturally enough, with

```perl
Package Person5;

my $Population;

sub headcount { return $Population; }
```

the package variable $Population is declared at the top of the package, and is therefore visible everywhere in the package. Even though you call headcount() from another package, it accesses a variable in its own package.

Similarly, when you increment its value as part of new(), you're accessing a variable in the same package. Since it's a package variable, it stays around for as long as the package does, which is why it doesn't lose its value when you do things in your main program.

Let's make one more addition and create the Person6 class: you'll allow your main program to process all of the names of people in your contacts database, and you'll have a class method to return to us an array of the objects created. Instead of keeping a separate variable for the population, you'll reimplement $Population in terms of the scalar value of that array.

```perl
package Person6;
# Person6.pm

# Class for storing data about a person

use strict;

my @Everyone;

sub new {
    my $class = shift;
    my $self = {@_};
    bless $self, $class ;
    push @Everyone, $self;
    return $self;
}

# Object accessor methods
sub address   { $_[0]->{address  } = $_[1] if defined $_[1]; $_[0]->{address  } }
sub lastname  { $_[0]->{lastname } = $_[1] if defined $_[1]; $_[0]->{lastname } }
sub firstname { $_[0]->{firstname} = $_[1] if defined $_[1]; $_[0]->{firstname} }
sub phone_no  { $_[0]->{phone_no } = $_[1] if defined $_[1]; $_[0]->{phone_no } }
sub occupation  {
   $_[0]->{occupation}=$_[1] if defined $_[1]; $_[0]->{occupation}
}

# Class accessor methods
sub headcount { return scalar @Everyone; }
sub everyone  { return @Everyone;        }

1;
```

Note that you're pushing one reference to the data onto the array, and you return another reference. There are now two references to the same data, rather than two copies of the data. This becomes important when it comes to destruction. Anyway, this time you can construct your objects and loop through them.

```perl
#!/usr/bin/perl
# classattr2.pl
```

```
use warnings;
use strict;
use Person6;

print "In the beginning: ", Person6->headcount(), "\n";
my $object = Person6->new(
    lastname    => "Galilei",
    firstname   => "Galileo",
    address     => "9.81 Pisa Apts.",
    occupation  => "bombadier"
);
print "Population now: ", Person6->headcount(), "\n";

my $object2 = Person6->new(
    lastname    => "Einstein",
    firstname   => "Albert",
    address     => "9E16, Relativity Drive",
    occupation  => "Plumber"
);
print "Population now: ", Person6->headcount(), "\n";

print "\nPeople we know:\n";
foreach my $person(Person6->everyone()) {
    print $person->firstname(), " ", $person->lastname(), "\n";
}
```

```
$ perl classattr2.pl
In the beginning: 0
Population now: 1
Population now: 2

People we know:
Galileo Galilei
Albert Einstein
$
```

Normally, you won't want to do something like this. It's not the class's business to know what's being done with the objects it creates. Since you know that in these examples you'll be putting all the Person6 objects into a database, it's reasonable to get the whole database with a single method. However, this isn't a general solution—people may not use the objects they create, or may use them in multiple databases, or in other ways you haven't thought of. Let the user keep copies of the object themselves.

Privatizing Your Methods

The things you did with your class attributes in new() in the two preceding examples were a bit against the OO philosophy: you directly accessed the class variables, instead of going through an accessor method. If another class wants to inherit from this class, it has to make sure it too carries a package variable of the same name in the same way.

What you usually do in these situations is to put all the class–specific parts into a separate method, and use that method internally in the class. Inheriting classes can then replace these *private methods* with their own implementations. To mark a method as private, for use only inside the class, it's customary to begin the method's name with an underscore. Perl doesn't treat these methods any differently—the underscore means nothing significant to Perl but is purely for human consumption. Think of it as a "keep out" sign to mark the method as for use by authorized personnel only!

Typically, the constructor is one place where you'll want to do a private setup, so let's convert the code for adding to the @Everyone array into a private method in the class Person7:

```perl
package Person7;
# Person7.pm

# Class for storing data about a person

use strict;

my @Everyone;

# Constructor and initialization
sub new {
   my $class = shift;
   my $self = {@_};
   bless $self, $class;
   $self->_init();
   return $self;
}

sub _init {
   my $self = shift;
   push @Everyone, $self;
}

# Object accessor methods
sub address   { $_[0]->{address  } = $_[1] if defined $_[1]; $_[0]->{address  } }
sub lastname  { $_[0]->{lastname } = $_[1] if defined $_[1]; $_[0]->{lastname } }
sub firstname { $_[0]->{firstname} = $_[1] if defined $_[1]; $_[0]->{firstname} }
sub phone_no  { $_[0]->{phone_no } = $_[1] if defined $_[1]; $_[0]->{phone_no } }
sub occupation  {
   $_[0]->{occupation}=$_[1] if defined $_[1]; $_[0]->{occupation}
}

# Class accessor methods
sub headcount { return scalar @Everyone; }
sub everyone  { return @Everyone;        }

1;
```

What you have now is pretty much the standard constructor. Let's go over it again:

```perl
sub new {
```

First, you retrieve your class name, which will be passed to you automatically when you do `Class->new()`, by using `shift` as a shorthand for `shift @_`.

```
my $class = shift;
```

Then you put the rest of the arguments, which should be a hash with which to initialize the attributes, into a new hash reference.

```
my $self = {@_};
```

Now you `bless()` the reference to tell it which class it belongs to, making it an object.

```
bless $self, $class;
```

Do any further initialization you need by calling the object's private `_init()` method. Note that due to inheritance, this private method may be provided by a subclass.

```
$self->_init();
```

Finally, return the constructed object.

```
    return $self;
}
```

Utility Methods

Your methods have mainly been accessors so far, but that's by no means all you can do with objects. Since methods are essentially subroutines, you can do almost anything you want inside them. Let's now add some methods that do things—*utility methods*:

```
package Person8;
# Person8.pm

# Class for storing data about a person

use strict;

my @Everyone;

# Constructor and initialization
#...

# Object accessor methods
#...

# Class accessor methods
#...

# Utility methods
sub fullname {
    my $self = shift;
    return $self->firstname() . " " . $self->lastname();
}
```

```perl
sub printletter {
    my $self      = shift;
    my $name      = $self->fullname();
    my $address   = $self->address();
    my $firstname = $self->firstname();
    my $body      = shift;
    my @date      = (localtime)[3,4,5];
    $date[1]++;      # Months start at 0! Add one to humanize!
    $date[2]+=1900;  # Add 1900 to get current year.
    my $date      = join "/", @date;

    print <<EOF;
$name
$address

$date

Dear $firstname,

$body

Yours faithfully,
EOF
    return $self;
}

1;
```

This adds two methods, `fullname()` and `printletter()`. `fullname()` returns the full name of the person the object describes. `printletter()` prints out a letter with a body supplied by the user. Notice that to print the name in the text of the letter, `printletter()` itself calls `fullname()`. It's good practice for utility methods to return the object if they have nothing else to return. This allows you to string together calls by using the returned object as the object for the next method call, like this: `$object->one()->two()->three();`.

Here's an example of those utility methods in use:

```perl
#!/usr/bin/perl
# utility1.pl

use warnings;
use strict;
use Person8;

my $object = Person8->new(
    lastname   => "Galilei",
    firstname  => "Galileo",
    address    => "9.81 Pisa Apts.",
    occupation => "bombadier"
);
$object->printletter("You owe me money. Please pay it.");
```

This produces our friendly demand:

```
$ perl utility1.pl
Galileo Galilei
9.81 Pisa Apts.

4/5/2004

Dear Galileo,

You owe me money. Please pay it.

Yours faithfully,
$
```

Death of an Object

You've seen how you construct an object, and we've made ourselves a constructor method that returns a blessed reference. What happens at the end of the story, when an object needs to be destructed? Object destruction happens in two possible cases, either implicitly or explicitly:

- Explicit destruction happens when no reference to the object remains. Just like when dealing with ordinary references, you may have more than one reference to the data in existence. As you saw in Chapter 11, some of these references may be lexical variables, which go out of scope. As they do, the reference count of the data is decreased. Once it falls to zero, the data is removed from the system.

- Implicit destruction happens at the end of your program. At that point, all the data in your program is released.

When Perl needs to release data and destroy an object, whether implicitly or explicitly, it calls the method DESTROY() on the object. Unlike other utility methods, this doesn't mean Perl is telling you what to do. Perl will destroy the data for you, but this is your chance to clean up anything else you have used, close any files you opened, shut down any network sockets, and so on.

If Perl doesn't find a method called DESTROY(), it won't complain but will silently release the object's data.

The Finished Class

Let's put all the pieces of the class together and examine the class all the way through:

```
package Person8;
```

First of all, let's reiterate that a class is nothing more than a package. You start off the class by starting a new package. As usual, you want to make sure this package is at least as pedantic as the one that called it, so you turn on strictness:

```
# Class for storing data about a person

use strict;
```

Next, you declare your class attributes. These are ordinary package variables.

```
# Class attributes
my @Everyone;
```

You provide a nice and general constructor, which calls a private method to do its private initialization. You take the class name, create a reference, and bless() it:

```
# Constructor and initialization
sub new {
    my $class = shift;
    my $self = {@_};
    bless $self, $class;
    $self->_init();
    return $self;
}
```

Your private method just adds a copy of the current object to a general pool. In more elaborate classes, you'd want to check that the user's input makes sense and get it into the format you want, open any external files you need, and so on.

```
sub _init {
    my $self = shift;
    push @Everyone, $self;
}
```

Next, you provide very simple object accessor methods to allow you to get at the keys of the hash reference where your data is stored. These are the only interfaces you provide to the data inside the object, and everything goes through them:

```
# Object accessor methods
sub address   { $_[0]->{address  } = $_[1] if defined $_[1]; $_[0]->{address  } }
sub lastname  { $_[0]->{lastname } = $_[1] if defined $_[1]; $_[0]->{lastname } }
sub firstname { $_[0]->{firstname} = $_[1] if defined $_[1]; $_[0]->{firstname} }
sub phone_no  { $_[0]->{phone_no } = $_[1] if defined $_[1]; $_[0]->{phone_no } }
sub occupation  {
    $_[0]->{occupation}=$_[1] if defined $_[1]; $_[0]->{occupation}
}
```

Accessing class attributes is even easier, since these are simple variables.

```
# Class accessor methods
sub headcount { return scalar @Everyone; }
sub everyone  { return @Everyone;        }
```

Finally, you have a couple of utility methods, which perform actions on the data in the object. The `fullname()` method uses accessors to get at the first name and last name stored in the object, and returns a string with them separated by a space.

```
# Utility methods
sub fullname {
   my $self = shift;
   return $self->firstname() . " " . $self->lastname();
}
```

Second, `printletter()` is a slightly more elaborate method that prints out a letter to the referenced person. It uses the address and first name accessors plus the `fullname()` method to get the object's details. Notice that in both methods you're using `my $self = shift` to grab the object as it was passed to you.

```
sub printletter {
   my $self      = shift;
   my $name      = $self->fullname();
   my $address   = $self->address();
   my $firstname = $self->firstname();
   my $body      = shift;
   my @date      = (localtime)[3,4,5];
   $date[1]++;      # Months start at 0! Add one to humanize!
   $date[2]+=1900;  # Add 1900 to get current year.
   my $date      = join "/", @date;

   print <<EOF;
$name
$address

$date

Dear $firstname,

$body

Yours faithfully,
EOF
}

1;
```

Do You Need OO?

Now that you have discussed the basics of OO in Perl, how do you decide whether or not you should be using a procedural or an OO style in your programs? Here are five guidelines to help you decide.

Are Your Subroutines Tasks?

If your program naturally involves a series of unconnected tasks, you probably want to be using a procedural style. If your application is *data-driven*, then you're dealing primarily with data structures rather than tasks, so consider using an OO style instead.

Do You Need Persistence?

After your task is completed, do you need somewhere to store data that you want to receive next time you process that data? If so, you may find it easier to use an OO interface. If each call to a subroutine is completely independent of the others, you can use a procedural interface.

For instance, if you're producing a cross–reference table, your cross–reference subroutine will need to know whether or not the thing it's processing has turned up before or not. Since an object packages up everything you know about a piece of data, it's easy to deal with that directly.

Do You Need Sessions?

Do you want to process several different chunks of data with the same subroutines? For instance, if you have two different "sessions" that signify database connections or network connections, you may find it easier to package up each session into an object.

Do You Need Speed?

Object-oriented programs generally run slower than equally well–written procedural programs that do the same job, because packaging things into objects and passing objects around is expensive both in terms of time spent and resources used. If you can get away with not using object orientation, you probably should.

Do You Want the User to Be Unaware of the Object?

If you want to hide the details of how a thing behaves, OO is a good approach. You can design the object to store the data in any way that you choose, then provide the user with an easy–to-use interface. The user can then use the object without having to know how the information about the object is implemented.

Are You Still Unsure?

Unless you know you need an OO model, it's probably better to use a procedural model to help maintenance and readability. If you're still unsure, go with an ordinary procedural model.

Summary

Object-oriented programming is another way of thinking about programming. You approach it in terms of data and the relationships between pieces of data, which we call *objects*. These objects belong to divisions called *classes*—these have properties (*attributes*) and can perform actions (*methods*).

Perl makes object–oriented programming neat and simple:

- An *object* is a reference that has been blessed into a class.

- A *class* is an ordinary Perl package.

- A *method* is an ordinary Perl subroutine that has the class name or object reference magically passed in.

From these three basic principles, you can start to build data–driven applications.

Exercises

1. Using `Person8.pm`, write a program to do the following:

    Create three different `Person8` objects.

    Print the number of `Person8` objects.

    Loop through the `Person8` objects and print a letter to each one.

CHAPTER 14

■ ■ ■

Introduction to CGI

The Common Gateway Interface (CGI) is a method used by web servers to run external programs (known as *CGI scripts* or *CGI programs*), typically to generate web content dynamically. Whenever a web page queries a database, or a user submits a form, a CGI script is usually called upon to do the work.

CGI is simply a specification that defines a standard way for web servers to run such scripts and for those programs to send their results back to the server. The job of the CGI script is to read information that the browser has sent (via the server), and to generate some form of valid response, usually (but not always) visible content. Once the script has completed its task, it finishes and exits.

Perl is a very popular language for this purpose, thanks to its unrivalled text-handling abilities, easy scripting, and relative speed. It is probably true to say that a large part of Perl's current popularity is due to its success in dynamic web-page generation. Moreover, there is an excellent module available for Perl that makes writing CGI scripts easy—CGI.pm.

■ **Note** Usually, when we refer to Perl modules we do not include the .pm. For instance, when we talk about the DBI module, we never call it "the DBI.pm module." However, with the CGI module, we call it "the CGI.pm module." We are not sure why this is, perhaps it is historical—once upon a time we CGI programmers used a set of functions in a file called cgi.pl. Since that file was named cgi.pl, we suppose everyone called the new object-oriented version CGI.pm. Or it could be an effort to distinguish the CGI.pm module from the CGI protocol. Whatever the reason, we will continue the tradition of calling it CGI.pm.

In this chapter we will discuss the basics of CGI, how data is sent to CGI scripts, how the server responds to the client, and how to make all of this simple using CGI.pm.

This chapter is not meant to be an exhaustive study of writing CGI scripts with Perl, but rather an introduction with enough information to get you started, and to suggest where to look for more information. The best place to find out all you need to know is by picking up a copy of the *Official Guide to Programming with CGI.pm* by Lincoln Stein (Wiley & Sons, 1998). Of course, the online documentation for CGI.pm is available by executing perldoc CGI. The most important thing to remember about CGI with Perl—it's fun! So let's get started.

We Need a Web Server

The first step in writing CGI programs is to obtain access to a web server. While there are several options, such as obtaining an account with an ISP that provides a web server, a common solution is to install a web server on your machine and work locally.

The web server we suggest is the most popular server used on the Internet: Apache. As this chapter is being written (January 2010), Apache has about 47% of the web server market (you can see a comparison of all the different servers at `http://news.netcraft.com/archives/web_server_survey.html`). Apache is popular because it is a solid program, extensible, highly securable, and open source (meaning free!).

To download Apache, visit `http://httpd.apache.org/` and click the download link. As of January 2010, the latest version is 2.2.14. Follow the installation directions at `http://httpd.apache.org/docs/2.2/install.html` to install it on your machine. Or, better yet, get a copy of *Pro Apache, Third Edition* by Peter Wainwright (Apress, 2004) for an excellent guide that will help you get Apache up and running in no time.

A note to Unix users: chances are, Apache is installed and running on your machine—yet another reason to like Unix! To verify that your machine is ready to serve a web client, point your browser to `http://127.0.0.1/`, a special address that points to the machine you're sitting in front of. This address is also known as *localhost*. If you see a response page that tells you Apache is up and running, you are ready to go! You can replace `127.0.0.1` with `localhost`, as you'll see in the examples in this chapter, which all use `http://localhost/`. But beware—if your machine does not have a web server running, you are likely to end up at `http://www.localhost.com/`.

■ **Note** If you install Apache on Windows, it is possible that the path to Perl used in the examples:

`#! /usr/bin/perl`

will have to be changed to the location of Perl on the Windows installation, such as:

`#!c:/Perl/bin/perl.exe`

Creating a CGI Directory

Once Apache is installed, you need to create and configure a CGI directory. To learn how to do this, see `http://httpd.apache.org/docs/2.2/howto/cgi.html`. The location of this directory will vary from machine to machine, but common Unix locations are `/usr/local/apache/cgi-bin/` and `/home/httpd/cgi-bin/`.

Writing CGI Programs

Now that Apache is installed and the CGI directory is configured, let's write some CGI scripts. We often say that writing CGI in Perl is so easy—if you can print "hello, world!" you are halfway there! We will illustrate this with our first example.

All the examples in this chapter should be placed in the directory that `/cgi-bin/` points to. So, for instance, if you write a program named `foo.pl` and place it in your CGI bin directory, you can execute the program by loading this URL in your browser:

```
http://localhost/cgi-bin/foo.pl
```

"hello, world!" in CGI

Here's our first example—a program that sends "hello, world!", our Zen-like greeting, to the browser:

```perl
#!/usr/bin/perl
# hello.pl

use warnings;
use strict;

print "Content-Type: text/plain\n";
print "\n";
print "hello, world!\n";
```

If this program is located in the CGI directory and has the proper executable permissions (755 in the Unix world), we can view the result by loading `http://localhost/cgi-bin/hello.pl` in our browser, as shown here:

After the first familiar lines in this program, we see the statement

```perl
print "Content-Type: text/plain\n";
```

This print statement is very important—it contains the content type of the information that follows. This is sent to the client in what is known as the *HTTP header*—the mechanism the server uses to tell the client what kind of information it is sending. In this case, we are telling the client that what follows is to be treated as plain text, and to deal with it appropriately, which is normally by displaying it in fixed-width font.

The next line is:

```
print "\n";
```

prints a blank line. Printing a blank line is very important. The header must be followed by a blank line so the client knows that the header is complete and that the following information is the body, the main part of the information. If you forget to print the blank line, you will generally get a "Server Error" message on the browser.

Then we print the message we want the world to see:

```
print "hello, world!\n";
```

What to Do If Things Go Wrong

What if you don't see the warm, friendly greeting in your browser? There are many things that can go wrong with CGI scripts; here are some things you can do to troubleshoot the problem:

- The file must be located in the directory in which Apache is looking. Double-check that it is, and if not, move it to the appropriate place and try again.

- Make sure the permissions on the file are set so that the server can execute the program. In Unix, the permissions are usually set to 755, so chmod the file and test it again.

- The script might have a syntax error (hey, it happens!). An easy way to check this is to execute the program on the command line using the -c option:

  ```
  $ perl -c hello.pl
  hello.pl syntax OK
  ```

  This should tell you that the syntax is OK. If not, fix the problem and try again.

  That blank line is really important—if you forgot to print it, a server error is the normal result. A simple way to make sure the all-important-gotta-have-it blank line is there: simply execute the program from the command line:

  ```
  $ perl hello.pl
  Content-Type: text/plain

  hello, world!
  ```

  Do you see the blank line? If not, print that extra \n.

- Make sure that content type is something expected. For this program, it should be text/plain.

- It is possible that Apache is not configured properly. This is harder to fix—you will have to read through the Apache configuration documents to troubleshoot this problem.

- When all else fails, have a look in Apache's error log file (normally found in a directory named logs in the file named error_log). Apache reports errors to this file—it might tell you why the script failed.

If you still can't figure out the problem, head over to www.perlmonks.org. This is a great site where Perl programmers can ask other Perl programmers questions and expect polite, useful answers. Emphasis on polite. There are many places on the web where a question can result in a fiery response—Perl Monks is not one of them.

The CGI Environment

When the web server executes a CGI program, it makes available to that program a considerable amount of information through exported environment variables. To grab the environment variables in a Perl program, we look in %ENV. Here is a program that uses %ENV to show several important facts the server knows about the client requesting the CGI program:

```
#!/usr/bin/perl
# env1.pl

use warnings;
use strict;

print "Content-Type: text/plain\n";
print "\n";

print "your hostname is:      $ENV{REMOTE_ADDR}\n";
print "your outbound port is: $ENV{REMOTE_PORT}\n";
print "your browser is:       $ENV{HTTP_USER_AGENT}\n";
```

If you point your browser to http://localhost/cgi-bin/env1.pl, you'd see

As this program shows, the server knows the Internet address of the client, the port number of the machine the client is coming from, and the web browser it is using.

You may be wondering what other environment variables the server has available. This program will show you:

```perl
#!/usr/bin/perl
# env2.pl

use warnings;
use strict;

print "Content-Type: text/plain\n";
print "\n";

foreach (sort keys %ENV) {
    print "$_ = $ENV{$_}\n";
}
```

Loading http://localhost/cgi-bin/env2.pl will display all of our environment variables as shown in this example:

Generating HTML

Our CGI programs will not normally print plain text. Instead, they will print HTML to the client and the browser will render that text appropriately. To tell the client that our CGI program is generating HTML is as simple as changing the Content-Type:

```
#!/usr/bin/perl
# env3.pl

use warnings;
use strict;

print "Content-Type: text/html\n";
print "\n";

foreach (sort keys %ENV) {
    print "$_ = $ENV{$_}";
    print "<br />";
}
```

Changing the content type to text/html tells the browser that what follows is HTML and to handle the text as it would any other HTML. Note that when printing the environment variables and their values, we don't use newline characters since the browser treats them in HTML as simple whitespace characters. To get the line break we want, we must print the break tag <br />.

If we look at http://localhost/cgi-bin/env3.pl, we'll see something like

Since we can generate arbitrary HTML, let's make this output a bit more readable by putting it in a table:

```perl
#!/usr/bin/perl
# env4.pl

use warnings;
use strict;

print "Content-Type: text/html\n";
print "\n";

print "<table border=\"1\">";
foreach (sort keys %ENV) {
    print "<tr><th>$_</th><td>$ENV{$_}</td>";
}
print "</table>";
```

Ah, that's better (look at http://localhost/cgi-bin/env4.pl):

Take a moment to view the output from the program that the browser sees and renders by viewing the source: select the View menu in the browser and then pull down to Source (it might be Page-> Source or View-> Source, depending on your browser). This pops up a window that contains the HTML source code, which is the output from the CGI script. Handy tool, this View -> Source—the web is what it is in large part due to the fact that you can see the HTML that others create. This is an excellent way to learn what it takes to code good web pages.

Introducing CGI.pm

As you can see from these examples, writing CGI programs is straightforward: generate standard output with `print()` function calls, remembering to start the output with the `Content-Type` line followed by a blank line (don't forget the blank line!), followed by whatever you want to display in the browser: text, HTML, etc.

We will now introduce one of the most popular Perl modules (perhaps the most popular module): `CGI.pm`. This module, written by Lincoln Stein, makes it easy to generate HTML and process form data by providing some helpful methods. (We'll talk about form data a little later in this chapter.)

Let's jump right into this module by looking at an example. First, we'll present a program to generate a web page by printing plain HTML without the use of `CGI.pm`, then we'll see exactly the same web page generated by a program using `CGI.pm`.

Here is the non-`CGI.pm` version:

```perl
#!/usr/bin/perl
# html1.pl

# this program generates HTML without the use
# of CGI.pm

use warnings;
use strict;

print "Content-Type: text/html\n";
print "\n";
print "<html>\n";
print "<head>\n";
print "<title>Generating HTML</title>\n";
print "</head>\n";
print "<body>\n";
print "<h1>Now Is:</h1>\n";
print "<p>\n";
print "The current date and time is: ";

print scalar(localtime);

print "</p>\n";
print "<hr />\n";
print "<h1>Our CGI Scripts</h1>\n";
print "<p>\n";
print "By the time this chapter is over, you will write all of \n";
print "these scripts:\n";

print "<br />$_\n" foreach <*.pl>;

print "</p>\n";
print "<h1>Go Here For Excellent Books!</h1>\n";
print "<p>\n";
print "Check out the \n";
print "<a href=\"http://www.apress.com/\">Apress Home Page</a>.\n";
print "</p>\n";
print "</body>\n";
print "</html>\n";
```

Most of this code simply prints HTML. Let's look at two lines in detail. First:

```perl
print scalar(localtime);
```

The `localtime()` function called in scalar context returns a nice, readable string showing the current date/time stamp on the computer.[1] This program prints that string to standard output, which will be displayed in the body of the browser. The next line of interest is

```
print "<br />$_\n" foreach <*.pl>;
```

This code uses the expression modifier form of the `foreach` command, looping through all files that match the glob pattern `*.pl`. Each of the files is printed with a preceding `<br />` tag.

Loading this page (`http://localhost/cgi-bin/html1.pl`) into your browser should display something like the following:

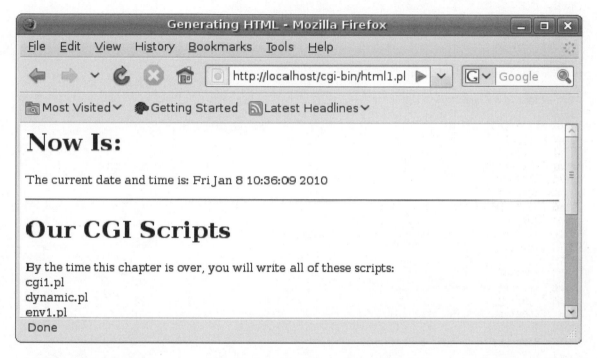

As you can see, all those `print()` functions with the double quotes, newlines, and semicolons make the code a bit hard to read. This program might be better written with a here-document as shown in this example (`html2.pl`):

```
#!/usr/bin/perl
# html2.pl
```

---

[1] In list context, `localtime()` returns something similar but different. See `perldoc -f localtime` for all the useful information that `localtime()` returns.

```perl
# this program generates HTML without the use
# of CGI.pm - this time with a here document

use warnings;
use strict;

print "Content-Type: text/html\n";
print "\n";

print <<EOHTML;
<html>
<head>
<title>Generating HTML</title>
</head>
<body>
<h1>Now Is:</h1>
<p>
The current date and time is:
EOHTML

print scalar(localtime);

print <<EOHTML;
</p>
<hr />
<h1>Our CGI Scripts</h1>
<p>
By the time this chapter is over, you will write all of
these scripts:
EOHTML

print "<br />$_\n" foreach <*.pl>;

print <<EOHTML;
</p>
<h1>Go Here For Excellent Books!</h1>
<p>
Check out the
<a href="http://www.apress.com/">Apress Home Page</a>.
</p>
</body>
</html>
EOHTML
```

Notice that here-documents are useful when printing static text. However, when we print scalar(localtime) and loop through all the .pl files, we need to make sure those executable statements are outside of a here-document.

This content can be generated by using CGI.pm and its methods. First, let's look at the program (cgi1.pl) and then we'll step through the code line by line:

```perl
#!/usr/bin/perl
# cgi1.pl

# this program generates HTML with the use
# of CGI.pm

use warnings;
use strict;
use CGI ':standard';

print header();
print start_html('Generating HTML');
print h1('Now Is:');
print p('The current date and time is:', scalar(localtime));
print hr();
print h1('Our CGI Scripts');

my $file_listing = '';
$file_listing .= "<br />$_" foreach <*.pl>;

print p('By the time this chapter is over, you will write all of',
        'these scripts:', $file_listing);
print h1('Go Here For Excellent Books!');
print p('Check out the',
        a({ href => 'http://www.apress.com/' }, 'Apress Home Page'));
print end_html();
```

The first part of this program is like any other Perl program: the shebang followed by optional comments followed by use warnings; and use strict;. Then comes the line that makes the use of CGI.pm possible:

```perl
use CGI ':standard';
```

This statement looks slightly different from other use statements we have seen since it adds ':standard'. This string tells CGI.pm that we want to use the methods in the module without having to call them using an object. In other words, if we use the :standard mode, we can call the header() method like this:

```perl
print header();
```

instead of like this:

```perl
my $q = new CGI;
print $q->header();
```

The header() method is very convenient—it prints the header (clever name, eh?). In other words, it generates the text

```
Content-Type: text/html
```

Yep, there is a blank line after the Content-Type line; the header() generates that all-important, gotta-have-it blank line, so we don't have to remember to do it. Next comes a method that generates the start of the HTML:

```
print start_html('Generating HTML');
```

which generates this HTML:

```
<html xmlns="http://www.w3.org/1999/xhtml" lang="en-US" xml:lang="en-US">
<head><title>Generating HTML</title>
</head><body>
```

Notice that the argument to `start_html()` is placed between the `<title>...</title>` tags.

Next up is

```
print h1('Now Is:');
```

This method generates the `<h1>...</h1>` tags with the argument to the method placed between the open and close tags.

```
<h1>Now Is:</h1>
```

Then we see

```
print p('The current date and time is:', scalar(localtime));
```

Like `h1()`,`p()` generates `<p>...</p>` with the argument(s) between the tags. This method has two arguments—a string and a function call separated by a comma. `CGI.pm` is smart enough to take these two arguments and concatenate the string and the function return value, automatically adding a space to separate them. This method, therefore, generates something that resembles

```
<p>The current date and time is: Fri Jan 18 19:02:48 2010</p>
```

The next method:

```
print hr();
```

generates `<hr />`. This is similar to `h1()` and `p()`.

A couple of lines later we see this code:

```
my $file_listing = '';
$file_listing .= "<br />$_" foreach <*.pl>;

print p('By the time this chapter is over, you will write all of',
        'these scripts:', $file_listing);
```

The code creates a variable `$file_listing` that will include all the Perl scripts in the current directory. For each Perl file, we append a `<br />` tag along with the file's name to `$file_listing`. That variable is then included as an argument to `p()`. This generates the text:

```
<p>By the time this chapter is over, you will write all of  these scripts:
<br />cgi1.pl<br />env1.pl<br />env2.pl<br />env3.pl<br />env4.pl<br />hello1.pl<br
/>html1.pl<br />html2.pl</p>
```

Next is a call to `p()` that includes a call to `a()`:

```
print p('Check out the',
        a({ href => 'http://www.apress.com/' }, 'Apress Home Page'));
```

This method generates

```
<p>Check out the <a href="http://www.apress.com/">Apress Home Page</a></p>
```

We will discuss the first argument to the `a()` method in detail a little later in this chapter. Finally, we see

```
print end_html();
```

This method generates the ending HTML tags:

```
</body></html>
```

Conventional Style of Calling Methods

The `cgi1.pl` program has several different `print()` function calls—one for each method that produces HTML. That's way too many. The conventional way of using `CGI.pm` is to combine all the prints into one as shown in `cgi2.pl`:

```perl
#!/usr/bin/perl
# cgi2.pl

# this program generates HTML with the use
# of CGI.pm using the conventional style

use warnings;
use strict;
use CGI ':standard';

print
    header(),
    start_html('Generating HTML'),
    h1('Now Is:'),
    p('The current date and time is:', scalar(localtime)),
    hr(),
    h1('Our CGI Scripts');

my $file_listing = '';
$file_listing .= "<br />$_" foreach <*.pl>;

print
    p('By the time this chapter is over, you will write all of',
      'these scripts:', $file_listing),
    h1('Go Here For Excellent Books!'),
    p('Check out the',
      a({ href => 'http://www.apress.com/' }, 'Apress Home Page')),
    end_html();
```

This generates exactly the same output as the other examples we've seen. Note how all the methods are arguments to a single `print()` function call. Many programmers consider this to be more readable than having a separate `print()` for each method call.

■ **Note** A word of caution: if the `h1()` method, for instance, is followed by a semicolon instead of a comma (a very common mistake!):

```
h1('Here Is An Example Web Page');
```

that semicolon would terminate the `print()`, so the following methods (`p()`, `hr()`, and so forth) would not be printed. It is our experience that when only a portion of the web page is displayed, it is often the result of a misplaced semicolon.

CGI.pm Methods

Many `CGI.pm` methods generate a number of tags, while others generate only one.

Methods That Generate Several Tags

We have seen methods that generate more than one tag, such as `start_html()`, which generates `<html><head><title>...</title></head><body>`. This method is used to generate all the HTML that is at the top of the HTML content. We invoked the method with one argument, and that argument was understood by the method to be the title of the web page and was placed between the `<title>...</title>` tags.

Named Parameters

There is another way to invoke the method—using *named parameters*. Since `start_html()` generates the `<body>` tag, we would like to be able to easily set certain attributes of that tag when we invoke the method. Here is an example that gives our web page a title, background color, and text color:

```
start_html(
    -title   => 'Generating HTML',
    -bgcolor => '#cccccc',
    -text    => '#520063'
),
```

This sets the title to "Generating HTML", the background color to a nice gray, "#cccccc", and the text color to an excellent shade of purple, "#520063."[2]

---

[2] How excellent? Go to www.northwestern.edu to see.

There are many different named parameters available to `start_html()`; check out `perldoc CGI` for a complete list.

Methods That Generate One Tag

We saw several methods that generate just one tag, including `h1()`, `p()`, and `hr()`. These methods generate the tags that use their name: `h1()` produces `<h1>...</h1>`, `p()` produces `<p>...</p>`, and `hr()` generates `<hr />`.

There are many other such methods—more or less one for each tag available in HTML. Examples include `i()` (`<i>...</i>`), `b()` (`<b>...</b>`), `li()` (`<li>...</li>`), and many others.

Providing Attributes

Many of the tags have optional attributes. You can provide these attributes to the methods by passing an anonymous hash containing the attributes and their values as the first argument to the method. For instance, let's say we want the `<h1>` tag to be aligned in the center of the page; to do this, we would call the `h1()` method like this

```
h1({ align => 'center'}, 'Here Is An Example Web Page'),
```

which generates

```
<h1 align="center">Here Is An Example Web Page</h1>
```

Providing more than one attribute is simply a matter of specifying more than one key/value pair to the anonymous hash. This method invocation generates an `<hr />` tag with a pixel size of 10 and no shading set:

```
hr({ size => 10, noshade => 1 }),
```

which generates

```
<hr size="10" noshade="1" />
```

Now we can see the magic involved in the `a()` method we saw earlier.

```
a({ href => 'http://www.apress.com/' }, 'Apress Home Page'),
```

generates

```
<a href="http://www.apress.com/">Apress Home Page</a>
```

Processing Form Data

CGI scripts don't merely generate HTML—they usually do some back-end, server-side processing. One major type of processing is gathering information from users by grabbing the data posted to a *form*. A form is a collection of *widgets* that allow the user to input data, select options, click buttons, and so forth. Most of us have filled out forms on the web when we've purchased books from an online store, filled out a survey, or created an account at `www.slashdot.org`.

Forms are created by surrounding one or more widgets with the `<form>` and `</form>` tags. The most important attribute to the `<form>` tag is the *action*, or CGI script, that is to be invoked when the user clicks the submit button.

Here is a simple form (`form.html`) that lets a user to enter her name and age:

```
<html>
  <head>
    <title>A Simple Form</title>
  </head>
  <body>
    <h1>Please Enter Your Name</h1>
    <form action="http://localhost/cgi-bin/form.pl">
      First name: <input type="text" name="firstname">
      <br>
      Last name: <input type="text" name="lastname">
      <br>
      <input type="submit">
    </form>
  </body>
</html>
```

This generates the form shown here after a user enters some text:

The CGI program associated with this form, as indicated by the `action=` attribute, is `http://localhost/cgi-bin/form.pl`. This program obtains the information the user entered into the form and processes it. The key to this program is the important `param()` method.

The param() Method

You can invoke the `param()` method with one argument, or with none. When invoked with no argument, `param()`returns a list of all the *parameters* in the form. A parameter is simply the name of the widget indicated by the `name=` attribute. In our `form.html`, there are two named widgets: `firstname` and `lastname`. The `param()` method invoked with no arguments would produce the list

```
('firstname', 'lastname')
```

When invoked with one argument, the `param()` method returns the value of that parameter. So, if the user enters his first name as Frodo, then `param('firstname')` returns Frodo. If he enters his first name as Bilbo, the method returns Bilbo. Likewise, `param('lastname')` returns the last name entered by the user into the form.

And now the code to process the form (`form.pl`):

```perl
#!/usr/bin/perl
# form.pl

use warnings;
use strict;
use CGI ':standard';

my @params     = param();
my $firstname = param('firstname') || 'you have no first name!';
my $lastname  = param('lastname')  || 'you have no last name!';

print
    header(),
    start_html(
        -title    => 'Welcome!',
        -text     => '#520063'
    ),
    h1("Hello, $firstname $lastname!"),
    end_html();
```

This program produces this result, assuming the user enters "Frodo" for the first name and "Baggins" for the last name:

The important lines in this program are

```
my @params    = param();
my $firstname = param('firstname') || 'you have no first name!';
my $lastname  = param('lastname')  || 'you have no last name!';
```

The first statement assigns to @params a list of all the parameters, or widget names, in the form that was posted. In our example, they are 'firstname' and 'lastname'. This line is followed by two assignments that are very similar. The first assigns $firstname the value that was entered into the firstname field in the form. The || operator ensures that the variable $firstname has a meaningful value—if the user does not enter a name, param('firstname') will be the empty string, which is false, so the || will evaluate the operand on the right and assign 'you have no first name!' to $firstname. A similar assignment is made to $lastname, and the print() function prints the two variables.

Dynamic CGI

The example we just looked at had an HTML file that was separate from the CGI program. The HTML was stored in form.html and the CGI program was stored in form.pl. This is known as a *static* CGI program—where the CGI program is loaded as a result of the action= in a static HTML file.

Sometimes keeping the HTML and CGI program in separate files creates a situation that is difficult to manage. It may be better to have the HTML generated by the same program that processes the posted data, that is, a *dynamic* CGI program.

A dynamic CGI program does one of two things:

- If there is posted data, process the data.

- If there is no posted data, build the form.

Recall that the `param()` method returns a list of all the parameters posted by the form. If this list is empty, the CGI program was invoked with no parameters. Thus, a dynamic CGI program has this general form:

```
if (param()) {
    # the program was invoked with parameters,
    # process the posted data
} else {
    # the program was invoked with no parameters,
    # build the form
}
```

Here is an example of a dynamic CGI program that implements the scenario we saw previously: it either builds a form that accepts a user's name and age, or it processes the form data (`dynamic.pl`):

```
#!/usr/bin/perl
# dynamic.pl

use warnings;
use strict;
use CGI ':standard';

if (param()) {
    # we have parameters, so process the form data

    my @params    = param();
    my $firstname = param('firstname') || 'you have no first name!';
    my $lastname  = param('lastname')  || 'you have no last name!';

    print
        header(),
        start_html(
            -title  => 'Welcome!',
            -text   => '#520063'
        ),
        h1("Hello, $firstname $lastname!"),
        end_html();

} else {
    # no parameters, so build the form

    print
        header(),
        start_html('A Simple Form'),
        h1('Please Enter Your Name'),
        start_form(),
        'First name: ',
        textfield(-name => 'firstname'),
        br(),
        'Last name: ',
```

337

```
        textfield(-name => 'lastname'),
        br(),
        submit(),
        end_form(),
        end_html();
}
```

This program generates the same form as `form.html` and it processes the form the same as `form.pl`. Note that it builds the form using `CGI.pm` methods. There are a few methods worth noting. First, the `start_form()` method builds the beginning `<form>` tag. The action can be specified with `{ -action => '/cgi-bin/whatever.pl' }`, but we're using the default action, which is the same CGI program that built the form. The form is eventually closed with `end_form()`.

The text form widget is created with `textfield(-name => 'lastname')`. The `textfield()` method is one of many methods used to create form widgets. Basically, there's a method for each different type of widget available. For a complete list, see `perldoc CGI`.

Let's Play Chess!

It's time to roll all the topics we have discussed into a single example. This CGI script will be a web implementation of the chess program, `chess.pl`, we discussed in Chapter 11. Since we are playing chess on the Web, we'll call this CGI script `webchess.pl`. This program will illustrate that with just a little bit of additional code, we can web-enable a program we wrote for the shell.

Before we look at the program, it is important to note that a CGI script is *stateless*. That means the CGI script itself can't remember anything about the most recent execution, or state, of the script. As a result, we somehow have to remember the recent state of the chessboard so we can pick up the game from the last move the user made. This is different from the `chess.pl` program—each move was made within the same execution of the program, so `chess.pl` always knew the state from move to move.

We will keep track of the state of the chessboard in a file named `webchess.dat`. This file will be an eight-line file, with each line being one row on the board. Each row will have its eight pieces, colon separated. Here is the initial state of the chessboard:

```
WR:WN:WB:WQ:WK:WB:WN:WR
WP:WP:WP:WP:WP:WP:WP:WP
:::::::
:::::::
:::::::
:::::::
BP:BP:BP:BP:BP:BP:BP:BP
BR:BN:BB:BQ:BK:BB:BN:BR
```

We can see that the first, second, seventh, and eighth rows have pieces. The middle four rows are empty—if two colons are right next to one another, that square does not have a piece on it.

If `webchess.pl` is going to keep its state in `webchess.dat`, we need some code to read from the data file and to write to the data file. These operations are placed within two functions: `read_in_chessboard()`, which will, you guessed it, read in the chessboard. The equally well-named function `write_out_chessboard()` will write it out. Let's jump into the code:

```
#!/usr/bin/perl
# webchess.pl
```

```perl
use warnings;
use strict;
use CGI ':standard';

my @chessboard = read_in_chessboard();

# grab the posted data, if any:
my $start = param('start') || '';
my $end   = param('end')   || '';

my $startx = '';
my $starty = '';
my $endx   = '';
my $endy   = '';

# time to make our move!
if ($start and $end) {
    if ($start =~ /^\s*([1-8]),([1-8])/) {
        $startx = $1 - 1;
        $starty = $2 - 1;
    }
    if ($end =~ /^\s*([1-8]),([1-8])/) {
        $endx = $1 - 1;
        $endy = $2 - 1;
    }
    if ($startx ne '' and $starty ne '' and
        $endx ne ''    and $endy ne '' ) {
        # put starting square on ending square
        $chessboard[$endy][$endx] = $chessboard[$starty][$startx];
        # remove from old square
        undef $chessboard[$starty][$startx];

        # we have changed the chessboard, so write
        # back out
        write_out_chessboard(@chessboard);
    }
}

# time to print to the browser
print
    header(),
    start_html('Web Chess'),
    h1('Web Chess');

# start the table that will contain the board
print '<table>';

# loop, printing each piece
foreach my $i (reverse (0..7)) { # row
    print '<tr>';
    foreach my $j (0..7) {        # column
```

```
        print '<td>';
        if (defined $chessboard[$i][$j]) {
            print $chessboard[$i][$j];
        } elsif ( ($i % 2) == ($j % 2) ) {
            print "..";
        }
        print '</td>';
    }
    print "</tr>";      # end of row
}

# we are done with our table
print '</table>';

# print a form for the next move
# and end the html
print
    hr(),
    start_form(),
    'Starting square [x,y]:',
    textfield(-name => 'start'),
    br(),
    'Ending square [x,y]:',
    textfield(-name => 'end'),
    br(),
    submit(),
    end_form(),
    end_html();

### function definitions ###

sub read_in_chessboard {
    # this function opens webchess.dat and builds
    # the chessboard
    # an example line from webchess.dat is:
    # BR:BN:BB:BQ:BK:BB:BN:BR

    # this is our local copy of the chessboard,
    # we'll return this later
    my @cb;
    open FH, '<', 'webchess.dat';

    foreach my $i (0..7) {
        my $line = <FH>;
        # split the line on a : or any whitespace
        # which will take care of the \n at the
        # end of the line
        my @linearray = split /[:\s]/, $line;
        # $#linearray should be 7!
        foreach my $j (0..$#linearray) {
            # if the text between the colons is
```

```
                    # not the empty string, we have a piece,
                    # so assign it to our chessboard
                    if ($linearray[$j]) {
                        $cb[$i][$j] = $linearray[$j];
                    }
                }
            }
        }
    close FH;

    # time to return back the chessboard
    return @cb;
}

sub write_out_chessboard {
    # the chessboard is passed in as our
    # argument
    my @cb = @_;

    # write the chessboard to webchess.dat
    # so that each piece on a row is colon separated
    open FH, '>', 'webchess.dat';
    foreach my $i (0..7) {
        foreach my $j (0..7) {
            if (defined $chessboard[$i][$j]) {
                print FH $chessboard[$i][$j];
            }
            if ($j < 7) {
                print FH ':';
            }
        }
        print FH "\n";
    }
}
```

Wow, that's a lot of code. Let's look at it a chunk at a time. We'll start at the bottom of the program with the functions to read from and write to the input data file. First, the relevant code in read_in_chessboard():

```
# this is our local copy of the chessboard,
    # we'll return this later
    my @cb;
    open FH, '<', 'webchess.dat';

    foreach my $i (0..7) {
        my $line = <FH>;
        # split the line on a : or any whitespace
        # which will take care of the \n at the
        # end of the line
        my @linearray = split /[:\s]/, $line;
        # $#linearray should be 7!
        foreach my $j (0..$#linearray) {
```

```
            # if the text between the colons is
            # not the empty string, we have a piece,
            # so assign it to our chessboard
            if ($linearray[$j]) {
                $cb[$i][$j] = $linearray[$j];
            }
        }
    }
    close FH;

    # time to return back the chessboard
return @cb;
```

This function creates a my() variable @cb that will hold a local copy of the chessboard. The input data file is opened in read mode. Then, for the eight rows on the board, a line of text is read from the input file and split on either the colon or whitespace character. split()breaks the line into eight parts—the pieces for that row. Then we loop for each square in the row. If there is a piece in the square, the square on the chessboard is assigned the piece. (No piece in the square is represented by the empty string, which is false, so any true value indicates a piece is present.) After each square in each row is assigned, the input file is closed and the chessboard is returned to whoever called it.

Now let's look at the function that writes the chessboard back out to the file:

```
sub write_out_chessboard {
    # the chessboard is passed in as our
    # argument
    my @cb = @_;

    # write the chessboard to webchess.dat
    # so that each piece on a row is colon separated
    open FH, '>', 'webchess.dat';
    foreach my $i (0..7) {
        foreach my $j (0..7) {
            if (defined $chessboard[$i][$j]) {
                print FH $chessboard[$i][$j];
            }
            if ($j < 7) {
                print FH ':';
            }
        }
        print FH "\n";
    }
}
```

This function opens the data file in write mode. It then loops eight times, once for each row. For each row, it loops eight times, once for each square in the row. If there is a defined value, it is printed (the value will be either the piece, such as "WB", or the empty string). A colon is printed after all but the last square on the row. After the row is printed, we end the line with \n. When all rows are printed, the output file is closed.

Now, let's look at the main code in the program. First, we create a variable to hold the chessboard by calling the function that reads from the data file:

```
my @chessboard = read_in_chessboard();
```

Then, we read in the posted data, if there is any. This data will be the starting and ending coordinates (such as 4,2). Note that if there is no posted data for either the start or end square, the variable will be assigned the empty string:

```
# grab the posted data, if any:
my $start = param('start') || '';
my $end   = param('end')   || '';
```

Now that $start and $end have the starting and ending square if they were entered, let's break those up into the X and Y coordinates. First we check to make sure we have both a starting and ending pair, otherwise there's no reason to do this work:

```
my $startx = '';
my $starty = '';
my $endx   = '';
my $endy   = '';

# time to make our move!
if ($start and $end) {
    if ($start =~ /^\s*([1-8]),([1-8])/) {
        $startx = $1 - 1;
        $starty = $2 - 1;
    }
    if ($end =~ /^\s*([1-8]),([1-8])/) {
        $endx = $1 - 1;
        $endy = $2 - 1;
    }
    if ($startx ne '' and $starty ne '' and
        $endx ne ''   and $endy ne '' ) {
        # put starting square on ending square
        $chessboard[$endy][$endx] = $chessboard[$starty][$startx];
        # remove from old square
        undef $chessboard[$starty][$startx];

        # we have changed the chessboard, so write
        # back out
        write_out_chessboard(@chessboard);
    }
}
```

Note that we are doing several checks here. First, we check to see if the user entered any coordinates. Then, we make sure we have good values for X and Y for both the starting and ending square. Only when we determine that we have to make a move do we modify the chessboard. And only when the chessboard has been modified do we write the chessboard back out to the data file.

Next, we start printing to the browser, starting with the initial HTML stuff:

```
# time to print to the browser
print
    header(),
```

```
        start_html('Web Chess'),
h1('Web Chess');
```

Then we print the chessboard. It is almost identical to the code that prints the chessboard in `chess.pl` except that we are going to put the board into an HTML table, so we have to print the necessary table tags:

```
# start the table that will contain the board
print '<table>';

# loop, printing each piece
foreach my $i (reverse (0..7)) { # row
    print '<tr>';
    foreach my $j (0..7) {          # column
        print '<td>';
        if (defined $chessboard[$i][$j]) {
            print $chessboard[$i][$j];
        } elsif ( ($i % 2) == ($j % 2) ) {
            print "..";
        }
        print '</td>';
    }
    print "</tr>";      # end of row
}

# we are done with out table
print '</table>';
```

First, we start the table. For each row, we print `<tr>` to start the row. For each column in the row, we wrap either the chessboard piece, "..", or nothing at all, inside `<td>..</td>`. We end the row with `</tr>` then finalize the table with `</table>`.

Next we see the code to print the form to read in the user's move:

```
# print a form for the next move
# and end the html
print
    hr(),
    start_form(),
    'Starting square [x,y]:',
    textfield(-name => 'start'),
    br(),
    'Ending square [x,y]:',
    textfield(-name => 'end'),
    br(),
    submit(),
    end_form(),
    end_html();
```

Whew! That was a long program. Enough talk—now it is time to play chess. Load `http://localhost/cgi-bin/webchess.pl` into your browser and you will see

Let's make an opening move: the white pawn from 4,2 to 4,4:

Improvements We Can Make

There are many enhancements we can make to this script—beyond the fact that we haven't built in any chess rules. This program is a good start for a chess game, but we should consider the following:

- *More error checking*: Error checking is good, especially for web programs—the last thing we want is a user to come to our web site, run a program, and have that program fail. One thing we should do is handle any failure to open the file when we read or write. This requires more than simply using the `die()` function because the output from `die()` goes to standard error, which does not end up in the browser. There are several ways to address this including a helpful module called `CGI::Carp`.

- *The design of the web page*: This page is OK, for geeks. But for consumption by the general public, we would want a slick, professional-looking site that is easy to navigate and pleasant to look at. This requires the help of a graphic artist and web designer—more art than HTML. To illustrate the difference, check out `www.bware.org`—that is a web page designed by a geek. Compare that to `www.onsight.com`, which was developed by a graphic artist.

- *An even more appealing design*: Speaking of an appealing web page, it would be nice to replace those letters with pictures. Wouldn't it be cool if instead of seeing BP we saw a picture of a black pawn? Again, we need an artist.

- *Every user gets his own game*: As this program is written, there is only one game. If you are playing, and you make a move, your friend can run the program and see the result. He can then make a move, which you will see the next time you run the program. Then another friend can come along, run the program, and you and your initial friend would see this new move. Not such a great thing. To resolve this we could add authentication with a username/password and store a unique copy of the game state for each user.

Hopefully this example has shown how easy it is to write CGI scripts in Perl. By adding a little bit of code, we were able to transform a program that ran in a shell to a program that has a web interface. Not only was it easy, it was fun! Speaking of fun, it's time to play some chess . . .

What We Did Not Talk About

Since this chapter can't possibly cover everything there is to know about CGI programming, there are many things we did not talk about. Some of these are very important topics you should take time to learn about, eventually:

- *Web security*: Running a web server that is connected to the Internet allows anyone who can reach your site to run your program. If the program is insecure, anyone who wants to can execute it, possibly doing nasty things. There are individuals in the world who like to try to break CGI scripts and crack into machines—that is the reality of the world we live in.[3] The good news is that it is possible to write secure CGI programs applying just a few techniques.

- *HTML*: This chapter is not a primer on HTML, so we did not discuss all the available tags and form widgets. There are many books and web sites devoted to HTML—read one and learn all about it. Then check out *Official Guide to Programming with CGI.pm* written by Lincoln Stein, the author of `CGI.pm`, to see how to use `CGI.pm` to build any HTML you want.

- *Other features*: There are many other aspects of CGI and HTTP we didn't cover, including JavaScript, SSL, authentication, and `mod_perl`.

---

[3] These individuals are often called hackers, but that is a misuse of the term. A hacker is one who creates a useful program, usually quickly, in an artistic way; it's what many of us programmers aspire to be. A person who breaks into other people's computers is called a *cracker*.

- *Database access*: Most modern web sites contain content that is generated dynamically by reading the data out of a database. In order to achieve any level of sophistication with Perl and databases, we need the excellent Perl module DBI. And that is the topic of the next chapter.

- *Templating*: Most modern web sites have a consistent look and feel. In other words, every page in the site has the same general layout—perhaps the same logo and links along the top, the same navigation links on the left side of the page, and the same information on the bottom of the page. If this were hard-coded for each page, then changing the look and feel of the web site would require a change to every single CGI script on the site. The solution is to create a template—a general layout for every page. Each CGI script uses the template for the basic look of the page, then adds the specific content for its purpose. Then, when the look and feel changes (as it probably will, eventually), the changes are made in one place—the template—and they are immediately applied to every CGI program. Perl offers many ways to template your web site including HTML::Template, the Template Toolkit, Mason, and Embperl.

Summary

CGI is the cornerstone of programming for the web, and Perl is *the* language to use to write CGI programs. In this chapter we discussed the CGI protocol, CGI.pm, forms, and form data. We saw that CGI programs are essentially a bunch of print() functions that generate standard output. We learned that CGI.pm can help make our lives easier by providing helpful methods to generate this output.

Form data can be processed using the param() function. Dynamic CGI scripts generate the form and/or process the form, depending on whether they were invoked with or without form data.

You now know enough about CGI programming to get started. So get going! And happy hacking.

Exercises

1. Write a CGI script that asks users to enter their names, addresses, and phone numbers. Respond to the users with a nice message thanking them for filling out the form, and append their information to a file.

2. Make the changes to webchess.pl that were made to chess.pl in the exercises at the end of Chapter 11.

CHAPTER 15

■ ■ ■

Perl and DBI

Now it's time to talk about the Database Independent (DBI) module, one of Perl's best. The module provides an easy-to-use API that's portable across operating systems and databases. It allows you to connect to a wide variety of databases—Oracle, Sybase, Informix, MySQL, mSQL, Postgress, ODBC, and many others—and even to files with comma-separated values. Using this module you can access and administer databases from your Perl programs, combining the power of the language with the usefulness of databases.

This chapter introduces Structured Query Language (SQL) and discusses the most common ways to use it. Following that, we'll look at DBI and the related DBD (Database Driver) modules, then write some Perl code to access and update a MySQL database. Finally, we'll take our newfound knowledge, connect it with what we learned in the previous chapter, and create a simple web interface to a database by combining Perl, DBI, and CGI. It should be fun, so let's get to it.

SQL, (pronounced *ess-que-el* by some and *sequel* by others, but we'll use the first) is a language that allows programmers to access *relational databases*—collections of information tables whose contents are interconnected. It's relatively easy to use—compared with Perl, SQL is a snap. We'll talk about some of the most common SQL *queries*—statements that interrogate a database—and in doing so we'll describe the language to the point that learning the remaining details requires nothing more than referring to an SQL book or web site. But we're getting ahead of ourselves. Before we can talk about SQL we need to discuss relational databases.

Introduction to Relational Databases

There are two important facts about relational databases. First, the content is *persistent*—it continues to exist after the execution of the program that accesses or modifies it. Second, relational databases, unlike files on a disk, allow concurrent access and updates from multiple users and processes. The database server makes sure changes are made to the data in a safe way.

As noted earlier, a relational database consists of tables. These hold data in rows, each of which is composed of fields. A field contains one basic piece of information, and from row to row, fields in the same position hold the same type of data. There are a lot of buzzwords here, so let's describe each of these with an example.

Let's say we want to keep some information about our favorite musicians: their names, phone numbers, and the instruments that they play. We might start by creating a list of the musicians like this:[1]

Name	phone
Roger Waters	555-1212
Geddy Lee	555-2323
Marshall Mathers III	555-3434
Thom Yorke	555-4545
Lenny Kravitz	555-5656
Mike Diamond	555-6767

This list shows six lines of data—the rows in relational-database-speak. When we take these and place them together into one collection of data, we have a table. Normally, for each row we want to create a unique identifier—the *primary key*, or simply the *key* (just in case we have two different Marshall Mathers III in our table). We can access the MMIII we're interested in using this unique value. We'll name the field column containing the key `player_id` and name the other fields, as well:

player_id	name	phone
1	Roger Waters	555-1212
2	Geddy Lee	555-2323
3	Marshall Mathers III	555-3434
4	Thom Yorke	555-4545
5	Lenny Kravitz	555-5656
6	Mike Diamond	555-6767

So now we've created a table (let's name it `musicians`) with three fields—`player_id`, `name`, and `phone`—and six rows of information.

---

[1] These aren't their real phone numbers. Sorry about that.

Normally when we build a database, we spread the information among several tables that connect to one another in some way, usually by the key, but you can use another field. To illustrate, let's expand our information about musicians to describe what each plays and some important facts about those instruments.

We could add each instrument to the row in the `musicians` table, but we'd duplicate a lot of information. For instance, three of our performers play guitar, so any guitar data we provide we'd have to be repeat for each musician. Also, several of our musicians have multiple talents—for instance, Thom Yorke plays guitar and keyboards and sings. If we enter data for each instrument Thom plays, our table will become big and difficult to work with. Instead, let's create another table, named `instruments`, to hold this information:

inst_id	instrument	type	difficulty
1	Bagpipes	reed	9
2	Oboe	reed	9
3	Violin	string	7
4	Harp	string	8
5	Trumpet	brass	5
6	Bugle	brass	6
7	keyboards	keys	1
8	Timpani	percussion	4
9	Drums	percussion	0
10	Piccolo	flute	5
11	Guitar	string	4
12	Bass	string	3
13	conductor	for-show-only	0
14	Vocals	vocal	5

Now that we've defined some instruments along with our opinion of their associated degrees of difficulty, we somehow need to map the instrument information to the information stored in the `musicians` table. In other words, we need to indicate how the `instruments` and the `musicians` tables relate. We could simply add the `inst_id` value to the `musicians` table like this:

player_id	Name	phone	inst_id
1	Roger Waters	555-1212	12

and so on, but remember that many of our musicians play more than one instrument. We would then need two rows for Roger Waters (he sings, too) and three rows for Thom Yorke. Repeating their information is a waste of memory and makes the database too complex. Instead, let's create another table that will connect these two tables. We will call it `what_they_play` and it will have two fields: `player_id` and `inst_id`.

player_id	inst_id
1	11
1	14
2	12
2	14
3	14
4	7
4	11
4	14
5	11
5	14
6	9

To read all this information and make sense of how it relates, we would first look in the `musicians` table and find the musician we want—for instance Geddy Lee. We find his `player_id`, 2, and use that value to look in the `what_they_play` table. In that table, two entries for his `player_id` map to two `instr_ids`: 12 and 14. Taking those two values, we use them as the keys in the `instruments` table and find that Geddy Lee plays the bass and sings for his band.[2]

---

[2] `www.rush.com`

This example illustrates that the `musicians` relates to `instruments` through the `what_they_play` table. Breaking the data into separate tables allow us to list the information that we need only once and is often more logical than keeping all the information in a single table—this is called *normalization*.

We Need an SQL Server—MySQL

Before we can show examples of SQL, we need an SQL server. There are many available—some cost money, some cost a *lot* of money, and some are free. One of the best, most powerful SQL servers, MySQL (`www.mysql.com`), is free. Given that we like free, we'll choose it. MySQL is open source, available for many different operating systems, and relatively easy to install and administer. It's also well documented (`http://dev.mysql.com/doc/refman/5.1/en/`) and there are many good books available including the excellent *The Definitive Guide to MySQL 5, Third Edition* by Michael Kofler (Apress, 2005). MySQL is an excellent choice for small, medium, and large databases. And did we mention it's free?

If you're a Linux user, chances are MySQL is already installed on your system. Do a quick check to see. If not, you'll find installation instructions at the MySQL web site (`http://dev.mysql.com/doc/refman/5.1/en/installing.html`). Since it's so well documented there, we won't repeat that information here.

Testing the MySQL Server

Just to be sure all is well, let's enter a few MySQL commands at the shell prompt to see if everything is working. The following examples assume that the MySQL `root` user (not to be confused with the Unix `root` user) has been given a password. This is a very good idea if your server will be available over the network—you don't want a pesky cracker logging in and carrying out destructive actions such as modifying or deleting data. Let's say `root`'s password is "RootDown".[3]
First, let's show all the tables set up on the server:

```
$ mysqlshow -u root -p
Enter password: RootDown
+-------------------+
|    Databases      |
+-------------------+
| mysql             |
| test              |
+-------------------+
```

---

[3] This is a very bad password for many reasons, the least of which is that it is published in this book. For information on creating good passwords, see *Hacking Linux Exposed*, *Second Edition*, Brian Hatch, Osborne Press (2002).

Next, we'll list all the tables in the database named `mysql`:

```
$ mysqlshow -u root -p mysql
Enter password: RootDown
Database: mysql
+---------------+
|     Tables    |
+---------------+
| columns_priv  |
| db            |
| func          |
| host          |
| tables_priv   |
| user          |
+---------------+
```

If these commands work (as they have in our example), then all's well with the MySQL server. Now we can create a database to store our musician information.

Creating a Database

After starting the MySQL server, we need to issue a MySQL command to create the database, which we'll call `musicians_db`. First, let's log into the MySQL command line interface (CLI):

```
$ mysql -u root -p
Enter password: RootDown
```

A few lines of information about the server will print, then we'll see the MySQL prompt:

```
mysql>
```

SQL CASE SENSITIVITY

Before we start working with the MySQL database, we should take a moment to talk about the case-sensitivity rules for SQL commands. Unlike Perl commands, those in SQL are not normally case sensitive. But in parts of the command that refer to what the programmer has created, case counts. Though this may sound confusing, it's quite simple. For example, later in this chapter we'll be working with the table we named musicians, which has a field we called name. To show the names in the table we could write an SQL command that would look like this:

```
SELECT name FROM musicians;
```

The two uppercase terms are the SQL parts. We created the lowercase words. Since the SQL parts of the command aren't case sensitive, we could have written:

```
select name from musicians;
```

But *name* and *musicians*, which we created, are case sensitive. So this command would not work:

```
SELECT NAME FROM MUSICIANS;
```

For clarity, in this chapter we'll use all uppercase for SQL terms in a command and all lowercase for terms we've defined.

The CREATE DATABASE Command

Creating a database is as simple as executing the CREATE DATABASE command:

```
mysql> CREATE DATABASE musicians_db;
Query OK, 1 row affected (0.01 sec)
```

The USE Command

Next we need to tell MySQL that we want to work with the newly created database. We do so with the USE command.

```
mysql> USE musicians_db;
Database changed
```

The CREATE TABLE Command

Now we have to create some tables. The first is musicians. Recall that it has three fields: player_id, an integer that serves as the key; name, a character string; and phone, a character string. The command to create a table is, not surprisingly, CREATE TABLE.[4] The syntax is:

```
CREATE TABLE table_name (field_definition, field_definition...)
```

The value of table_name is up to us—in our example we're using musicians. The field definitions comprising the comma-separated list within the parentheses follows this basic form:

field_name type

We make up the field names and choose the value for *type* from one of many different that MySQL supports, including INT. We specifiy strings in the form CHAR(n) where n is the number of characters in the string. Here's the command to create our table of musicians:

```
mysql> CREATE TABLE musicians (
    ->    player_id INT PRIMARY KEY,
    ->    name CHAR(50),
    ->    phone CHAR(12));
```

The player_id field will hold an integer that will serve as the key into the table. Both name and phone are strings.

---

[4] This MySQL stuff is easy!

■ **Note** There are many different SQL data types and ways in which we can create keys. For all the information on this subject, see the online documentation or the recommended textbook.

The DESCRIBE Command

The DESCRIBE command displays all the fields in the table and their types. This will show us if the musicians table was created correctly:

```
mysql> DESCRIBE musicians;
+-----------+----------+------+-----+---------+-------+
| Field     | Type     | Null | Key | Default | Extra |
+-----------+----------+------+-----+---------+-------+
| player_id | int(11)  |      | PRI | 0       |       |
| name      | char(50) | YES  |     | NULL    |       |
| phone     | char(12) | YES  |     | NULL    |       |
+-----------+----------+------+-----+---------+-------+
3 rows in set (0.00 sec)
```

From the output of the DESCRIBE command, everything looks okay, so let's create the other two tables—what_they_play and instruments:

```
mysql> CREATE TABLE what_they_play (
    ->    player_id INT,
    ->    inst_id INT);
Query OK, 0 rows affected (0.01 sec)

mysql> CREATE TABLE instruments (
    ->    inst_id INT PRIMARY KEY,
    ->    instrument CHAR(40),
    ->    type CHAR(20),
    ->    difficulty INT);
Query OK, 0 rows affected (0.00 sec)
```

Creating a Non-root User with the GRANT Command

It's important to create a non-**root** user to access the database—performing normal non-admin MySQL activities as the **root** user is a bad idea for security reasons, so let's create a user that will be allowed to perform basic queries on the musicians_db database:

```
mysql> GRANT SELECT, INSERT, UPDATE, DELETE
    ->    ON musicians_db.*
    ->    TO musicfan@localhost
    ->    IDENTIFIED BY "CrimsonKing";
Query OK, 0 rows affected (0.03 sec)
```

You can trust us that this creates a user who's named musicfan, has the password CrimsonKing[5], and can select, insert, update, and delete records from the database. Or you can check out the documentation and read all about the GRANT command.

We're going to start inserting data into our musicians_db database, so we need to log out as the root user and log back in as the newly created musicfan user:

```
mysql> quit
Bye
$ mysql -u musicfan -p
Enter password: CrimsonKing

mysql>
```

The INSERT Command

Now we're ready to put data into the table. We'll use the SQL command INSERT. The basic syntax is

```
INSERT INTO table_name (field1, field2, ...) VALUES (value1, value2, ...);
```

First the command line identifies the table into which MySQL should insert a row of data. The comma-separated list in the first set of parentheses indicates the fields that will get values. The parenthetical list after the term VALUES specifies the fields' values in their respective order. Roger Waters is deserving of a row of data in our table, so let's insert him, as key 1, along with his phone number:

```
mysql> INSERT INTO musicians (player_id, name, phone)
    -> VALUES (1, "Roger Waters", "555-1212");
Query OK, 1 row affected (0.01 sec)
```

The SELECT command can tell us if the row was inserted correctly (more on SELECT later).

```
mysql> SELECT * FROM musicians;
+-----------+--------------+----------+
| player_id | name         | phone    |
+-----------+--------------+----------+
|         1 | Roger Waters | 555-1212 |
+-----------+--------------+----------+
1 row in set (0.00 sec)
```

---

[5] Another bad password, but a snippet of lyrics from a great song.

Let's enter the other musicians:

```
mysql> INSERT INTO musicians (player_id, name, phone)
-> VALUES (2, "Geddy Lee", "555-2323");
Query OK, 1 row affected (0.00 sec)

mysql> INSERT INTO musicians (player_id, name, phone)
-> VALUES (3, "Marshall Mathers III", "555-3434");
Query OK, 1 row affected (0.00 sec)

mysql> INSERT INTO musicians (player_id, name, phone)
-> VALUES (4, "Thom Yorke", "555-4545");
Query OK, 1 row affected (0.00 sec)

mysql> INSERT INTO musicians (player_id, name, phone)
-> VALUES (5, "Lenny Kravitz", "555-5656");
Query OK, 1 row affected (0.00 sec)

mysql> INSERT INTO musicians (player_id, name, phone)
-> VALUES (6, "Mike Diamond", "555-6767");
Query OK, 1 row affected (0.00 sec)

mysql> SELECT * FROM musicians;
+-----------+----------------------+----------+
| player_id | name                 | phone    |
+-----------+----------------------+----------+
|         1 | Roger Waters         | 555-1212 |
|         2 | Geddy Lee            | 555-2323 |
|         3 | Marshall Mathers III | 555-3434 |
|         4 | Thom Yorke           | 555-4545 |
|         5 | Lenny Kravitz        | 555-5656 |
|         6 | Mike Diamond         | 555-6767 |
+-----------+----------------------+----------+
6 rows in set (0.00 sec)
```

Excellent! Our musicians are entered. Now for the commands to enter data into the other two tables. Read along and follow the bouncing ball.

```
mysql> INSERT INTO what_they_play (player_id, inst_id)
    -> VALUES (1, 11), (1, 14), (2, 12), (2, 14), (3, 14),
    -> (4, 7), (4, 11), (4, 14), (5, 11), (5, 14), (6, 9);
Query OK, 11 rows affected (0.00 sec)
Records: 11  Duplicates: 0  Warnings: 0
```

```
mysql> SELECT * FROM what_they_play;
+-----------+---------+
| player_id | inst_id |
+-----------+---------+
|         1 |      11 |
|         1 |      14 |
|         2 |      12 |
|         2 |      14 |
|         3 |      14 |
|         4 |       7 |
|         4 |      11 |
|         4 |      14 |
|         5 |      11 |
|         5 |      14 |
|         6 |       9 |
+-----------+---------+
11 rows in set (0.00 sec)
```

Notice that we used an alternative form of INSERT to add multiple rows, in this case all of them, at the same time.

```
mysql> INSERT INTO instruments
    ->     (inst_id, instrument, type, difficulty)
    ->     VALUES
    ->     (1, "bagpipes", "reed", 9),
    ->     (2, "oboe", "reed", 9),
    ->     (3, "violin", "string", 7),
    ->     (4, "harp", "string", 8),
    ->     (5, "trumpet", "brass", 5),
    ->     (6, "bugle", "brass", 6),
    ->     (7, "keyboards", "keys", 1),
    ->     (8, "timpani", "percussion", 4),
    ->     (9, "drums", "percussion", 0),
    ->     (10, "piccolo", "flute", 5),
    ->     (11, "guitar", "string", 4),
    ->     (12, "bass", "string", 3),
    ->     (13, "conductor", "for-show-only", 0),
    ->     (14, "vocals", "vocal", 5);
Query OK, 14 rows affected (0.00 sec)
Records: 14  Duplicates: 0  Warnings: 0
```

```
mysql> SELECT * FROM instruments;
+---------+------------+--------------+------------+
| inst_id | instrument | type         | difficulty |
+---------+------------+--------------+------------+
|       1 | bagpipes   | reed         |          9 |
|       2 | oboe       | reed         |          9 |
|       3 | violin     | string       |          7 |
|       4 | harp       | string       |          8 |
|       5 | trumpet    | brass        |          5 |
|       6 | bugle      | brass        |          6 |
|       7 | keyboards  | keys         |          1 |
|       8 | timpani    | percussion   |          4 |
|       9 | drums      | percussion   |          0 |
|      10 | piccolo    | flute        |          5 |
|      11 | guitar     | string       |          4 |
|      12 | bass       | string       |          3 |
|      13 | conductor  | for-show-only|          0 |
|      14 | vocals     | vocal        |          5 |
+---------+------------+--------------+------------+
14 rows in set (0.00 sec)
```

Now that we've created the three tables and populated them, let's talk about how we pull information out of the database.

The SELECT Command

SELECT allows us to query the database. The command examines the table we indicate and returns the information that matches the criteria we specify. We've seen several SELECT commands in this form:

```
mysql> SELECT * FROM musicians;
+-----------+---------------------+-----------+
| player_id | name                | phone     |
+-----------+---------------------+-----------+
|         1 | Roger Waters        | 555-1212  |
|         2 | Geddy Lee           | 555-2323  |
|         3 | Marshall Mathers III | 555-3434  |
|         4 | Thom Yorke          | 555-4545  |
|         5 | Lenny Kravitz       | 555-5656  |
|         6 | Mike Diamond        | 555-6767  |
+-----------+---------------------+-----------+
6 rows in set (0.00 sec)
```

By using the * (star) character, we've had SELECT ask for all fields and their contents ordered as they appear in the table. To ask for specific fields, we list their names in comma-separated format instead of using the star.

```
mysql> SELECT player_id, name, phone FROM musicians;
+-----------+----------------------+----------+
| player_id | name                 | phone    |
+-----------+----------------------+----------+
|         1 | Roger Waters         | 555-1212 |
|         2 | Geddy Lee            | 555-2323 |
|         3 | Marshall Mathers III | 555-3434 |
|         4 | Thom Yorke           | 555-4545 |
|         5 | Lenny Kravitz        | 555-5656 |
|         6 | Mike Diamond         | 555-6767 |
+-----------+----------------------+----------+
6 rows in set (0.01 sec)
```

We can select the fields in any order.

```
mysql> SELECT name, phone, player_id FROM musicians;
+----------------------+----------+-----------+
| name                 | phone    | player_id |
+----------------------+----------+-----------+
| Roger Waters         | 555-1212 |         1 |
| Geddy Lee            | 555-2323 |         2 |
| Marshall Mathers III | 555-3434 |         3 |
| Thom Yorke           | 555-4545 |         4 |
| Lenny Kravitz        | 555-5656 |         5 |
| Mike Diamond         | 555-6767 |         6 |
+----------------------+----------+-----------+
6 rows in set (0.00 sec)
```

We can also request specific fields—we don't need to show all of them.

```
mysql> SELECT name, phone FROM musicians;
+----------------------+----------+
| name                 | phone    |
+----------------------+----------+
| Roger Waters         | 555-1212 |
| Geddy Lee            | 555-2323 |
| Marshall Mathers III | 555-3434 |
| Thom Yorke           | 555-4545 |
| Lenny Kravitz        | 555-5656 |
| Mike Diamond         | 555-6767 |
+----------------------+----------+
6 rows in set (0.00 sec)
```

The WHERE Clause

So far, all of our SELECT queries have shown every row in the table, but often we want only specific rows. The WHERE clause tells SELECT to show only those that match our criteria. For instance, to see all the information in the musicians table for the musician with player_id 1 we could enter the command as:

```
mysql> SELECT * FROM musicians WHERE player_id = 1;
+-----------+---------------+----------+
| player_id | name          | phone    |
+-----------+---------------+----------+
|         1 | Roger Waters  | 555-1212 |
+-----------+---------------+----------+
1 row in set (0.00 sec)
```

Or how about selecting only the name of player_id 1:

```
mysql> SELECT name FROM musicians WHERE player_id = 1;
+--------------+
| name         |
+--------------+
| Roger Waters |
+--------------+
1 row in set (0.00 sec)
```

And here's how to grab Thom Yorke's phone number:

```
mysql> SELECT phone FROM musicians WHERE name = "Thom Yorke";
+----------+
| phone    |
+----------+
| 555-4545 |
+----------+
1 row in set (0.00 sec)
```

Maybe we're interested in all instruments with difficulties of 8 or higher:

```
mysql> SELECT instrument FROM instruments WHERE difficulty >= 8;
+------------+
| instrument |
+------------+
| bagpipes   |
| oboe       |
| harp       |
+------------+
3 rows in set (0.00 sec)
```

or the easiest instruments:

```
mysql> SELECT instrument FROM instruments WHERE difficulty <= 2;
+------------+
| instrument |
+------------+
| keyboards  |
| drums      |
| conductor  |
+------------+
3 rows in set (0.00 sec)
```

We can also combine conditions. Here's a SELECT query that returns all the percussion instruments with a difficulty less than or equal to 3:

```
mysql> SELECT instrument FROM instruments
    ->   WHERE type = "percussion" AND difficulty <= 3;
+------------+
| instrument |
+------------+
| drums      |
+------------+
1 row in set (0.00 sec)
```

■ **Note** There are many different ways to use the WHERE clause in SELECT. See the docs for all the details.

We could go on forever describing all the different uses of WHERE, but let's move on to sorting the output.

The ORDER BY Clause

The ORDER BY clause allows us to specify which field to sort the output by. Let's say we want to show all the musician information, but with the output in name order:

```
mysql> SELECT * FROM musicians ORDER BY name;
+-----------+---------------------+----------+
| player_id | name                | phone    |
+-----------+---------------------+----------+
|         2 | Geddy Lee           | 555-2323 |
|         5 | Lenny Kravitz       | 555-5656 |
|         3 | Marshall Mathers III| 555-3434 |
|         6 | Mike Diamond        | 555-6767 |
|         1 | Roger Waters        | 555-1212 |
|         4 | Thom Yorke          | 555-4545 |
+-----------+---------------------+----------+
6 rows in set (0.00 sec)
```

How about showing all the instruments and their difficulty from easiest to hardest:

```
mysql> SELECT instrument, difficulty FROM instruments ORDER BY difficulty;
+------------+------------+
| instrument | difficulty |
+------------+------------+
| drums      |          0 |
| conductor  |          0 |
| keyboards  |          1 |
| bass       |          3 |
| timpani    |          4 |
| guitar     |          4 |
| trumpet    |          5 |
| piccolo    |          5 |
| vocals     |          5 |
| bugle      |          6 |
| violin     |          7 |
| harp       |          8 |
| bagpipes   |          9 |
| oboe       |          9 |
+------------+------------+
14 rows in set (0.00 sec)
```

Let's list all the percussion instruments sorted by their names:

```
mysql> SELECT instrument FROM instruments
    ->    WHERE type = "percussion"
    ->    ORDER BY instrument;
+------------+
| instrument |
+------------+
| drums      |
| timpani    |
+------------+
2 rows in set (0.00 sec)
```

Can we reverse that order? Yup. Use the qualifier DESC:

```
mysql> SELECT instrument FROM instruments
    ->    WHERE type = "percussion"
    ->    ORDER BY instrument DESC;
+------------+
| instrument |
+------------+
| timpani    |
| drums      |
+------------+
2 rows in set (0.00 sec)
```

More Complicated SELECTs

Sometimes selecting information from our database requires criteria that are a bit more complicated than what we've seen so far. Here's one example: Satisfying the purpose for which we really created our database—finding out what instrument a particular musician plays.

If, for instance, we want to know what Lenny Kravitz plays, we'd first have to find out his player_id by querying the musicians table. Next, using that player_id, we'd select the inst_ids from what_they_play. Then, for each of those inst_ids, we'd get the instrument name from the instruments table.

First, let's get Lenny Kravitz's player_id:

```
mysql> SELECT player_id FROM musicians WHERE name = "Lenny Kravitz";
+-----------+
| player_id |
+-----------+
|         5 |
+-----------+
1 row in set (0.00 sec)
```

Now, using his player_id of 5, we'll grab the inst_ids from what_they_play:

```
mysql> SELECT inst_id FROM what_they_play WHERE player_id = 5;
+---------+
| inst_id |
+---------+
|      11 |
|      14 |
+---------+
2 rows in set (0.00 sec)
```

Finally, for each of the inst_ids, 11 and 14, we query the instruments table for the instrument:

```
mysql> SELECT instrument FROM instruments WHERE inst_id = 11;
+------------+
| instrument |
+------------+
| guitar     |
+------------+
1 row in set (0.02 sec)
```

```
mysql> SELECT instrument FROM instruments WHERE inst_id = 14;
+------------+
| instrument |
+------------+
| vocals     |
+------------+
1 row in set (0.00 sec)
```

Whew, that seems like a lot of work just to find the instruments Lenny plays, especially since we created this database to do just that kind of query. There must be a better way, right? There is.[6] We can do all four in one query using a *table join*.

Table Joins

MySQL is a relational database, so we must be able to query information from more than one table. By joining the tables, we can use more than one in a single SELECT. The best way to illustrate table joins is with an example. Take the complex SELECT, in the previous section, that let us discover the instruments Lenny Kravitz plays. We could have stated the request like this: "Give me all the instrument names in the instruments table that match the inst_ids in the what_they_play table for the player_id in the musicians table associated with the musician with the name Lenny Kravitz."

In SQL, we can indicate the instrument field in the instruments table using the table and field names in the format instruments.instrument. Likewise, inst_id in what_they_play is what_they_play.inst_id. With these fully qualified names we can use player_id in both the musicians table and the what_they_play table—SQL can keep them separate because we'll call them musicians.player_id and what_they_play.player_id.

Given that bit of good news, let's translate the query we just stated in English into SQL:

```
mysql> SELECT instrument
    ->     FROM instruments
    ->     JOIN what_they_play ON instruments.inst_id = what_they_play.inst_id
    ->     JOIN musicians ON what_they_play.player_id = musicians.player_id
    ->     WHERE musicians.name = "Lenny Kravitz";
+------------+
| instrument |
+------------+
| guitar     |
| vocals     |
+------------+
2 rows in set (0.00 sec)
```

The big difference between this query and those in our previous method, where we used multiple separate queries, is that we've listed more than one table in the FROM part: instruments, what_they_play, and musicians. Also, our WHERE clause has several conditions ANDed together. We're using more than one table and comparing values in one table with those in another, so we're joining the data together. Hence the term *table join*.

Let's do one more table join. Here's a query that will show all the musicians that play percussion instruments:

---

[6] TMTOWTDI in SQL too!

```
mysql> SELECT player_id
    ->     FROM what_they_play
    ->     JOIN instruments on what_they_play.inst_id = instruments.inst_id
    ->     WHERE instruments.type = "percussion";
```

```
+-----------+
| player_id |
+-----------+
|         6 |
+-----------+
```

```
1 row in set (0.00 sec)
```

As you can see, the SELECT combinations are endless! SQL is quite flexible—we can pull out exactly the information we need in exactly the order we want from the specific tables we're interested in. We've explored only a few SQL commands—there are so many more to learn. Check out the documentation and Kofler's book for more information.

But while using the MySQL command line interface is enjoyable, it's much more fun to query our database using Perl and DBI.

Introduction to DBI

DBI is the Database Independent module, which was written by Tim Bunce. It's a collection of APIs that allow programmers to connect to and access databases. As the name implies, the module allows you to write programs that access databases regardless of their type. You can write a program to query databases based on Oracle, Sybase, MySQL, Postgres, ODBC—the list goes on and on. All you need is the DBI module and the appropriate Database Driver (DBD).

■ **Note** Each of the mentioned databases has its own SQL dialect. Most implement the basic commands such as INSERT and SELECT in similar ways, but they sometimes implement the details of specific commands slightly differently. Keep this in mind if you're creating a Perl script that you want to port from one type of database to another—use the common form of each command even if a database has a nifty feature—but one that's not supported elsewhere.

We're using MySQL server in this chapter, so we need to install DBI and the MySQL DBD modules.

Installing DBI and the DBD::mysql

To use DBI you must install the appropriate modules. The first is DBI. As this is being written, the latest version of DBI on CPAN is 1.609, but as usual, that may have changed by the time you read this. You can easily check to see if DBI is installed on a system by executing the following at the command line:

```
$ perl -e "use DBI"
```

If there's no output, DBI is installed. If this command produces errors, follow the instructions, in Chapter 12, on installing the modules needed to install DBI. When that's done, you can install the MySQL driver. The name of module is DBD::mysql.

Connecting to the MySQL Database

Our first Perl program will simply connect to the MySQL database. If that works, we know that DBI and DBD::mysql are installed correctly and the real fun can begin. Let's look at an example we'll call connect.pl:

```perl
#!/usr/bin/perl
# connect.pl

use warnings;
use strict;
use DBI;

my $dbh = DBI->connect("DBI:mysql:musicians_db", "musicfan", "CrimsonKing");

die "connect failed: " . DBI->errstr() unless $dbh;

print "connect successful!\n";

$dbh->disconnect();
```

After the first four lines (the one with the shebang followed by the comment and then use warnings; and use strict;) we use the DBI module. Next we see a call to the DBI->connect() method. When we talked about object-oriented programming in Chapter 13, we mentioned that most modules use the method new() as their constructor. DBI, however, employs connect(). This is fine—any method name we choose can be the constructor, and since constructing a DBI object requires that we connect to a database, connect() seems a logical choice.

There are three arguments to connect(): the DSN, also known as the *data source name*, the username of the user, and the person's password. In this invocation, the data source name is

"DBI:mysql:musicians_db"

All data sources will start with DBI followed by a colon, the term mysql (since we're using MySQL server and DBD::mysql), a colon, and the database to which we're connecting—in this case, musicians_db.

■ **Note** Let's say that one day we want to port our database from MySQL to some other database server such as Oracle. In this script, all we need to do is change the text mysql in the data source to oracle. Provided that DBD::oracle is installed on our machine and we don't use any MySQL-specific queries, the script will work perfectly. Talk about portable!

The return value of DBI->connect() is an object that we can use to do things with the database. We call this the *database handler,* so we name it $dbh (but of course we can name it whatever we want). After the call to DBI->connect(), we check the value of $dbh.

```
die "connect failed: " . DBI->errstr() unless $dbh;
```

This makes sure $dbh has a true value. If DBI->connect() fails, it returns a false value to $dbh, so we die(), complaining that something went wrong with the database connection. The function DBI->errstr() reports the error, so to help the user we include this information in the string that die() prints. If all is well, we print a cheerful message and disconnect from the database.

```
print "connect successful!\n";
```

```
$dbh->disconnect();
```

We use the disconnect() method to disconnect from the database. Though not really necessary, since Perl will disconnect us when the script terminates, it's polite.

Here's what happens when we execute this program:

```
$ perl connect.pl
connect successful!
$
```

Now that we can connect, let's execute an SQL query.

Executing an SQL Query with DBI

From the previous example, connect.pl, we know how to connect to the database. Now we need to learn how to perform SQL queries.[7] Let's look at showmusicians.pl, a program that connects to the database musicians_db and displays all the rows in the musicians table. This program connects as before, prepares and executes an SQL query, and then loops through the result of the query.

```
#!/usr/bin/perl
# showmusicians.pl

use warnings;
use strict;
use DBI;

my $dbh = DBI->connect("DBI:mysql:musicians_db", "musicfan", "CrimsonKing");

die "connect failed: " . DBI->errstr() unless $dbh;
```

---

[7] As usual, there are a lot of ways to execute an SQL query and retrieve its results using Perl and DBI. We'll look at the easiest and most common way, but you can read about all the various ways by typing perldoc DBI at the shell prompt.

```
# prepare the query to get the data out
# of the musicians table
my $sth = $dbh->prepare("SELECT player_id,name,phone FROM musicians")
            or die "prepare failed: " . $dbh->errstr();

$sth->execute() or die "execute failed: " . $sth->errstr();

my($player_id, $name, $phone);

# loop through each row of data, printing it
while (($player_id, $name, $phone) = $sth->fetchrow()) {
    print "$player_id : $name : $phone\n";
}

$sth->finish();

$dbh->disconnect();
```

The database handler, $dbh, executes the **prepare()** method, which we show by itself here:

```
# prepare the query to get the data out
# of the musicians table
my $sth = $dbh->prepare("SELECT player_id,name,phone FROM musicians")
            or die "prepare failed: " . $dbh->errstr();
```

The method takes its argument, an SQL query, compiles it, and prepares it for execution. The query, SELECT player_id,name,phone FROM musicians, chooses three fields from the musicians table. If the prepare() method succeeds, it returns an object, known as the *state handler*, that's assigned to $sth. If the prepare() method fails, it returns false, and in that case, we die() printing $dbh->errstr(), the reason for the failure. If all is well, though, we execute the query.

```
$sth->execute() or die "execute failed: " . $sth->errstr();
```

The execute() method performs the query, storing the result into the $sth object. If the method fails, we die() and issue an explanation by executing $sth->errstr(). The $sth object has the result of the query stored within it, so we have to retrieve that information, which fetchrow() does.

```
# loop through each row of data, printing it
while (($player_id, $name, $phone) = $sth->fetchrow()) {
    print "$player_id : $name : $phone\n";
}
```

The fetchrow() method returns the next row of information supplied by the query. We then take that row and copy it memberwise into three variables. Since the query asked for the player_id, name, and phone from the musicians table, we take those pieces of information and store them in $player_id, $name, and $phone, respectively, then print the variables. After we're done with the state handler, we want to adhere to good practices, so we finish with:

```
$sth->finish();
```

Executing the query we've just described produces the following:

```
$ perl showmusicians.pl
1 : Roger Waters : 555-1212
2 : Geddy Lee : 555-2323
3 : Marshall Mathers III : 555-3434
4 : Thom Yorke : 555-4545
5 : Lenny Kravitz : 555-5656
6 : Mike Diamond : 555-6767
$
```

A More Complex Example

Earlier in this chapter we created a complex query that determined the instruments Lenny Kravitz played. The process required several steps. First we found his player_id from the musicians table. Next we used the player_id to read the inst_ids from the what_they_play table. Then, for each of those inst_ids, we read the instrument name from the instruments table. Here's how we might do the same with Perl and DBI:

```perl
#!/usr/bin/perl
# showinstruments1.pl

use warnings;
use strict;
use DBI;

my($who, $player_id, $inst_id);

print "Enter name of musician and I will show you his/her instruments: ";
chomp($who = <STDIN>);

my $dbh = DBI->connect("DBI:mysql:musicians_db", "musicfan", "CrimsonKing");

die "connect failed: " . DBI->errstr() unless $dbh;

# first, grab the musicians player_id
my $sth = $dbh->prepare("SELECT player_id FROM musicians WHERE name = '$who'")
            or die "prepare failed: " . $dbh->errstr();

$sth->execute() or die "execute failed: " . $sth->errstr();

($player_id) = $sth->fetchrow();

die "player_id not found" unless defined $player_id;

# given the player_id, grab their inst_ids from what_they_play
$sth = $dbh->prepare("SELECT inst_id FROM what_they_play
                          WHERE player_id = $player_id")
            or die "prepare failed: " . $dbh->errstr();
```

```
$sth->execute() or die "execute failed: " . $sth->errstr();

# foreach inst_id, grab the instrument name from the
# instruments table and print it
while (($inst_id) = $sth->fetchrow()) {
    my $sth = $dbh->prepare("SELECT instrument FROM instruments
                                     WHERE inst_id = $inst_id")
            or die "prepare failed: " . $dbh->errstr();

    $sth->execute() or die "execute failed: " . $sth->errstr();

    my($instrument) = $sth->fetchrow();
    print "    $instrument\n";

    $sth->finish();
}

$sth->finish();

$dbh->disconnect();
```

Let's look at each step of this process. After connecting to the database, as we've been doing in the previous examples, and asking for the user to enter the name of a musician, we construct and execute a query to obtain that musician's `player_id`.

```
# first, grab the musicians player_id
my $sth = $dbh->prepare("SELECT player_id FROM musicians WHERE name = '$who'")
            or die "prepare failed: " . $dbh->errstr();

$sth->execute() or die "execute failed: " . $sth->errstr();

($player_id) = $sth->fetchrow();

die "player_id not found" unless defined $player_id;
```

Let's look at the pertinent code, starting with the query to get the `player_id` of the artist:

```
# first, grab the musicians player_id
my $sth = $dbh->prepare("SELECT player_id FROM musicians WHERE name = '$who'")
            or die "prepare failed: " . $dbh->errstr();
```

Notice that we've constructed the SQL query using the variable `$who`. We need the outer double quotes of the query string to take the value of `$who`. And since the name is a string, the SQL query must wrap single quotes around `$who`.

The next lines of code

```
$sth->execute() or die "execute failed: " . $sth->errstr();

($player_id) = $sth->fetchrow();
```

execute the query. This should return only one row (it could return none if the musician isn't found in the table) so we only have to call fetchrow() once. We take the return value of that method, which is a list of one value, and assign it to the assignable list ($player_id). As a result, $player_id will contain either the player_id of the musician the user entered at standard input or undef if the musician wasn't found. The program die()s if $player_id is undefined.

Now we use $player_id to construct a query asking for the inst_ids:

```
# given the player_id, grab the inst_ids from what_they_play
$sth = $dbh->prepare("SELECT inst_id FROM what_they_play
                            WHERE player_id = $player_id")
            or die "prepare failed: " . $dbh->errstr();

$sth->execute() or die "execute failed: " . $sth->errstr();
```

Notice how the query string contains $player_id, the value we just read out of the database. Since player_id is an integer, it doesn't need to appear in quotes within the SQL query. When executed, this should return all the inst_ids for that player_id. We then loop through the result a row at a time:

```
# foreach inst_id, grab the instrument name from the
# instruments table and print it
while (($inst_id) = $sth->fetchrow()) {
    my $sth = $dbh->prepare("SELECT instrument FROM instruments
                                    WHERE inst_id = $inst_id")
            or die "prepare failed: " . $dbh->errstr();

    $sth->execute() or die "execute failed: " . $sth->errstr();

    my($instrument) = $sth->fetchrow();
    print "    $instrument\n";

    $sth->finish();
}
```

As we loop through each row of output from the previous query, we prepare() another query to read the name of the instrument from the instruments table. Notice that in the while loop, $sth will receive the return value from prepare() and that we've declared this variable with a my(). The my() here is important—it creates a new copy of $sth within the while loop, preventing us from clobbering the previous value of $sth (the result of the query of the what_they_play table) outside the while loop.

If we'd failed to declare $sth with a my(), that previous query would've been overwritten and we would have processed just one row of output from the what_they_play query. As an alternative to declaring $sth with my(), we could have selected a different variable name, but while that's fine, convention calls for sticking with $sth as the state-handler (besides, that new variable would have to have needed the my()as well). Now lets execute the code we've just discussed to see what happens.

```
$ perl showinstruments1.pl
Enter name of musician and I will show you his/her instruments: Roger Waters
    guitar
    vocals
$
```

Looks excellent—but not so fast. There's a problem with this program, as this example demonstrates:

```
$ perl showinstruments1.pl
Enter name of musician and I will show you his/her instruments: Chris O'Rourke
DBD::mysql::st execute failed: You have an error in your SQL syntax near
'Rourke'' at line 1 at showinstruments1.pl line 20, <STDIN> line 1.
execute failed: You have an error in your SQL syntax near 'Rourke'' at line 1 at
showinstruments1.pl line 20, <STDIN> line 1.
$
```

Can you see what the problem is? The query that uses $who, the name entered, looks like this:

```
$dbh->prepare("select player_id from musicians where name = '$who'")
```

Since $who is single-quoted in the SQL query string, the single quote in the name "Chris O'Rourke" makes SQL think that the string it's comparing to name is "Chris O". SQL then sees "Rourke", which is totally out of place, causing a syntax error. You could escape the single quote and turn $who into "Chris O\'Rourke", but while that would work, there's a better way.

Use Placeholders

To see how we deal with the problem just discovered, notice how we've changed the showinstrument1.pl SQL query strings in this new version, showinstrument2.pl:

```perl
#!/usr/bin/perl
# showinstruments2.pl

use warnings;
use strict;
use DBI;

my($who, $player_id, $inst_id);

print "Enter name of musician and I will show you his/her instruments: ";
chomp($who = <STDIN>);

my $dbh = DBI->connect("DBI:mysql:musicians_db", "musicfan", "CrimsonKing");

die "connect failed: " . DBI->errstr() unless $dbh;

# first, grab the musicians player_id
my $sth = $dbh->prepare("SELECT player_id FROM musicians WHERE name = ?")
            or die "prepare failed: " . $dbh->errstr();

$sth->execute($who) or die "execute failed: " . $sth->errstr();

($player_id) = $sth->fetchrow();

die "player_id not found" unless defined $player_id;

# given the player_id, grab their inst_ids from what_they_play
```

```perl
$sth = $dbh->prepare("SELECT inst_id FROM what_they_play
                              WHERE player_id = ?")
            or die "prepare failed: " . $dbh->errstr();

$sth->execute($player_id) or die "execute failed: " . $sth->errstr();

# foreach inst_id, grab the instrument name from the
# instruments table and print it
while (($inst_id) = $sth->fetchrow()) {
    my $sth = $dbh->prepare("SELECT instrument FROM instruments
                                    WHERE inst_id = ?")
            or die "prepare failed: " . $dbh->errstr();

    $sth->execute($inst_id) or die "execute failed: " . $sth->errstr();

    my($instrument) = $sth->fetchrow();
    print "    $instrument\n";

    $sth->finish();
}

$sth->finish();

$dbh->disconnect();
```

We've modified the first call to **prepare()** and **execute()** so that it now reads:

```perl
my $sth = $dbh->prepare("SELECT player_id FROM musicians WHERE name = ?")
            or die "prepare failed: " . $dbh->errstr();

$sth->execute($who) or die "execute failed: " . $sth->errstr();
```

Instead of using the variable $who in the query string, we use a question mark. This acts as a *placeholder* for a variable or value we'll provide later. And what we provide later ends up being an argument to the **execute()** method: $sth->execute($who). DBI will take the $who argument and plug it into the question mark in the query string. The nice thing about using this feature is that we don't have to worry about escaping the single quote. Much better!

What happens, though, if there's more than one variable in the query string? In that case, all their values are provided in the **execute()** method and plugged into the placeholders memberwise, as shown in this snippet:

```perl
$sth = $dbh->prepare("SELECT * FROM data WHERE name = ? AND age = ?");
$sth->execute($name, $age);
```

Wait a minute, though! Both showinstruments1.pl and showinstruments2.pl use three SQL queries. But we learned earlier in this chapter that with a table join we could obtain the same information using one query.

DBI and Table Joins

You can perform any SQL query using DBI, and this includes table joins. Let's modify the previous example showinstruments2.pl to do a table join as shown here in showinstrument3.pl:

```perl
#!/usr/bin/perl
# showinstruments3.pl

use warnings;
use strict;
use DBI;

my($who, $instrument);

print "Enter name of musician and I will show you his/her instruments: ";
chomp($who = <STDIN>);

my $dbh = DBI->connect("DBI:mysql:musicians_db", "musicfan", "CrimsonKing");

die "connect failed: " . DBI->errstr() unless $dbh;

# use a table join to query the instrument names
my $sth = $dbh->prepare("SELECT instrument
    FROM instruments
    JOIN what_they_play ON instruments.inst_id = what_they_play.inst_id
    JOIN musicians ON what_they_play.player_id = musicians.player_id
    WHERE musicians.name = ?")
            or die "prepare failed: " . $dbh->errstr();

$sth->execute($who) or die "execute failed: " . $sth->errstr();

# loop through them, printing them
while (($instrument) = $sth->fetchrow()) {
    print "    $instrument\n";
}

$sth->finish();

$dbh->disconnect();
```

The big change is the preparation and execution of the query:

```perl
# use a table join to query the instrument names
my $sth = $dbh->prepare("SELECT instrument
    FROM instruments
    JOIN what_they_play ON instruments.inst_id = what_they_play.inst_id
    JOIN musicians ON what_they_play.player_id = musicians.player_id
    WHERE musicians.name = ?")
            or die "prepare failed: " . $dbh->errstr();

$sth->execute($who) or die "execute failed: " . $sth->errstr();
```

Here we've constructed one large query, as we did previously in this chapter, that joins the musicians, what_they_play, and instruments tables. Notice how we use a placeholder when we compare musicians.name and how the variable $who is provided within the execute() method.
Does this table join work? Yep. Take a look:

```
$ perl showinstruments3.pl
Enter name of musician and I will show you his/her instruments: Thom Yorke
    keyboards
    guitar
    vocals
$
```

Perl and DBI give us an easy way to create programs that query our database. We can do anything with Perl that we can with SQL, and that includes execution of many SQL commands we haven't talked about in this chapter.

Perl, DBI, and CGI

Perl and DBI are enjoyable, but now let's take our exploration to another level of fun by combining our new skills with what we learned in the previous chapter: CGI. We'll develop a CGI script that will interface with the musicians_db database. We'll make it a dynamic CGI program that will present the user with a form, and when the person submits data (by clicking a button), the program will provide a response. We'll let the user choose to see one of two responses—a musician's phone number or the instruments the artist plays.
The program will follow this general flow:

```
if (param()) {
    if (param('Show phone number')) {
        # query database and show the musicians phone number
    } elsif (param('Show instruments')) {
        # query the database and show the instruments played by the musician
    }
} else {
    # query the database and build the initial form with all the musicians names
}
```

We'll look at the full code in all its glory, first, then examine the specific pieces in detail:

```
#!/usr/bin/perl
# musicians.pl

use warnings;
use strict;
use CGI ':standard';
use DBI;

if (param()) {
```

```
    # we have parameters, go grab the musicians
    # name
    my $musician = param('musician') || '';

    if (param('Show phone number')) {
        # the user wants to see the musician's phone number
        # print first part of HTML
        print
            header(),
            start_html("Phone Number for $musician"),
            h1("Phone Number for $musician");

        # query the database and get the phone number
        my $dbh = DBI->connect("DBI:mysql:musicians_db", "musicfan",
                                "CrimsonKing");
        my $sth = $dbh->prepare("SELECT phone FROM musicians
                                    WHERE name = ?")
                    or die "prepare failed: " . $dbh->errstr();

        $sth->execute($musician) or die "execute failed: " . $sth->errstr();

        my($phone);

        ($phone) = $sth->fetchrow();

        # print number and end HTML
        print
            "Call $musician at $phone.",
            end_html;
} elsif (param('Show instruments')) {
        # the user wants to see the instruments the musician
        # plays, start the HTML
        print
            header(),
            start_html("Instruments played by $musician"),
            h1("Instruments played by $musician"),
            "$musician plays:",
            '<ul>';

        # query the database with a table join and retrieve the
        # instruments played by musician
        my $dbh = DBI->connect("DBI:mysql:musicians_db", "musicfan",
                                "CrimsonKing");
my $sth = $dbh->prepare("SELECT instrument
            FROM instruments
            JOIN what_they_play ON instruments.inst_id = what_they_play.inst_id
            JOIN musicians ON what_they_play.player_id = musicians.player_id
            WHERE musicians.name = ?")
                    or die "prepare failed: " . $dbh->errstr();

        $sth->execute($musician) or die "execute failed: " . $sth->errstr();
```

```perl
            my($instrument);

            # print all the instruments in a bullet list
            while (($instrument) = $sth->fetchrow()) {
                print "<li>$instrument</li>";
            }

            # finish the HTML
            print
                '</ul>',
                end_html;
        }

    } else {
        # no data was posted, so print the initial form to the user
        # allowing to select the musician and whether they want
        # to see the phone number or the instruments
        print
            header(),
            start_html('My Favorite Musicians'),
            h1('Select a Musician'),
            start_form(),
            '<select name="musician">';

        # grab all the musician's names out of the database
        my $dbh = DBI->connect("DBI:mysql:musicians_db", "musicfan", "CrimsonKing");
        my $sth = $dbh->prepare("SELECT name FROM musicians")
                    or die "prepare failed: " . $dbh->errstr();

        $sth->execute() or die "execute failed: " . $sth->errstr();

        my($name);

        # loop through each row of data, printing it as an option
        # in the select widget
        while (($name) = $sth->fetchrow()) {
            print qq{<option value="$name">$name</option>};
        }

        # finish the select widget, print the submit buttons
        # and end the HTML
        print
            '</select>',
            br(),
            submit('Show phone number'),
            submit('Show instruments'),
            end_form(),
            end_html();
    }
```

When we run the program (`http://localhost/cgi-bin/musicians.pl`) the first time, we see this initial page:

This form allows users to select a musician from a drop-down list. When you execute the program, you'll see that the menu contains all the musicians we've inserted into our table—in fact, the menu is built by reading from the database. You'll also see two buttons—one indicates clicking on it will produce the selected musician's phone number. The other shows that, when clicked, it will display the instruments the selected musician plays. The `else` part of the program, which builds this page, starts with:

```
} else {
    # no data was posted, so print the initial form to the user
    # allowing them to select the musician and whether they want
    # to see the phone number or the instruments
    print
        header(),
        start_html('My Favorite Musicians'),
        h1('Select a Musician'),
        start_form(),
        '<select name="musician">';
```

The code prints the header first, followed by the start of the HTML for the page. Within the code for the form we see the creation of a `<select>` widget—this is a drop-down menu that allows us to choose one of the provided options. After that, the code says:

```
# grab all the musicians names out of the database
    my $dbh = DBI->connect("DBI:mysql:musicians_db", "musicfan", "CrimsonKing");
    my $sth = $dbh->prepare("SELECT name FROM musicians")
                    or die "prepare failed: " . $dbh->errstr();

    $sth->execute() or die "execute failed: " . $sth->errstr();
```

which connects to the database, then prepares and executes the query that retrieves all the musician names. Next comes the code that displays the names:

```
    my($name);

    # loop through each row of data, printing it as an option
    # in the select widget
    while (($name) = $sth->fetchrow()) {
        print qq{<option value="$name">$name</option>};
    }
```

This loops through all the rows of output (the musician names) and prints them in an <option> widget, adding them to the drop-down menu so they can be selected. Finally, the code finishes the page by closing the <select> widget, then printing two submit buttons:

```
    # finish the select widget, print the submit buttons

    # and end the HTML
    print
        '</select>',
        br(),
        submit('Show phone number'),
        submit('Show instruments'),
        end_form(),
        end_html();
}
```

Now let's say someone selects a name from the drop-down menu and clicks the button "Show phone number". Our user hasn't talked to Geddy Lee for a while, so he's the choice, which produces the following screen:

Let's look at the part of the program that built this page. It starts with:

```
if (param('Show phone number')) {
        # the user wants to see the musician's phone number
        # print first part of HTML
        print
            header(),
            start_html("Phone Number for $musician"),
            h1("Phone Number for $musician");
```

When the `if` determines the user wants to see the musician's phone number, the program starts the HTML for the page and then accesses the database:

```
        # query the database and get the phone number
        my $dbh = DBI->connect("DBI:mysql:musicians_db", "musicfan",
                               "CrimsonKing");
        my $sth = $dbh->prepare("SELECT phone FROM musicians
                                    WHERE name = ?")
                    or die "prepare failed: " . $dbh->errstr();

        $sth->execute($musician) or die "execute failed: " . $sth->errstr();
```

This looks familiar by now—the code connects to and queries the database using the placeholder for the musician's name, a process that returns the phone number for the musician. Now we need to fetch the row, read the data into $phone, print to the browser, and end the HTML:

```
my($phone);

($phone) = $sth->fetchrow();

# print number and end HTML
print
    "Call $musician at $phone.",
    end_html;
```

After calling Geddy Lee, our music fan might want to see the instruments Thom Yorke plays, so our curious person goes back to the initial page, select Thom from the drop-down menu, and clicks *Show instruments*. That produces this page:

And here's the code that builds the page:

```
} elsif (param('Show instruments')) {
    # the user wants to see the instruments the musician
    # plays, start the HTML
    print
        header(),
        start_html("Instruments played by $musician"),
        h1("Instruments played by $musician"),
        "$musician plays:",
        '<ul>';
```

We see that the user wants to show the musician's instruments, so we start the HTML, print some text, and then start an unordered list (a bullet list). Then we go to the code that queries the database:

```
    # query the database with a table join and retrieve the
    # instruments played by musician
    my $dbh = DBI->connect("DBI:mysql:musicians_db", "musicfan",
                            "CrimsonKing");
my $sth = $dbh->prepare("SELECT instrument
            FROM instruments
            JOIN what_they_play ON instruments.inst_id = what_they_play.inst_id
            JOIN musicians ON what_they_play.player_id = musicians.player_id
            WHERE musicians.name = ?")
                    or die "prepare failed: " . $dbh->errstr();

    $sth->execute($musician) or die "execute failed: " . $sth->errstr();
```

Using the table join we've seen a few times in this chapter, we find all the instruments that the musician plays, bringing us to the code that prints the instruments:

```
    my($instrument);

    # print all the instruments in a bullet list
    while (($instrument) = $sth->fetchrow()) {
        print "<li>$instrument</li>";
    }
```

Notice that each instrument is printed within an <li> tag, which makes it into a bullet item in the list. Finally we get to the end of the unordered list and the end of the HTML:

```
    # finish the HTML
    print
        '</ul>',
        end_html;
}
```

That was fun! And using Perl, CGI, and DBI it was easy as well. Such is the power and practicality of Perl revealed.

What We Didn't Talk About

This chapter isn't meant to be an exhaustive discussion of SQL and DBI. There are many topics we didn't talk about that you should learn if you want to harness the maximum power of SQL. First, there are several essential commands, including the following:

- UPDATE: Allows data in a table to be modified. An example might be

    ```
    UPDATE musicians SET phone = "555-9999" WHERE player_id = 3;
    ```

- **DELETE**: Deletes a row from a table. An example might be

  ```
  DELETE FROM instruments WHERE inst_id = 13;
  ```

  Be careful! If you don't use the **WHERE** clause, you'll delete all rows in the table.

- **REPLACE**: If the key provided does not exist, the data is inserted; otherwise the row with that key is first deleted, then the new row is inserted. An example might be

  ```
  REPLACE INTO musicians (player_id, name, phone)
          VALUES (1, "Neil Peart", "555-8888");
  ```

Just as knowing these SQL commands is important, so is understanding table indexing. Indexing can significantly increase the speed of **SELECT** statements with large tables. See the docs for more information. Also, be sure to check out Michael Kofler's excellent book, and remember to look at the online documentation for MySQL at `http://dev.mysql.com/doc/refman/5.1/en/`.

Summary

In this chapter we described how to access a database using Perl and the **DBI** module. We started with a description of a relational database and followed with a brief introduction to SQL. We then installed MySQL, created a database with three tables, and talked about several SQL commands. **INSERT** and **SELECT** were the most important ones. We also discussed using table joins as a way to implement the relations in relational databases. After that, we introduced **DBI** and **DBD::mysql** and wrote several Perl scripts to access and query the database. We ended with an example that showed how easily you can create dynamic web content by connecting Perl, **DBI**, and **CGI.pm**. And in the middle of that discussion, we took time out of our busy day to call one of our favorite musicians.

Exercises

1. Write a Perl script that prompts the user for an instrument and then prints all the musicians that play that instrument.
2. Write a CGI program similar to `musicians.pl` that serves as a web interface to the script you created for exercise 1.

Exercise Solutions

This appendix contains the answers to the chapter exercises. An important note: each solution is *an* answer, not *the* answer. Remember that in Perl, there is more than one way to do it, and that applies to these solutions as well.

Chapter 1

1.

```perl
#!/usr/bin/perl
# chap01ex1.pl

use warnings;

print "Hi Mom.\nThis is my second program.\n";
```

Chapter 2

1.

```perl
#!/usr/bin/perl
# chap02ex1.pl

use warnings;
use strict;

print "Currency converter\n\n";

print "Please enter the exchange rate: ";
chomp(my $yen = <STDIN>);
```

```perl
print "Enter first price to convert: ";
chomp(my $price1 = <STDIN>);

print "Enter second price to convert: ";
chomp(my $price2 = <STDIN>);

print "Enter third price to convert: ";
chomp(my $price3 = <STDIN>);

print "$price1 Yen is ", ($price1/$yen), " dollars\n";
print "$price2 Yen is ", ($price2/$yen), " dollars\n";
print "$price3 Yen is ", ($price3/$yen), " dollars\n";
```

2.

```perl
#!/usr/bin/perl
# chap02ex2.pl

use warnings;
use strict;

print "enter a hex number: ";
chomp(my $hexnum = <STDIN>);
print "converted to an int: ", hex($hexnum), "\n";

print "enter an octal number: ";
chomp(my $octal = <STDIN>);
print "converted to an int: ", oct($octal), "\n";
```

3.

```perl
#!/usr/bin/perl
# chap02ex3.pl

use warnings;
use strict;

print "enter a value less than 256: ";
chomp(my $bin = <STDIN>);

print((128 & $bin) / 128);
print((64 & $bin) / 64);
print((32 & $bin) / 32);
print((16 & $bin) / 16);
print((8 & $bin) / 8);
print((4 & $bin) / 4);
print((2 & $bin) / 2);
```

```
print((1 & $bin) / 1);

print "\n";
```

4.

```
(2 + (6 / 4) - (3 * 5) + 1) = -10.5
(17+((-(3**3))/2)) = 3.5
((26+3)^(4*2)) = 21
(((4 + 3) >= 7) || (2 & ((4 * 2) < 4))) = 1
```

Chapter 3

1.

```
#!/usr/bin/perl
# chap03ex1.pl

use warnings;
use strict;

my $target = 12;
print "Guess my number!\n";
print "Enter your guess: ";

my $guess;
while ($guess = <STDIN>) {
    if ($target == $guess) {
        print "That's it! You guessed correctly!\n";
        last;
    } elsif ($guess > $target) {
        print "Your number is more than my number\n";
    } elsif ($guess < $target) {
        print "Your number is less than my number\n";
    }
    print "Enter your guess: ";
}
```

2.

```
#!/usr/bin/perl
# chap03ex2.pl
```

```perl
use warnings;
use strict;

for (my $i = 1; $i <= 10; $i++) {
    print "$i square is: ", $i*$i, "\n";
}
```

3.

```perl
#!/usr/bin/perl
# chap03ex3.pl

use warnings;
use strict;

for (my $i = 1; $i <= 50; $i++) {
    if ($i % 5 == 0) {
        print "$i is evenly divisible by 5\n";
    }
}
```

Chapter 4

1.

```perl
#!/usr/bin/perl
# chap04ex1.pl

use warnings;
use strict;

my @a = (2, 4, 6, 8);

foreach (@a) {
    print "$_ ** 2 = ", $_ ** 2, "\n";
}

foreach (reverse @a) {
    print "$_ ** 2 = ", $_ ** 2, "\n";
}
```

3.

Here is a program that illustrates the answer to this question.

```perl
#!/usr/bin/perl
# chap04ex3.pl

use warnings;
use strict;

my @a = ('aa' .. 'bb');
print "first array:\n";
print "@a\n";

@a = ('a0' .. 'b9');
print "------------\n";
print "second array:\n";
print "@a\n";
```

Chapter 5

1.

```perl
#!/usr/bin/perl
# chap05ex1.pl

use warnings;
use strict;

my %hash = (
    scalar => 'dollar sign',
    array  => 'at sign',
    hash   => 'percent sign'
);

foreach (sort keys %hash) {
    print "$_: $hash{$_}\n";
}
```

2.

```perl
#!/usr/bin/perl
# chap05ex2.pl
```

```perl
use warnings;
use strict;

my %phonenumbers = (
    John  => '555-1212',
    Sue   => '555-2222',
    Larry => '555-3232',
    Moe   => '555-4242'
);

print "enter name: ";
while (<STDIN>) {
    chomp;
    if (exists $phonenumbers{$_}) {
        print "$_ has the phone number: $phonenumbers{$_}\n";
    } else {
        print "$_ is not in the phone book\n";
    }
    print "enter name: ";
}
```

3.

```perl
#!/usr/bin/perl
# chap05ex3.pl

use warnings;
use strict;

my %jokes = (
    Java   => "None. Change it once, and it's the same everywhere.",
    Python => "One. He just stands below the socket and the world " .
              "revolves around him.",
    Perl   => "A million. One to change it, the rest to try and do it in " .
              "fewer lines.",
    C      => '"CHANGE?!!"'
);

print "enter programming language: ";
while (<STDIN>) {
    chomp;
    if (exists $jokes{$_}) {
        print "How many $_ programmers does it take to change a lightbulb?\n";
        sleep 2;
        print $jokes{$_}, "\n";
    } else {
        print "That language is not funny...\n";
    }
```

```perl
    print "enter programming language: ";
}
```

Chapter 6

1.

```perl
#!/usr/bin/perl
# chap06ex1.pl

use warnings;
use strict;

print "enter a number: ";
chomp(my $input_num = <STDIN>);
if ($input_num < 0) {
    print "please enter a positive number!\n";
} else {
    my $result = factorial($input_num);
    print "$input_num! = $result\n";
}

sub factorial {
    my $num = shift;

    if ($num == 0) {
        return 1;
    } else {
        my $answer = 1;
        foreach (2 .. $num) {
            $answer = $answer * $_;
        }
        return $answer;
    }
}
```

2.

```perl
#!/usr/bin/perl
# chap06ex2.pl

use warnings;
use strict;

print "enter a number: ";
```

```perl
chomp(my $input_num = <STDIN>);
if ($input_num < 0) {
    print "please enter a positive number!\n";
} else {
    my $result = factorial_recursive($input_num);
    print "$input_num! = $result\n";
}

# here is the solution using recursion -
# a recursive function is a function that calls
# itself
sub factorial_recursive {
    my $num = shift;

    if ($num == 0) {
        return 1;
    } else {
        return $num * factorial_recursive($num - 1);
    }
}
```

3.

```perl
#!/usr/bin/perl
# chap06ex3.pl

use warnings;
use strict;

my $number_of_seconds;

prompt_user();
my ($hours, $minutes, $seconds) = secs2hms($number_of_seconds);
print "$number_of_seconds seconds is $hours hours, $minutes ",
      "minutes and $seconds seconds";
print "\n";

sub prompt_user {
    print "please enter the number of seconds: ";
    chomp($number_of_seconds = <STDIN>);
}

sub secs2hms {
    my ($h,$m);
    my $seconds = shift;;     # defaults to shifting @_
    $h = int($seconds/(60*60));
    $seconds %= 60*60;
    $m = int($seconds/60);
    $seconds %= 60;
```

```
    ($h,$m,$seconds);
}
```

Chapter 7

1.

Match "hello" followed by zero or more and any character but \n followed by "world"; or, in other words, any string that contains "hello" followed later by "world".

Match one or more digits at the beginning of the string followed by one whitespace character followed by zero or more word characters followed by the end of the string.

Match an uppercase letter at the beginning of a word followed by zero or more lowercase letters to the end of a word; or, in other words, match a word that begins with an uppercase letter followed by any number of lowercase letters.

Match a character, remember it in \1, followed by any number of any characters but \n, followed by the character remembered. In other words, match any string with two occurrences of the same character.

2.

```
/^\d.*\d$/

/^[\s\w]+$/

/^\S*$/
```

3.

```
#!/usr/bin/perl
# chap07ex3.pl

use warnings;
use strict;

while (<>) {
    print if /[aeiouy][aeiouy]/i;
}
```

4.

```
#!/usr/bin/perl
# chap07ex4.pl
```

```perl
use warnings;
use strict;

while (<>) {
    print if /^[^aeiouy]*[aeiouy][^aeiouy]*[aeiouy][^aeiouy]*$/i;
}
```

Chapter 8

1.

```perl
#!/usr/bin/perl
# chap08ex1.pl

use warnings;
use strict;

open(INFH,  '<', 'gettysburg.txt') or die $!;
open(OUTFH, '>', 'ex1out.txt')     or die $!;

while (<INFH>) {
next if /^\s*$/;
    my @words = split;
    print OUTFH "$_\n" foreach @words;
}

close INFH;
close OUTFH;
```

2.

```perl
#!/usr/bin/perl
# chap08ex2.pl

use warnings;
use strict;

unless (@ARGV) {
    @ARGV = qw(file1.dat file2.dat file3.dat);
}

print <>;
```

3.

```perl
#!/usr/bin/perl
# chap08ex3.pl

use warnings;
use strict;

my $target;
while (1) {
    print "What file should I write to? ";
    $target = <STDIN>;
    chomp $target;
    if (-d $target) {
        print "No, $target is a directory.\n";
        next;
    }
    if (-e $target) {
        print "File already exists. What should I do?\n";
        print "(Enter 'r' to write to a different name, ";
        print "'o' to overwrite or\n";
        print "'b' to back up to $target.old)\n";
        my $choice = <STDIN>;
        chomp $choice;
        if ($choice eq "r") {
            next;
        } elsif ($choice eq "o") {
            unless (-o $target) {
                print "Can't overwrite $target, it's not yours.\n";
                next;
            }
            unless (-w $target) {
                print "Can't overwrite $target: $!\n";
                next;
            }
        } elsif ($choice eq "b") {
            if (-e "$target.old") {
                print "Backup $target.old exists.  Overwrite it? [y|n] ";
                my $choice = <STDIN>;
                chomp $choice;
                if ($choice ne 'y') {
                    next;
                }
            }
            if ( rename($target, $target.".old") ) {
                print "OK, moved $target to $target.old\n";
            } else {
                print "Couldn't rename file: $!\n";
                next;
            }
        } else {
```

```
            print "I didn't understand that answer.\n";
            next;
        }
    }
    last if open(OUTPUT, '>', $target);
    print "I couldn't write to $target: $!\n";
    # and round we go again.
}

print OUTPUT "Congratulations.\n";
print "Wrote to file $target\n";

close OUTPUT;
```

Chapter 9

1.

```
#!/usr/bin/perl
# chap09ex1.pl

use warnings;
use strict;

open(FH, '<', 'ex1.dat') or die $!;

while (<FH>) {
    my $name    = substr $_,  0, 24;
    my $address = substr $_, 25, 18;
    my $city    = substr $_, 52, 20;
    my $state   = substr $_, 72,  2;
    my $zip     = substr $_, 75,  5;


    print <<EOT;
Record:
name    : $name
address : $address
city    : $city
state   : $state
zip     : $zip
EOT

}

close FH;
```

2.

```perl
#!/usr/bin/perl
# chap09ex2.pl

use warnings;
use strict;

while (<>) {
    tr/a-zA-Z/n-za-mN-ZA-M/;
    print;
}
```

Chapter 10

1.

```perl
#!/usr/bin/perl
# chap10ex1.pl

use warnings;
use strict;

my $dir  - shift || '';
my $size = shift || '';

die "usage: chap10ex1.pl <dir> <size>\n" unless $dir and $size;

chdir $dir or die "can't chdir: $!";

# first, a file glob
# this gets hidden files too
print "using glob:\n";
foreach (glob('.* *')) {
    if (-f $_ and -s _ >= $size) {
        print '    ', $_, ' ' x (30 - length($_)), -s _, "\n";
    }
}

# now using a directory handle
print "\n\nusing directory handle:\n";
opendir DH, '.' or die "opendir failed: $!";
while ($_ = readdir(DH)) {
    if (-f $_ and -s _ >= $size) {
        print '    ', $_, ' ' x (30 - length($_)), -s _, "\n";
```

```
    }
}
closedir DH;
```

Chapter 11

1.

```perl
#!/usr/bin/perl
# chap11ex1.pl

use warnings;
use strict;

my @chessboard;
my @back = qw(R N B Q K B N R);
foreach (0..7) {
    $chessboard[0][$_] = "W" . $back[$_]; # White Back Row
    $chessboard[1][$_] = "WP";            # White Pawns
    $chessboard[6][$_] = "BP";            # Black Pawns
    $chessboard[7][$_] = "B" . $back[$_]; # Black Back Row
}

while (1) {
    # Print board
    foreach my $i (reverse (0..7)) { # Row
        foreach my $j (0..7) {        # Column
            if (defined $chessboard[$i][$j]) {
                print $chessboard[$i][$j];
            } elsif ( ($i % 2) == ($j % 2) ) {
                print "..";
            } else {
                print "  ";
            }
            print " ";  # End of cell
        }
        print "\n";     # End of row
    }

    print "\nStarting square [x,y]: ";
    my $move = <>;
    last unless ($move =~ /^\s*([1-8]),([1-8])/);
    my $startx = $1-1; my $starty = $2-1;

    unless (defined $chessboard[$starty][$startx]) {
        print "There's nothing on that square!\n";
        next;
```

```perl
}
print "\nEnding square [x,y]: ";
$move = <>;
last unless ($move =~ /([1-8]),([1-8])/);
my $endx = $1-1; my $endy = $2-1;

# detect if a piece is about to be taken
if (defined $chessboard[$endy][$endx]) {
    print "\n$chessboard[$endy][$endx] at (", $endx + 1, ",",
            $endy+1, ") is being taken!\n\n";
}

# Put starting square on ending square.
$chessboard[$endy][$endx] = $chessboard[$starty][$startx];
# Remove from old square
undef $chessboard[$starty][$startx];
}
```

2.

```perl
#!/usr/bin/perl
# chap11ex2.pl

use warnings;
use strict;

my @chessboard;
my @back = qw(R N B Q K B N R);
foreach (0..7) {
    $chessboard[0]->[$_] = "W" . $back[$_]; # White Back Row
    $chessboard[1]->[$_] = "WP";            # White Pawns
    $chessboard[6]->[$_] = "BP";            # Black Pawns
    $chessboard[7]->[$_] = "B" . $back[$_]; # Black Back Row
}

while (1) {
  # Print board
  foreach my $i (reverse (0..7)) { # Row
      foreach my $j (0..7) {        # Column
          if (defined $chessboard[$i][$j]) {
              print $chessboard[$i][$j];
          } elsif ( ($i % 2) == ($j % 2) ) {
              print "..";
          } else {
              print "  ";
          }
          print " ";  # End of cell
      }
      print "\n";      # End of row
```

```perl
    }

    print "\nStarting square [x,y]: ";
    my $move = <>;
    last unless ($move =~ /^\s*([1-8]),([1-8])/);
    my $startx = $1-1; my $starty = $2-1;

    unless (defined $chessboard[$starty][$startx]) {
        print "There's nothing on that square!\n";
        next;
    }
    print "\nEnding square [x,y]: ";
    $move = <>;
    last unless ($move =~ /([1-8]),([1-8])/);
    my $endx = $1-1; my $endy = $2-1;

    if (defined $chessboard[$endy][$endx]) {
        # can't take your own piece
        if (substr($chessboard[$endy][$endx], 0, 1) eq
            substr($chessboard[$starty][$startx], 0, 1)) {
            print "\nyou can't take your own piece!\n\n";
            next;
        }
        # can't take a king
        if ($chessboard[$endy][$endx] =~ /K/) {
            print "\nyou can't take a king!\n\n";
            next;
        }
    }

    # Put starting square on ending square.
    $chessboard[$endy][$endx] = $chessboard[$starty][$startx];
    # Remove from old square
    undef $chessboard[$starty][$startx];
}
```

3.

```perl
#!/usr/bin/perl
# chap11ex3.pl

use warnings;
use strict;

my %addressbook;

sub menu {
    print <<EOT;
```

```
Please make a choice:
    1  add an entry
    2  view an entry
    3  view all entries
    4  delete an entry
    5  exit

Your choice:
EOT
}

sub add_entry {
    print "Enter name: ";
    chomp(my $name = <STDIN>);
    if (exists $addressbook{$name}) {
        print "Name alread exists in the address book!\n";
    }
    print "Address:    ";
    chomp(my $address = <STDIN>);
    print "Phone:      ";
    chomp(my $phone = <STDIN>);
    $addressbook{$name} = {
        address => $address,
        phone   => $phone
    };
}

sub view_entry {
    print "Enter name to view: ";
    chomp(my $name = <STDIN>);
    if (exists $addressbook{$name}) {
        print "Address: $addressbook{$name}{address}\n";
        print "Phone:   $addressbook{$name}{phone}\n\n";
    } else {
        print "$name is not in address book!\n\n";
    }
}

sub view_all {
    foreach my $name (sort keys %addressbook) {
        print "Name:    $name\n";
        print "Address: $addressbook{$name}{address}\n";
        print "Phone:   $addressbook{$name}{phone}\n\n";
    }
}

sub delete_entry {
    print "Enter name to delete: ";
    chomp(my $name = <STDIN>);
    if (exists $addressbook{$name}) {
        delete $addressbook{$name};
```

```perl
    } else {
        print "$name is not in address book!\n\n";
    }
}

while (1) {
    menu();
    chomp(my $answer = <STDIN>);
    SWITCH: {
        $answer == 1 and add_entry(),    last SWITCH;
        $answer == 2 and view_entry(),   last SWITCH;
        $answer == 3 and view_all(),     last SWITCH;
        $answer == 4 and delete_entry(), last SWITCH;
        $answer == 5 and exit(0);
    }
}
```

Chapter 13

1.

```perl
#!/usr/bin/perl
# chap13ex1.pl

use warnings;
use strict;
use Person8;

my $object1 = Person8->new(
    lastname    => "Galilei",
    firstname   => "Galileo",
    address     => "9.81 Pisa Apts.",
    occupation  => "bombadier",
    phone_no    => "312.555.1212"
);

my $object2 = Person8->new(
    lastname    => "Wall",
    firstname   => "Larry",
    address     => "123 Perl Ave.",
    occupation  => "Programmer",
    phone_no    => "312.555.2323"
);

my $object3 = Person8->new(
    lastname    => "Torvalds",
    firstname   => "Linus",
```

```perl
    address       => "593 Linux Ave.",
    occupation  => "Programmer",
    phone_no    => "312.555.3434"
);

print "There are ", Person8->headcount(), " Person8 objects\n";

foreach my $person (Person8->everyone()) {
    print "\n", '-' x 80, "\n";
    $person->printletter("You owe me money. Please pay it.");
}
```

Chapter 14

1.

```perl
#!/usr/bin/perl
# chap14ex1.pl

use warnings;
use strict;

use CGI ':standard';

print
    header(),
    start_html('Exercise 1');

if (param) {
    my $name    = param('name')    || '';
    my $address = param('address') || '';
    my $phone   = param('phone')   || '';

    print
        h1('Thanks for your information!'),
        'Thanks for entering the following information:',
        br(),
        $name,
        br(),
        $address,
        br(),
        $phone;

    open FH, '>>', '/tmp/ex1.dat';
    print FH '-' x 80, "\n$name\n$address\n$phone\n";
    close FH;
} else {
```

```
    print
        h1('Please enter some information'),
        start_form(),
        'Name: ',
        textfield(-name => 'name'),
        br(),
        'Address: ',
        textarea(-name => 'address', rows => 3),
        br(),
        'Phone number: ',
        textfield(-name => 'phone'),
        br(),
        submit(),
        end_form();
}

print
    end_html();
```

2.

The solution to this problem is to include the changes shown previously in the section for Chapter 11, exercises 1 and 2.

Chapter 15

1.

```perl
#!/usr/bin/perl
# chap15ex1.pl

use warnings;
use strict;
use DBI;

my($instrument, $musician);

print "Enter instrument: ";
chomp($instrument = <STDIN>);

my $dbh = DBI->connect("DBI:mysql:musicians_db", "musicfan", "CrimsonKing");

die "connect failed: " . DBI->errstr() unless $dbh;

# use a table join to query the instrument names
```

```perl
my $sth = $dbh->prepare("SELECT musicians.name
    FROM musicians,what_they_play,instruments
    WHERE instruments.instrument = ? AND
        musicians.player_id = what_they_play.player_id AND
        what_they_play.inst_id = instruments.inst_id")
            or die "prepare failed: " . $dbh->errstr();

$sth->execute($instrument) or die "execute failed: " . $sth->errstr();

# loop through them, printing them
while (($musician) = $sth->fetchrow()) {
    print "    $musician\n";
}

$sth->finish();

$dbh->disconnect();
```

2.

```perl
#!/usr/bin/perl
# chap15ex2.pl

use warnings;
use strict;
use CGI ':standard';
use DBI;

if (param()) {
    my $instrument = param('instrument') || '';

    print
        header(),
        start_html("Musicians who play $instrument");
        h1("Musicians who play $instrument");

    my $dbh = DBI->connect("DBI:mysql:musicians_db", "musicfan",
                        "CrimsonKing");
    my $sth = $dbh->prepare("SELECT name
                FROM musicians, what_they_play, instruments
                WHERE instruments.instrument = ? AND
                    instruments.inst_id = what_they_play.inst_id AND
                    what_they_play.player_id = musicians.player_id")
                or die "prepare failed: " . $dbh->errstr();

    $sth->execute($instrument) or die "execute failed: " . $sth->errstr();

    my($name);

    while (($name) = $sth->fetchrow()) {
```

407

```
            print "$name plays the $instrument.<br>";
    }
    print
        end_html;
} else {
    print
        header(),
        start_html('My Favorite Instrument'),
        h1('Select an Instrument'),
        start_form(),
        '<select name="instrument">';

    my $dbh = DBI->connect("DBI:mysql:musicians_db", "musicfan",
                            "CrimsonKing");
    my $sth = $dbh->prepare("SELECT instrument FROM instruments")
                or die "prepare failed: " . $dbh->errstr();

    $sth->execute() or die "execute failed: " . $sth->errstr();

    my($instrument);

    while (($instrument) = $sth->fetchrow()) {
        print qq{<option value="$instrument">$instrument</option>};
    }

    print
        '</select>',
        br(),
        submit('Show musician(s)'),
        end_form(),
        end_html();
}
```

Index

■ Symbols

\ backslash, 17, 37, 232

' ' single quotes, for strings, 17

-- auto-decrement operator, 41

- hyphen metacharacter, 161, 167

- subtraction operator, 23

- unary minus operator, 25

! (not) operator, 31, 61

!~ operator, 37, 155

!= comparison operator, 29

indicating comments, 3, 6

$ dollar sign

    as metacharacter, 159

    prefixing scalar variables, 38

$! variable, 180

$#array, 99

$_ variable, 46

    regular expressions and, 155, 158

    substitution and, 170

    while loop and, 68

$| variable, 195

$ARGV variable, 190

% modulo operator, 25

% percent sign, prefixing hashes, 115

< left angle bracket, indicating read mode, 180, 182

< less-than operator

    comparing numbers and, 29

    comparing strings and, 35

<< operator, 20, 37

<> angle brackets, enclosing filehandles, 183

<> diamond. See diamond

<= less-than-or-equal-to operator, 30, 71

<STDIN> (standard input), 49, 55, 67

> greater-than operator

    comparing numbers and, 29

    comparing strings and, 35

> right angle bracket, indicating write mode, 182

>> operator, 37

>> two right angle brackets, indicating append mode, 183

>= greater-than-or-equal-to operator, 30

%ENV hash, 215

& ampersand, 137

& AND operator, 26

&& (and) operator, 31, 61

() parentheses. See parentheses

* asterisk metacharacter, 165, 166, 167

* multiplication operator, 21, 23

* star, SELECT command and, 361

** exponentiation operator, 24

. concatenation operator, 32

. period metacharacter, 163, 167

/ division operator, 23

/ forward slash, 18

/ forward slash metacharacter, 155

; semicolon

    statements and, 7

    subroutine declaration and, 136

? question mark metacharacter, 165, 166, 167

: colon, data sources and, 369

" " double quotes, for strings, 17

@ at sign, prefixing arrays, 91

@_, passing arguments to subroutines and,
    137–142, 147–152

@ARGV array variable

    command-line arguments and, 187

    diamond (<>) and, 189

@INC path, 260, 262

[] square brackets. *See entries at* square
    brackets

^ carat metacharacter, as anchor, 159, 160, 167

^| XOR operator, 27

_ underscore. *See* underscore

` backquotes, 227

{} curly braces. *See* curly braces

| either-or operator, 163

| OR operator, 27

| pipe. *See* pipe

|| (or) operator, 31, 61, 336

    default values and, 150

~ NOT operator, 27

+ addition operator, 23

+ plus sign metacharacter, 165, 166, 167

++ auto-increment operator, 41

<=> spaceship operator, 30, 113

= assignment operator

    array assignments and, 91

    multiple assignments and, 43

    operator precedence and, 40

    scalar assignments and, 38

=> operator, 36, 116

=~ operator, 37, 155, 158, 170

== comparison operator, 28, 56, 237

-> arrow notation, 241, 245, 289

■ Numbers

0 prefix, 22

0x prefix, 22

■ A

\a escape sequence (alarm), 8

a() method, 331, 333

abstraction (encapsulation), 290, 293

accessing

    arrays, 95–109

    list values, 87–91

accessor methods, 302, 312

action at a distance, variables and, 146

action attribute, CGI programs and, 334, 338

ActivePerl

    module installation and, 280

    Win32 modules and, 276

addition operator (+), 23

address book (sample program), 250–255

alphabetic range, 87

alternatives, 163

ampersand (&), 137

anchors, 159, 175

and (&&) operator, 31, 61

AND operator (&), 26

angle brackets <>, enclosing filehandles, 183

anonymous data, 232, 234

anonymous references, reference counts and, 244

Apache web server, 318

append mode, 179, 182, 183

applications. *See* programs

arguments, 7, 137
    default values for, 150
    how they are passed, 147–152
    named parameters and, 151

arithmetic operators, 23–25

array elements, references and, 238

array indexes (array subscripts), 97

array slices, 101

arrays, 81, 91–114, 231–235
    accessing, 95–109
    adding elements to, 95, 109
    anonymous, 234, 251
    attributes and, 298
    converting to hashes, 116
    exists() function and, 124
    for loop and, 100
    foreach loop and, 101, 103
    functions for, 109
    looping through with indexes, 100
    matrices and, 245
    naming conventions for, 91
    scalar context vs. list context and, 94
    subroutines and, 149
    tree-like data structures and, 250
    variable interpolation and, 93
    while loop and, 100

arrow notation (->), 241
    matrices and, 245
    methods and, 289

ASCII character set, 8

ASCII values, 34

assignable lists, 90

assignment operator (=)
    array assignments and, 91
    multiple assignments and, 43
    operator precedence and, 40
    scalar assignments and, 38

associative arrays. *See* hashes

asterisk (*) metacharacter, 165, 166, 167

at sign (@), prefixing arrays, 91

attributes, 288
    classes and, 304–307, 312
    providing, 300
    storing, 298

audio, Win32::Sound and, 276

autoclosing files, 180

auto-decrement operator (--), 41

auto-increment operator (++), 41

automatic conversion of scalars, 21, 34

autovivification, 245–249

■ B

\b escape sequence (backspace), 8

b metacharacter, 163, 167

backquotes (``), 227

backreference variables, 167, 171, 176

backslash (\), 17, 37, 232

backwhacking characters, 17–20

barewords, 16

base 10 (decimal system), 10

base 16 (hexadecimal system), 10

base 2 (binary system), 10

base 8 (octal system), 10

BEGIN subroutine, 262

Benchmark, 275

best practices, 6

bidirectional pipes, 200

binary numbers, 10, 15, 21

bits, 10

bitwise operators, 25–28

blank line, header and, 320, 325, 329

bless() function, 288, 293, 296

Boole, George, 28

Boolean logic, 28, 55

Boolean operators, 28, 31

breaking out of loops/blocks, 74

browsers, CGI and, 317–348

buffering, 195

bugs, 11

built-in functions, 221–225, 228

Bunce, Tim, 368

Bundle::libnet, 285

Bundle::LWP, 284

bundles, 284

BY ORDER clause (SELECT command), 364

■ C

-c option, for checking Perl syntax, 4

canonpath() function, 273

carat (^) metacharacter, as anchor, 159, 160, 167

Carp module, 285

carp() function, 285

case sensitivity

    classes and, 289

    lc() function and, 199

    loop labels and, 78

    regular expressions and, 157

    SQL commands and, 355

    subroutines and, 132

    uc() function and, 199

    variable names and, 46

catdir() function, 273

catfile() function, 273

CGI (Gateway Interface), 317–348

    CGI directory and, 318

    CGI.pm methods and, 332, 338

    CGI.pm module and, 317, 325–333

CGI programs, 317, 318–332

    DBI module and, 378–385

    static vs. dynamic, 336

    troubleshooting, 320

    writing, 318–325

character classes, 161–163

character sets (character encoding), 8

chdir() function, 221

checksum, modules and, 283

chess game (sample program), 231

    basic representation of, 245–249

    making enhancements to, 346

    web implementation of, 338–347

chmod command, 4

chmod() function, 224

chomp() function, 50, 69

chop() function, 50

chunking large integers, 14

class methods, 289, 291

classes, 289, 292

    attributes for, 304–307, 312

    case sensitivity and, 289

    constructors and, 291

    inheritance and, 290

    making your own, 295–313

    polymorphism and, 290

CLI (command line interface), 354

close() function, 180

code for this book, downloading, 12

colon (:), data sources and, 369

columns, extracting fields from strings and, 210

command line interface (CLI), 354

command-line arguments

    @ARGV variable and, 187

    Getopt::Std/, 271

    reading files and, 186

comments, 3, 6

comparing

    numbers, 28, 56

    strings, 34, 58

comparison operator (==), 28, 56, 237

comparison operators, 28

Comprehensive Perl Archive Network. *See* CPAN

computer program name and version (sample program), 133

concatenation operator (.), 32

concurrency, relational databases and, 349

conditional operator, 36

conditions

    if statement for, 54–66

    short-circuited evaluation and, 66

connect() function, 369

constants, 13

constructors, 291, 293, 298–301, 312

control flow constructs, 53–79

    if statement and, 54–66

    loop control constructs and, 74–79

    looping constructs and, 66–74

control variables, 72, 103

conversion utility (sample program), 140–142

counting items

    via hashes, 126–129, 198

    pitfalls to avoid with, 176

    pluralizing items and, 200

CPAN (Comprehensive Perl Archive Network), modules and, 257, 267, 278–286

    installing modules, 281–283

    submitting your own module, 285

CPAN module, 281–283

CPAN shell, 281

crackers, 347

CREATE DATABASE command, 356

CREATE TABLE command, 356

croak() function, 285

curly braces ({})

    anonymous hashes and, 234

    array elements and, 238

    arrays and, 239

    dereferencing data and, 236

    foreach loop and, 103

    hashes and, 117, 241

    if statements and, 54, 61

    as metacharacter, repetition and, 166, 167

    statements and, 7

    subroutines and, 132

    variables and, 47

currency converter (sample program), 48

cwd() method, Net::FTP and, 294

■ D

-d metacharacter, 162, 167

D metacharacter, 162, 167

d option, for debugger, 11

data

    anonymous, 232

    files and, 179–206

    human-readable, via hashes, 125

    types of, 13–22

data source name (DSN), 369

data structures

    complex, 244–255

    references and, 231

    trees and, 250–255

Data::Dumper, 268

Database Driver modules (DBD modules), 349, 368

database handler, 370

Database Independent module. *See* DBI module

databases. *See* relational databases

data-driven applications, 314

date, displaying current, 226

DBD modules, 349, 368

DBI module, 349–386

    CGI programs and, 378–385

    installing, 368

    SQL queries and, 370–375

    table joins and, 377

DBD::mysql module, 282, 368

debugger, 11

decimal system, 10

decisions, regular expression engine and, 170

default values, for arguments, 150

defensive programming, 200

defined() function, 59

definite loops, 66

DELETE command, 386

delete() function, 118, 123

delete() method, Net::FTP and, 294

deleting

    directories, 223

    files, 222

delimiters, 19, 85, 172

dereferencing data, 236, 242, 251

DESCRIBE command, 357

DESTROY() method, 292, 311

destructors, 292, 311

DeviceInfo() function, 277

Devices() function, 277

diamond (<>), 161, 196, 185–191

die() function, 51, 285

    file-opening errors and, 180

    newlines and, 181

Digest::MD5, 283, 284

directories, 217–225

    File::Find and, 270

    functions used with, 221–225

    reading, 220

    for sample programs, setting up, 2, 3

directory handles, 220

disconnect() function, 370

division operator (/), 23

do statement, 260

do..until loop, 72

do..while loop, 72

documentation, perldoc and, 268

documenting your programs, 6

dollar sign ($)

    as metacharacter, 159

    prefixing variables, 38

double quotes (" "), for strings, 17

double-quoted strings, 17, 46

    => operator and, 116

    array variable interpolation and, 93

    here-documents and, 20

    within lists, 84

downloads

    Apache web server, 318

    code for this book, 12

DSN (data source name), 369

dynamic CGI, 336

■ E

each() function, 123, 200

eagerness, regular expression engine and, 169

either-or operator (|), 163

elements, 81

    arrays, adding to, 95, 109

    hashes and, adding/reassigning/removing, 118

    within lists, accessing, 87–91

else keyword, 61

elsif keyword, 62

emacs text editor, 2

empty lists, 82

encapsulation (abstraction), 290, 293

end of file (EOF), 20

end of text (EOT), 20

end_form() function, 338

environment variables

    %ENV hash and, 215

    CGI and, 321

EOF (end of file), 20

EOT (end of text), 20

eq (equal to) string comparison operator, 35

equality, comparing numbers for, 28

error checking, 259

error messages, 5, 59, 87

error status, program execution and, 225

errors

    die() function and, 51

    file-opening, 180

errstr() function, 370, 371

escape sequences, 4, 8

    \a, 8

    \b, 8

    \E, 159

    \n, 8

    \Q, 159

    \r, 8

    \t, 8, 17

    \x, 8

escaping characters, 17–20, 158, 168

examples. *See* sample programs

exclusive OR operator (^), 27

execute() function, 371, 376

executing programs, 2, 225–228

exercises

    answers to, 387–408

    arrays, 114

    CGI programs, 348

    control flow constructs, 79

    DBI module, 386

    files, 205

    first steps in Perl, 12

    hashes, 129

    object-oriented programming, 315

    references, 255

    regular expressions, 177

    scalars, 52

    string processing, 213

    subroutines, 152

exists() function, 124

exit() function, 50, 58, 64

explicit destruction, 311

exponentiation operator (**), 24

exporters, 265

expression modifiers

    foreach loop and, 108, 327

    if statement and, 65

    while loop and, 74

external programs, executing, 225–228

■ F

false, 28, 54–60

fetchrow() function, 371

fields, 349

    extracting from strings, 210

    field names and, 356

    ORDER BY clause and, 364

    SELECT command and, 361

File::Find, 270

file paths, 173, 180

file slurps, 190, 196, 276

File::Spec, 273

file tests, 200–205, 219

filehandles, 179–185

    angle brackets <> enclosing, 183

    buffering and, 195

    closing files and, 180

    opening files and, 179, 181

    pipe (|) connecting, 196–200

    writing to files and, 192

filenames, File::Spec and, 273

files, 179–206, 217–225

    autoclosing and, 180

closing, 180

deleting, Hoover program and, 270

do statement and, 260

file gobbing and, 217

File::Find and, 270

file size and, 219

file slurps and, 190, 196, 276

File::Spec and,

file tests and, 219, 200–205

filehandles for accessing, 179–185

functions used with, 221–225

opening, 179, 181, 193

package hierarchies for modules and, 264

require statement and, 261

sorting content and, 193, 198

use statement and, 262

writing to, 192–195

find() function, 270

finish() function, 371

finite loops, 66

flags, 271, 272

flattened lists, 84, 86, 95

floating-point numbers, 14, 15, 21

flock() function, 259

flow charts, 53

flow of execution, of programs, 53

for keyword, 72, 108

for loop, 71

arrays and, 100

breaking out of, 75

foreach keyword, 72, 103, 108

foreach loop, 71

arrays and, 101, 103

breaking out of, 75

counting items, hashes and, 128

expression modifiers and, 108

syntax for, 103

fork() function, 228

Format() function, 277

forms, 333–338, 378–385

forward definitions, subroutines and, 136

forward slash (/), 18

forward slash (/) metacharacter, 155

functions, files/directories and, 221–225

■ G

/g global match regexp modifier, 171, 173

Gateway Interface. *See* CGI

ge (greater than or equal to) string comparison
 operator, 35

get() function, 284

get() method, Net::FTP and, 294

Getopt::Long, 271, 272

Getopt::Std, 271

getopts() function, 272

getprint() function, 284

getpwent() function, 228

get-set methods, 288, 303

getstore() function, 285

glob() function, 217

global variables, 43, 142

goto statement, caution for, 79

GRANT command, 357

greater-than operator (>)

number comparisons and, 29

string comparisons and, 35

greater-than-or-equal-to operator (>=), 30

greediness, regular expression engine and, 169

grouping

parentheses for, 163, 165

pitfalls to avoid with, 175

gt (greater than) string comparison operator, 35

guessing game (sample program), 57

■ H

h1() method, 330, 333

hackers, 347

hard links, 222

hash keys, 116, 118

hash() method, Net::FTP and, 294

hashes, 115–130, 231–246

%ENV hash and, 215

anonymous, 234

converting to arrays, 116

counting items and, 126–129

creating, 115–119

elements and, adding/reassigning/removing, 118

examples of using, 125–129

functions for, 121–124

human-readable data and, 125

list context and, 119

objects and, 288

references and, 241, 242

reversing, 126

scalar context and, 120

tree-like data structures and, 250

head() function, 284

header() method, 329

"Hello, world!", 319

here-documents, 20, 328

hex() function, 21

hexadecimal numbers, 15, 21

hexadecimal system (hex system), 10

hr() method, 333

HTML

attributes and, 333

CGI.pm module and, 325–332, 338

form processing, CGI and, 333–338

generating, CGI and, 323

resources for further reading, 347

HTTP header, 319

human-readable data, hashes and, 125

hyphen (-) metacharacter, 161, 167

■ I

/i case-insensitive regexp modifier, 157, 161, 173

if . . . else statement, 61

if . . . elsif . . . else statement, 61–64

if statement, 54–66

expression modifiers and, 65

multiple choice statements and, 61–64

unless statement and, 64

implicit destruction, 311

indefinite loops, 66

indentation, 7, 9

index() function, 208

indexes (indices), 207

looping through arrays with, 100

pitfalls to avoid with, 176

indexing into strings, 207

inequality, comparing numbers for, 29

infinite loops, 66–70

inheritance, 290, 299

init_expression, 71

INSERT command, 358–361

integers, 14

interpolation, 17, 46, 157

iterator variables, 103–108

■ J

join() function, 175

joke machine (sample program), 98, 106

■ K

keys() function, 121

keys, databases and, 350

keywords, 6

kill() function, 228

Kleene, Stephen, 154

Kleene's star (* asterisk metacharacter), 165

Knuth, Donald, 11

■ L

last index, of an array, 99

last keyword, 74, 77

lc() function, 199

LDS (Leaning Toothpick Syndrome), 18

le (less than or equal to) string comparison operator, 35

Leaning Toothpick Syndrome (LDS), 18

least significant bit, 26

left angle bracket (<), indicating read mode, 180, 182

length() function, 208

less-than operator (<)

number comparisons and, 29

string comparisons and, 35

less-than-or-equal-to operator (<=), 30, 71

letters, ranges of, 85

lexical scope, 146

lexical variables, 43, 142, 146

libwin32 modules, 276

link() function, 222

links, 222

list context

backquotes and, 227

file gobbing and, 218

hashes and, 119

reading in, 183, 186, 190

vs. scalar context, 94

list slices, 90, 91

lists, 81–91

arrays and, 91–114

elements within, accessing, 87–91

flattened, 84, 86, 95

qw// (quote words operator) for creating, 84–87, 89

return values and, 140

subroutines and, 149

literals, 13

local scope, 146

local variables, 142, 146

localtime() function, 226, 284, 327

log levels, 258

logical operators, 31, 60, 65

login() method, Net::FTP and, 293, 294

long flags, 272

loop control constructs, 74–79

loop labels, 77, 78

looping constructs, 54, 66–79

    loop control constructs and, 74–79

    reexecuting the loops, 76

    while loop and, 66–74

ls() method, Net::FTP and, 294

lt (less than) string comparison operator, 35

LWP, Bundle::LWP and, 284

■ M

/m multiple lines regexp modifier, 173

Makefile.PL, modules and, 281

matrices, 245, 249

McIlroy, Doug, 196

memory

    backreference variables and, 167

    file size and, 191

message printing (sample program), 68

metacharacters, 158–167

    list of, 166

    pitfalls to avoid with, 176

methods, 288

    accessor, 302, 312

    CGI.pm, 332, 338

    creating, 301–313

    polymorphism and, 290

    private, 307, 312

    utility, 309, 313

mirror() function, 285

misspellings, strict pragma and, 45

mkdir() function, 223

modules, 257–286

    bundles and, 284

    classes, adding to, 295

    creating, 258

    distributions of, 283

    installing, 280

    package hierarchies for, 263

    reasons for using, 257

    resources for further reading and, 286

    searching CPAN for, 257, 278, 283

    standard, 267–278

    true value and, 260

    using, 260–265

modulo operator (%), 25

most significant bit, 26

moving files, 222

multiple choice statements, 61–64

multiplication operator (*), 21, 23

munging, 173

musicians database (sample program), 378–385

my() function, 44, 45, 142, 374

    arrays and, 92

    foreach loop and, 72

    hashes and, 117

MySQL database

    connecting to, 369

    DBD::mysql module for, 368

    resources for further reading and, 386

    SQL queries and, 370–375

MySQL server, 353–368

creating databases and, 354–361

installing, 353

testing, 353

■ N

\n escape sequence (new line), 8

named parameters, 151, 332

namespaces, 144

naming conventions

for arrays, 91

for filehandles, 180

for subroutines, 132

for variables, 6, 46, 146

ne (not equal to) string comparison operator, 35

nedit text editor, 2

negative indexes (indices), 207

Net::FTP, 292

Net::Telnet, 281

networks, Bundle::libnet and, 285

new() function, 291, 369

next keyword, 75, 77

non-root users, relational databases and, 357

nonword characters, 163

normalization, 353

not (!) operator, 31, 61

NOT operator (~), 27

Notepad text editor, 3

number systems, 9

numbers, 14–16

automatic conversion of, 21, 34

comparing, 28, 56

list slices and, 90

ranges of, 85

types of, 14

numeric operators, 22–32, 36, 114

■ O

object methods, 289, 301–313

object-oriented programming (OO), 287–315

classes and, 295–313

reasons for using, 313–314

resources for further reading and, 291

terminology and, 287–292

objects, 287, 292, 314

constructors and, 291

creating, 298–301

destructors and, 292, 311

encapsulation and, 290

polymorphism and, 290

oct() function, 21

octal numbers, 15, 21

octal system, 10

one-dimensional feature of lists/arrays, 84

OO. *See* object-oriented programming

open() function

executing external programs and, 225

for files, 179, 181, 193

for pipes, 196

opendir() function, 220

operating system (OS), interfacing with, 215–229

built-in functions and, 221–225

files/directories and, 217–225

operator precedence, 24

auto-increment/auto-decrement operators and, 41

list of operators and, 37

logical operators and, 61

operators, 22–38, 55–61

   file test, 201

   list of, 37

   numeric comparisons and, 56

   numeric, 22–32

   operator precedence and, 24

   string comparisons and, 58

   string, 32–36

   syntax for, 40

or (‖) operator, 31, 61, 150

OR operator (|), 27

OS (operating system), interfacing with, 215–229

   built-in functions and, 221–225

   files/directories and, 217–225

out of scope, 44

■ P

p() method, 330, 333

package hierarchies, 263

package operator, 145

packages, 144, 258, 289, 295, 311

param() function, 335, 337

parameters, forms/widgets and, 335

parentheses (())

   arguments and, 7

   foreach loop and, 103

   lists and, 82

   as metacharacters, for grouping, 163, 167

operator precedence and, 24, 38

   in subroutines, 133–137, 139

passing arguments, 8

password tester (sample program), 58

path() function, 274

patterns, 154–170

percent sign (%), prefixing hashes, 115

performance, object-oriented programming and, 314

period (.) metacharacter, 163, 167

Perl

   homepage for, 12

   object-oriented programming and, 287–315

   Perl Monks and, 321

   your first program in, 2, 12

Perl Monks, 321

Perl Package Manager (PPM), module installation and, 280

perldoc, 268

permissions

   chmod() function and, 224

   file tests and, 201

persistence

   object-oriented programming and, 314

   relational databases and, 349

pipe (|), 196–200, 225

piped data, receiving and sending, 196

placeholders, 375, 378

Play() function, 277

pluralizing items, 200

plus sign (+) metacharacter, 165, 166, 167

.pm file extension, 295

pointers (C/C++), 231

polymorphism, 290

pop() function, 109, 240

post-increments, 42

PPM (Perl Package Manager), module installation and, 280

predeclaring subroutines, 136

pre-decrements, 42

pre-increments, 42

prepare() function, 371, 374

primary keys, databases and, 350

print() function, 4, 327, 331

private methods, 307, 312

procedural programming, vs. object-oriented programming, 287, 313

program name and version (sample program), 133

programming, procedural vs. object-oriented, 287, 313

programming languages, 1

programs. *See also* sample programs

    data-driven applications and, 314

    documenting, 6

    external, executing, 225–228

    flow of execution and, 53

    running/executing, 2

    terminating, 50

push() function, 109, 240

put() method, Net::FTP and, 294

pwd() method, Net::FTP and, 294

■ Q

q// and qq// (quote-like operators), 19

quantifiers, 164

question mark (?) metacharacter, 165, 167

quote-like operators (q// and qq//), 19

quote words operator (qw//), 84–87, 89

quotes, for strings, 17–20

qw// (quote words operator), 84–87, 89

■ R

\r escape sequence (carriage return), 8

range operators, 36

ranges, 85

    alphabetic range and, 87

    combining with list slices, 91

read mode, 179, 182, 193

readdir() function, 220

readlink() function, 222

records, extracting fields from strings and, 210

redo keyword, 76, 77

ref() function, 296

reference counts, 243

references, 231–255

    attributes and, 298

    bless() function and, 288, 293, 296

    creating, 232–239

    defined, 231

    destroying, 243

    hashes and, 241, 242

    life cycle of, 232–244

    reference counts and, 243

    using, 236, 244–255

regexp modifiers, 157, 173

the registry, Win32::TieRegistry and, 277

regular expression engine, how it works, 169

regular expressions (regexes), 153–177

defined, 153

learning to read, 159

modules and, 283

patterns and, 154–170

substr() function and, 210

working with, 170–176

relational databases, 349–353

creating, 354–361

example illustrating, 378–385

SQL dialects and, 368

table joins and, 367

remainder operator (%), 25

rename() function, 204, 222, 226

rename() method, Net::FTP and, 294

repetition, 164

repetition operator (x), 32

REPLACE command, 386

require statement, 261

resources for further reading, 226

Apache web server, 318

bidirectional pipes, 200

built-in functions, 228

CGI, 317

character sets, 8

data structures, 255

file tests, 201

form widgets, methods for, 338

HTML, 347

modules, 286

MySQL, 353, 386

named parameters, 333

object-oriented programming, Perl and, 287, 291

passwords, creating, 353

regular expressions, 176

SQL data types, 357

standard modules, 267

return statement, 141

return values, 139–142

reverse() function, 126

arrays and, 109

lists and, 87

right angle bracket (>), indicating write mode, 182

right angle brackets, two (>>), indicating append mode, 183

rindex() function, 210

rmdir () function, 223

root user, relational databases and, 357

rows, databases and, 349, 362

running programs, 2

■ S

s metacharacter, 162, 167

S metacharacter, 162, 167

/s single line regexp modifier, 173

s/// (substitute) operator, 170

sales results for tile shop (sample program), 102

sample programs

address book, 250–255

chess game, 231, 245–249, 338–347

computer program name and version, 133

conversion utility, 140–142

currency converter, 48

directory for, setting up, 2, 3

file download, illustrating object-oriented programming, 292

guessing game, 57

HTML generation and, 325–332

joke machine, 98, 106

message printing, 68

musicians database, 378–385

password tester, 58

Person class, illustrating object-oriented programming, 295–313

summing utility, 137–140

tile shop sales results, 102

weather querying, 62

scalar context

backquotes and, 227

file gobbing and, 218

hashes and, 120

vs. list context, 94

reading in, 183, 186, 193

scalars, 13–52

automatic conversion of, 21, 34

defined, 13

lists and, 81

operators and, 22–38

return values and, 139

types of data and, 13–22

variable interpolation and, 46

variables and, 38–46

scoping, 43, 142–147, 305

script pragma, foreach loop and, 72

search-and-replace operations, 170

security

root user, relational databases and, 357

web security and, 347

SELECT command, 361–367

INSERT command and, 358

table joins and, 367

semicolon (;)

statements and, 7

subroutine declaration and, 136

sendmail, 198

sessions, object-oriented programming and, 314

set methods, 288, 303

shebang, 3, 329

shift, 300

shift() function, 112, 188, 192, 240

short circuiting, 150

short-circuited evaluation, 65

shuttle operator (<=>) , 30, 113

single-quoted strings, 17, 47

here-documents and, 20

within lists, 84

single quotes (' '), for strings, 17

slicing, 90, 91

soft links, 222

sort() function, 112

sorting content, 193, 198

sound, Win32::Sound and, 276

source code, 2, 275

spaceship operator (<=>), 30, 113

special variables, 46

split() function, 154, 174

splitdir() function, 274

splitpath() function, 274

SQL (Structured Query Language), 349

SQL commands, 354–367

    case sensitivity and, 355

    SQL dialects and, 368

SQL data types, 357

SQL queries, 349, 370–375

SQL servers, 353

square brackets ([])

    anonymous arrays and, 234

    arrow notation and, 243

    for elements, 87, 96

square bracket ([]) metacharacters, 161, 167

standard input (<STDIN>), 49, 55, 67

star (*), SELECT command and, 361

start_form() function, 338

start_html() method, 330, 332

starting index, 208, 210

state handler, 371

statelessness, CGI programs and, 338

statements, 7, 31

static CGI, 333–336

static data, 289

static methods, 289

STDERR (standard error) filehandle, 179

STDIN (standard input) filehandle, 179

STDOUT (standard output) filehandle, 179

Stein, Lincoln, 317, 325, 347

step_expression, 71

strict pragma, 44

    arrays and, 92

    hashes and, 117

string functions, 208–213

string operators, 32–36, 114

stringifying, 268

    array elements, 99

    arrays, 102

    variables, 94

strings, 4, 13, 17–22

    automatic conversion of, 21, 34

    comparing, 34, 58

    comparison operator (==), caution for, 56

    defined, 17

    list slices and, 90

    processing, 207–214

    quotes for, 17–20

    ranges and, 86

    string functions and, 208–213

    string operators and, 32–36

Structured Query Language (SQL), 349

sub keyword, 132

subroutines (subs), 43, 131–152

    body of, 134

    defining, 132

    invoking, 133–137

    naming conventions for, 132

    object-oriented programming and, 314

    order of declaration for, 134–137

    passing arguments and, 147–152

    passing arguments to, 137

    return statement and, 141

    when to use them, 131

substitution, 170

substr() function, 210

substrings, 208

subtraction operator (-), 23

summing utility (sample program), 137–140

symbolic links, 222

symlink() function, 222

syntax errors, 16

sysread() function, 228

system() function, 225

syswrite() function, 228

■ T

\t escape sequence (tab), 8, 17

table indexing, 386

table joins, 367, 377

tables, databases and, 349–353

    table joins and, 367

    table names and, 356

telnet, Net::Telnet and, 281

templates, CGI programs and, 348

Term::Readline, 284

test_expression, 71

testing

    Benchmark and, 275

    Test module and, 285

text editors, 2

text processing, 207–214

textfield() function, 338

timethese() function, 275

timethis() function, 275

timing code, Benchmark and, 275

tmpdir() function, 274

tr/// operator (transliteration operator), 212

trees, data structures and, 250–255

true, 28

true value, modules and, 260

true, 54–60

type() method, Net::FTP and, 294

■ U

uc() function, 199

unary minus operator (-), 25

undef variables (undefined variables), 59

underscore (_)

    in array names, 91

    for chunking large integers, 14

    private methods and, 308

    subroutines and, 132

    in variable names, 46

Unicode character set, 8, 12

Unicode values, 34

unless statement, 64, 65

unlink() function, 222, 226

unshift() function, 112, 240

until loop, 70, 75

UPDATE command, 385

USE command, 356

use statements, 262, 329

use strict;, 44, 250, 329

use warnings;, 5, 329

utility methods, 309, 313

■ V

values() function, 122

variable interpolation, 17, 46

variables, 38–46

anonymous data and, 232, 234

backreference, 167, 171, 176

defined, 13

global, 43, 142

lexical, 43, 142, 146

modifying, 39

naming conventions for, 6, 46, 146

special, 46

undefined (undef variables), 59

vi text editor, 2

Volume() function, 277

■ W

w metacharacter, 162, 167

W metacharacter, 162, 167

-w option, for warnings, 4

Wall, Larry, 55, 79

wanted() function, 270

warn() function, 285

warning messages, 5, 59, 87

.wav files, Win32::Sound and, 276

weather query (sample program), 62

Web, Bundle::LWP and, 284

web forms, 333–338, 378–385

web security, 347

web servers, CGI and, 317–348

WHERE clause (SELECT command), 362, 367

whereis command (Unix), 216

while loop, 66–74

arrays and, 100

breaking out of, 75

expression modifiers and, 74

for loop and, 71

whitespace, 4, 7, 9

widgets, 333, 338

Win32 modules, 276

Win32::Registry, 277

Win32::Sound, 276

Win32::TieRegistry, 277

Windows, Win32 modules and, 276

Windows paths, 17

word boundaries, 163

WordPad text editor, 2

write mode, 179, 182

writing to files, 192–195

■ X

\x escape sequence (Unicode character), 8

/x readability regexp modifier, for comments/whitespace, 173

x repetition operator, 32

XOR operator (^), 27

You Need the Companion eBook

Your purchase of this book entitles you to buy the companion PDF-version eBook for only $10. Take the weightless companion with you anywhere.

We believe this Apress title will prove so indispensable that you'll want to carry it with you everywhere, which is why we are offering the companion eBook (in PDF format) for $10 to customers who purchase this book now. Convenient and fully searchable, the PDF version of any content-rich, page-heavy Apress book makes a valuable addition to your programming library. You can easily find and copy code—or perform examples by quickly toggling between instructions and the application. Even simultaneously tackling a donut, diet soda, and complex code becomes simplified with hands-free eBooks!

Once you purchase your book, getting the $10 companion eBook is simple:

❶ Visit **www.apress.com/promo/tendollars/**.

❷ Complete a basic registration form to receive a randomly generated question about this title.

❸ Answer the question correctly in 60 seconds, and you will receive a promotional code to redeem for the $10.00 eBook.

233 Spring Street, New York, NY 10013

Offer valid through 8/10.